Freak Show
Legacies

Freak Show Legacies

*How the Cute, Camp and Creepy
Shaped Modern Popular Culture*

Gary Cross

BLOOMSBURY ACADEMIC
LONDON • NEW YORK • OXFORD • NEW DELHI • SYDNEY

BLOOMSBURY ACADEMIC
Bloomsbury Publishing Inc
50 Bedford Square, London, WC1B 3DP, UK
1385 Broadway, New York, NY 10018, USA
29 Earlsfort Terrace, Dublin 2, Ireland

BLOOMSBURY, BLOOMSBURY ACADEMIC and the Diana logo are trademarks of
Bloomsbury Publishing Plc

First published in Great Britain 2021

Copyright © Gary Cross, 2021

Cover Design by Terry Woodley
Cover image: Allen Lester, Untitled (Boys looking at fat lady banner), circa 1941, detail.
Black & White Photo Print, 9 3/8 x 7 9/16 in. (23.8 x 19.2 cm). Ringling Museum
Tibbals Circus Collection, ht0000060

A catalogue record for this book is available from the British Library.

A catalog record for this book is available from the Library of Congress.

Names: Cross, Gary S., author.
Title: Freak show legacies: how the cute, camp and creepy shaped modern
popular culture / Gary Cross.
Description: London; New York: Bloomsbury Academic, 2021. |
Includes bibliographical references and index. |
Identifiers: LCCN 2020056475 (print) | LCCN 2020056476 (ebook) |
ISBN 9781350145139 (hardback) | ISBN 9781350145122 (paperback) |
ISBN 9781350145146 (epub) | ISBN 9781350145153 (ebook)
Subjects: LCSH: Freak shows–Social aspects–United States.
Classification: LCC GV1835.5 .C76 2021 (print) | LCC GV1835.5 (ebook) |
DDC 791.3/5–dc23
LC record available at https://lccn.loc.gov/2020056475
LC ebook record available at https://lccn.loc.gov/2020056476

HB: 978-1-3501-4513-9
PB: 978-1-3501-4512-2
ePDF: 978-1-3501-4515-3
ePub: 978-1-3501-4514-6

Typeset by Deanta Global Publishing Services, Chennai, India

To find out more about our authors and books visit www.bloomsbury.com
and sign up for our newsletters.

CONTENTS

List of Figures vi
Prologue: Our Thing about Monsters viii

1   Freaking Out 1

2   Carnival Culture and the Challenge of Gentility 23

3   Marginalizing the Freak 69

4   The Cute: Domesticating the Freak 103

5   Countercultures of the Freakishly Camp 141

6   The Creepy: Freaks as Flesh-Eating Zombies 175

7   Taking the Sideshow to the Big Top: Freak Culture in the
Mainstream 207

Bibliography 221
Index 225

FIGURES

1.1   Studio publicity shot of Tod Browning and sideshow performers in *Freaks* 5

1.2   Theatrical poster advertising *Night of the Living Dead* 10

2.1   Woodcut of a two-headed monster *c.* 1495 25

2.2   P.T. Barnum and General Tom Thumb, *c.* 1850 31

2.3   Krao, "The Missing Link" 38

2.4   Cover of *History of Sexual Wonders: The Great Lala Coolah* (1916) 40

2.5   Oft-published image of the Frank Lentini as a young man with his parasitical twin 43

2.6   Cover of *Isaac W. Sprague, The Living Skeleton* (1870) 45

3.1   "Giraffe Burmese Women" at leisure from their circus sideshow in London 72

3.2   Drawings of Robert Ripley from *Believe it or Not* (1929) 75

3.3   The conjoined twins Violet and Daisy Hilton as young performers 78

3.4   An example of the trend toward the grotesque in carnival sideshows 84

3.5   Grace McDaniels (1888–1958), victim of elephantiasis of the lip 86

3.6   A "geek" performing at a fair in Donaldsonville, Louisiana, 1938 92

3.7   Famed sideshow impresario Ward Hall (with the red top hat), shown in 2002 with cast members 94

4.1   Admiral Dot, *c.* 1875 107

4.2   Tom Thumb, *c.* 1848, dressed to impress his genteel audience 110

4.3   "Lady Little, The Doll Lady," *c.* 1911 116

4.4   Three of the "Doll family," *c.* 1924 117

4.5   Anita "The Living Doll," *c.* 1910 119

4.6   Schaefer's Fairy Tale Town, 1933, in Lubeck, Germany 122

5.1   Ed "Big Daddy" Roth's Beatnik Bandit customized car, 1960 148

5.2   Classic poster from the grindhouse cinema 152

5.3   Poster for *The Screaming Skull* (1958) 155

5.4   A gathering of costumed fans for the final viewing of *Rocky Horror Picture Show* at the Roxy Theater in Toronto (May 8, 1983) 158

5.5   "The Enigma" 164

5.6   Latter-day Coney Island freak show (2006) 168

6.1   A promotional poster for Universal's 1935 remake of the famous *Frankenstein* by Karoly Grosz 183

6.2   Poster for *I Was a Teenage Werewolf* (1957) 188

6.3   Zombies on the march in *Night of the Living Dead,* 1968 193

6.4   Cast of *Texas Chainsaw Massacre* posing in costume (1974) 194

6.5   Robert Englund portrayed as Freddy Krueger in *A Nightmare on Elm Street, c.* 1989 199

PROLOGUE

OUR THING ABOUT MONSTERS

Monsters are everywhere. Romantic teen stories turn to scenes of vampires or werewolves (*Twilight Saga* series, 2005–8). A cartoon movie for kids, featuring the classic nerd misfit and his dog, ends up being a redo of the Frankenstein saga (*Frankenweenie*, 2012). And there is an absolute fixation on the zombie (usually with an apocalyptic backdrop). The AMC series *The Walking Dead*, first shown in 2010, is based on a comic book. On the screen, it interlaces melodramas and conflicts of survivors of an apocalyptic event, with confronting and smashing the skulls of mindless zombies. Inevitably by 2015, a sequel appeared with the not-too-imaginative title *Fear of the Walking Dead*; but it was still popular, especially with the eighteen- to forty-nine-year demographic.[1] The novel (and later film) *Warm Bodies* (2013) tells a familiar story of the nerd getting the girl, even though he is a zombie and has eaten the brains of her boyfriend (whose memories the zombie absorbs). A curious turn for a romance! The long-standing popularity of the medieval fantasy *Game of Thrones* isn't content with fantastic battles and occasional nudity along with elaborate plotlines and complex characters. It also featured at various points in the series the Warlocks of Qarth with blue lips and White Walkers, who were hidden for thousands of years before returning to reanimate the dead and kill the living. All this is certainly a world away from the Westerns and even police procedurals that were enough to engage and even excite audiences a generation or so ago.

More subtly certainly, TLC, a cable channel that began as The Learning Channel, has long offered an evening array of quintuplets, the morbidly obese (in *My 600 Lb. Life*), midgets, and the "Body Bizarre." We are dared not to be "creeped out" as the stars of these reality shows behave as ordinary people striving to solve day-to-day problems and at times to overcome their disabilities. We are told to treat them with respect. Yet the producers cannot help tempting us with feelings of discomfort as we witness a 600-pound woman showering ("tastefully" blurred). These creepy characters are not at the margins of today's culture—shown in back street grindhouse movie houses or drive-ins or more recently on the secondary streaming channels on TV (e.g., Shutter). They are right up there on HBO, AMC, and CW and watched by millions, especially the young.

And this is not restricted to cinematic fantasy. Lady Gaga and other performers revel in the image of the monster or freak as in her Monster Ball Tour of 2009, placing a premium on the shocking or at least the pretense of the horrifying. And, of course, since *Doom* (1993), the video game industry has featured the virtual encounter between the player and flesh-eating monsters in shoot-up games that offer the pulsating thrill of the kill-or-be-killed. The *Plants vs. Zombies* video game of 2009 has "homeowner" players use a variety of plants to avoid having their brains eaten out by zombies. An amazing thing about the modern popular imagination is the prevalence of monsters. Creepiness is everywhere.

But there are some curious variations in all of this. As we survey the boneyards of modern horror, we find that a good deal of it is tongue-in-cheek, purposefully exaggerated and "ironic," that is, campy. You will be forgiven for not having seen movies like *Redneck Zombies* (1989), *Monsturd* (2003), *Shaun of the Dead* (2004), or *Zombieland* (2009). And these movies are not just victims of their often-low-budget special effects and makeup; they are intended to be a joke. Consider for a moment the violent video games that mock themselves (like *Grand Theft Auto*). Hipster irony, perhaps, but I think more.[2]

At least as common, the creepy is sometimes set in a context of innocence, childhood, and even wondrousness. Often the creepy character is also cute or at least begins that way—a curious combination really of adorably but also edgy cuteness, sometimes morphing into the bizarre. Note *Happy Tree Friends* (from 1999), an adult-oriented animated video series that is disguised as a children's web show seen on YouTube. *Happy Tree Friends* offers cute cartoon anthropomorphic forest animals, often with eyes shaped like Pac-Man figures, buckteeth, and pink heart-shaped noses. Yet they are subject to extreme, graphic violence in each episode. At one point, there was a warning given to the site "Cartoon Violence: Not recommended for small children or big babies."[3]

Is this nothing more than a desire of horror mongers to appeal to a market of jaded youth or extend it to the kiddies? In a world of multiple TVs, individualized video streaming, and overworked (or overindulgent) parents, what the kids are watching is often just overlooked. But I think that there is more, especially when we think of the creepy, the camp, and the cute as three dominant and curiously interrelated terms of popular taste or aesthetics.

What is going on? Why so many monsters? And why these odd fusions of the cute and camp with the creepy?

Evolutionary anthropologists tell us that that our attraction to monsters and the fear and disgust is biologically programmed. Others add that this allure is culturally engrained in us. Yet civilization has condemned most forms of these engagements: gladiator fights (since the Middle Ages), public executions (in America, the last one in 1936), and even the street appearance of the grotesquely malformed beggar (banned by law in some places in the United States, beginning in the 1920s). There is nothing inevitable about "the walking dead." Much in our culture condemns the zombie allure.

Nevertheless, human fascination with the monster has found refuge for centuries in freak shows and carnivalesque festivals as well as more recently in films. Some older observers might even say all the contemporary monsters and thrills they evoke amount to little more than a carnival moved from the midways of old. They are modernized versions of the traditional freak show where hucksters promised rubes a glimpse of the bizarre or forbidden. For a century up to about forty years ago, millions of Americans (and others) flocked to laugh at the antics of dancing midgets, gawk at conjoined twins and fat ladies, and watch in amazement and disgust as men swallowed swords and live mice while women intertwined their half-bare bodies with slithering snakes. In the past two generations, these encounters with the traditional carnival have retreated to the tawdriest scenes of county fairs or disappeared from sight and memory. But they have now returned with greater force in the modern era in the electronic media as zombies and other monsters. There is a lot of truth to this argument. There is much of the carnival, and especially its side or freak show, on cable and streaming services. But isn't there a world of difference between a midget or even conjoined (Siamese) twins and flesh-eating zombies?

Maybe modern monster shows are no more than the old horror film on steroids—updated versions of those old black-and-white monster movies produced in the early 1930s, seen by boomers on late (Saturday) night TV, and occasionally rediscovered by millennials on streaming channels. In fact, the film industry has long offered fantasy replacements for real encounters with freakish monsters, fulfilling our desire to have our viscera excited in sudden exposures to the frightening and shocking. The unreality of film not only spares viewers of much stress but allows for special forms of emotional and physical excitement. Silent films like *Nosferatu* (1922) did the job with limited sensuality; then came voice with *Dracula* (1931) and color with the Hammer series of gothic horror remakes in the late 1950s, each phase progressively intensifying the experience. While self-censorship in the film industry from the 1930s limited the thrills, the lifting of those controls in 1968 with the rating system accelerated that intensity. And, increased "realism" in digital imaging since the 1990s has invited more "creative" expressions of the grotesque, disgusting, and frightening. We can laugh at the crude rubber *Creature from the Black Lagoon* (1954) while being terrified by the digital update: *Godzilla, Mothra, and King Ghidorah: Giant Monsters All-Out Attack* (2001). Modern monster makers have a lot of tools to toy with our emotions and a lot of incentives for doing so. But why hasn't this trend toward intensified terror been challenged? Why have the monsters, rather than the censors, won?

Some may see the escalation of horror as simply a mass retrogression to the Roman mob cheering the slaughter in the arena. Others might envision this intensification as the liberation of natural and evolved needs to encounter the frightening and disgusting. Still others can even just explain the monster mania as the abdication of genteel culture and the abandonment of its standards of decency—just another step in the West's "slouching toward Gomorrah" to adopt the title of conservative judge Robert Bork's critique of modern culture and liberal politics.[4]

As a historian, who habitually looks for explanations of the present in the past, I want to delve a bit deeper than these common arguments. Regression, liberation, and abdication don't explain much. They often assume that the "masses" rebelled against their cultured and civilized betters (or oppressors) in unleashing the monster, a thumb in the eye of refinement and a release of libidinal energy and frustration. But this often hides class prejudice. And these arguments entirely neglect to explain how the cute and camp have been added to the mix today. Most important, this story can be told in a new way by beginning not with Dracula or other monsters of the movies, but with their cousins, the freaks of the nineteenth-century sideshow.

First, I argue that the roots of the present popular culture with its monsters can be found, not in the so-called emotionally primitive masses, but rather in middle-class culture. This seems to be nonsensical because it was the respectable modern and progressive bourgeoisie (as we shall see presently) who rejected the popular attraction to the abject, censored horror in the movies, and marginalized the freak show, seeing such fascination as bestial and primitive, a throwback to an unenlightened age.

Yet, it was not only the country rubes and thrill-seeking working class that continued to gawk at the freak shows and delight in graphic horror. A portion of the modernizing middle class itself (along with others) held on to freakishness by rejecting the genteel values of bourgeois elites. This diverse group did so by adding the cute and the camp to the creepiness of the monster/freak. And, in so doing, they radically transformed popular culture.

This focus on the middle class isn't a new idea exactly. In the 1960s and 1970s, writers like Daniel Bell (*Cultural Contradictions of Capitalism*) and Christopher Lasch (*The Culture of Narcissism: American Life in an Age of Diminishing Expectations*) believed that the middle-class youth counterculture of that era, with its embrace the moniker of the "freak," was engaged in an dangerous rebellion against the constraints and refinements of bourgeois/liberal culture. Others shared this basic analysis but insisted instead that the revived carnival was a positive sign of cultural liberation.[5] I want to stand apart from this debate, which has become sterile anyway. Instead, I want to take this idea of the middle-class rejection of its own values in a different direction—exploring how that rebellion shaped today's popular culture as seen in its monster shows. The middle class did this by transforming the traditional freak show and freakishness into the cute, camp, and creepy.

Beginning in nineteenth century, freaks like midgets, fat and bearded ladies, and conjoined twins appeared in "dime museums," fairs, and circuses, challenging middle-class ideas about normalcy and nature's regularity. But, by the twentieth century a genteel portion of the middle class withdrew from the freak show, making it more rural and working class. From the 1930s, the freak show was relegated to the world of the naïve and credulous but also the uninhibited thrill-seeker. In time and for many reasons, the time-worn freak show would largely disappear from American life, but freakishness would not.

What happened? First, the middle class, or at least a portion, did not throw out carnival altogether. These respectable people bowdlerized the Saturnalian midway by continuing to embrace "abnormality" in the cute—those freaks that evoked both neediness and harmless impishness, especially midgets; and they passed this delight on to their kids an amazingly diverse and novel commercial culture of cartoons, toys, and fantasy narration. The middle-class crowd (if not all of its literate elite) wanted more than order and beauty; they wanted the sensuality and the fun that the sideshow had brought, especially if it could be seen through the "innocent" eyes of their children.

Second, sections of the middle class (especially its youth) re-embraced the freak, not in gawking awe or credulity, but in the half-serious play of camp. In a culture of increasing intensity and sophistication, the rubes' thrills and naïve imagination were rejected, but not without conceding a certain need for recovering their excitement and fantasy. Camp was the solution: a replacement for the unsophisticated gawking of the rube with the half-serious engagement of jaded youth. And, in the process, camp offered a protest against convention, with little cost or consequence.

Finally, the middle class's initial rejection of the freak was an unwillingness to confront the disturbing and frightening. But the desire and need to experience fear and even disgust could not be suppressed, even with middle-class (especially young) audiences. Aided by a loosening of constraints on media, the result was a revival and extension of the creepy in horror films and other experiential entertainments. And the creepy, unconstrained by the freak show's (or old horror story's) traditionalism, became extremely diverse—and far ghastlier—as the dynamic of consumer culture accelerated the horrifying and the escalation of sensuality.

All three of these middle-class responses had fully blossomed by the 1960s, even if they cannot be fully explained by the 1960s countercultural youth movement. Since then, independent of this movement, they have expanded from the impulse of a minority to the mainstream through commercialization. And these responses have combined and transformed in dynamic ways, giving birth to cuteified horror and campy zombies.

Thus, the roots of omnipresence monster in contemporary popular culture may be found in the history of the freak show and the complex response of the modern middle class to it. The creepiness of *Frankenweenie, The*

Walking Dead, and *My 600 Lb. Life* reflects several generations of middle-class youth rejecting the rationalized order of their parents' aesthetic. More subtly, through the added lenses of the camp and the cute, the creepy has taken on a distinctly modern character. The history of the creepy, camp, and cute reveals much about middle-class modernity and its contradictions. This story is an important way of understanding today's popular culture and its many critics. Both beginning, and as a bridge along the road of, this story is the film *Freaks,* the central theme of my first chapter.

Notes

1 A. S. Hamrah, "Now Streaming: The Plague Years," *The Baffler,* no. 28, July 2015. https://thebaffler.com/salvos/now-streaming-plague-years.

2 Jasie Stokes, "Ghouls, Hell and Transcendence: The Zombie in Popular Culture from 'Night of the Living Dead' to 'Shaun of the Dead,'" PhD Dissertation, Department of Humanities, Classics and Comparative Literature, Brigham Young University, 2010; Tyll Zyvura, "Zombie Studies Bibliography Scholarly Research on Zombies in Popular Culture," Updated: September 14, 2016, https://www.zotero.org/groups/zombie_studies_bibliography/items.

3 Susanne Ylönen, "Lower than Low? Domesticating the Aesthetics of Horror in Childish Remakes," in *Aesthetics of Popular Culture,* M. Ryynänen and J. Kovalcik, eds. (Bratislava: Academy of Fine Arts and Design; SlovArt Publishing, 2014), 124–49.

4 Robert Bork, *Slouching Toward Gomorrah: Modern Liberalism and American Decline* (New York: Regan Books, 1996).

5 One of many reviews of this vast literature is Mikita Brottman, *High Theory/Low Culture* (New York: Palgrave, 2005).

1

Freaking Out

In the depth of the Depression in January of 1932, *Freaks* opened in San Diego. This film was an unusual tale of a circus midget and his misguided love for a trapeze artist, set in the world of sideshow human oddities. The bigger story was of the public hostility to this movie and how this puts us on a journey across decades of American popular culture that sets the stage for this book: This is a story first of middle-class rejection of the freak and the carnival, and subsequently the revival of some elements of the freakish in popular culture.

The freak was hardly a marginal figure in American popular culture. Most were born with or developed aberrations from the biological norm (though some were ethnic or racial minorities); they were gazed, even gawked, at as objects of pity but also wonder; and they were frequently made more interesting (or tolerable) when they were "normalized" in dress, demeanor, and skills. Broadly, they personified the carnival—a culture of difference where the unexpected is expected and where sensual wonder prevails over rational order. The freak symbolized a broader culture of "freakery"— presentations and persons (real and virtual) so abject as to evoke a disturbing response. And they were part of a world that middle-class modernity would eventually marginalize, though never destroy. *Freaks* and its fate provide a window on the fate of freakery in modern America.

This film was directed and produced by Tod Browning, a Hollywood veteran, first as an actor in the 1910s and then as a screenwriter and director. As a youth, he had been a "talker" in carnival sideshows and had long been intrigued with the life and art of freaks. Gaining the support of MGM's powerful executive, Irving Thalberg, *Freaks* promised audiences a backstage view of the lives and personalities of the midgets, bearded ladies, pinheads, hermaphrodites, and Siamese twins that commonly appeared in circus sideshows. However, the movie was really a horror show.

Browning's portrayal was shaped by his recent experience as a maker of films of the grotesque and gruesome drama, including a 1925 silent feature called *The Unholy Three* involving a crime spree by a trio of circus performers, including a midget. In 1931, Browning contributed to the new craze for horror (that included the smash hits of *Frankenstein* and *King Kong*) with his version of *Dracula*. His next film, *Freaks*, would continue down that horrific path with a story that culminated with a band of angry freaks creeping through mud on a rainy night to attack the villain, the "normal" trapeze artist Cleopatra and her strongman lover, Hercules. In the course of the movie, Cleopatra had humiliated the gentle and sympathetic midget Hans who foolishly has fallen in love and married her. After his money all along, Cleopatra and Hercules plot to murder Hans. After being mocked at the wedding party and learning of the plot, the freaks band together to seek revenge. No violence is shown as the freaks attack Cleopatra, but the results are—her reduction to a legless squawking duck-like figure—as evidence of the potent rage of freaks when one of their kind is mistreated.[1]

Viewed by modern eyes, the film is not very horrifying (just as *King Kong and Frankenstein* are not). Like other horror films of the 1930s, there is more melodrama than terror on the screen. Much of the film is the story of a sympathetic, but naïve, Hans and a caring, if sometimes pitiful, Frieda, his midget girlfriend whom he leaves for Cleopatra. Despite its horrifying climax, *Freaks* was pretty tame. It had to be, produced as it was under the mainstream logo of MGM rather than a low-class "Grindhouse" studio that specialized in exploitation movies. In most ways, *Freaks* was a familiar melodrama for its time: the story of a misguided desire for love, a manipulative female, and ultimately the reconciliation of an appropriate couple (albeit midgets). We sympathize with the freaks, at least the midget couple. They become monsters only when provoked.[2]

And yet the film incited outrage from its first appearance. Women were reported screaming as they ran from the theater; one allegedly had a miscarriage while watching the movie. *Freaks* was a lightning rod for opponents of horror and sexually suggestive movies in 1932. While viewed favorably by a few critics (including famed Hollywood reporter Louella Parsons), negative reception came quickly. The *Kansas City Star* summed up many reviews: "It took a weak mind to produce it and it takes a strong stomach to look at it." MGM studio head, Louis B. Meyer, concerned that the film would sully the reputation of his respectable company, pulled *Freaks* from theaters by the early summer of 1932 after a delayed showing in New York. It was banned in England (reversed only thirty years later), but also in Nazi Germany and Stalin's Russia. Worst of all (from Hollywood's point of view) the film cost $316,000 to produce but lost $164,000.[3]

All this might seem simply to suggest that sensibilities were less jaded in 1932 than they are now. On the eve of the enforcement of Motion Picture Production Code in 1934 that banned sexually suggestive and gangster-glorifying movies and ushered in the age of costume dramas and Shirley Temple, this horrified reaction might have been predicted. In fact, by 1936, in this new conservative cultural climate horror films had become rarer. The National Association of Women raised concerns about the sexual innuendo in *Freaks* when it complained to the Code Administration about the suggestive scenes regarding the love life of the conjoined Hilton twins and the hermaphrodite. Recognizing this popular reaction, ads for the movie tried to tone down the horror and sexuality; instead, they stressed the normality of the freaks and the rights of the twins to love.[4]

Digging deeper, the audience's reaction is hard to explain. After all, the freak had been a mainstay in the culture of popular curiosity since the nineteenth century, having been successfully commercialized in a package of spectacles wrapped in a richly evocative narrative. Freak shows had challenged, but also confirmed, the values of a largely upwardly mobile crowd since the 1840s. The display of the individual freak, especially the giant and the dwarf, had been part of a long and even ancient culture of aristocratic presentation—markers of luxurious exoticism and eccentricity. In many ways, the domesticated freak shared a history with the aristocratic invention of the lap or house dog as a pet rather than a work animal. Hardly a horror show.[5]

The cast of *Freaks* was disturbing to some perhaps, but all were familiar, often famous, figures in the sideshows of circuses and even Vaudeville. Americans had long paid good money to see these unusual people. Harry Earles plays Hans, while his midget sister took the role of his lovelorn female lead, Frieda. This pair were celebrities, originally from Germany, who, with their other midget siblings, became the "Doll" family, long headliners with the Ringling Brothers and Barnum and Bailey Circus. Hans had a leading role in the cast of Munchkins in the famous *Wizard of Oz* of 1939.

Others in the cast included the Living Skeleton, Pete Robinson, who married a "fat lady." Robinson was widely known as a "Jack Sprat" in the flesh. The armless women, Francis O'Conner and Martha Morris, were famous in sideshows for signing picture cards of themselves with their feet. O'Conner crocheted and even was a sharpshooter. Schlitzie was one of several pinheads in the movie, a victim of microcephaly (characterized by a smaller than average head and mental retardation). Living to eighty, he was noted for being cheerful and accommodating, even though he always needed the help of a caregiver, who, like others, treated Schlitzie as a child. More disturbing was Prince Randian, unusual in the sideshow for he lacked both arms and legs. Known as the human torso, human caterpillar, or even human worm, Prince Randian was famous for rolling and smoking cigarettes with his mouth. His articulate speech often disarmed onlookers. The conjoined twins, Daisy and Violet Hilton, might also have bothered audiences in 1932. But their story of exploitation by "guardians" from whom they had been recently liberated, along with their fame on the Vaudeville circuit as skilled musicians (playing the piano and saxophone), made them anything but terrifying. Olga Roderick (aka Jane Barnell) was a natural bearded woman, well known for her regular appearances at Hubert's Museum in New York City. Koo Koo, the Bird Girl, suffered from bad vision (thus sometimes labeled the Blind Girl from Mars) and a bone deformity that produced a birdlike appearance. This was exaggerated when she was dressed in feathers, sometimes with huge chicken feet. Odd, but hardly, horrifying. Johnny Eck was also featured. Although a legless "half man," he was handsome and a great talker. All traditional sideshow fare.

Perhaps more disturbing was Josephine/Joseph, who had a brief role in *Freaks* as a hermaphrodite. Still, the half male/half female figure (often a fake) was a common exhibit in sideshows (sometimes offered as a "blow-off" act at the end of the show for an extra charge). He or she was usually dressed in a costume that suggested both sexes with half of the body tanned and muscled and the other half pale. Some half-and-half artists were skilled at faking the possession of both male and female genitals (revealed in some blow-offs in carnival sideshows). But the movie left this out, of course.[6]

Nevertheless, the prevailing American popular culture of 1932 found *Freaks* anathema. The movie itself offers clues why. It shows a break from a century of American fascination with anomalies of the sideshow. From the opening scene, the talker deviates from the common spiel of the sideshow. He does not tell us that the freaks are amazing curiosities who have transcended their disadvantages, but "living breathing monstrosities"—even if he also reminds the audience that "but for the accident of birth you might be as they are" and that "They didn't ask to be brought into the world." They live by "a code of their own" and even more ominously, the talker warns us: "Offend one and you offend them all." This sets up the main thread of the story: These humiliated Others take revenge on ordinary people, a frequent theme of horror stories (like in *Frankenstein*). Freaks are to be feared. They are creepy. But even more, they are to be pitied. And displaying these pathetic creatures on film was a central objection of genteel critics like the National Association of Women who was appalled that MGM would "stoop to the disgrace of making money out of hurt, disfigured and suffering humanity." A new attitude toward the freak was emerging in a middle-class culture that was beginning to reject and want to hide the abject and pitiful.[7]

Freaked Out by Freaks: Origins

By 1932, the freak had become a subject of a horror show, disgusting in appearance and behavior, dangerous when riled up, pitied yes for the hurt caused them by nature, but never to be brought into the happy home of humanity. Even if the movie condemns the mockery of the "abled" Cleopatra and Hercules, the attitudes of the trapeze artist and strong man aren't far from what the movie expects from the audience. Most viewers, no doubt, found absurd the sight of a three-foot, three-inch man with a high-pitched voice pursuing a beautiful trapeze artist, especially when he was competing with the man's man, Hercules. While the freak had fascinated several generations of Americans, by 1932, movie goers were beginning to find them repulsive.

FIGURE 1.1 *Studio publicity shot of Tod Browning and sideshow performers in* Freaks. *Note the "pinheads" and the "half man" Johnny Eck on the left, Bettmann, Getty Images.*

This break from the past signaled the decline of the freak show and all that it represented, especially in genteel and aspiring middle-class circles. Up to this point, dwarfs, giants, and numerous other human curiosities had attracted monarchs and aristocrats who, for centuries, had displayed these oddities. But even medical and scientific chroniclers viewed these people as mysteries or even separate species. Similarly, they had fascinated ordinary crowds at festivals and fairs. In the 1840s, P.T. Barnum introduced a range of human curiosities at his American Museum in New York. The circus sideshows that followed featured individuals with unusual bodies (mostly from birth) but also self-made freaks (tattooed ladies), performers (fire-eaters), and gaff (fake) freaks. These performers drew millions of Americans in the late nineteenth century, and did so across class and cultural lines, enticing the gawking voyeur with back stories of exotic origins and the respectable with claims that these special people were of superior intelligence and abilities.[8]

But, by the end of the Victorian era, there were signs of disenchantment: By 1900, genteel values of restraint, respect, and normality challenged and marginalized the carnival culture, reducing the three-legged wonder to a pitiful victim and condemning audiences who gawked at jars of two-headed fetuses or pinheads at sideshows as both naïve and boorishly insensitive. This change also reflected an emerging unwillingness of Americans to face stigma and confront their anxiety about the fragility of human existence in much the same way as modern Americans became unwilling to confront the physical reality of death or the disturbance of the disturbed individual. Little people and other human oddities could no longer be stared at. Reinforcing these genteel standards were changing views of scientists and medical experts. With advances in embryology, obstetrics, and endocrinology, no longer could three-legged men, bearded ladies, and giants be treated as curiosities and mysteries. Rather they became victims of birth defects and glandular abnormalities.[9] This made freaks pitiful rather than fascinating. To be accepted by "respectable" middle-class audiences, they had to be entertaining. The most successful form of this had roots in the late Victorian sideshow—the midget who disarmed the unease of viewers with song, dance, and fantasy. And this freak was *cute.*

Snow White's Cuteified Dwarfs

Just five years after the disastrous showing of *Freaks,* in December 1937, another film pointed to this new way of seeing the freak as cute: *Snow White and the Seven Dwarfs.* Walt Disney's iconic first animated feature film was anything but a horror show (though there were frightening elements in it). The movie became a children's classic, the first of many Disney animations featuring "princess" figures, often prevailing over a jealous female adult, and, in the end, finding a Prince Charming with whom to live "happily ever after."

Central, however, to this familiar story is the seven dwarfs. By any measure, they were freaks, but they were cuteified freaks. Like sideshow midgets or even Browning's little people, the seven dwarfs are childlike men. The seven dwarfs are comic relief to the tensions of the story. Still, their singing, dancing, and personalities almost steal the show. Like the Doll family of real midgets, the seven dwarfs are entertaining in ways that only a cuteified midget could be, by their looks and behavior.

In Neal Gabler's account, Walt Disney and his crew toiled for months to find the desired look for the dwarfs, even hiring three professional midgets to present animators with models of movement and appearance. Walt was disappointed with the result: "To me," he complained, these midget performers "are not very cute. I can't help but feel sorry for these guys." While circus audiences might have found the seven dwarfs appealing, Disney wanted them to be even more cute. He wanted his cartoon dwarfs to be "imaginary," exaggerations of the small people of the freak show, like the childlike cartoon and comic characters of the era. Dopey was especially important. One animator on the Disney team suggested that Dopey have a "kid personality with a small nose and eyes fairly large, a little outward slant to make him elfish." Dopey was not to be stupid (despite his name), but to suggest that "he hasn't grown up—sort of childish." Most of the dwarfs, however, were to be rather old men, but definitely not to be models of masculine maturity. Rather they were to be comical, but in endearing ways: Doc was to be a "windbag," clumsy and tongue tied (reminiscent of the comic Ed Wynn). Grumpy was supposed to be a women-hating grouch with a heart of gold, crying when he witnessed the poisoning of Snow White.[10] These dwarfs were like predictable comic male characters (diminished but made charming by their traits—Sleepy, Sneezy, and Bashful); and, in the form of lovable little people, becoming even more comical and adorable. Disney insisted that the dwarfs sing "quaint" songs even yodel, suggesting a vague nostalgia for a premodern world rather than perform the "hot" pop music of the 1930s. They were cute: childlike and comically endearing, always full of character, loveble, and huggable. In effect, Disney transformed the freak show midget with its many meanings into the quintessential cute.[11]

Midgets and dwarfs may have appealed to adults as little people had for centuries. However, Disney did more: He made the dwarfs appealing to small children (as well as to their parents) in an increasingly child-focused world. Kids saw the dwarfs in a special way: Though appearing to be adult, the seven dwarfs remain, little not just in stature, but in grownupness—in fact, smaller than the children in the audience. More important, to kids, the dwarfs were cute, just as kids were increasingly cute to adults (small, dependent, endearing, and huggable, easily turned into Disney-licensed toys or figurines, ideal for the female child consumers). When first coming to the dwarfs' cottage, Snow White says that it is "just like a doll's house," and when she enters the empty cottage she sees dirty dishes and cobwebs; she is convinced that the inhabitants must be "untidy little children," in fact, "orphans" who don't have a mother. Like many girls in the audience would have responded, Snow White pretends to be the mother, insisting, when the dwarfs return home, that they wash up for dinner and clean up their cottage. Though the little men are protective and care for her when Snow White is "killed" by the stepmother's poisoned apple, the dwarfs are really just cute little kids. Curiously, this is done in part by making the dwarfs seem like old men with double chins, corns on their feet, red noses, white beards, and possessing oldish attitudes (like Grumpy with his fears of Snow White's "women's wiles"). By the 1930s, the grandfatherly was often portrayed comically as childlike (note the comical elder in Westerns like Gabby Hayes). Such old characters were shown as going through a second childhood that kids could patronize as much as young adults.[12]

The dwarfs and Snow White reversed the big-small, grownup-child relationship for child viewers. Doc, the leader of the dwarfs, was anything but an authority. A bit different, Dopey was like a little brother to the eight-year-old viewer. Again, this made the child audience delight in the feeling of superiority. In the end, Snow White is awakened by the Prince's kiss and prepares to go off with him (all grown up). She offers the dwarfs an endearing but innocent kiss on their mostly bald heads, as she would a child, leaving them behind in their doll's house. Snow White goes on to a romantic grownup world, the dream of many children. The dwarfs do not. They remain cute kids in the imagination of real kids who knew that they themselves would eventually transcend cuteness and grow up.

For all ages, Disney's dwarfs were not pitiful like Hans; certainly not frightening or disgusting as were many in *Freaks*. They were part of a broad cuteification of small children (and some animals) toward the end of the nineteenth century. In the process, at least some freaks were made cute, especially those who resembled children. This made midgets (and even some giants, especially the gentle and childlike ones and even pinheads) adorable. And part of this phenomenon was parental indulgence of kids' fantasies, a bowdlerization of the freak show.

Freaks Revived: The Coming of Camp

Three decades after *Snow White*, we see another legacy of the freak show in the curious revival of Browning's *Freaks*. In the 1960s and 1970s, the movie was viewed by a new generation, but with very different eyes than those terrorized by the film in 1932. Its audience was not the country rube who so long had patronized carnival sideshows. Rather, *Freaks* attracted the "freaks" of the late 1960s and early 1970s countercultural youth. In 1970, they thronged (admittedly in small numbers) to the Midnight Movies in big cities and the film societies in college towns, where *Freaks* became a favorite of hip youth. Even earlier avant-garde critics changed views. No longer was *Freaks* a horror show. For the critics of the 1960s, it was a forgotten masterpiece. For many youth viewers, it was camp.

Freaks had undergone a checkered history. In 1947, MGM licensed it to a small distributor, Dwain Esper. Removing the MGM logo, Esper made it part of the underground grindhouse movie circuit that combined lurid themes about sexual disease and drugs with moralistic covers (*Damaged Lives* and *Reefer Madness*, for example). Esper exhibited *Freaks* in small down-market theaters and even drive-ins in the late 1940s under the deceptive name of *Forbidden Love*. Esper soon added an "educational" prologue to *Freaks* (also retitling again as *Nature's Mistakes*), noting the "long conditioning of our forefathers," that made modern audiences abhor the deformed despite their "normal thoughts and emotions." This was, of course, typical of grindhouse fare, using an educational or moralistic cover to get passed censors and exhibit what was still widely considered horrific or, at least, distastefully grotesque. *Freaks* had gone down-market, attracting the same "rubes" to whom the freak show had been relegated when the middle class abandoned it.

This changed, however, when *Freaks* was shown and favorably reviewed at the 1962 Venice Film Festival. High-minded critics from *Sight and Sound* and *Spectator* wrote of how Browning's depiction of the freak community enlarged the audience's sympathy for the Other. Recognizing its renewed potential for ticket buyers, MGM reclaimed its rights to the movie. After seeing *Freaks* at a New York art theater, the famed photographer Diane Arbus followed this revisionist perspective in her documentations of urban oddities. Arbus was one of many celebrants of the bizarre in the 1960s (including Andy Warhol and Federico Fellini).[13]

But central to the revival of *Freaks* and freakishness itself was the audience—predominately youth who had rejected, at least temporarily, the middle-class culture of their suburban *Readers' Digest* upbringings, happily embracing the term "freak" for themselves. These young people refused to be disgusted by Browning's dwarfs, pin heads, Siamese twins, and human worms without limbs. The 1960s counterculture gave human oddities a positive image, especially on college campuses; freaks were no longer the pitied, the disgusting, the not-to-be-gawked-at; and the name "freak" was a proud badge of disengagement of the middle-class youth from middle-class suburban culture. Yet, for many viewers of *Freaks*, this was more than a thumb in the eye of bourgeois respectability. In the context of the cult viewing in an avant-garde setting, the crowd treated the spectacle as a joke, perhaps feigning shock, but from a knowing distance, really just pretending to be appalled. This was the beginning of modern camp.[14]

Increasingly repeated from the 1960s, camp was famously documented in Susan Sontag's "Notes on Camp" of 1964. We see this mockery of middle-class sensibility in the Batman TV show of 1966 with its overwrought posing of the virtuous pair of Batman and Robin and the over-the-top villain, the Penguin. Other cult films of camp appeared in the 1970s, including John Waters's *Pink Flamingos* (1972) and *Rocky Horror Picture Show* (in 1973 as a stage musical and in 1975 as a film).[15]

In embracing *Freaks,* modern camp audiences in effect were putting on the rube who had attended the freak show of old, responding with a range of simulated emotions. Like the cute, camp introduced still another way by which the freak had become irrepressible, living on in everything from the outlandish interview TV shows of Jerry Springer that featured incestuous relationships to sideshow revivals that evoked disgust with performers pouring beer down their noses. In the opening decades of the twenty-first century, camp became practically the norm on adult TV cartoons like *Family Guy* and many reality shows.

The Creepiness of *Freaks* Intensified with Zombies

Coming out of the 1960s was still another slap at the face of genteel restraint and another form of freakishness. This was best represented in the movie *Night of the Living Dead* (1968). Quickly after its release, it became a cult classic and was often viewed by the same crowd that flocked to the revivals of *Freaks*. But *Night of the Living Dead* went much further: Replacing the aggrieved freaks attacking the vile Cleopatra are zombies who swarm helpless and innocent victims. This movie was truly exceptional for its unrelenting horror, what I call simply the creepy. Produced on the cheap by George Romero of Pittsburgh, *Night of the Living Dead* was far different from the old horror films—often predictable variations on the Victorian Gothic novels, upon which they were based, with their standard repertory of mad scientists, spooky castles, dumb villagers, and not-so-frightening monsters.[16]

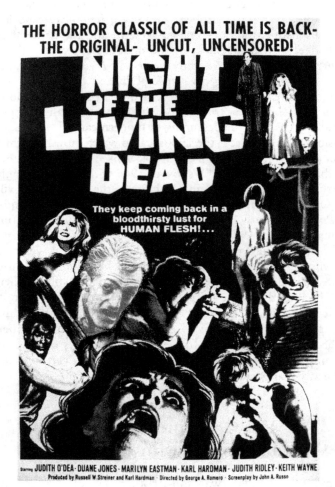

FIGURE 1.2 *Theatrical poster advertising* Night of the Living Dead, *Universal History Archive, Getty Images.*

By contrast, *Night of the Living Dead* was an unrelenting assault on the senses with the onslaught of flesh-eating, walking dead zombies, giving little time for a sophisticated plot, much less character development. Gone was the fog and atmospheric castles. Instead most of the action takes place on an ordinary Pennsylvania farm with a contemporary cast of characters, all perfectly identifiable by audiences of 1968. The same is true of the zombies. There is no real explanation of where the zombies come from. It hardly mattered. The point was their unyielding swarming the farmhouse. And, no one survives. The horror is unrelieved by a happy ending. There is no moral uptake as in many previous horror movies, including, of course, *Freaks*. The zombie apocalypse has found a persistent audience, including the long-running series on AMC cable TV, *The Walking Dead*. Of course, there had been many cheap horror films that preceded *Night of the Living Dead*, many of which appeared in drive-ins and late-night TV hosted by local campy celebrities. *Night of the Living Dead*, however, stood out for its unvarnished terror.[17]

However, while *Freaks* was treated as disgusting horror in 1932, *Night of the Living Dead* of 1968, with far creepier freaks, was a huge hit, copied many times in a new wave of gross out horror. So what had changed in thirty-six years since the condemnation of *Freaks*? The obvious answer is the lowering of taboos in the new cultural climate that accompanied the new Hollywood rating system, allowing more explicit violence. But why did this occur in the late 1960s?

To be sure, *Night of the Living Dead* was an extension in a long developing trend in the fantasy industry—the gradual embrace of the "freak-out" creepy. We see this in increasingly bizarre freak shows from the 1930s on with displays of two-headed fetuses in a jar, for example. Similar are the so-called grindhouse films from the same time that drew mostly lower-class and slumming audiences with the promise of the grotesque, violence, and sex. However, the audience for the creepy by the late 1960s seems to have broadened to include also a decidedly more middle class and youthful mix. That audience rebelled against the restraint and cuteified Kitsch of their parents; and, as increasingly jaded youth in ever more intense consumer culture, that crowd found pleasure in accelerated creepiness.

Moreover, *Night of the Living Dead* signaled another trend in cinema—an intensification of the creepy. Narrative and character development gave way to a more visceral appeal: a package of emotional hits or "compressions" that audiences dared filmmakers to throw at them on the screen.[18] And this trend in horror followed a similar pattern of stepped-up violence in the action-adventure genre in the 1970s and 1980s.[19] As we shall see, intensity led to more intensity into the twenty-first century. The creepy became more so.

Carnival and Freaks Marginalized

These four media events—the 1932 reception of *Freaks*, the 1937 smash hit of *Snow White and the Seven Dwarfs*, the late 1960s revival of *Freaks*, and cult success of the 1968 *Night of the Living Dead*—reveal a curious transformation: An advancing culture of middle America had ostracized the freak from early in the twentieth century, rejecting it as a respectable object of cultural gazing. But then the freak show reappeared in radically new forms as early as 1937 as the cuteified freaks of Disney for the middle class and their children and then at the end of the 1960s in a variety of forms in the freakishly camp and creepy for youth, notably from the rebellious middle class.

This rejection and reintegration of the freak has a long history, closely linked to that very middle class and its evolving popular culture. This process is part of a wider phenomenon—the flight from and yet survival (in new forms) of the carnival in popular culture. The rejection of the popular, traditional folk festival, of which the freak show was a vital component, has long been associated with the formation of the middle and professional classes. The historical analysis of this flight often begins with the Russian literary theorist M. M. Bakhtin in his famous *Rabelais and His World* (1968 in English) and has been developed by many social and cultural historians, especially Peter Burke and Robert Malcolmson.[20]

Let us pause for a moment to recall the character of this mostly lost festival tradition and why the middle class rejected it—along with the freakshow. Festivals often had links to religious traditions though usually festivals occurred in breaks in the agricultural work cycle (the pre–Lenten Carnival and Yuletide, for example). Carnival festivals were boisterous, shocking, and mocking. They rejected the church's insistence on contemplation, prayer, and respect for the holy (and authority). Carnival was saturnalian (after the ancient Roman holiday where social rules were freely broken), providing a safety value in repressed societies by releasing the common folk temporarily from the onerous expectations of bosses and the church. As Bakhtin emphasizes (followed by dozens of others), carnival was a celebration of the body, not the soul; and that was not an admiration for the Greek idea of physical beauty, but a fascination with the scatological, the monstrous, and the outlandish. The traditional festival then was the perfect venue for freaks with their extraordinary bodies and behaviors and for the audiences enthralled by them.[21]

It was this carnival culture that was opposed by the ancestors of the modern middle class. Like others, Bakhtin roots this animosity in religious reformers, who during the sixteenth and seventeenth centuries attacked the corruption of the sacred with the carnivalesque.[22] However, opposition to carnival also came from the desire of an emerging bourgeoisie to withdraw from this saturnalian public culture to the serenity of their homes and families with private and individualistic activities like card games, restrained music, and reading. The object was orderly families and disciplined inner-directed offspring. Again, as noted by Max Weber and many followers, these religious (and new cultural) values produced a capitalist spirit of competitive self-control.[23]

This epochal withdrawal from the carnival has taken a large number of forms: from the bourgeois invention of the "(with)drawing room" for sedate family pleasures and the coffee house (as an alternative to the grog house) for the emerging sober businessman in the late seventeenth century to the transformation of community-focused, but often violent, ball games into highly controlled sports like modern soccer or football in the late nineteenth century.[24] Lawrence Levine describes this phenomenon in *High Brow/Low Brow* as part of the late nineteenth-century rise of a genteel elite, insistent on serious performances of Shakespeare and on building scientific museums in opposition to the aesthetic frivolity of Vaudeville and P.T. Barnum's shows.[25] The idea went much further—to drive out the boisterous sensuality of the bar, brothel, gambling den, and even youthful rebellion in schools and on Halloween. And these aggressions on carnival peaked around the beginning of the twentieth century.

All this gets us to my main point: The attack on the freak show was part of a larger middle-class assault on carnival—a rejection of "abnormality" and the abject. There were many reasons for this rejection, and it took a long time. As we shall see, Victorian-era Americans, even from the "respectable" classes, could still gaze (if not openly gawk) as midgets and conjoined twins if they were presented as basically "normal" (middle-class) or objects of religious or "scientific" observation.

The discrediting of the freak show came only in the twentieth century when the mystery of the unnatural and the abnormal lost credibility, first and more thoroughly in the educated middle class. In the case of the freak, this took the special form of medicalizing "deformity." Zip (aka What Is It?), a famed pinhead long touted in freak shows as the exotic "missing link" between humans and apes, had fascinated decades of gawking audiences. But in the twentieth century, he became simply a microcephalic, a victim of intellectual disability, motor dysfunction, and a short life expectancy due to chromosomal abnormalities in vitro.

While science demystified the freak, middle-class tastemakers introduced new standards of propriety that transformed acceptable behavior and attitudes of sideshow crowds. Old habits of gawking at the abnormal or openly feeling superior to exotics from the tropics with elongated necks or victims of birth anomalies became taboo. Respectable people could pity the freak, but not be fascinated by the oddity.

Most of all, however, upholders of this new standard wanted the freak out of sight. The expulsion of the freak reveals the unease that the modern middle class experienced when encountering differences that contradicted their standards of the rational, orderly, and beautiful. This attitude has long been associated with the "dark side" of the rational/enlightenment revolution of the late seventeenth century where those people who challenged "reason" (like the insane or otherwise abnormal) were incarcerated in asylums.[26] The banishment of the freak show is still another manifestation of this trend. How all this took place is part of my story.

Of course, genteel tastemakers failed to entirely suppress the freak show; for many years, they just marginalized it. Many Americans never adopted the genteel value system and instead adhered consciously or not to a truncated carnival culture, even the freak show. It lingered on through the twentieth century in ever smaller carnivals and circuses in rural America, increasingly patronized by the country "rube," the poor, and the poorly educated. And the shows became more down-market and dwindled to a mere shadow. In the long run, the genteel assault on the freak show (like its rejection of the traditional festival) seems to have succeeded.

The Irrepressible Freak

But there is another side to the freak show story. The culture of the human oddity has survived and even flourished in popular culture. It had origins in the old freak shows but reappeared in radically new forms. The new freak took three expressions: The cuteified midget that made freakishness delightful; the parody of the freak in the aesthetic of camp; and a dramatic extension of the horror of the freak in the creepy. All three were products of late modern middle-class culture, especially in the young. The carnival was revived in part by the descendants of that genteel class which had once condemned it.

The midget became the quintessential domesticated oddity, part of a broad complex of looks, responses, and attitudes that came with the introduction of the *cute* in modern culture. The cuteified midget was one form of the Barnumesque world of the sideshow, to which middle-class culture remained loyal. Small people were not disgusting like the "human worm." Like the seven dwarfs, midgets could be integrated into the world of the delightful and adorable.

Part of the appeal of the cute (in the freak and well beyond) came from a transformation of adult attitudes toward the child toward the end of the nineteenth century. The once fragile child (all-too-often becoming angels in unavoidable premature death) or urchin youth (who, without sufficient parental discipline, gave in to sin) became the vital and delightful innocent, sometimes naughty, but always nice. The child became cute, as did many of their playthings and fantasy heroes in comic books and cartoons. And so did some freaks. While, of course, the cute extended far beyond the freak, when cuteified the freak was welcome back into "respectable" middle-class culture.[27]

The cuteified midget was the one form of the freak show that the middle class could embrace. This reveals the limits of genteel project: A large share of the middle class simply did not want to abandon wonder for the often formal and austere culture of gentility and the highbrow. There were many forms of "wonder"—much of which elites would label Kitsch. Here, however, wonder came in the form of the "innocence" of the cute.

Middle-class moderns did not settle on the sublimity of Central Park, the Museum of Modern Art, and good books of their cultured elite, but craved and consumed a more corporeal, emotional, even zany culture in the shared experience of Disney's and later Jim Henson's weirdo "freaks," who were redeemed by their cuteness.

A second acceptable return of the freak show came in the form of a substitution of the now-taboo act of gawking at the oddity for camp. We have already noted campish response of young viewers of the 1960s and 1970s to "monster" shows (especially *Freaks*) of the 1930s and 1940s that were hardly intended to be camp. By the 1960s, cheap horror movies were deliberately exaggerated with cheesy dialog and crude graphics to appeal to a camp-seeking crowd of youth. By the 1990s, a new breed of freak performer appeared who exaggerated the old routine of eating glass or fire while claiming at least to be trying to shock viewers. But, far from being appalled by all this, some viewers distanced themselves emotionally from the act, even treating it as a joke. The audience also pretended half-seriously to be amazed and even digested, joining in the game of the put-on as they put on the role of the country rube or old carnival crowd. Though camp had antecedents, modern camp was embraced by a mostly young rebellious middle class. In it, we see a rejection of the gawking gaze for both bemused disengagement and a playful embrace of a lost carnival culture. It mocked the highbrow (or kitsch) of their parents, while pretending to play the freak.

A third form of the return of the freak was more indirect—the revival of the *creepy* or, at least, its turn to the mainstream. The fear and disgust experienced by viewers of the creepy freaks in Browning's film and many other Gothic tales of dread continued decades after *Freaks*, but often in muted ways and (like the freak show) often were produced for down-market audiences. But in the late 1960s, as a new generation became jaded by the promises of consumer culture, these emotions took more intense forms in *Night of the Living Dead* and then with a ratcheting up of sensual intensity in an avalanche of fright, gore, and unrelenting predation in slasher and zombie films. A postmodern delinking of aesthetic and emotional themes from traditional contexts and narratives meant that the creepy could be mixed with camp and even the cute, but it often was expressed in the pure form of shock.

Some Preliminary Explanations

This revival of freak culture demands explanations. This will be a major burden of this book. But as a foretaste of what's to come, let me offer some preliminary thoughts. Most obviously, the decline and reformulation of freakishness is part of the historic ambiguity of bourgeois culture. A rich summary of this ambiguity is offered in Daniel Bell's famous *Cultural Contradictions of Capitalism* (1976). Bell argues that the rational efficiency of bourgeois industrialism has been challenged by a hedonistic culture that came not from a proletariat or traditional elite but within the bourgeoisie itself (originally in the Romantic Movement). He suggests that in the modern age of mass consumption the hedonistic side of bourgeois culture has come to dominate. An unleashing of desire is vital to expanding consumer markets and thus the survival of capitalism, but this hedonistic impulse undermines the production values of the industrious bourgeoisie. The genteel culture of the Western middle class, then, is vibrant, but also contradictory, and for Bell, dangerously so.[28]

Bell's argument is relevant in explaining the late modern bourgeois (or genteel) rejection of the carnival—in its revulsion of the grotesque, sensual, irrational, and abnormal, for example. This rejection has become part of middle-class identity. But Bell finds that at least a portion of that middle class has abandoned genteel detachment for a culture of escalating sensual fulfillment. And, this is found in a revived carnival. Bell and others like Leslie Fiedler were alarmed by the rise of the countercultural "freak" among the youth of the late 1960s and early 1970s. These self-declared oddities, widely recognized to be the offspring of the middle class, rejected genteel conventions and sought to make themselves in the image of the human oddity of old, willing to be gazed at and standing in solidarity with the Other—at least in a gesture of camp. As inheritors of this hedonistic side of the rise of the bourgeoisie and capitalism, the countercultural "freaks" freely embraced the camp and its irony as well as the creepy with its promotion of emotional intensity.[29]

Another explanation for the middle-class revival of the freak show may come from the theory of postmodern hypercapitalism. According to this perspective, since the 1970s, the increasingly rapid pace of production and purchase has fragmented and intensified change in consumer markets. At the same time, new digital technologies have produced an experiential consumer economy that is equally ephemeral and fragmented. The result is a fast consumer capitalism. Sianne Ngai has more recently expanded this analysis in her oblique literary studies of modern emotions and aesthetics. She argues that hypercapitalism has produced a jaded culture that, among much else, combines the quest for the shocking with the response of boredom ("stuplimity"). This seems to be manifested in the modern appeal of the creepy and the distancing aesthetic of the camp. Her analysis of the contradictory attraction to the cute suggests also how hypercapitalism has produced commodified and passive, even immobilizing, sensibilities.[30] I might add also that hypercapitalism leads to the intensification of sensuality manifested in the unrelenting push of the emotional buttons of horror in the creepy.

An alternative to the two cultural theories above is a biological analysis that explains the recent rise of the creepy. This explanation is based on the observation that horror stories and movies meet an irrepressible psychological need, rooted in evolutionary adaptations, to encounter the predator and to derive pleasure from surviving this experience (as a fantasy and simulation). The bourgeois attempt to ban this longing to be scared and to show that one can "take it" ran against our evolved nature. These desires are manifested throughout human history in many forms (gladiator fights, executions, and even real battle). I think there are limits to the evolutionary argument—especially its limited ability to explain the nuance of historical change. Still, I think cultural historians have too long ignored the sciences (and the reverse).[31]

Finally, I would like to offer a fourth avenue of explanation that is closer to my own work and is often neglected by other writers: The re-embrace of the freak show is part of a complex change in childrearing and generational identity that has emerged over the past 120 years. This has been manifested in several ways: First, as suggested above, the linkage between the cute and the midget is deeply intertwined with the reconfiguring of the young child into a spunky innocent—the cute—and the middlebrow embrace of wonder mediated through the cute child. Second, changes in the behaviors and values of the older child and youth are closely tied to the middle-class rejection of the genteel (especially in the young) in what I have elsewhere called the cool. A powerful expression of this is the appeal of the camp and creepy—rejections of genteel values of the serious and sublime refinement.

This book tells a big story of cultural revolution, ranging across the last hundred and more years. It is about the rise of the freak show in the mid-nineteenth century that attracted both the genteel middle- and working-classes and the subsequent marginalization of the freak show to the back corners of state fairs and carnivals as the expanding middle class rejected the oddity on display. Yet the second half of the twentieth century did not see the triumph of genteel culture, a clear split between the high- and low-brow, or even the hegemony of a conventional/conformist middlebrow. In diverse and even confusing ways, the freak show returned under new management (and new audiences) as the cute, camp, and creepy—often in movies and TV shows. And in this "second wave" of freakishness, much had changed. No longer did the audience for that show consist primarily of the rube or insecure, if often socially mobile, immigrant or ethnic. Since its revival, freak culture has been increasingly comprised of media-drenched and jaded middle-class youth reared in the postmodern world of fast capitalism, gleefully rejecting markers of genteel civilization.

In exploring this curious story, I will note how the Victorian middle class assimilated the freak to its culture, but then in the twentieth century withdrew from the sideshow as the genteel abandoned the carnival in general. I will show how part of the freak show survived in the cuteification of the carnival midget that was mirrored in the modern cartoon, dolls, and toys. I will explore the camp in the antics of crowds at self-mocking films like *Rocky Horror Picture Show*, new-style freak shows, and tabloid talk TV. I will show how the creepy went wild in pointed reference to the unrelenting onslaught of zombies and slashers in horror films in recent years and even how the creepy sometimes combined with the cute and campy. This book is an exploration of how the spectacle of freakishness challenged genteel culture from the twentieth and into the twenty-first centuries, creating a commercial spectacle culture shaped by the cute, the camp, and the creepy.

I will not focus on the *person* of the freak as the Other who represented changing ideas about identity and normalcy (as have others). Rather, I will consider the *audience* for the freakish and how its response to the freak changed. The result is a popular culture that is interlaced with freakish elements with roots in the late nineteenth-century circus but radically transformed after its marginalization from 1930. That culture sometimes confirms middle-class values, but in a particular form of the cute. At the same time, it often confronts bourgeois rationality without breaking from secularity and skepticism (as in camp). Finally, that popular culture challenges respectability in a jaded quest for ever more extremes of shocking sensuality (the creepy). And sometimes, the modern carnival culture pulls all three of these freakish elements together in a cacophonous blend of intensity.

All this brought not merely the titillating and pointlessly boundary-breaking. This infusion of the latter-day freak into contemporary popular culture added a dynamism and creativity that neither genteel nor traditional carnival culture could ever offer. No longer at the side, the new show is sometimes annoyingly, but often vitally, at the center of contemporary popular culture. It is a *side show* no longer.

But, as always, we need to understand where all this came from. We need to understand how people historically responded with wonder at the extraordinary body and how a rising middle class assimilated it and then rejected it. This is the task of the next chapter.

Notes

1   David Skal and Elias Savada, *Dark Carnival: The Secret World of Tod Browning* (New York: Anchor, 1995), Chapter 1, 87–153; Robin Larsen and Beth Haller, "The Case of *Freaks,*" *Journal of Popular Film and Television*, 29, 4 (2002): 164–73; Nancy Bombaci, *Freaks in Late Modernist America* (New York: Peter Lang, 2006), 98–100, 223; Eugenie Brinkema, "Browning. Freak. Woman. Stain," in *The Cinema of Tod Browning: Essays of the Macabre and Grotesque*, Bernd Herzogenrath, ed. (Jefferson, NC: McFarland, 2008), 158–74; Mikita Brottman, *Offensive Films: Toward an Anthropology of Cinéma Vomitif* (Westport, CT: Greenwood, 1997), 17–56; Rachel Adams, *Sideshow U.S.A.: Freaks and the American Cultural Imagination* (Chicago: University of Chicago Press, 2001), Chapter 3.

2   The screenplay was, in fact, a significantly toned-down version of a short story, "Spurs," (1923), where the midget is a nasty self-centered figure who torments the grasping female circus performer, making her carry him on her back after she thinks she has tricked him into marriage. Skal and Savada, *Dark Carnival*, 154, 166, 176; David Skal, *The Monster Show: A Cultural History of Horror*

(New York: Norton, 1995), 148–9. Note also Brottman, *Offensive Films*, Chapter 1.

3   Review of *Freaks, Kansas City Star* quoted in "*Freaks* Neither Amusing or Entertaining," *Cinema Digest*, August 8, 1932, 17; "Freaks," *Variety*, February 5, 1932; "Freaks Rouse Ire and Wonder: Horrified Spectators Write Scathing Letters," *Los Angeles Times*, February 14, 1932, 9; Louella Parsons, "'Freaks' Picture Grotesque and Sensational," *Los Angeles Examiner*, February 13, 1932, 3; Larsen and Haller, "Case of *Freaks*," 167–8; Skal and Savada, *Dark Carnival*, 176–81 and Skal, *Monster Show*, 155 for other reviews; Bombaci, *Freaks*, 86–7; Wheeler Dixon, *A History of Horror* (New Brunswick, NJ: Rutgers University Press, 2010), 53; Leslie Fiedler, *Freaks: Myths and Images of the Secret Self* (New York: Simon and Schuster, 1978), 16; Robin Larsen and Beth Hall, "Public Reception of Real Disability: The Case of Freaks," *Journal of Popular Film & Television*, 29, 4 (Winter 2002): 164–72.

4   Mrs. Ambrose Nevin Diehl, Letter to Will Hays, February 26, 1932, cited in Douglas Gomery, ed., *Will H. Hays Papers, Part II* (Frederick, MD: University Publications of America, 1986); Alison Peirse, *After Dracula: The 1930s Horror Film* (London: I.B. Tauris, 2013), 2–3; Skal and Savada, *Dark Carnival*, 17, 176–7; Fiedler, *Freaks*, 191–6.

5   Fiedler, *Freaks*, Chapter 1; Hy Roth, *The Little People* (New York: Everest House, 1980).

6   Warner Home Video, *Tod Browning's 'Freaks,' The Side Show Cinema*, Turner Entertainment 2004), https://www.youtube.com/watch?v=OPfgrN7ZfCY&t=2138s.

7   Film critic Eugenie Brinkema finds the "gaze" of the freaks the real horror of the movie. These special people have already been traumatized and thus make us feel guilty for our normality and fear that we might share in their fate (as, of course, Cleopatra does). Skal and Savada, *Dark Carnival*, 167–8; Skal, *Monster Show*, 153; Brinkema, "Browning," 164–6; Diane and Doon Arbus, *Diane Arbus, An Aperture Monograph* (New York: Aperture, 1972), 3.

8   A few of the many sources on the freak show before 1930 include: Robert Bogdan, *Freak Show: Presenting Human Oddities for Amusement and Profit* (Chicago: University of Chicago Press, 1988); Michael Chemers, *Staging Stigma: A Critical Examination of the American Freak Show* (London: Palgrave, 2008); Thomas Fahey, *Freak Shows and the Modern American Imagination* (London: Palgrave, 2006); Adams, *Sideshow U.S.A*; Andrea Dennett, "The Dime Museum Freak Show Reconfigured as Talk Show," in *Freakery: Cultural Spectacles of the Extraordinary Body*, Rosemarie Garland Thomson, ed. (New York: New York University Press, 1996), 315–26.

9   Chemers, *Staging Stigma, 19*.

10 Neal Gabler, *Walt Disney: The Triumph of the American Imagination* (New York: Knopf, 2007), 249–51.

11 Gabler, *Walt Disney*, 154.

12 David H. Fisher, *Growing Old in America* (New York: Oxford University Press, 1978), Chapter 3.

13   David Friedman, *A Youth in Babylon: Confessions of a Trash-Film
     King* (Buffalo, NY: Prometheus Books, 1990), 63; Tom Milne, "Tender
     Comprehension," *Sight and Sound*, 32, 3 (Summer 1963): 145; Isabel Quigley,
     "What the Cinema Might Do More Often," *Spectator,* June 21, 1963. Skal and
     Savada, *Dark Carnival*, 223–7; Mike Quarles, *Down and Dirty: Hollywood's
     Exploitation Filmmakers and their Movies* (Jefferson, NC: McFarland, 1993),
     111–20; L. Q. Hunter, "Trash Horror and the Cult of the Bad Film," in *A
     Companion to the Horror Film*, Harry Benshoff, ed. (Malden, MA: Wiley
     Blackwell, 2017), 482–500. Vincent Canby, "Why Is *Freaks* Still a Great
     Horror Film?" *New York Times*, November 1, 1970, 103; Modern reviews of
     Freaks can be found at https://www.rottentomatoes.com/m/freaks/reviews/?
     page=3&sort=.

14   James Hoberman and Jonathan Rosenbaum, *Midnight Movies* (New York:
     Da Capo, 1991); Stuart Samuels, *Midnight Movies: From the Margins to the
     Mainstream* (Video recording, Starz Media, 2007). A dated, but interesting,
     take on the 1960s "freak" is Daniel Foss, *Freak Culture* (New York: Dutton,
     1972).

15   Susan Sontag, "Notes on Camp," in *Susan Sontag Reader*, Susan Sontag,
     ed. (New York: Vintage, 1983), 105–19; Hunter, "Trash Horror," 482–500;
     Quarles, *Down and Dirty*, 57–66.

16   Mathias Clasen, *Why Horror Seduces* (New York: Oxford University
     Press, 2017), 93–102; Judith Halberstam, *Skin Shows: Gothic Horror and
     the Technology of Monsters* (Durham, NC: Duke University Press, 1995),
     Chapter 1; Skal, *Monster Show*, Chapters 8 and 9; Quarles, *Down and Dirty*,
     70–5; Glenn Ward, "Grinding Out the Grind House: Exploitation, Myth, and
     Memory," in *Grindhouse: Cultural Exchange on 42nd Street, and Beyond*,
     Austin Fisher, ed. (London: Bloomsbury Academic, 2016), 13–30; James
     Twitchell, *Dreadful Pleasures: The Anatomy of Modern Horror* (New York:
     Oxford University Press, 1985); Sinclair McKay, *A Thing of Unspeakable
     Horror: The History of Hammer Films* (London: Aurum Press, 2007).

17   Dixon, *History of Horror*, 116–17; David Konow, *Reel Terror: The Scary,
     Bloody, Gory Hundred-Year History of Classic Horror Films* (New York:
     Thomas Dunne Books, 2012), 99–112; Paul Gagne, *The Zombies That
     Ate Pittsburgh* (New York: Dodd, Mead, 1987); Julian Hanich, *Cinematic
     Emotion in Horror Films and Thrillers* (London: Routledge, 2010).

18   Dixon, *History of Horror,* 116–17 and William Paul, *Laughing Screaming:
     Modern Hollywood Horror and Comedy* (New York: Columbia University
     Press, 1994), 260–7.

19   Eric Lichtenfeld, *Action Speaks Louder: Violence, Spectacle, and the American
     Action Movie* (Westport, CT: Praeger, 2004), 59, 145. See also Yvonne Tasker,
     ed., *Action and Adventure Cinema* (New York: Routledge, 2004); Konow, *Reel
     Terror*, Chapter 6 and 268–78.

20   M. M. Bakhtin, *Rabelais and His World* (Cambridge, MA: MIT Press, 1968);
     Peter Burke, *Popular Culture in Early Modern Europe* (New York: Harper,
     1978); Robert W. Malcolmson, *Popular Recreations in English Society, 1700-
     1850* (Cambridge: Cambridge University Press, 1973).

21 As often noted, Bakhtin emphasized the vital, communal, and creative side of carnival, often neglecting its tribal, irrational, and violent dimensions.

22 Classics on this theme are Michael Walzer, *The Revolution of the Saints* (Cambridge, MA: Harvard University Press, 1982), Chapter 1 and 6; Burke, *Popular Culture*, 207–43; Robert Muchembled, *Popular Culture and Elite Culture in France, 1400-1750* (Baton Rough: LSU Press, 1985), 49–61.

23 Max Weber, *The Protestant Ethic and the Spirit of Capitalism* (New York: Oxford University Press, 2009, original: 1905).

24 I summarize all this in *A Social History of Leisure* (State College, PA: Venture Press, 1989) (that I hope to update and revise).

25 Lawrence Levine, *High Brow/Low Brow: The Emergence of a Cultural Hierarchy in America* (Cambridge, MA: Harvard University Press, 1988).

26 The obvious reference is to Michel Foucault's *Madness and Civilization: A History of Insanity in the Age of Reason* (New York: Norton, 1988, original: 1961); another very valuable source is Rosemarie Garland-Thomson, *Staring: How We Look* (New York: Oxford University Press, 2009), especially Chapter 6.

27 Gary Cross, *The Cute and the Cool: Wondrous Innocence and American Children's Culture* (New York: Oxford University Press, 2004).

28 Daniel Bell, *The Cultural Contradictions of Capitalism* (New York: Basic, 1976).

29 Leslie Fiedler, *Freaks: Myths and Images of the Secret Self* (New York: Simon and Schuster, 1979).

30 Sianne Ngai, *Our Aesthetic Categories: Zany, Cute, Interesting* (Cambridge, MA: Harvard University Press, 2012) and her *Ugly Feelings* (Cambridge, MA: Harvard University Press, 2005).

31 Clasen, *Why Horror Seduces*, 95; R. H. Dillard, "*Night of the Living Dead*: It's Not Just Like a Wind Passing Through," in *American Horrors*, George Walker, ed. (Urbana: University of Illinois Press, 1987), 14–9; Kendall Phillips, *Projected Fears: Horror Films and American Culture* (Westport, CT: Praeger, 2005), 82–3.

2

Carnival Culture and the Challenge of Gentility

Throughout history people have found wonder by encountering difference and imagining the marvelous in the unfamiliar. Probably every time and culture has had its freaks. Though these encounters and imaginings have changed over time and vary from place to place, they have remained surprising persistent, at least, until recently. Most designations of freakery are derived from human fascination with the boundaries between inside and outside groups, human and animal, conventional and unusual size, shape, and behavior, and between the normal and unexpected.

And yet part of the making of modernity has been the abandonment of the wondrous stare at the boundary and the debunking of the mysterious stories purported to explain that boundary. Science has demystified the dwarf and conjoined twin; but even more, modern bourgeois culture simply denies that stare and that mystery. However, the exchange between the "normal" viewer and the Other has not really disappeared, but rather this encounter has been transformed. To make sense of all this, we need to begin with the polymorphous responses of our ancestors to the human (or animal) oddity, how they met the freak with fear, delight, and repugnance.[1] As literary historian Rachel Adams notes, "freak shows performed important cultural work by allowing ordinary people to confront and master, the most extreme and terrifying forms of Otherness that they could imagine."[2]

Historic Encounters with the Extraordinary

The freak show has its origins in ancient stories and practices intended to explain the *unknown*—strange and alien creatures from distant and mysterious lands and, even more, shadowy wonders of unusual births that produced extraordinary *bodies*, exciting a wide and even contradictory range of emotions. Unusual *behavior*, especially in subjecting the body to pain or danger (as in sword swallowing), was yet another form of freakishness. Sometimes our predecessors found ways of containing and domesticating these strange jokes of nature (as freaks were often called). While confined to legends and to serving as the playthings of kings and aristocrats until relatively modern times, the freak had become a commodity in the commercial entertainment industry by the nineteenth century.

The world beyond the mountains or seas that protected self-assumed civilized people has often been believed to be inhabited by monsters and oddities. Herodotus thought that humans past the lands of the Scythians had goat's feet and that the Libyan deserts were inhabited by dwarfs. Even the medieval traveler Marco Polo claimed that the peoples of Sumatra sported tails. And Arab folklore promoted the idea that that in Java humans could be found with heads lodged in their breasts. Stories abound of monsters in dark forests or caves, giants atop misty mountain, and mermaids in deep waters. Throughout history, parents have told their children tales of many kinds of mysterious unknowns: Brownies with pointed ears were said to inhabit barns in Scotland, coming out only at night to play tricks on farmers. Never seen little people guarded treasure in mines (echoed in Disney's seven dwarfs) and demanded food and other favors in exchange for not harming humans or for warning them of danger. Some, like trolls, were said to be nasty, while others, like elves, were supposed to be friendly. This identification of the oddity with faraway, mysterious, and often dangerous places shaped narratives and appeals of unusual creatures through the centuries—even in the quest for the exotic in modern times, including the adventurous voyages of Robert Ripley recorded in his "Believe It or Not" cartoons from the 1920s.[3]

Even closer to the mystery of the "monster" is the extraordinary body, often linked to the uncertainty of birth. Ancient peoples saw portents of good or bad futures in abnormal birth: To the Babylonians of 2800 BCE, a baby with a foot of six toes promised affliction to the community. The birth defect had to have an explanation: God's wrath or glory, the sin of the parent or community. In 1599, Ambroise Paré added a natural explanation for the birth of giants or midgets: perhaps too much semen (if the child was oversized) or too little (if small). Such naturalistic analysis was as fact-free as the supernatural claim, but perhaps it was also less satisfying insofar as "superstitious" explanations long persisted. Many seem arbitrary: Ancient Greeks glorified androgynous babies but scorned hunchbacks or cripples. Stories abound of the birth of hybrids from humans mating with animals (or gods), producing werewolves, gargoyles, and minotaurs. Through the eighteenth-century observers like Carl Linnaeus listed albinos, babies with tails, and the like as separate species. They were not simple deviations from the human norm, but biologically unique. A common explanation of freakish birth was "maternal marking," where an often-stressful encounter of a pregnant woman, including the sight of fornicating dogs or a lion mauling a person, resulted in a dog- or lion-faced baby. Joseph Merrick, the famous "elephant man" of Victorian Britain, was said to have believed that his deformity was caused by his mother's fright during her pregnancy with him when she was nearly run over by an elephant. Such beliefs were doubtless encouraged by the ever-present fear of infant or maternal mortality at the point of birth. Such anxieties were compounded by the horror of deformity in the perilous years of maturation. Neither apprehension had widely held medical explanations until the late nineteenth century.[4]

Less common in the ancient world was behavioral freakishness— subjecting the body to extraordinary stress that violated common ideas of self-preservation. Sword swallowing along with walking on hot coals, handling dangerous snakes, and other forms of self-abnegation developed about 4000 years ago in India. They were practices of religious ascetics,

FIGURE 2.1 *Woodcut of a two-headed monster c.1495, Wellcome Collection, Attribution 4.0 International (CC BY 4.0).*

intended to show their spiritual power and ability to surmount the ordinary fragility of the human body. By 100 CE, these practices had passed to Greece and Rome as part of festival celebrations and then to medieval fairs. These spectacles were a regular part of sideshows and performances into the twentieth century and survive today in new age freak shows. These marvels did not always evoke fear or disgust, but often wonder. As historians of science, Lorraine Daston and Katherine Park note, the word "marvel" is derived from an Indo-European word for smile and it is related to the word "miracle." The freak has never been purely negative.[5]

In fact, feelings of horror and repugnancy toward the freak were sometimes mollified or even reversed in the pleasure of turning the monster into a pet. Roman emperors Augustus and Tiberius kept dwarfs or midgets at their courts. Treated as amusing objects of affection by the Romans, midgets were "manufactured" in a few cases by underfeeding small children. And Emperor Domitian sent dwarf gladiators into the coliseum for the crowd's amusement. Ancient Egyptian pharaohs seem to have a more positive view (and even apparently pictured little people as gods). The custom of making small people into pets or spectacles seems to have declined in the Middle Ages. However, in the increasingly lavish and self-aggrandizing courts of the Renaissance, ancient practices returned: The Medicis of Florence, along with Spanish, French, Russian, and Swedish kings, kept little people in their retinues, and often dressed them in the finest livery. Sometimes they were used as novel accessories in banquets (as were thirty-four for the Roman Cardinal Vitelli in 1566) or weddings (as in 1710 when Peter the Great embellished a marriage celebration with seventy dwarfs). Some midgets and dwarfs were allowed to roam about court displaying their wit and charm, as did jesters in the Middle Ages. Small people were sometimes assumed to be wise despite their size (and small heads). However, the English word "freak," dating from the 1560s, may suggest something about what these oddities did and how they were perceived. The word originally meant a "sudden turn of mind," and may be related to the Old English word *frician*, "to dance" or jump and make gestures. Even so, occasionally midgets were used as executioners (perhaps a bit of dark humor). By contrast, giants were rarer in court society and usually used as ceremonial guards or in symbolic displays of military might (such as with Frederick the Great of eighteenth-century Prussia).[6]

While court freaks disappeared in France after 1662 (presumably because of more enlightened culture), the custom persisted in Eastern Europe through the eighteenth century. It is noteworthy that domesticated freaks were mostly miniature men, rather than conjoined twins or armless women, for example. Midgets were bodily oddities, of course, but they were also often objects of delight. Sometimes the pleasure in court midgets was like the affection shown pet animal (also largely a creation of court society). Still, the practice of keeping a midget like a lap dog was usually an expression of status, a sign that the aristocratic or royal possessor had the capacity for conspicuous consumption (similar in function to the cabinets of curiosities collected by elites from the sixteenth century).[7] But the small person also brought a negative form of amusement, even mockery, to the court when these jokes of nature made the owner feel superior. In the paintings of Spanish painters of the seventeenth and eighteenth centuries (as in the Portrait of Sebastián de Morra by Diego Velázquez of 1645), court midgets were portrayed as laughable in their elegant dress and were associated with dogs. They were not yet considered "cute," as will develop later (Chapter 4).[8]

Inevitably perhaps, that which amused the elite "trickled down" to the crowd in the tavern or at the fair. By the end of the sixteenth century, dwarfs and midgets appeared at alehouses and sang at fairs in England, often accompanied by managers: In 1581, a seven-foot giant and a three-foot dwarf from Holland teamed up in an acrobatic dance for bemused English crowds. Oft-noted were the displays of anomalies at St. Bartholomew's Fair in London: In 1631, attractions included people born with four arms and three breasts; and, in 1662, conjoined female twins attracted crowds.[9] Long a venue for four days of frolicking, St. Bartholomew's Fair was finally closed in 1855 after years of complaint of disorder and debauchery, but not before it was immortalized by many authors (Ben Jonson, Samuel Pepys, and William Wordsworth). Charles Dickens in his Sketches by Boz (1836) describes another London fair at Greenwich, famed not only for the display of a dwarf and a giantess but also for the appearance of a living skeleton and albino, available to the masses for a mere penny admission.[10]

In colonial North America and the early United States, itinerate showmen offered an array of cheap amusements: from peep shows and organ grinders with trained monkeys to human oddities, including in 1809 in Salem, Massachusetts, an albino and handless woman who could make paper flowers. Armless Martha Ann toured northern states from 1798 to 1848, amazing audiences with her skill at cutting paper silhouettes with her feet. In 1838, Nathaniel Hawthorne wrote about his visit to a small wax works show in Salem, consisting of effigies of murderers and their victims that attracted mixed crowds of "half bumpkin half country squire." He noted in the audience a mechanic, and even "several decent-looking girls" as well as a "gentlemanly sort of person, who looks somewhat ashamed of himself for being there."[11]

In 1786, the type of oddities that rich collectors had gathered in their cabinets of curiosities became available to the public, albeit primarily a cultured elite, in the museum of Charles Willson Peale of Philadelphia. In 1814, his sons opened a second museum in Baltimore. The elder Peale was an amateur naturalist and painter, intent on educating the public about native birds and the bones of mastodons. In fact, he futilely sought government subsidies for his displays. While Charles Peale insisted that nature's oddities were to be shown rarely on request, he conceded to popular taste by displaying a five-legged calf (as well as the trigger finger of a murderer). After Charles Peale retired in 1810, his sons were somewhat more willing

to concede to popular taste. Lectures on natural science, emphasizing the
regularity of nature, gradually gave way to theatrical programs. By 1849,
Peale's offspring abandoned decades of attempting to foster "rational
amusement" and sold much of their collection to Moses Kimball of Boston
and P.T. Barnum of New York, who willingly accommodated popular taste
in their "dime" museums.[12]

These dime museums, sites of eclectic display and entertainment, evolved
from the failure of more serious institutions. Dime museums had their roots
in the first American Museum that opened in New York City in 1791. First,
it was only for members interested in American artifacts. This high-minded
institution failed by 1798, and, even though John Scutter partially restored
it 1810, he was obliged to offer a popular collection of wax figures, along
with his collection of stuffed animals, to succeed. But Scutter's museum
too failed in 1821. Later P.T. Barnum bought part of the collection for
his new American Museum of 1841. Unlike the museums of Peale and
Scutter, Barnum's dime museum was relentlessly commercial. It flourished
until 1865 when it burned down and was immediately rebuilt, only to
succumb once again to fire in 1868, after which Barnum shifted to traveling
shows, including the circus. Still other dime museums survived in urban
America, becoming homes of itinerate human anomalies who had formerly
displayed themselves on their own. Dime museum proprietors offered these
freaks lodging and made them centerpieces of a broadly popular venue
of entertainment that continued in storefront shows and circuses into the
twentieth century.[13]

Commercializing Difference: Entertainment for All with Barnum's Dime Museum

As so many historians have noted, Barnum (1810–1891) was the consummate
showman. He launched his career in 1835 by displaying an old ex-slave,
Joice Heth, presenting her as a 161-year-old, who had once been the nurse
of George Washington. Benjamin Reiss shows how Barnum's customers
responded to this racialized freak not only with condescension and disgust
but also with admiration for her presumed linkage to the Founding Father,
her humor, family loyalty, and love of religious music. Another authority,
James Cook, shows how Barnum fully expressed the methods and values of
a new age of commercialized entertainment, aptly combining an appeal to
popular sensation with middle-class sensibility.[14]

Barnum drew on new forms of publicity like newspapers and photos to
create novel appeals while popularizing formerly localized and traditional
entertainments. His early and often discussed displays of fraudulent
oddities—the "Feejee Mermaid," a monkey's head sewn onto the lower half
of a fish, for example—provided Barnum with much fame and notoriety.

With such displays, he attracted both the gullible and the bemused to his museum. Barnum recognized that he had created a subtle interaction between the yarn-spinning showman and an amused urban customer who often enjoyed the deception. Gradually this gave way to a more subtle approach, combining freakish novelties, family-oriented country fair acts like jugglers and magicians, and respectable middle-class melodramas (even temperance plays) along with lectures on electricity and natural history. His museum, followed by his three-ring circus, offered something for everyone in his culturally diverse crowd. Barnum's museum also presented a "perceptional overload," as Cook notes, a kind of serial intensity, as displays came one after another, anticipating the sensual assault of the ten-in-one sideshow and three-ring circus. Disney and other modern theme park impresarios have made this "overload" into an art. Even more, Barnum offered novelty, ginned up by intense publicity, creating commercial crazes like his tour of the Swedish Nightingale, Jenny Lind, or his display of dancing and singing native Americans. Ultimately, the diversity and range of his spectacle created the massified spectator that blended appeals across class, gender, geography, and race. And the freak show was at its heart.[15]

Barnum's dime museum provided a mix of new and old, mid- and lowbrow, as did much mid-nineteenth-century entertainment. Located on a very respectable corner (Broadway and Anne Street in the heart of Manhattan), it attracted 38 million visitors in its twenty-four-year run despite its relatively high price then of not a dime but twenty-five cents. Although Barnum insisted on well-behaved crowds, the audience was always part of the entertainment. Barnum's customers walked through rooms of displays, gawking at and reacting to what was shown. Many authors have noted this tension between Barnum's presumption of edification and concessions of popular entertainment. In fact, he walked a tightrope: First, he had to appeal to the aspiring middle class with its commitment to moderation and "rational recreation" and its rejection of the carnivalesque. Second, he had to make concessions to the more raucous and disrespectful plebeians who still embraced the traditional carnival blend of mockery, credulity, and fascination with the extraordinary body. This strategy not only brought him success but shaped the programing of other museums and later circuses and sideshows. Barnum displayed human oddities, often appealing to the plebeian prejudices of his audience. Yet he rejected the common idea that albinos, pinheads, and conjoined twins were non-human species, but instead insisted that they were capable of normal moral development. He often portrayed them with exceptional human talents and skills rather than as frightful monsters. While he won the working-class and immigrant crowd with carnival, this appeal to respectability made the oddity acceptable to genteel as well as popular audiences. And he did this at a time when the rising bourgeoisie in Europe had pulled away from the fair and festival. He created a mass, rather than class-divided, culture—even in his freak show.[16]

Barnum's acquisition of the five-year-old, twenty-six-inch-tall Charles
Stratton in 1843 for display at his museum illustrates this culturally
diverse appeal. While advertised as eleven years old (making his size more
astonishing), Stratton was at first dressed as a baby and was humorously
named Tom Thumb, a well-known English fairy tale figure dating from the
seventeenth century. But soon the midget was elevated with the uniform
of a general, delighting largely middle-class audiences with his comical
banter, singing, and dancing. In a famous visit to England, Tom Thumb was
ennobled with a highly publicized audience with Queen Victoria. Stratton
stood in sharp contrast to the misshaped dwarfs hawked as "monsters" in
traveling shows; instead, he offered an uncanny air of normality in manner,
exceptionality in talent. Barnum took advantage of new technology, posing
Stratton for a Daguerreotype photo in 1843 and later for mass-produced
carte de visite photos to spread his fame to an adoring audience of middle-
class consumers. Retiring at twenty, Stratton later returned to Barnum's
stage in 1863 in the media frenzy of his wedding with Lavinia Warren (after
a widely publicized, but contrived, rivalry with "Commodore Nutt"—
aka George Morrison Nutt). Attended by gilded New York (the Astors,
Vanderbilts, and Belmonts), their wedding took place at Grace Episcopal
Church in New York. Later, Barnum offered fans photos of the presumed
fruit of this union of midgets, a baby (faked).[17]

While Tom Thumb was a freak of nature, like the midgets of Renaissance
courts, he was domesticated, integrated into a respectable world of bourgeois
elegance, removing any uneasiness that especially the middle-class viewer
might have had in viewing a man with a high-pitched voice who was scarcely
forty inches tall as an adult. Other oddities were more troublesome to the
middle-class viewer (the pinhead portrayed as the "missing link" between
humans and apes, for example). But these freaks were set in a museum
where middle-class standards of rational recreation (lectures, natural history,
didactic plays, etc.) prevailed. They were not put in a dirty stall or pit in the
back of a rundown carnival or basement of an empty store front in a sleazy
part of town as might occur in later freak shows.

Of course, not all nineteenth-century dime museums were so genteel.
Inevitably some catered to a more down-market crowd in the lower
Manhattan district of the Bowery. Between 1876 and 1887, George
Bunnell operated a museum, which included a "Dante's Inferno" with
wax figures tormented in Hell (including prominent American plutocrats
and politicians like Jay Gould and Boss Tweed). George Huber's museum
(1888–1910) featured at one time Jo-Jo, the Dog-Faced Boy and a geek
who bit off the heads of snakes, along with a variety of low-quality
musical and comedy acts, stuffed birds, and war curios. Attending were
"women and children, men of the Bowery stamp, and sailors on shore
leave," notes the *New York Times* smugly at its closure in 1910, observing
that the crowds at Huber's museum had been shifting to the nearby movie
theater for several years. In 1891, Huber's former partner, E.M. Worth,

FIGURE 2.2 *P.T. Barnum and General Tom Thumb, c. 1850 when Charles Stratton was about twelve. Wikimedia Commons.*

opened a rival museum that offered a thrill-seeking crowd Charles Tripp, the armless man, famed veteran of Barnum shows, and Senoj, a twenty-seven-inch-tall man without legs and one webbed foot. The New York Museum of Anatomy on lower Broadway in 1848 presented viewers a quasi-medical, but ultimately voyeuristic, experience. Admitting only male customers (respecting the dignity of Victorian ladies), this museum featured an amalgam of sometimes scurrilous oddities: fetuses in jars illustrating human embryonic development but also wax figures depicting female sex organs accompanied by "doctors" delivering medical lectures as well as wax depictions of female beauty (Venus) and, for some reason, the skull of Henry VIII's jester. Though dime museums disappeared after 1910—no longer able to compete with movie houses and other sites of urban amusement—their attractions survived decades later in the form of storefront shows that cropped up in the downtowns of many American cities and in traveling carnivals.[18]

Freaks at Circuses, Fairs, and Carnivals

While freak appearances in dime museums and other urban venues were widespread in the Victorian era, the American encounter with oddities became a national experience in this still largely rural country only with the spread of the traveling circus and its sideshow. The modern circus's origin is commonly attributed to Philip Astley. An English horse trainer, Astley, transformed his riding school in London in 1768 into a ring in which trick horseback riding was offered to a paying audience. As additional entertainment, Astley displayed acrobats on trampolines and wire-walkers, who he hired from the popular theater. As early as 1793, John Ricketts, an English immigrant located in Philadelphia, copied Astley's formula with a show consisting of horseback riding, juggling, and, in 1795, a dwarf who rode standing up on a small horse. Small menageries of exotic animals, featuring elephants, appeared in the United States by 1815, and the circus ring and menagerie were commonly combined by 1850. The Spalding and Rogers Circus first toured by train in 1846.[19] At first, freaks appeared in shows independent of but nearby circuses (as sideshows). The first to combine a circus, menagerie, and freak show museum was Waring, Raymond, and Co. in 1837 (though most sideshows remained independent until the 1870s).[20]

By 1871, Barnum had abandoned his museum (which had at various times been a traveling show) for a rail-based traveling circus, bringing along famous acts from the museum to the sideshow. The sideshow became a regular feature, usually opened an hour before the big tent show. Freaks were combined with minstrel singers and a band, dancers (later often dressed in exotic costumes), jugglers, and ventriloquists. Despite much variety, the sideshow gradually was formalized: strolling crowds were greeted with a six-foot-high "bally" platform where a "talker" (not usually called a "barker") hyped the tented show that was usually behind him, often offering the audience a preview of a featured performer before directing the gathered crowd or "tip" (more manipulatively known as the "mark") to the ticket booth. After entering the sideshow tent, customers were introduced to each personality (some of whom performed; others were simply observed) followed often by a "blow-off" of a separately ticketed act to make room for the next group of viewers. From the 1870s, sideshows were decorated with garish banners individually painted to feature each act. Small and less "respectable" circuses had "grifters," who cheated customers with shell or card games and who offered girly shows (often as the blow-off) with varying degrees of female exposure. The sideshow was far more than a display of freaks, though they were a major draw.[21]

World's fairs and amusement parks were still another important site for the display of human oddities. Beginning with the Philadelphia Centennial Exhibition in 1876 and continuing with the 1893 Columbia Exhibition in Chicago, these fairs included amusement areas with freak shows that were separated from the scientific and artistic displays. The informal Shantyville in

Philadelphia included well-known attractions such as The Wild Children of Australia and a 602-pound woman. The more elaborately planned Midway Plaisance in Chicago featured not only the first Ferris Wheel and stereotyped miniature German and Irish "villages" but also exhibits of West African "natives" in the Dahomey Village and "cannibalistic" Samoans. Following on the success of the Chicago's Midway in 1893, the first American amusement parks appeared, the most famous of which were grouped at Coney Island, near New York City. There, in 1903, the most ambitious of these, Dreamland, was opened. Despite pretensions of middle-class respectability, Dreamland contained both a village of midgets, Lilliputia, and after 1908 a full-blown sideshow of freaks that survived the burning of this amusement park in 1911.[22]

Another venue for the freak show was the traveling carnival. Emerging after the Civil War with independent shows of wax works, food and game stalls, and mechanical rides, by the 1890s, national chains of carnivals emerged. The carnival was a modern adaptation of the amusement section of the traditional trade fair. The carnival was notable for its ability to move cheaper and faster than the circus (lacking elephants and big top tents, for example). By 1896, Frank Bostock's carnivals competed with the Ferrari Brothers. Along with state and county fairs, carnivals were often sponsored by fraternal organizations like the Elks; and by 1905 there were already forty-six touring carnivals.

About this time, ten-in-one freak shows joined the carnival. For a single price, crowds saw a mix of ten freaks and "working acts" like the bladebox (where a woman appeared to be stabbed by swords in a box). The shows differed greatly in size and quality. Variations were the "grind show" where the acts were continuous as customers passed through to view the featured figure, often in a pit. Later, single act shows (Single-Os) became common, especially in smaller carnivals. Because real Siamese twins and other born-oddities were rare and expensive, fake (or "gaffed") freaks were common. Following Barnum with his manufactured oddity, the Fejee Mermaid, faked features like the "serpent chicken" were common by the 1890s.[23]

Freaks were not necessarily treated poorly. The dime museums often provided onsite shelter and a measure of community. And some freaks earned good money. Well known is the success of Tom Thumb and the original Siamese Twins (Chang and Eng Bunker) who owned mansions and farms. Freaks often gained fame through newspaper features, biographical booklets, postcards, and photo cards (which they often sold to the crowd personally as a major source of their income).[24]

The Exotic Freak in the Victorian Moral World

The stories and cultures of the sideshow performers have often been chronicled by both scholarly historians and enthusiasts. But I am interested here mostly in teasing out the motives and culture of audiences rather than the lives of the actors. This is not easy because that audience from the beginning was diverse and market research was nonexistent. One way, at least, of indirectly identifying those differences and what appealed to freak-show goers is to explore the range of displayed freaks and how they were presented in the Victorian dime museum, circus sideshow, and early carnival (trusting, to a degree, that exhibitors knew their audiences). The goal is not to repeat the work of sideshow historians with full details of individual freaks, but to explore how the variety of oddities and their presentation to the public indicate what the audience was seeking.

Literary scholar Leslie Fiedler claims that freaks represent the "basic fears" and insecurities of viewers; encountered creatures evoke anxieties about "monsters" from distant and unknown places or who, but for the grace of God in birth and upbringing, members of the audiences might have been. And yet he also insists that "all freaks are perceived to one degree or another as erotic," appealing to the desire to transcend taboos. Oddities are attractive in their deviation from the conventional, the normal. This duality of fear and attraction runs through much of the freak encounter throughout history.[25]

Part of the attraction of the oddity was his or her setting in age-old mystery, ancient myths and fairy tales, and misty recollections of traditional fairs and spectacles in which both these anxieties and attractions were deeply bonded. On top of this residual cultural (and perhaps biological) response was the change brought in the nineteenth century: repositioning the freak in a socially fluid and highly commercialized entertainment venue. To win paying audiences, impresarios like Barnum had to make the freak intelligible to an emerging middle class with definite standards of propriety, often shaped by women. At the same time, the freak had to attract equally aspiring, but often culturally and socially insecure, working-class and immigrant customers who, while retaining some of the credulity and boisterous fascination of the old festival/fair crowd, also looked to the sideshow as a vindication of their racial and cultural superiority to the freaks. Show people accomplished this through producing "backstories" for the freaks in pitch booklets and photos (principally for a middle-class consumer) as well as by orchestrating animated freak performance along with crowd interaction (often for the lower orders). In a way, Barnum reversed (or delayed) the split between the genteel and carnival culture noted by Bakhtin in Europe.

Common Victorian freaks were the exotic feral child and wild man who presumably had been raised by and had lived among animals. Historically, of course, this is a common myth; and the return of these "savages" to civilization has long fascinated people. But, an age-old fear of the barbarian and monsters beyond the communal boundary had often given way to a sense of superiority by the white urban audiences of mid-nineteenth-century America. This helps explain why these Americans would have been willing to pay to see human oddities. In fact, they were really often local people with birth or developmental anomalies: midgets, pinheads, and white women with frizzy hair dressed in leopard skins or other outlandish garb to appear "foreign." They were described as exotics, rescued from the jungle or the horrors of Turkish harems. The freak without the dramatic story was merely someone out of place to be ignored or pitied.

Freak show talkers often presented these stories on the bally stage, but they were written also in pitch booklets. A common theme was the portrayal of victims of microcephaly (pinheads)—identified by their stunted growth, undersized craniums, and limited intelligence—as wild people from distant places. In 1850, John Steven published the booklet *Memoire of an Eventual Expedition in Central America, Resulting in the Discovery of the Idolatrous City of Iximaya. . . and the Remarkable Aztec Children.* It recounts how a boy and girl (about three feet tall) were liberated from the jungles of Central America, presumably from a "nearly extinct race" that somehow escaped Cortez's Spanish invasion. In fact, they were microcephalic midgets brought to the United States in 1849. Added to this romantic tale is a patronizing explanation of their diminutive size, resulting from the horrors of inbreeding (like that of the Hindu, we are told). While the boy seems "bird like" and idiotic, his "eyes show intelligence"; the girl curiously looks "Jewish," suggesting that the Aztec Children might possibly be redeemed by civilization. Lending this classic story of missionary rescue from savagery and mystery a measure of rationalist legitimacy, the author notes that these children "claim the attention of physiologist and all men of science." This story fits a common pattern—combining an appeal to curiosity for barbarous places and with a missionary impulse to civilize the captured wild child and identify what, if anything, makes the child human. As always, the freak is at the boundary between the human and the animal, the civilized and the savage.[26]

Another dimension of this fascination with liminality was the African albino. Rudolph Lucasie was one of these, presumably rescued in 1844 by a white man on the coast of Madagascar after being wounded by a lance by other Africans, who, the booklet insists, view albinos of their race as monsters. Though his speech was unintelligible to experts, he learned some Italian and was converted to Catholicism. Again, there is the conventional missionary and civilizing story. But more, Lucasie's African origins was mollified by his white skin and features.[27]

Similarly, in an 1872 booklet introducing the "Wild Australian Children," Captain J. Reid offers middle-class readers a backstory of rescue and liminal mystery, justifying the actual display of victims of birth defects. Reid, an agent for a menagerie on a hunt for specimens, joined a band of missionaries and hunters to explore the Australian outback inhabited by aboriginal cannibals. There, Reid's group found four feral children, presumably from a nearly "extinct" tribe (in fact, microcephalic siblings from Ohio). These children have a "monkey like-gait and small heads" that is belied by their "bright intelligent faces." Again, though the boy resists wearing clothing and speaks only a few words, he has learned to use a fork and comb (interesting markers of civilization). However, like other primitives, he has a "childish fondness for toys" and like his fellow savage, "he "moves on stage noiselessly as the skulking Indian in his native forest." These "Wild Children" are both alien and familiar, irredeemably primitive and potentially candidates for civilizing. They are, Reid argues, a link between the "ourang-outang" and the human.[28] The savage is a perpetual child, sharing traits with the familiar primitive, forested native American, all characteristics that tell us by contrast what it means to be human and civilized. This story gives expression to the anxiety and fascination of literate Victorian viewers, but it also reassures them of their place at the vanguard of civilization.

An 1875 booklet featured still another pair of savages, "Waino and Plutano, the Wild Men of Borneo," brought to civilization in the sideshow. It tells the tale of the discovery of twins in the "impenetrable jungle" of Borneo, where no missionary had dared to visit. The twins may have lived in caverns or, to suggest even greater savagery, "made nests in trees like birds" and were "hardly more elevated in social standing than ourang-outangs." Yet, unlike monkeys they were more agile. Again, suggesting these oddities represented the boundary between human and animal, the booklet notes that in captivity, they gradually learned manners (though they had no speech). Instead of appealing to the scientific interest of these rescued primitives, this booklet draws on another middle-class concern by insisting that these creatures are not animals but made in the "image of God" and "if they live blameless lives, they will go to heaven." Of course, Waino and Plutano were really Hiram and Barney Davis from New York or Connecticut and were pinheads and midgets. The booklet, doubtless purchased by more affluent and educated viewers, recognized the humanity of Waino and Plutano. However, in the sideshow, they were dressed in jungle costumes and expected to snarl and snap, perhaps accommodating expectations of a wider, predominately plebeian, crowd, which believed that these brothers were biologically inferior.[29]

Repeatedly microcephalics were displayed as "missing links" in the evolution from ape to human—still another example of the complex presentation of the exotic freak. "Zip," William Henry John (1843–1926) a black microcephalic from New Jersey, was advertised as a foundling, rescued naked from the River Gambia. Presumably, he was discovered "roving in the manner of the monkey" and walked like "a child beginning to acquire that accomplishment." Not only was he portrayed as a permanently immature but was a "connecting link between the wild native African and the brute creation."[30]

In this regard, these booklets follow a common popular belief that the "savage" represented a lower stage in human evolution that is duplicated in the development of the individual child as in Ernest Haeckel's theory (1866): "ontogeny [individual development] recapitulates phylogeny [species evolution]." This idea was later applied to child development in G. Stanley Hall's *Adolescence* (1904). Hall claimed children recapitulated humanity's evolution from "savagery" to "civilization," as they grew up.[31]

But these respectable Victorian ideas did not deter Barnum and others from dressing such childlike examples of human evolution in furry costumes to conform to popular expectations of what a "savage" should look like. Thus, for half a century Zip or "What Is It?" was exhibited in this way in sideshows and dime museums as an example of the "missing link" between ape and human in a popular understanding of Darwinian evolution.

A variation of exotic freaks are the "Circassian Beauties," usually ordinary *white* women with dramatically frizzled hair and dressed in exotic costumes, which became a rage on the freak show circuit in the 1860s and 1870s. Their backstory went through various editions, culminating in the 1860s: "Circassians" were said to be from a region of that name in the Caucasus Mountains (thus the term Caucasians for whites) of south-central Asia, a region Johann Blumenbach (1752–1840) claimed to be the original site of all humanity (assuming the evolutionary priority of whites). Added to the fascination with these "first" humans was the story that they had been forced into a Turkish harem but were rescued by Europeans. Again, popular racial and cultural prejudice was affirmed in this exotic take on the superiority of Caucasians, on deeply held European animosity toward the Turks, and in myths about the taboo sexuality of their rulers. Circassian women, sometimes said to have been rescued from the Constantinople "slave market," were featured in circuses through the 1890s. Though they were often dressed in exotic clothing, they were ordinary American young women with frizzy hair of various colors. Long-haired women and long-bearded men were still rare enough to attract cartes de visite and cabinet cards promoting their sideshow and museum appearances. Audiences were also more broadly fascinated with albinos like Etta Rogers with her "white hair like finely spun floss or threads of silver."[32]

Fascination with the exotic oddity of course grew with Western colonization of sub-Saharan Africa and parts of Asia from the 1870s. This culminated in Barnum and Bailey's "Ethnological Congress of Savage Peoples" of 1884, consisting of 73 "Bestial Australian Cannibals, Big-Lipped Botocudos, Wild Moslem Nubians, Annamite Dwarfs," but also "Burmese Priests, and Haughty Syrians." Fascination with the black "primitives" continued with African bushmen like Cliko in the 1920s, Ubangi people with saucer-lips in the early 1930s, and the "Darkest Africa" show at the Chicago World's Fair (1933–4).[33]

The backstories of exotic freaks reflected a common Victorian response to encounters with a widening world: a linkage of exotic dark-skinned people with animals and, with the popularization of Darwin, with a low rung on the evolutionary ladder. But sprinkled in these biases was often the missionary's admonition that all humanity shared a God-given soul and the Enlightenment conviction that through education even savages could share in European civilization (if only in a limited degree).

FIGURE 2.3 *Krao, "The Missing Link," drawing on a popular understanding of Darwin, was claimed to be found in Laos and exhibited in London in 1887. Wellcome Collection, Attribution 4.0 International (CC BY 4.0).*

The Extraordinary Body in Victorian America

Another type of oddity that appeared regularly in the sideshow were persons whose bodies were disturbingly different. The anxious attraction came not from their origin in the unknown place (or, at least, the myth of exotic origins), but rather from their plainly uncommon birth and bodily development. The ancient mysteries and uncertainties of birth and biological growth and its bodily anomalies continued to obsess Victorians. This was not merely a residual emotion, but a continued reality, changing only at the end of the nineteenth century as deaths and maladies at birth and during childhood declined sharply. Giving birth to an armless child was a real fear as was experiencing a growth-stunting disease in an offspring. Victorians paid to experience bodily anomaly, greeting it with a welter of emotions: pity, curiosity, superiority, and even admiration. But that response varied based on the class culture of the viewer.

While most bodily aberrations found their way into the freak show, they did so in different degrees and with distinct presentations. Persons with a surfeit of hair like Jo-Jo the Dog-Faced Boy (found in the "dense forest of Kostrama in the Russian Empire"), Lionel (the Lion-faced Boy), Alice Bounds (The Bear Lady), and Davey (the Man Bear) were all well-known fixtures of late nineteenth-century sideshows. Mostly victims of hypertrichosis, showmen often portrayed them as mysterious creatures on the boundary between human and animal. These presentations were in part throwbacks to earlier myths about creatures who breached this boundary as a result of in human–animal sexual unions. Even the ancient myth of maternal marking survived in the nineteenth century, as the case of the Bear Boy, whose booklet claimed that he was born bearlike because of a rather gruesome experience of his mother—his father cutting the throat of his pregnant mother's pet cub and throwing the body on her.[34]

However, many "born-freaks," despite their extraordinary appearance, were described as normal, even gifted in some way, reducing the discomfort of genteel audiences who were anxious not to openly display "carnival" attitudes in disparaging the unfortunate or showing excessive fascination in the exotic. Such was the case with another hirsute anomaly, the bearded lady, a gender-bending phenomenon. In pitch literature, she was usually pictured as a "normal" woman, often married with children, and in possession of exceptional intelligence and charm. She often spoke in a disarmingly soft voice and took pride in her appearance. In photos, she was often dressed in a conventionally feminine costume (all heightening the contradiction of a bearded female). Such was the 1854 description of Madame Clofullia, "Dame à Barbe" (in classy French yet), who presumably grew a beard only at fourteen years of age after a typical girlhood in Switzerland. When bearded, she left her village not to be displayed in a tawdry fair but to present herself in Geneva, sophisticated home of Rousseau, after which she visited the palace of Versailles. Later, she married a painter and traveled to New York to be shown by Barnum. The voyeuristic appeal of gender ambiguity was intensified by the lady-like description of Clofullia, but her "respectability" also increased her appeal to a genteel audience.[35]

Another form of gender ambiguity was the half-and-half or hermaphrodite. Although later commonly a gaffe or fake freak in the traveling carnival, early portrayals of this sexual wonder gave the hermaphrodite a respectable backstory. Such is seen in the printed account of Lala Coolah (1916), which insists that she was born female in 1870. She showed signs of a voice "harsh and coarse" only at twelve, after which doctors found both sex organs (the penis formerly being obscured in her flesh). Though she married a man, soon she divorced to adopt male clothes to appear in the Congress of Living Wonders. The tone of this booklet (no doubt purchased by the more affluent customer) was modest and respectable with no accounting for her sex life or personality, merely a brief account of her physical appearance, as if Lala was to be a "mystery of nature" rather than an object of sexual voyeurism.[36]

This contrasts with the more common (and perhaps realistic) portrayal of the hermaphrodite in post-Victorian carnival shows. These later half-and-halves showed more than contrasting female and male sides of the face and body. Sometimes their ambiguous sexual organs (enlarged clitorises appearing as penises, for example) were revealed on the stage of sex shows, especially at the "blow-off" (though often faked). The respectable portrayal of Lala contrasted with sexual stare of the working-class viewer, openly fascinated with the body's orifices and sexual characteristics, which, as Bakhtin notes, was central to centuries of European popular festivals.[37]

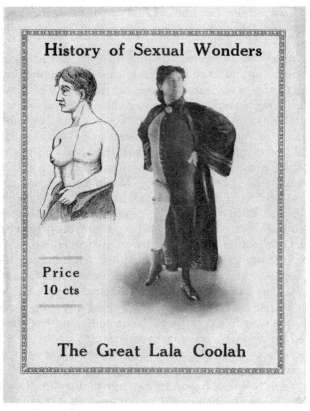

FIGURE 2.4 *Cover of* History of Sexual Wonders: The Great Lala Coolah *(1916), illustrating a sideshow hermaphrodite, Tibbals Circus Collection of Booklets, No 13, John and Mable Ringling Museum of Art Archives.*

Other corporeal freaks in the late Victorian period included individuals with rare, but dramatic, birth defects, who again were wrapped up in the genteel-crowd-pleasing rhetoric of improvement and normality. These included freaks with parasitical partial twins like Myrtle Corbin, a woman with four legs and two sets of sex organs, and Laloo (1874–1905), an Indian with a partial body of a twin attached to his chest (advertised as his "sister" but less romantically was, in fact, a vestigial male twin). Adding to the imagination of potential viewers, Laloo was presented as possessing twenty toes and twenty fingers, two bodies, but only one head. Yet this appeal to the popular fascination with the extraordinary body did not make Laloo horrific or disgusting. Rather he was presented as a good-looking intelligent boy with his "sister" (dressed in girl's clothes and shoes, suggesting that her head was buried in Laloo's chest).[38]

Among the most famous freaks with a partial twin was Francesco Lentini (1889–1966), who maintained a bourgeois elegance with his three legs to near the end of the sideshow era. Born into a presumably respectable Italian family and presented in pitch cards as "always kindly and courteous," his father didn't allow him to join the freak show until he was thoroughly educated (we are told that he knew four languages). Still, he appeared at circuses and his publicity booklet addressed common audience curiosity: He possessed four feet, sixteen toes, and two sets of male organs; and he always bought two sets of shoes for his three legs (giving one shoe to a one-legged friend). Legless freaks like Eli Bowen were advertised as half people, yet "able to move off very swiftly." Postcards and cartes de visite of legless freaks usually pictured them dressed as well-appointed bourgeois (although the black "turtle" boy, George Williams, in 1885 was pictured in shabby clothes), often posed on pedestals as if they were living busts. Even Heinrich Haag, featured as an "elastic skin man," was not shown as horrifying (though he stretched his eyelids over his cheeks), but as a "wonderful phenomenon, how his skin made him famous." The presumed autobiography of the armless Miss Ann E. Leak (1871) followed a similar pattern: She tells us that she was born in Georgia and obliged to "cast myself upon the sympathies and charities of the world" when her family lost everything during the Civil War, forcing her to reluctantly perform with Barnum in 1868. Still, we are told, she had lady-like skills that she used to overcome her adversity: She could write, crochet, and carve meat with her feet. She reminds her often pious readers that "My lot was not one of my own choosing but such as Providence has assigned me."[39]

Perhaps the most dramatic of born-freaks were the conjoined or Siamese twins, named after the most famous of nineteenth-century attached brothers, Chang and Eng Bunker (1811–74). They were among the first of a long line, but their fame was probably enhanced by their relatively happy story. The pair was discovered by an English merchant in Bangkok, Siam, in 1824 and brought to the United States in 1829. A "Captain Coffin" displayed them in New York and Philadelphia before they toured England and Europe. Noted for their business acumen (having a thriving business in duck eggs before leaving Siam), their fame and fortune grew. When they returned in 1836 from their globe-trotting, they were rich enough to retire a few years later to a farm in Mount Airy, North Carolina. They married sisters (daughters of a local clergyman) eventually producing twenty-two children between them. This arrangement required two houses as Chang and Eng split visits equally across the week. Having been on the losing side of the Civil War (and having to give up their slaves), the brothers returned for a time to touring.[40]

A pitch booklet featuring the Bunkers (1869) opens with the obvious question of idle curiosity: "Are they two men?" Yes, they have distinct body sensations for pain and pleasure, though they often have the same thought. Though they can plow, fish, and row together and sleep face to face, they seldom talk or play games with each other. The obvious question of their marriage and sex lives especially with two sisters is not discussed, though certainly it must have intrigued viewers. Chroniclers claimed that despite their conjoined state, the brothers were starkly different: Chang was fond of women and drank, while Eng led a sober life. Chang supposedly supported the South, while Eng was a Union man. All of this made the central issue more pressing. How did they manage as separate persons? This was a question that was vital in the nineteenth-century middle-class world, where individualism was a supreme value. Of all the freaks, the Siamese twins seemed to violate most genteel expectations—and this made them disturbing but also fascinating. This made their respectability all the more important.[41]

Other conjoined twins did not have such an uplifting, middle-class story to tell. Millie and Christina McKoy (1851–1912), the "Two-Headed Nightingale" joined from the lumbar vertebrae to the sacrum were black, born in slavery and were exploited by their owner/managers. Still, they drew big paying crowds because of their sweet singing duets, dancing, and intelligence. These talents also made them conventional and acceptable, reducing the uneasiness of viewers staring at them. Millie and Christina still raised a common question: Were they a single person (with two heads)? This was made more pressing when they spoke of themselves as one person, even though they had different pulses and slept independently (as noted by the doctors who frequently examined them). As Rosemary Garland-Thomson notes, the conjoined twin challenges a common assumption: "a fundamental aspect of humanness: our separateness," made even more disturbing when the conjoined twins were dicephalic—sharing a single lower body.[42]

Most presentations of freaks were prosaic and factual; and many offered a middle-class image of uplift. However, in the case of Isaac Sprague (1841–87), the "living Skeleton" (or ossified man) we read about a pitiful sufferer. Sprague was a victim of a rare condition (fibrodysplasia ossificans progressiva) where bone formed around muscles, ligaments, and tendons eventually immobilized him. The ossified man was a popular freak type, in part because it was easy to fake. Sprague offers a sentimental story, appealing to the pious Victorian—a tale of a normal birth and childhood gone wrong:

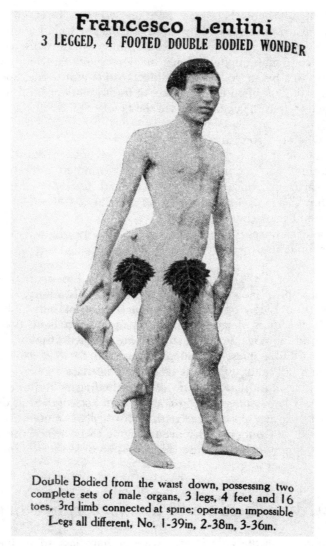

Francesco Lentini
3 LEGGED, 4 FOOTED DOUBLE BODIED WONDER

Double Bodied from the waist down, possessing two
complete sets of male organs, 3 legs, 4 feet and 16
toes, 3rd limb connected at spine; operation impossible
Legs all different, No. 1-39in, 2-38in, 3-36in.

FIGURE 2.5 *The oft-published image of the Frank Lentini as a young man with his parasitical twin. Life History of Francesco Lentini, (np, 1939), 5, Tibbals Circus Collection of Booklets no. 13, John and Mable Ringling Museum of Art Archive.*

Recalling a happy youth at school and the pleasures of swimming, Sprague tells how, at twelve years of age, he became a "wreck of nature" as he started losing flesh and control of his muscles as his body turned to "stone." While his father attempted to help him, both parents died by the time he was twenty-three. Unable to run a store as had his father, he reluctantly joined the circus in 1864 (suggesting a noble, rather than money-grubbing, heart, again pleasing to a genteel audience). Within two years, he was jobless when the circus burned down. Aided by saintly people, he found a job at a dime museum, eventually working for Barnum, only to lose work again when Barnum's second museum burned in 1868. Eventually returning to Barnum, his only joy was his marriage. In addition to this pitiful tale, Sprague was not above making a pitch that echoed the traditional appeal to religion by street beggars—that the charitable win the favor of God:

> People who are strong and robust,
> And can look at mystery.
> Do you think you're doing wrongly
> When you are patronizing me?
> If not, buy this book I sell,
> And remember when you buy,
> God makes miracles to please you.
> Never should his power die.[43]

In a later booklet (1878), another ossified man, W.T. Sapp, makes an even more pitiful appeal. However, instead of stressing his misery, Sapp affirms conventional bourgeois optimism. Until he was seven, he was happy; but then the "dark clouds of sad misfortune" plagued him as his body became "as solid and unmovable as a stone." He resisted displaying himself, but boredom and a quest for independence and the "spirit of ambition" overtook him (all admirable traits to the middle-class viewer at the time). Though lacking more than the "aid of only the fingers and one shoulder," he flourished when others with lost "health and strength sink downward discouraged" and waste "their strength in cowardly complaint." He claims to feel blessed "teaching others more fortunate them myself the lessons of patience and gratefulness."[44] The freak here is an object lesson in bourgeois virtue to be admired.

Further Freaks and the Victorian Norm

Other oddities with body deviations were perhaps less adaptable to these moral lessons but were still portrayed as content and approachable. Consider the obese: Most images of fat people in the sideshow before about 1900 were dressed in street clothes and often shown from the waist up or seated in a dignified position. However, increasingly thereafter, obese ladies were described regularly as "jolly" (though, in fact, they were often distressed by their frequent inability to stop gaining weight) or made to seem comical. Fat ladies were often dressed as babies to accentuate the contrast between their childlike appearance and their bodily mass. They were given infantile names like Baby Irene or Dolly Dimples. Postcards showed them in dainty dresses and often childish hats, usually sitting revealing overflowing flesh.

FIGURE 2.6 *Cover of Isaac* W. Sprague, The Living Skeleton *(1870), Tibbals Circus Collection of Booklets, no. 13, John and Mable Ringling Museum of Art Archives.*

Especially after 1930, they smiled (as did celebrities, politicians, and others) to reveal their cheerful nature.[45]

Fat men were treated differently—sometimes portrayed as jolly, but not the butt of jokes. In Victorian America, obese males were often associated with giants. In 1859, Daniel Lambert was merely described as a "wonderful extraordinary heavy man." In 1879, John Powers "the Wonderful Giant Boy" who, at seventeen years of age weighing 525 pounds, was simply called a "phenomenon of nature," outshining "all the giants of fairy land." He was said to be benevolent, well educated, and a "staunch friend."[46] Even later fat men were not portrayed as babies. Absent in the images and back stories of either the fat man or woman was any suggestion of gluttony or greed (in contrast to a common image of the fat man in literature as the tyrannical king or later the rich man). The obese in sideshows were always benevolent, if sometimes patronized—never creepy, at least, in their presentation, again reflecting a genteel accommodation.

While I'll discuss the midget in more detail in a later chapter, the little person was central to the nineteenth century dime museum and sideshow. The dwarf had disproportionately short limbs, in contrast with the midget who was a miniature but proportionally a normal adult. Both are products of abnormal prenatal or childhood development (and experienced a variety of growth patterns). And, while stories abound of the trials of small people in coping with the normal-sized world of furniture, tools, and people, Victorian descriptions of little people generally emphasized their normality, even superiority in intelligence, talent, and personality. Midgets came in many forms: displayed as toy soldiers (General Mite and Tom Thumb), as fairies (if female), and as exotics (Che-Mah from China and, of course, the Wild Men from Borneo). Often their size was only one part of their appeal. The Wild Men from Borneo, Waino and Plutano, recited poems in English, but also (perhaps for the lowbrow element in the crowd) lifted barbells and wrestled.[47]

Giants—again, in contrast to myths and fairy tales—were said to be friendly and, in contrast to reality (where their height produced circulatory problems and short lives), were portrayed as strong and protective. According to a pitch book, the Cape Breton Giant (seven feet, four inches) possessed a "stern and shrewd mind, tempered with kindness," but basically he was an ordinary farmer who drank and smoked. Many descriptions of giants stressed their statistics rather than personalities; or their size was punctuated with their wearing oversized cowboy hats or top hats. Cartes de visite from the 1880s and 1890s show giants of exotic backgrounds, especially Chinese, Icelandic, and Russian. Rarer were female giants such as Anna Swan, "The Nova Scotia Giant Girl," who was amusingly shown with her husband who came up to her waist. Despite the size of these giants that may have been threatening to viewers, sideshows stressed their benevolence, humanity, and humor or their exotic, rather than intimidating, demeanor.[48]

The sideshow presentation leaned toward the comfortably amusing: While in folklore, giants and dwarfs were often set against each other, in the sideshow the positive was emphasized, posing the tall and short as best friends, humorously paired together both to magnify their extremes and to assure crowds of their benevolence. Nineteenth-century freak shows endeavored to assuage viewers' anxieties rather than to excite them. Later this would change.

Another, though small, category of freak in the nineteenth century was the self-made deviant from the conventional use of the body. These exceptional people might be admittedly awkwardly called body-invasive (or simply behavioral) oddities. This group included the tattooed and those who subjected their bodies to unnecessary penetration with seemingly painful or damaging objects: fire eaters, sword swallowers, blockheads (who submitted to blows to the body), pincushions (who punctured their faces, tongues, limbs, and even eyelids with needles), or even iron tongues (who lifted weights from the tongue or skin). Few of these seem to have been immortalized with postcards or pitch booklets, probably because they were less appealing to the more affluent attendee.[49]

Most of this group were tattooed men and women. Subjecting the body to subcutaneous ink to form permanent illustrations has, of course, been a form of human decoration for centuries in certain islands in the Pacific Ocean. These exotics had been displayed in France and England from the end of the seventeenth century. In the 1820s and 1830s, a white sailor, John Rutherford, who went "native" by being tattooed on his South Sea voyages, exhibited himself in England. The curiosity of inked skin, especially when combined with the exotic story of adventure, had an obvious appeal to provincial English town and country folk. The most famous tattoo performer in Victorian America was Captain George Costentenus. He offered a colorful story that conformed to popular prejudices of Asians: He claimed to be a descendant of a Greek noble from Turkish Albania, who was involuntarily tattooed by central Asians from Tartary as punishment for participating in a rebellion of miners. After years of displaying himself in Europe, as nearly naked as allowed to show the full extent of his bodily art, he toured with Barnum in 1876 and others, being especially a draw in the 1880s.[50]

Tattooed females were particularly popular, appearing as living contradictions to Victorian propriety. Perhaps most famous was Nora Hildebrandt who had a strangely romantic, if racist, backstory: She and her father (a seafaring man with tattoos) in 1878 were said to have been captured by the indigenous American chief Sitting Bull. When her father was stripped in preparation of being burned alive, the tribe was so enchanted by his tattoos that they offered to spare him if he tattooed his daughter. According to the pitch booklet, for a year, she was tied to a tree and subjected to 365 designs. Alas, the father was burned when he refused to tattoo her further. Presumably rescued thereafter, the daughter joined the dime museum. In fact, Hildebrandt was voluntarily tattooed by her father, a Civil War–era tattoo artist from New York City. The key to both her and Costentenus's stories is the subjection of the adventurer to the diabolical Other, making the tattoo a mark of imposed Otherness. These exotic stories enhanced the romantic taboo of viewing the tattooed freak. By the twentieth century, the tattooed exhibitor no longer was expected to be involuntarily subjected to the ink and needle, but the shock of seeing this violation of the "temple of God," the human body, remained an object of both revulsion and attraction. But gradually the wonder wore off, especially as new tattoo artists (including those with machines) increased the supply of tattooed people eager to be displayed.[51]

Although sword swallowers were common by mid-century and were easy to train, other "self-made" body-invasive freaks arrived later to the stage (often a hybrid between the freak and the skilled circus performer).

These oddities offered more extreme off-putting behavior that seemed to contradict "natural" bodily integrity and care. Signor Lawanda (1849–1934), known as "The Iron Jawed Man," lifted two large men on a barrel with his teeth. Blockheads like Billy Wells subjected themselves to having granite blocks broken on their heads with a sledgehammer in both circuses and dime museums. Human ostriches (who ate a variety of non-foods like nails, coins, and broken glass) as well as well geeks who bit off the heads of chickens and other animals appeared fairly often by 1900. Most famous of the human ostriches was Alfonso, a black man presumably from Barbados, who worked at dime museums, Barnum and Bailey, and later at Buffalo Bill's Wild West Show. Perhaps to add to his respectability for a middle-class viewer, he did not play the exotic card, but rather wore a business suit in his act. By 1897, Ringling Brothers included a human pincushion who stabbed himself with needles. Less appalling were the strongmen and women who joined the bally stage at the end of the nineteenth century. As with the fat lady, the female oddity in strength was treated as a joke: "Tyana, The Earth's Strongest Woman" was shown in a postcard holding up seven men in suits on a beam from her legs. All this suggests that the sideshow gradually shifted to fostering stronger emotions of disgust but also mockery and whimsy. And this was just the beginning.[52]

The Freak's Place in Victorian Culture

From the 1840s through the end of the century, freaks were offered to both the genteel/salon and popular/carnival crowd as displays of difference. I have covered many forms of this appeal. But more generally we should ask: Why was difference an attraction (and repulsion)? As disability scholar Lennard Davis notes, the concept of the "norm" as the statistical average emerged in the mid-nineteenth century (promoted by the Belgian statistician Adolphe Quetelet). This reinforced the idea of the middle class as the standard that was at neither extreme (in wealth, body, and behavior). This made the freak stand out as different and reinforced the "normality" of the viewer. George Oddell in 1927 argued what has become a common view, that gawking at the midget or double-bodied man made ordinary people feel superior, more secure in their mediocrity. In the eyes of these gazers, they were, at least, "normal."[53]

The idea of the average also provided standards for the freak's acceptance in "normal" society—as sideshow impresarios continually tried to find points of normalcy in the otherwise extraordinary freaks. However, in the long run, the norm became the standard for defining deviance. The eugenics movement in the early twentieth century made the freak simply abnormal, not a mystery. The concept of the norm had hardened. But in the nineteenth century, the freak remained ambiguous, partially different, but still normal in some ways.

Finally, it is important to recognize that the Victorian freak was only a part of a wider culture of entertainment, a fact that softened their freakishness. Circus sideshows of the Sells Brothers, Ringling Brothers, and Barney and Bailey, in the 1880s, for example, featured Punch and Judy puppet shows for children, minstrel bands and dancers, magicians, contortionists, comics, snake charmers, performing birds, mind readers, ventriloquists, strong people, and boxing monkeys. Ringling in 1897 even offered cat minstrels, a woman whistler, and, in 1903, "rag picture makers." Barney and Bailey included a "Vegetable King," who carved flowers from vegetables.[54] Human oddities were only part of a wider venue of variety entertainment that reached a broad audience, divided by age, gender, and culture. In this way, sideshows were similar to Vaudeville. It's probably fair to assume that the shock of the freak was thus mollified. And, this variety allowed a blending of low- and highbrow culture, as historian Lawrence Levine noted.[55] But, this will change.

It is hard to establish a clearly defined history of the Victorian sideshow and when it changed. But a few revealing patterns are evident in circuses: Sideshows in the 1870s featured conventional "born-freaks" (midgets, giants, fat people, Siamese twins, and other victims of birth defects and developmental aliments). Also typical were rescued "savages" like Zip. By the 1880s, reflecting the global expansion of Western imperialism, a wider range of exotic oddities appeared. Zulus become more common, reflecting the influence of Darwin and the global imperialism of white nations. Still, the older tradition of the rescued savage remained with Waino and Plutano, the Wild Boys of Borneo, and Maximo and Bartolo, the "Aztec Lilliputians" (microcephalics). These exotic exhibitions continued through the 1920s in displays of Australian bushmen, Zulus, and Indian rubber men (contortionists). Another form of exoticism were the tattooed. All this confirms a traditional fascination with the body anomalies and the mysterious and disturbing exotic.

However, beyond the conventional figures of fire-eaters, sword swallowers, and the exotic tattooed person, body-invasive freaks were rare in Victorian America. The sideshow was quite conservative, offering the same spectacles year after year, though individual acts came and went.[56] It is only at the end of the nineteenth century that oddities like blockheads, sword walkers, and pincushions with their stress on the disgusting begin to appear. This suggests the eclipse of the Victorian ideal of genteel respectability and signals the beginning of the end of the Victorian freak show.[57]

This brief review of the freak phenomenon in its Victorian heyday suggests a complex set of expectations of viewing crowds. As Garland-Thomson observes, staring at these "breaches of the common human scale and shape" ranged "from delightful to spiteful."[58] But this was always only part of the story. Displays of the human oddity's body, as Garland-Thomson again shows, were also "publicly staged staring encounters." This meeting was always ambiguous. It still required a physical and cultural distance between the viewer. Sometimes this meant that "human deviance [was]. . . enhanced, dressed, coiffed, and propped up," making the freak more freakish. This encounter created a disturbing excitement at the sight of the alien savage, reminding viewers of their animal linkages (as well as their superiority) or the fact that extraordinary bodies can appear in the normal course of human birth and development. Finally, audiences experienced stressful agitation at the sight of the ways that humans can impose seemingly hurtful objects on their bodies. Yet these abnormalities were often made into the normal and the distance was erased in their backstories and friendly self-presentations.

What is particularly striking about the Victorian freak show was the need to mollify audience feelings of discomfort or disgust. A common word used to identify the freak was "wonderful." Often the extraordinary person was described simply as an ordinary human being except for some odd trait; and that condition was addressed not in horror or disgust, but in wonderment or sometimes in plain statistics. Often the freak was piously said to have "lived for a purpose," be it to advance science or faith, or "to amaze, to entertain, and to instruct" humanity, as a booklet of 1871 describes the life of an ossified man. The same booklet tells us of a fat lady who "rises grandly before us" and a "cannibal child" who nevertheless is "an almost angelic child."[59] And, while their backstories were often designed to accentuate the mystery or marvel of the freak, they were also to assure the viewer of the oddity's ultimate humanity and normality.

These booklets surely addressed the values of a genteel crowd more than the popular, working-class crowd. The plebeians also attended the dime museums and sideshows and their presence also shaped the presentation of the oddity, sometimes perpetuating carnival behaviors in raucous or even disruptive actions. But an overriding theme of these freak shows was clearly in sync with the ethos of that middle-class culture. These misfortune persons on stage or in the pit had learned the lesson of nineteenth-century individualism, that of doing well or at least as well as possible with what they had. Though the freak challenged genteel values of moderation and the norm, the freak as presented in Victorian entertainment was ultimately assimilated into those values.

The Genteel Challenge to Freak Culture

Barnum reconciled a cultural clash: For the middle class, he offered stories of uplift and even of education and science to assuage bourgeois anxiety at indulging in the stare at the different; for the popular classes, he presented a touch of carnival, the right to stare and indulge in disturbing excitement. This contradictory appeal across class cultures was key to the secret of Barnum's success and ultimately the formula for much of America's "mass" commercial culture in the second half of the nineteenth century. But in the case of the freak show that combination broke down not long after

1900. The veneer of scientific and moral respectability that made Victorian freaks acceptable to the educated middle class disappeared. And, with it, permission to gawk at them. This relegated the freak show to the plebeians and their culture.

This is a complex story, the contours of which I can only survey here. At its core was a decisive change in the understanding of nature, ultimately based on scientific discovery. However, the collapse of the Victorian multiclass encounter with difference followed also a cultural shift—a rejection of fascination with the mystery of the extraordinary for the logic and predictability of the regular, fostered by the popularization of science, but also by secular values that severed elites from popular practices and beliefs. This change began with a narrow cultural vanguard, whose spiritual descendants formed a genteel elite. This group shaped, but ultimately did not control, a broad middle class, producing the modern distinction between high- and middlebrow culture.

Noted historians of science Daston and Parkin identify key elements of this shift that began in the intellectual history of early Modern Europe. In the seventeenth century, extraordinary bodies (commonly labeled "monsters") were still mostly understood as originating outside of predictable nature. They were marvels, sometimes understood as portents for fortune telling, or signs of the devil, or even opportunities for charity and even a sign of holiness. Some intellectuals had long attributed these deviations to natural causes, though often inconsistently. By the end of the eighteen century, however, Western Europe intellectuals and their educated and affluent followers more clearly broke from the folk culture that had nurtured the idea of the marvelous by removing "moral" or supernatural understandings of difference. But Daston and Park argue that the rise of repugnance to the popular expression of "wonder" was not a direct result of scientific discovery (such as in biological explanations of freaks of birth and development). Scientists and the cultured despisers of folk belief "abandoned open mouthed wonder for skeptical sangfroid" as a cultural stance. Jokes of nature were no longer either funny or marvelous. They were repugnant in their irregularity. Instead of seeing deviations from the norm as wondrously "mysterious" or some sign from a supernatural realm, this cultural community saw these oddities as reaffirmations of order, explainable and usually lamentable accidents of deviation from that order. This intellectual split from traditional belief paralleled an increasing social and cultural divide. Over the course of the eighteenth century, elites withdrew from popular festivals and folk culture to which rural and poor urban people clung. The Enlightened split from the "vulgar" and rejected the "marvelous."[60]

We certainly see signs of all this in 1853, when the dime museums were first winning large crowds. Notably, Horace Greeley, a New York newspaper celebrity, mocked the "Disgusting Exhibitions," of "a woman full five times heavier than she ought to be" or the "hideous little dwarf . . . a pale and trembling little whiffet—a living abortion—an idiot old at twenty months—a caricature at once of age and babyhood."[61]

Yet, despite the spread of the general principle of the intelligibility of nature and the understanding of the biological marvel as mere exceptions to its laws, naturalists persisted through the Enlightenment and into the nineteenth century in treating biological oddities as separate species. The English naturalist John Hunter continued to collect and catalog specimens of natural eccentricities and published *On Monsters* (1775). The French scientist Geoffroy Saint-Hilaire developed the field of teratology, the study of abnormal anatomy in the early nineteenth century. These efforts were almost entirely empirical, without much effort to explain the natural causes of these deviations from the norm. So, while Saint-Hilaire rejected as myth old stories of three-headed monsters, he still cited sensational stories of anomalies as part of a comprehensive effort to classify, rather than explain, the causes of abnormality or even to argue for a norm.[62]

This ambiguity continued well into the nineteenth century as physicians lent credibility to commercial freak shows when they appeared at well-publicized visits of human oddities to medical and scientific institutions. Sometimes physicians produced their own versions of freak shows as did Dr. Kahn in his Museum on Leicester Square in London in the 1850s, which featured live and wax monstrosities and models of sexual anatomy (with separate viewing for ladies). This exhibit was similar to Hunter's collection of oddities. It was purchased by the Royal College of Medicine in 1783 (open to physicians and the public upon application). The porous wall between science and carnival wonder was subtly confirmed by scientific journals like *Lancet* (1865), which continued to refer to a "double monstrosity" of a three-legged man with two penises as "remarkable"; and the *Journal of the American Medical Association* (1888) found a four-legged child as a "curious manifestation." Only slowly did the language and approach change as human oddities became "cases," subject, according to Steven Miles, to "measurement, clinical methodology and scientific anatomical vocabulary."[63] Science and freak culture coexisted through the nineteenth century because it benefited both groups, legitimizing show people and providing scientists with subjects to study. The crowning example of this collaboration were the baby incubator shows of Dr. Couney at Coney Island, where premature children were displayed in a medical setting to a paying crowd of gawkers who made the doctor's preemies into freaks.[64]

Gradually, however, scientists learned not to gawk at these exceptions and to explain them strictly in clinical terms. Even when they still retained a religious point of view, two late nineteenth-century teratologists, George Gould and Walter Pyle, were willing to accept oddities as simply part of the "clumsiness" of mother nature. Oddities served as the exceptions that proved the rule and were useful for doctors and scientists to diagnosis birth defects and offer treatment.[65] Garland-Thomson eloquently describes this shift in thinking about freaks "from wonder to error, from message to mistake, from street to laboratory, from stage to asylum." The change occurred over decades as origins of various oddities in birth defects or developmental diseases slowly were uncovered by science.[66]

The rise of eugenics, especially after 1900, contributed to the demystification of the oddity in still other ways. It fostered not only a call for breeding better babies but the demand that future generations of freaks be eliminated by limiting the procreation of parents with hereditary genetic disorders. The identification of the pinhead with mental retardation (and consequently moral inferiority) did much to demystify a key feature of the freak show. Equally important was the scientific linkage of freaks to the environment, including mother's diet and behavior in the prenatal stage (breaking from the mysterious stories of maternal marking).[67] Freaks became mundane victims of hard-to-pronounce medical conditions or of accidents or careless parenting, before and after birth.

By 1908, there were signs that an educated public at least was aware that most freaks were victims of medical disorders. In an article in *The Nation*, "Amusement and the Abnormal," Oswald Garrison Villard, a grandson of the famous New Englander William Lloyd Garrison, argued that freak shows were "making public sport of what was merely pathological." The giant was no superman; he was the victim of a disease that kills: "something at the base of his brain is responsible for the extraordinary and disproportionate growth." Though Villard saw these extraordinary people as defective humans, he focused his attack on the freak show audience, whose disgusting humiliation of these wretches recalled the appalling inhumanity of crowds cheering the slaughter in the Roman coliseum.[68]

An even more famous article appeared in April 1908 in *Scientific American,* the leading scientific journal for educated laypeople at the time. Entitled "Circus and Museum Freaks, Curiosities of Pathology," it was originally published in the *New York Medical Journal.* The article defines freaks as those "humble and unfortunate individuals whose sole means of livelihood is the exhibition of their physical infirmities to a gaping and unsympathetic crowd." These human oddities were "pathological rarities" who should be understood not as "ossified men" but victims of polyarthritis deformans and not as bearded ladies but sufferers from the rare condition of hypertrichosis. Yet, the object of the article was not simply to evoke pity or to advocate clinical confinement or treatment. Rather, it was to condemn the naiveté (rather than inhumanity as with Villiard) of the audience as the authors recall their own "attendance at sideshows in our unsophisticated younger days." To gawk was not only to humiliate the Other, it was to be childish and behind the times.[69] While disability historian Michael Chemers notes that these ideas hardly killed the freak show, they were part of a broader "medicalization of all human difference" and, with it, the separation of the medically abnormal from the normal through institutionalization or normalization via surgery or drugs.[70]

Still, only gradually was this medicalization reflected in law and behavior: A Florida statute in 1921 prohibited freak shows, but it was ignored. It was only in 1938 that Robert Moses, the powerful New York City official, prosecuted sideshows in Coney Island for violating an ordinance against bally talkers in an attempt to drive out the freak show. By the 1950s, only four states had outlawed the display of mentally retarded people (like pinheads).[71]

Nevertheless, normality becomes increasingly "enforced" in the twentieth century. This is seen in a growing public revulsion to street begging and the advent of "ugly laws" from the 1920s, especially in hostility to the maimed and diseased or even just people who "will incite staring." These freak-like people needed to be off the sidewalk because they created gawkers who elites found as disgusting as the freaks. The middle-class abandonment of the freak show, be it on stage or on the street, was well underway long before the oddity was marginalized.[72]

Debunking the freak show mystique extended far beyond the medical establishment and their enlightened bourgeois supporters. As James Cook notes in his study of Barnum's dime museum, even the uneducated "rube" did not always buy into Barnum's ballyhoo.[73] It shouldn't be a surprise that an early twentieth-century writer, Hereward Carrington, produced cheap booklets in 1912 explaining the trickery behind sideshow acts. Likely, many readers were adolescents and youth, enjoying a revelation of their elders' deceit and, even more, how they deceived, much in the way that *Mad Magazine* appealed to rebellious youth later in the century. Echoing the *Scientific American* article, Carrington asserts that "the sideshow is practically a thing of the past." If his readers wondered what had happened to the "Wild Men of Borneo," he informs them that the last of them had died in Waltham, Massachusetts, "which was about as close as he had ever been to Borneo." He really had come from the "wilds of Ohio." As for the giant, Carrington mockingly notes that he is no longer a "paragon of strength as in the fairy tales, he is considered a pathological specimen whose pituitary gland is diseased." Carrington went on to demystify the glass dancers, whose feet are never cut, but touch only specially prepared glass harmless to the skin. Performers on the blade or sword ladder are mere tricksters: They have tough feet that are pressed on, but not drawn across, the blade and thus not cut.[74]

In the 1920s and 1930s, popular magazines explained how freaks were really victims of glandular malfunctions.[75] More interesting is how biology textbooks began to illustrate the workings of the endocrine system by demystifying the sideshow oddity. One high school text of 1928 raises the question to its young readers: "Have you ever strolled through a circus menagerie and seen the 'freaks'. . .?" They are not "queer freaks of nature," but victims of "the character of glandular excretions." Overactive pituitary glands lead to giants and underactive ones, to midgets. Even textbooks for elementary school ask kids to recall seeing "funny little dwarfs" and the fat lady "as fat as a hippopotamus" and to question why these oddities have "not grown up normally the way most people do." The answer again is abnormal glands. The lesson learned was not merely the scientific origins of these physical differences, but to transform the child's understanding of the freak from "mysterious" to "abnormal."[76] The sideshow to the wide-awake youth by the 1930s was a trick or even a joke when the talker asked for money to view sick people. The gawkers had become the unsophisticated, the uneducated.

And there were signs that these rubes were in decline, especially in the cities. In the first decade of the twentieth century, New York newspapers had reported the latest additions to the freak shows in a tone similar to announcements of the newest Broadway show. By 1929, however, the *New York Times* reported that freak shows were growing "more conservative" because of the "marked slump in the credulousness of metropolitan throngs." Another *Times* article in 1928 notes that only the freshly landed immigrant or the "holiday maker from Harlem" still gawked at the three-legged man. The article claims the final victory of enlightened civilization, even at Coney Island: "A few hundred years have so developed our sense of decency that what was customary with the gentlemen of [the past]. . . would now be scandalous to the most proly of the proletariat."[77] The condescension of this writer is obvious, but a decline in the credulity of the newly urbanized masses was inevitable with the cutoff of most immigration in 1924 and the decline of the "insecure" crowd that once stared at Zip or Baby Irene.

Still another challenge to the freak show came from advocates of the natural history museum. As early as 1757, with the founding of the British Museum, enlightened elites tried to separate the collection and observation of nature from the carnival crowd's quest for sensation in the extraordinary. Early attendance at the British Museum was granted only to those applying for admission. Peale's Museum in Philadelphia in 1786 was first intended to be for gentlemen seeking knowledge of nature, but, as we have seen, economic pressure forced it and its successors to give in to the carnival culture of the dime museum.

In the United States, only when the natural history museum gained government and philanthropic support was an alternative possible. In 1856, Congress chartered the Smithsonian Institution, giving the resulting series of museums freedom from the carnival crowd, creating sites of genteel uplift. In 1850, Joseph Henry, head of this new collection, made that clear when he declared that the Smithsonian was "not for the curiosity of the casual visitor." Twenty years later, William Ruschenberger of the Academy of Natural Science made a similar point, arguing that the museum of natural history offered "artistic" displays. However, it "stirs no sensual emotions . . . but inclines the observer to perceive that the truth, nature itself is more worthy of respect and admiration than any imitation or likeness of it." Often the founders of natural history museums were not modern secularists who admired the logic of nature, much less simply proponents of an evolutionary understanding of the biological world. Historian Steven Conn shows how mid-nineteenth-century proponents of the science museum wanted to glorify God by giving visitors a vision of the "book of nature free from error." Such sites would not display God's "jokes" as if the deity played tricks by intervening in nature to create freaks. While this deistic perspective gradually gave way to a more secular one, museum leaders still insisted that the goal was to present, not the extraordinary, but a sense of order. Science museums offered visitors representative objects, not oddities. These museums rejected the carnival's sensuality and taste for the exceptional, the irregular, artificial, and bizarre. Instead, they offered the sublimity of nature's regularity.[78]

Directors of natural history museums also expected their institutions to be sites that gathered and even encouraged orderly and respectful crowds and uplifted the masses. While observing this "book of nature," visitors would presumably regulate themselves (again in contrast to the carnival or popular festival). Karen Rader and Victoria Cain note how museum leaders dreamed that their public institutions would become "physical experiments in republican ideas" in spaces that "ordered natural objects and fostered tentative mingling between the social classes." The idea was to "increase the attractiveness of knowledge and the ease of acquiring it" so as to make the natural history museum "an agency for better citizenship and for more stability of civic conditions," in the words of Norman Harris, financier and booster of Chicago's Field Museum at the turn of the twentieth century.[79] This idea was a fantasy perhaps, but reflected the progressivist idea that uplifting entertainment (rational recreation) as offered in museums would create social harmony and soften the class strife of industrialization.

However, ordinary visitors at the emerging natural history museums in New York, Chicago, Philadelphia, and Milwaukee, were not willing to buy the vision of their highbrow founders. What attracted crowds from the 1860s was the dramatic exhibition of dinosaur fossils, not the orderly displays of stuffed birds behind glass. The broad middle-class audience did not embrace the whole highbrow package. There were limits to that middlebrow crowd's interest in knowledge. They still wanted wonder and entertainment. As Rader and Cain note, early curators recognized the need for accommodating popular taste and learned that exhibits could not be just random specimens but had to offer interesting and intriguing alternatives to the "burdens" of school and book learning. At the same time, they still insisted that natural history displays be distinct from the "corrupted versions of science proffered by popular culture."[80]

This was a genteel compromise offered by the classes to the masses. One popular accommodation was to offer displays that addressed questions that ordinary visitors might ask (rather than scientists' queries) in order to induce the visitor to linger. Exhibits were to be attractive, such as in the grouping of birds or mammals, even if this neglected the reality of and the ugly in nature (as in the neglect in displaying insects, perhaps?). Some museums even took guidance from the presentation of objects in department store windows.

By the mid-1920s, science museums were, relatively speaking, becoming "places of entertainment and amusement," featuring dioramas and dramatic displays rather than mere collections of specimens and lessons in science.[81]

If the museums had to compromise with popular taste, this did not mean capitulation to the carnival. Instead, the compromise was with a middle class who wanted their edification to be entertaining. By the 1920s, this did not include freaks and their gawkers. And it excluded the boisterous carnival crowd. These museums (along with recently opened neighborhood parks and zoos), as Rachel Adams notes, "sought to enlighten their visitors through the strict organization of space and the regulation of behavior." These institutions made concessions to an entertainment culture that was still enlightened and largely middle class. Finally, as I argue elsewhere, museums and parks often focused on children, offering them parent-pleasing innocent "wonder."[82] The middlebrow could reject the freak show, but still have marvel and delight apart from the sober edification, preferred by highbrow elites.

The Challenge of Civility

Still another factor explains this rebuff of the freak—the crystallization of middle-class opposition to the very act of staring or gawking, not just the freakish object of the stare. Historian John Kasson identifies a distinctly urban and bourgeois attitude about staring that emerged in Victorian America in his classic *Rudeness and Civility: Manners in Nineteenth Century Urban America*. Advice manuals insisted that readers avoid "overinvolvement in the affairs of others" as well as "gestures of self-engrossment." A certain distance between individuals ("civil inattention") was required of the "civil" (i.e., socially acceptable) person. Bourgeois culture required reduced interpersonal conflict and restrained physical and emotional outbursts. This distancing and self-control was also essential for maximizing personal autonomy. An essential component of this comportment was the condemnation of staring at another person or making oneself the object of others' gaze (such as the dandy who made himself the center of attention). Leering at women "was to violate the modesty and honor of the lady" while the lady was told "not to acknowledge ogling or encourage it." This bourgeois ethic governing social interaction had long roots and impact: It was shared by the eighteenth-century gentry (as in George Washington's admonition not to look a man "full in the face") but was also reflected in the early twentieth-century etiquette manuals that warned businessmen to be inconspicuous and mothers to tell their children not to stare. Gawking was a marker of class: The lower classes stared; those up that scale did not. And as the middle class expanded, so did the ethos of not staring—and, with this, the acceptability of the freak show declined.[83]

But the stare was more than an assault on bourgeois individualism and the requirements of "proper" social interaction. It was also inherently ambiguous, a fact that made gawking all the more awkward and anxiety causing. Again, as Garland Thomson notes, while modern middle-class Americans had long been told not to stare, they were also told to be curious—just not be idly curious. But what was the difference? Children were told about the "evil eye" as a curse and also warned not to "turn a blind eye" to evil. All this made "looking" a source of anxiety. At the heart of this problem was finding a balance between acknowledging the other's special individuality and reducing the other's dignity and autonomy when "pinned down by a stare." Or from another point of view, the trick was "knowing how to declare yourself without revealing too much of yourself." Giving or receiving a "stare" was to upset these balances. And freak shows were all about staring and thus made middle-class crowds anxious.[84]

Even more problematic is that fact that staring can be, and often is, a form of asserting dominance as in the male gaze at the female nude (noted by art historian John Berger) or the "colonizing gaze" at the display of the "native" in alien dress or body (tattooed, elongated neck, or saucer-shaped lips, for example). Such staring "stigmatizes" the object of the look as noted by the famous sociologist Erving Goffman. Moreover, it became inadmissible to stare at the disabled as it violated a valued "spirit of benevolence" (Garland-Thomson). Signs of this were evident in Barnum's mid-nineteenth-century dime museum—thus the "normalizing" pitch of the backstories and bally publicity were designed to reduce this unease when gazing at midgets or conjoined twins. However, that anxiety had become unbearable by the twentieth century. The outright condemnation of the stare was evident already in the *Scientific American* article of 1908 cited above, at least, when the stare was at the born freak. In time, especially with the spread of the new anthropology of Franz Boas, which condemned old ideas of the cultural inferiority of non-western "savages," this censure applied also to exotic freaks.[85]

All of this produced confusion even among the freaks themselves. Human oddities sometimes objected to the gawking (though more commonly they tolerated it as a cost of business and even stared back at the wild-eyed rubes who paid to see them). If rare, however, this resistance to the gaze suggests something of the ambiguity caused by this challenge to the carnival. Famously, in 1899 the human oddities at the Barnum and Bailey Circus, while touring in London, were reported to be angry at being called "freaks." Forty members of the show met with the press in December 1898. A month later a resolution was prepared by the bearded lady, claiming that members of the sideshow were endowed "with extraordinary attributes not apparent to ordinary human beings" and should not be called freaks. Letters flowed into the various newspapers with 102 alternative names for "freak" that were more humane and respectful. Although arguably this was a publicity stunt arranged by the circus management, it did tap into a nerve as "respectable" Britons in the "spirit of benevolence" responded to this call. The term "prodigy" was selected by the Parliamentary chaplain and accepted by the circus management. Though this word never caught on, this episode signals a measure of discomfort among freaks at the gaze as well as bourgeois guilty conscience at their humiliating gawking, however limited its impact at the time.[86]

At the same time Edward Sandow, a widely heralded American strongman, pointedly rejected any association with the sideshow (though some of these shows included strongmen or women). He sought to link his extraordinary body and its presentation to high culture. In commercial photos, he posed as if he were a statue from ancient Greece or a historical hero, appealing to the genteel tastes of his day rather than the often lighthearted performances of the sideshow strong people (as noted above). And yet, as John Kasson finds, Sandow was never freed from the carnival brush. His image was captured in photo collections that differed little from the postcards and cartes de visite sold by freaks at the sideshow. For his fans (many of which were female), he was still the "spectator's pet," the victim of his fans' stare.[87]

Finally, and tragically, there is the story of Robert Wadlow, a small-town boy from Illinois (born in 1918) who grew to be eight-feet, eleven-inches tall and to weigh 491 pounds by the time of his death at twenty-two. Projecting an image of a mild-mannered and respectable youth who went to church, joined the Scouts, and read *Popular Mechanics*, his biographer claims his parents avoided publicity, though at six he was the size of a full-grown man and at twelve, he was sent on the road exhibiting himself as a boy giant. Wadlow made personal appearances in dozens of towns, large and small (often in advertising campaigns of shoe companies). He refused to join sideshows or to be dressed in anything but a respectable business suit. He declined to wear a top hat or raised shoes to make him look even taller than he was, and he abhorred circus garb. By 1937, Wadlow briefly accepted a spot in the Ringling Brothers Barnum and Bailey Circus but demanded to be lodged in first-class hotels with his parents and wear street clothes under the Big Top. Though he answered numerous newspaper reporters' questions about how he coped with his size dealing with beds, furniture, ceilings, and the like, Wadlow insisted on his normality. He bristled at the claim of a physician who briefly interviewed him in February 1937 that he, like other giants, was slow witted. Wadlow hated the stare of the doctor as much as that of the carnival crowd and refused to be treated as a specimen. When the doctor published an unflattering article in the *Journal of the American Medical Association* about him, Wadlow sued. Like Barnum's "prodigies" and Sandow, the upscale strongman, Wadlow used the anti-gawking values of the middle-class culture to define himself in an act in which his job was to be gawked at. Such was the logic of the carnival culture as it faced its challengers in the early twentieth century.[88]

By the 1930s, the carnival culture was beginning to be marginalized, but not destroyed. Middle-class viewers were retreating from it, ending the dynamic composite that comprised the freak show of Barnum's day. This, we have already seen, in the popular response to the film *Freaks* in 1932.

The emerging abhorrence to the freak show effectively disrupted older ways of relating to the Other. Giants and dwarfs became less amazing than pitiful. Discoveries in genetics turned physical anomalies into intelligible accidents of nature and fostered a eugenic movement that called for the sterilization of those with inheritable abnormalities. The medicalization of freaks reduced them to medical cases, rejecting the Victorian idea that freaks, through their fortitude and good humor, could rise to a measure of normality. The medical gaze reduced freaks to specimens to be poked, analyzed, and institutionalized, even as Wadlow resisted. And, for the enlightened laity who accepted this diagnosis, the freak was reduced to pity and even disgust. In the meantime, scientific display of nature, formerly intertwined with the carnival, dispensed with oddities in the publicly supported and professionally credentialed museum. Gawking may have still been tolerated in increasingly marginalized sideshows (as we shall see in the next chapter), but such staring and the objects of that gaze were increasingly associated with the past, that of the immigrant or country rube who was conned by a sideshow talker into spending a dime to see pitiful creatures who claimed to be something that they weren't.

This change transformed the meaning, and even more, the trajectory of the freak show. By the 1930s, the desertion of the middle class, combined with the decline of immigration and the rise of a new generation (often children of immigrants) who joined the middle class, led to the decline of crowds at the bally stage. The remaining audience of the freak show demanded new sensations and abandoned much of the old genteel cloak of respectability. As we shall see, the increasingly marginalized freak shows changed, often becoming more grotesque.

Notes

1   Lorraine Daston and Katherine Park, *Wonders and Orders of Nature, 1150-1750* (New York: Zone Books, 1998), 175.

2   Rachel Adams, *Sideshow U.S.A.: Freaks and the American Cultural Imagination* (Chicago: University of Chicago Press, 2001), 2–3.

3   C. J. S. Thompson, *Mystery and Lore of Monsters* (New York: Macmillan, 1931), Chapters 16, 23; Hy Roth and Robert Cromie, *Little People* (New York: Everest House, 1980), ix–xi; Jack Hunter, *Freak Babylon: An Illustrated History of Teratology and Freakshows* (New York: Creation, 2014), 5; Margrit Shildrick, *Embodying the Monster: Encounters with the Vulnerable Self* (London: Sage, 2002), Chapter 1; Roslyn Poignant, *Professional Savages: Captive Lives and Western Spectacle* (New Haven, CT: Yale University Press, 2004).

4   Joe Nickell, *Secrets of the Sideshows* (Lexington: University of Kentucky Press, 2008), 119; Leslie Fiedler, *Freaks: Myths and Images of the Secret Self* (New York: Simon and Schuster: 1978), 21, 230; Thompson, *Mysteries and*

Lore, 27, 39–54; Hunter, *Freak Babylon,* 7; George Gould and Walter Pyle, *Anomalies and Curiosities of Medicine* (New York: Julian Press, 1956, 1896), 45; Philip Wilson, "Eighteenth Century 'Freaks:' Reading the Maternally Marked Child," *Literature and Medicine,* 21, 1 (Spring 2002): 1–25.

5   Daston and Park, *Wonders and the Order of Nature,* 16–17.

6   Definition of "freak," https://www.dictionary.com/browse/freak.

7   Oliver Impey and Arthur MacGregor, eds., *The Origins of Museums: The Cabinet of Curiosities in Sixteenth- and Seventeenth-Century Europe* (London: House of Stratus: 2001).

8   Thompson, *Mysteries and Lore,* 23, 39–54; Gould and Pyle, *Anomalies,* 329, 337; Roth and Cromie, *Little People,* 3; Hunter, *Freak Babylon,* 9–12; Michael Chemers, *Staging Stigma: A Critical Examination of the American Freak Show* (London: Palgrave, 2008), 6–9; Fiedler, *Freaks,* 56, 63–4.

9   Richard Altick, *Shows of London: A Panoramic History of Exhibitions, 1600-1862* (Cambridge, MA: Harvard University Press, 1978), 37; Roth and Cromie, *Little People,* 7–9.

10 Charles Dickens, *Sketches by Boz Illustrative of Everyday Life and Everyday People* (original: 1836; London: Wordsworth Editions, 2001), 86.

11 Richardson Wright, *Hawkers and Walkers in Early America* (New York: Frederick Ungar, 1927), 179–80, 189–91; Nathaniel Hawthorne, *Hawthorne's Lost Notebook, 1835-41* (University Park: Pennsylvania State University, 1978) cited in *From Traveling Show to Vaudeville,* Robert M. Lewis, ed. (Baltimore: Johns Hopkins University Press, 2003), 27. George Groce and David Wallace, *Dictionary of Artists in America* (New Haven, CT: Yale University Press, 1957), 324.

12 Charles Sellers, *Mr. Peale's Museum* (New York: Norton, 1980), 22, 42, Chapter 3 especially; David Brightman, *Public Culture in the Early Republic: Peale's Museum and Its Audience* (Washington, DC: Smithsonian Institution Press, 1995); Robert Bogdan, *Freak Show: Presenting Human Oddities for Amusement and Profit* (Chicago: University of Chicago Press, 1988), 29–32.

13 Andrea Dennett, *Weird and Wonderful: The Dime Museum in America* (New York: New York University Press, 1997), 23–4.

14 Note the imaginative study by Benjamin Reiss, *The Showman and the Slave: Race, Death, and Memory in Barnum's America* (Cambridge, MA: Harvard University Press, 2001); James Cook, ed., *The Colossal P.T. Barnum Reader* (Urbana: University of Illinois Press, 2005), 1–9.

15 Chemers, *Staging Stigma,* 72–3; Dennett, *Weird and Wonderful,* 4, 6, 25–8; Neil Harris, *Humbug: The Art of P.T. Barnum* (Chicago: University of Chicago Press, 1973), Chapters 2 and 3; Cook, *The Colossal P.T. Barnum,* 9.

16 Cook, *The Colossal P.T. Barnum,* 6; Dennett, *Weird and Wonderful,* 6; Wilson, "Eighteenth Century 'Freaks'" 6–8.

17 Among the many sources that will be explored more fully in chapter 4 are: P. T. Barnum, *Struggles and Triumphs,* Vol. 11 (New York: Knopf, 1927), 541–65; "General Tom Thumb," *Frank Leslie's Ladies' Magazine,* 12 (1863): 263–71; *An Account of the Life, Personal Appearances, Character and Manners of*

Charles S. Stratton (London: np, 1844), 23; Sylvester Bleeker, *General Tom Thumb's 3 Years Tour Around the World* (1872, reprinted Charleston, SC: Nabu Press, 2011); Lewis, *From Traveling Show,* 36–40; Chemers, *Staging Stigma,* Chapter 2; Roth and Cromie, *Little People,* 46–8, 80–2; Frederick Drimmer, *Very Special People* (New York: Citadel Press, 1991), 179.

18 "Huber's Museum Closes Its Doors," *New York Times,* July 16, 1910, 7; Dennett, *Weird and Wonderful,* 57, 64.

19 Dominique Jando, *Philip Astley & The Horsemen Who Invented the Circus* (San Francisco: Circopedia Books, 2018); Mike Rendell, *Astley's Circus: The Story of An English Hussar* (self-published, 2014); Peter Verney, *Here Comes the Circus* (London: Paddington Press, 1978); Chapter 1; Isaac J. Greenwood, *The Circus: Its Origin and Growth Prior to 1835* (New York: Abbat, 1909), 86; Wright, *Hawkers and Walkers,* 190–6.

20 From 1851 to 1865, Barnum's Asiatic Caravan, Museum, and Menagerie featured both wild animals and human oddities, including Tom Thumb. Verney, *Here Comes the Circus,* Chapter 1; Bogdan, *Freak Show,* 40–2; Richard Flint, "Promoting Peerless Prodigies to the Curious," *The Amazing American Circus Poster,* Kristen Spangenberg and Deborah Walk, eds. (Cincinnati: Cincinnati Art Museum, 2011), 49–55.

21 Richard Arnold, *For the Season of 1873: Statistics of P.T. Barnum's Great Travelling Exposition* (Philadelphia, PA: William Mann, 1873); Flint, "Promoting Peerless Prodigies," 50; Fred D. Pfening, Jr., "Sideshows and Bannerlines," *Bandwagon,* March 4, 1985, 17–20; A. W. Stencell, *Seeing Is Believing: America's Sideshows* (Toronto: ECW Press, 2002), 51–5; Bogdan, *Freak Show*, Chapter 3.

22 Bogdan, *Freak Show,* 47–58; Robert Rydell, *All the World's a Fair: Visions of Empire at American International Expositions, 1876-1916* (Chicago: University of Chicago Press, 1987); John Kasson, *Amusing the Million: Coney Island at the Turn of the Century* (New York: Hill and Wang, 1978); Gary Cross and John Walton, *The Playful Crowd: Pleasure Places in the Twentieth Century* (New York: Columbia University Press, 2005), Chapters 2 and 3.

23 Joe McKennon, *Pictorial History of the American Carnival* (Sarasota, FL: Carnival Publishers of Sarasota, 1971), vol. 1, 22, 47–50; Nickell, *Sideshows,* 121, 48–50; Stencell, *Seeing Is Believing,* 25–6, 36–7, 51–5; Bodgan, *Freak Show,* 58–60.

24 Pfening, "Sideshows," 21; Van Matre, "Gold Dust in the Sawdust," *Bandwagon,* January 1, 1982, 7; Stencell, *Seeing Is Believing,* 25.

25 Fiedler, *Freaks,* 34, 137.

26 John Stevens, *Memoire of an Eventual Expedition in Central America Resulting in the Discovery of the Idolatrous City of Iximaya . . . and the Remarkable Aztec Children* (New York: E.F. Applegate, 1850), Tibbals Circus Collection of Booklets, no. 13, John and Mable Ringling Museum of Art Archives (hereafter cited as JMRMA); F. J. Mateen and C. J. Boes, "'Pinheads': The Exhibition of Neurologic Disorders at 'The Greatest Show on Earth,'" *Neurology,* 30 (November 2010): 2029. For details on the Aztec children, see Bogdan, *Freak Show,* 127–34; Marc Hartzman, *American Sideshow: An*

Encyclopedia of History's Most Wondrous and Curiously Strange Performers (New York: Tarcher/Penguin, 2005), 10–12.

27 *History of Rudolph Lucasie* (New York: np, 1860), Robert L. Parkinson Library & Research, Circus World Museum (hereafter Circus World Museum).

28 Captain J. Reid, *Adventures of an Australian Traveler in Search of the Wild Australian Child, Tom and Hettie* (Buffalo: Warren, Johnson, and Co., 1872), 11, 13, 14, Tibbals Circus Collection of Booklets, no. 14, JMRMA; Bogdan, *Freak Show,* 120.

29 *What We Know about Waino and Plutano, The Wild Men of Borneo* (New York: Simon and Peets, 1875), Tibbals Circus Collection of Booklets, no. 13, JMRMA; Mateen and Boes, "'Pineheads,'" 2029–31.

30 *What Is It?* (New York: Popular Press, 1884); Jay Teel, *True Facts and Pictures of Sideshow Freaks and Features* (Ansted, WV: Portland Press, 1930), 13, both in Tibbals Circus Collection of Booklets, no. 14, JMRMA; Cook, *The Colossal P.T. Barnum,* 134–5; Bogdan, *Freak Show,* 134–42; Janet Davis, *The Circus Age: Culture and Society Under the American Big Top* (Chapel Hill: University of North Carolina Press, 2002), 182–3.

31 Robert Richards, *The Tragic Sense of Life: Ernest Haeckel and the Struggle over Evolutionary Thought* (Chicago: University of Chicago Press, 2008) and Stephen Gould, *Ontogeny and Phylogeny* (Cambridge, MA: Belknap Press of Harvard University Press, 1977).

32 For example, Zaluma Agra, "Star of the East" nd, and Lula Zileake, 1896, Tibbals Circus Collection of Cartes de Visite, Oddities, JMRMA; Robert Bogdan, "Circassian Beauties: Sideshow Fabrications," *Bandwagon,* May 6, 1986, 22–4; Bogdan, *Freak Show,* 235–41; Circassian Beauty Archives, https://lostmuseum.cuny.edu/archive/exhibit/star; *The Wonderful History of a Wonder Lady, Miss Etta Rogers, The Albino* (New York: Darmon Peets, 1877), Tibbals Circus Collection of Booklets, no. 12, JMRMA; Etta Rogers, 1883, Tibbals Circus Collection of Cartes de Visite, Oddities, JMRMA. For a curious assortment of late nineteenth-century photos of long-haired women, some of which flow to the floor and images of men with floor dragging beards, see Tibbals Circus Collection of Cabinet Cards, Sideshows, JMRMA and Tibbals Circus Collection of Photographs, Sundry, JMRMA.

33 Barnum and Bailey, *Route Book,* 1894, 28, Circus World Museum; Bogdan, *Freak Show,* 185–99; Lewis, *From Traveling Show,* 135; Davis, *Circus Age,* 179–87.

34 A good recent survey is Lillian Craton, *The Victorian Freak Show: The Significance of Disability and Physical Differences in 19th-Century Fiction* (Amherst, NY: Cambria Press, 2010); Nicholas Foster, *Greatest Wonder of the World: History and Life of Jo-Jo, The Dog Face Man* (New York: Popular Press), 1885, Circus World Archive, Small Collection; Teel, *Sideshow Freaks,* 7; *The Nondescript Davey, Called the Man Bear* (New York: Popular Press, ca. 1870), Tibbals Circus Collection of Booklets, no. 14, JMRMA; Alice Bounds, *The Bear Lady* (ca., 1911), Tibbals Circus Collection of Booklets, no. 13, JMRMA. Another variation was Elle Harper, "The Camel Girl" with

legs joined forward and a hump on her back. Tibbals Photograph Collection, Sideshow Sundry, JMRMA.

35 *Madame Clofullia: Dame à Barbe* (New York: Popular Press, 1854), Tibbals Circus Collection of Booklets, no. 13, JMRMA; Bearded Ladies, Tibbals Circus Collection of Cartes de Visite, JMRMA; Teel, *Sideshow Freaks*, 14. Fiedler, *Freaks,* 143–4, 151; Davis, *Circus Age,* 120.

36 *History of Sexual Wonders: The Great Lala Coolah* (1916), Tibbals Circus Collection of Booklets, no 13, JMRMA; Fiedler, *Freaks,* 180–90; "He/She Scrapbook," *Freaks* (fanzine by Chris Fellner, Ringling Museum Art Library), no. 7, November 1996, 4–5; M. M. Bakhtin, *Rabelais and His World* (Cambridge, MA: MIT Press, 1968).

37 Fiedler, *Freaks,* 180–90; "He/She Scrapbook," *Freaks,* no. 7, November, 4–5; Bakhtin, *Rabelais and His World.*

38 Even more disturbing was Jean Libbera (1884–1930), dubbed "The Double-Bodied Man" with his parasitic brother protruding from his chest/stomach area. Laloo Cabinet Cards, nd, Tibbals Circus Collection of Cabinet Cards, Misc. Sideshow Collection, JMRMA; "Jean Libbera, The Double Bodied Man," Tibbals Circus Collection of Postcards, Sideshows, JMRMA.

39 Nickell, *Sideshows,* 128–37; *Life History of Francesco Lentini* (np, 1939), Tibbals Circus Collection of Booklets no. 13, JMRMA; George Williams cabinet card, Tibbals Circus Collection of Photographs, JMRMA; "Francesco Lentini," (ca 1915), Tibbals Collection of Postcards, Sideshows, JMRMA, *My Life's History by Miss Gabriele, The Only ½ Lady by Birth,* (np, 1910?), Circus World Archive, Small Collection; Bogdan, *Freaks Show,* 212–15; *Life of Herr Heinrich Haag, Elastic Skin Man* (New York: Popular Publications, 1880); *Autobiography of Miss Ann E. Leak, Born without Arms,* (New York Press of Wynkoop and Hallenbeck, 1871), 11, Tibbals Circus Collection of Booklets, no. 13 and no. 14, JMRMA. Similar is *Sketch of the Life of Barney Nelson: The Armless Phenomenon* (New York: Popular Publ., 1883), Tibbals Circus Collection of Booklets, no. 12, JMRMA; Hartzman, *American Sideshow,* 55.

40 See especially *Siamese Twins: Chang and Eng, A Biographical Sketch* (London: J.W. Last, 1869), Tibbals Circus Collection of Booklets, no. 14, JMRMA; J. N. Moreheid, *Domestic Habits of the Siamese Twins* (Raleigh, NC: E.E. Barclay, 1850), 1–11, Circus World Museum. Among the many biographies of the Bunkers are Yunte Huang, *Inseparable: The Original Siamese Twins and Their Rendezvous with American History* (New York: Liveright, 2018). Joseph Orser, *The Lives of Chang and Eng: Siam's Twins in Nineteenth-Century America* (Chapel Hill: University of North Carolina Press, 2014). Brief summaries are in Teel, *Sideshow Freaks,* 15–17; Fiedler, *Freaks,* 204–5.

41 *Historical Account of The Siamese Twin Brothers* (New York Elliot and Palmer, 1832); *A Few Particulars Concerning Chang-Eng, The United States Siamese Brothers* (New York: J.M. Elliott, 1836); *Siamese Twins, Chang and Eng* (London: J.W. Last, 1869); all in Tibbals Circus Collection of Booklets, no. 12 and 14, JMRMA; Moreheid, *Siamese Twins,* 12–24; Brief summaries are in Teel, *Sideshow Freaks,* 15–17; Fiedler, *Freaks,* 204–5.

42 "The Rare Female Pygopagus," *Bandwagon*, November 12, 1995, 46–9; Hartzman, *American Sideshow*, 65–6; Fielder, *Freaks*, 208–9; Rosemarie Garland-Thomson, *Staring: How We Look* (New York: Oxford University Press, 2009), 179.

43 Isaac W. Sprague, *The Living Skeleton* (New York: Damon and Peets, 1870), 1–16, Tibbals Circus Collection of Booklets, no. 13, JMRMA.

44 *Life of W. I. Sapp. The World Famous Ossified Man, Written by Himself* (Danville, VA: Dance Bros. & Co., 1897?), Tibbals Circus Collection of Booklets, no. 13, JMRMA; Teel, *Sideshow Freaks*, 9, 12–13; *The Lives of Three Very Remarkable Persons: Mr. John Battersby, Skeleton, Mrs. Battersby, Mammoth Lady, Zanobia, The Renowned African Cannibal Child* (Philadelphia: np, 1871), Tibbals Circus Collection of Booklets, no. 12, JMRMA.

45 Tibbals Circus Collection of Photographs, Sideshow includes a large group of late nineteenth-century cabinet cards of sideshow fat men and women, JMRMA; Tibbals Circus Collection of Post Cards, Sideshow contains a large collection of fat people (mostly women in the early twentieth century, JMRMA); Davis, *Circus Age*, 26, 119–20.

46 *Life of Daniel Lambert* (New York: Newcombe, 1809); Henry Blacker, *"Edward Bright the Fat Man of Malden," Remarkable Persons* (London, 1819); 35–7; *John H. Powers: The Wonderful Giant Boy* (Cincinnati: Cincinnati Courier, 1873), Tibbals Circus Collection of Booklets, no. 13 and 14, JMRMA; Davis, *Circus Age*, 121–3.

47 Roth and Cromie, *Little People*, 16, 20–7; Nickell, *Sideshows*, 111; Fielder, *Freaks*, 60–2, 116; Hunter, *Freak Babylon*, 80–1; Hartzman, *American Sideshow*, 27, 99–100.

48 *Biography of Captain H. Ureck, The Great German Giant* (New York: Popular Press, 1887), 27; Jas. D. Gillis, *The Cape Breton Giant* (Halifax: np, 1926), both in Tibbals Circus Collection of Booklets, no. 14, JMRMA; *Life of Chang the Chinese Giant* (New York: Popular Publ, 1881), Tibbals Circus Collection of Booklets, no. 12, JMRMA; Chang-Yu-Sing cabinet cards, Tibbals Circus Photograph Collection, Sundry, JMRMA; Note also Tibbals Circus Collection of Cartes de Visite, Midgets/Giants and Tibbals Circus Collection of Photographs, Sideshows, JMRMA; "Anna Swan, The Nova Scotia Giant Girl," Tibbals Circus Collection of Cartes de Visite, Oddities, JMRMA.

49 Circus historian Richard Flint finds that of the 800 American sideshow performers that he identified up to 1950 about half were born-freaks and 43 percent were "working acts" (like magicians but also sword swallowers). Few were "made freaks" like the tattooed. Flint, "Promoting Peerless Prodigies," 51.

50 *Life and Adventures of Captain Costentenus, The Tattooed Greek Prince, Written by Himself,* (New York: Popular Press, 1881), 1–14, 23, Tibbals Circus Collection of Booklets, no. 14, JMRMA.

51 "Miss Nora Hildebrandt," *The Tattooed Lady* (New York: Brunell Museum, 1884), Tibbals Circus Collection of Booklets, no. 13, JMRMA; Hartzman, *American Sideshow*, 46; Bodgan, *Freak Show*, 252–54.

52 Sig Lawanda, Cabinet Card, (1880s?); Tibbals Circus Collection of Cabinet Cards, Oddities, JMRMA; "Blockhead Billy Wells," *Bandwagon,* April 15, 1982, 7; Ringling Brothers' Circus, *Route Book,* 1897-99, 3, JMRMA; "Tyana," Postcard, (1890?), Tibbals Circus Collection of Postcards, Sideshow, JMRMA; Bodgan, *Freak Show,* 114, 263.

53 Lennard Davis, "Constructing Normalcy: The Bell Curve, the Novel, and the Invention of the Disabled Body in the Nineteenth Century," in *Disability Studies Reader,* L. Davis, ed. (New York: Routledge, 1997), 13–15; George C. D. Odell, *Annals of the New York Stage,* Vol. 15 (New York: Columbia University Press, 1927-29), 455.

54 Route Book Collection, Circus World Archive: Sells Brothers 1883, 5; 1886, 7; Barnum and Bailey, 1890, 22; Ringling Brothers, 1890, 5; 1891, 12; 1893, 23; 1896, 36; 1897, 34; 1900, 24; 1903-4, 27; 1905, 27; 1906, 21; 1907, 34; Sells Brothers, 1891, 11; John Robinson, 1921, 4; Hagenbeck Wallace, 1921, 4; 1924, 6; A. G. Barnes, 1922, 2. Note also Ringling Brothers, 1903, 51; Barney and Bailey, 1903, 27, both in Route Book Collection, JMRMA.

55 Lawrence Levine, *Highbrow, Lowbrow: The Emergence of Cultural Hierarchy in America* (Cambridge, MA: Harvard University Press, 1988), Chapter 1.

56 Route Book Collection, Circus World Archive: P. T. Barnum, 1876, 14; Sells Brothers, 1878, 7; P. T. Barnum, 1879, 6; P. T. Barnum, 1880, 8; Sells Brothers, 1881, 5; Sells Brothers 1883, 5; 1886, 7; Barnum and Bailey, 1888, 20. Note also in the same collection: Barnum and Bailey, 1890, 22; Ringling Brothers, 1890, 5; 1891, 12; 1992, 26; 1893, 19; 1893, 23; 1894, 18; Sells Brothers, 1891, 11; 1892, 5; Barnum and Bailey, 1897, 34; Forepaugh and Sells, 1896, 12; 1898, 13; John Robinson, 1824, 6; A. G. Barnes, 1924, 6. Note also the extensive collection of images of female snake "enchantresses" in Tibbals Circus Collection of Cabinet Cards, Sideshows, JMRMA.

57 In my wide but incomplete survey of route books, the sword walker first appears with Forepaugh and Sells in 1896, 12. The "impalement" act appears at Barnum and Bailey in 1903–04, 27 (both in the Route Book Collection, Circus World Museum). These acts, however, seem to be rare in the route books into the 1920s.

58 Garland-Thomson, *Staring,* 161.

59 *The Lives of Three Very Remarkable Persons* (1871), Tibbals Circus Collection of Booklets, no. 12, JMRMA.

60 Daston and Park, *Wonders and the Order of Nature,* 14, 18–19, 205–12, 329.

61 Horace Greeley, "Disgusting Exhibitions," *New York Tribune,* September 22, 1853, 4 cited in Lewis, *From Traveling Show,* 47.

62 Hunter, *Freak Babylon,* 7–8; Gould and Pyle, *Anomalies,* Chapter 1–4; Chemers, *Staging Stigma,* 47–69.

63 Lisa Kochanek, "'Reframing' the Freak: From Sideshow to Science," *Victorian Periodicals Review,* 30, 3 (Fall, 1997): 227–8, quotation, 232; Steven Miles, "Medical Ethics, Human Curiosities, and the New Medical Midway," *American Journal of Bioethics,* 4, 3 (Summer 2004): 39.

64 Dawn Raffel, *The Strange Case of Dr. Couney* (New York: Penguin/Blue Rider Press, 2018).

65 Gould and Pyle, *Anomalies*, 8.

66 Garland-Thomson, *Staring*, 178; Mateen and Boes, "'Pinheads,'" 20, 28–32; Hunter, *Freak Babylon*, 76.

67 For example, Harry Laughlin, "The Socially Inadequate: How We Shall Designate and Sort Them?," *American Journal of Sociology*, 27 (1921): 54–70; Ashley Montagu, *Prenatal Influences* (Springfield, IL: Charles Thomas, 1962); R. C. Scheerenberger, *A History of Mental Retardation* (Baltimore: Paul Brooks, 1983), 156, 183; Peter Conrad and Joseph Schneider, *Deviance and Medicalization: From Badness to Sickness* (St. Louis: C.V. Mosby, 1980), 263–6.

68 Oswald Villard, "Amusement and the Abnormal," *The Nation*, March 19, 1908, 254; Rosemary Garland-Thomson, *Extraordinary Bodies* (New York: Columbia University Press, 1997), 18. Chemers, *Staging Stigma*, 86–8.

69 "Circus and Museum Freaks, Curiosities of Pathology," *Scientific American Supplement*, April 4, 1908, 222; Sheila Rothman and David Rothman, *Pursuit of Perfection, The Promise and Perils of Medical Enhancement* (New York: Pantheon, 2003), 238.

70 Chemers, *Staging Stigma*, 91.

71 Mateen and Boes, "'Pinheads,'" 2032; Bogdan, *Freak Show*, 58.

72 Garland-Thomson, *Staring*, 18–19, 30, 75.

73 James W. Cook, *The Arts of Deception: Playing with Fraud in the Age of Barnum* (Cambridge, MA: Harvard University Press, 2001).

74 Hereward Carrington, *Side-Shows and Animal Tricks* (Kansas City: A.M. Wilson, 1913), 7–8, 11; Hereward Carrington, *Side-Show Tricks Explained* (np, Little Blue Book no. 1279, 1928), 8–9, Tibbals Circus Collection of Booklets, no. 14, JMRMA.

75 Leslie Gilliams, "Side-Show Freaks as Seen by Science," *Illustrated World*, 38 (1922): 213–15; Hannah Lees, "Side Show Diagnosis," *Colliers*, 99 (1937): 224.

76 J. Mace Andress et al., *Health Essentials* (Boston: Ginn, 1928), 152–3; Dorothy Baruch and Oscar Peiss, *My Body and How It Works* (New York: Harper Brothers, 1934), 89 cited in Rothman, *Pursuit of Perfection*, 18.

77 Bertram Reinitz, "Coney Enters its Steel Age," *New York Times*, June 16, 1929, XX2; Jan and Cora Gordon (English artists), "Coney Island as a World Showplace," *New York Times*, June 3, 1928, SM 7.

78 Steven Conn, *Museums and American Intellectual Life, 1876-1926* (Chicago: University of Chicago Press, 1998), 8 (quotation of David Murray, 35–7, quotation of Henry Ruschenberger, 40–1); Karen Rader and Victoria Cain, *Life on Display: Revolutionizing U.S. Museums of Science in the Twentieth Century* (Chicago: University of Chicago Press, 2014), Chapter 1. See also Curtis Hensley, *Savages and Scientists: The Smithsonian Institution and the Development of American Anthropology, 1846-1910* (Washington, DC: Smithsonian Institution Press, 1981).

79   Rader and Cain, *Life on Display*, quotation of Norman Harris, 23. See also
     Tony Bennett, "The Exhibitionary Complex," in *Culture/Power/History:
     A Reader in Contemporary Social Thought*, N. Dirks ed. (Princeton, NJ:
     Princeton University Press, 1994), 131.

80   Rader and Cain, *Life on Display*, 32.

81   Conn, *Museums*, 245; Rader and Cain, *Life on Display*, 19, 22, 27.

82   Adams, *Sideshow U.S.A.*, 26–7; Cross and Walton, *Playful Crowd*, Chapter 7.

83   John Kasson, *Rudeness and Civility: Manners in Nineteen Century Urban
     America* (New York: Harper Collins, 1990), 126–7; Garland-Thomson,
     Staring, 66, 69, 71–2.

84   Garland-Thomson, *Staring*, 3, 13, 25, 42, 64, 66–8.

85   Garland-Thomson, *Staring*, 41–5. See also Erving Goffman, *Behavior in Public
     Places* (New York: Free Press, 1966); Erving Goffman, *Stigma: Notes on the
     Management of Spoiled Identity* (New York: Touchstone, 1986); John Berger,
     Ways of Seeing (New York: Penguin, 1990); Reiss, *Showman and the Slave*;
     Rydell, *All the World's a Fair*.

86   "Uprising of the Freaks, January 6, 1898," in *Barnum and Bailey in the World*
     (London: np, 1897-1901), 21, Circus World Museum; Bogdan, *Freak Show*,
     271–5; John Lentz, "Revolt of the Freaks," *Bandwagon*, September 10, 1977,
     26–8.

87   John Kasson, *Houdini, Tarzan, and the Perfect Man* (New York: Hill and
     Wang, 2001), 8, 60–7.

88   Frederic Fadner, *The Gentleman Giant: The Biography of Robert Pershing
     Wadlow* (Boston, MA: Bruce Humphries, 1944), 5, 35, 41, 47, 56, 96, 111–13,
     151–6. For another perspective, see Bogdan, *Freak Show*, Chapter 10.

3

Marginalizing the Freak

By the 1980s, the freak show was a shadow of its former self. Sideshow operators and old hand performers have longed blamed this decline on rising costs and growing scarcity of personnel (especially with medical interventions that have reduced the availability of born-freaks). In carnivals, mechanized rides drew more customers at lower costs. Some veteran showpeople have admitted that "political correctness" (PC) has impeded their ability to display freaks (hermaphrodites and deformed fetuses, for example) and to make money from the customers' gawking at extraordinary bodies. Still, old freak show operators have long insisted that the basic impulse to stare at the oddity and even willingly to be taken in by an illusion or a showman's exaggerated pitch has scarcely changed.

While I won't deny that these economic and "political" factors have played a role in the decline and that there is still a demand for viewing the oddity, I insist that there is more to what happened to the freak show. The withdrawal of the educated middle classes from the audience explains part of the fate of freaks. Still, from the 1930s especially, the show itself changed and, with it, a new aesthetic emerged, as show operators strove to meet the demands of new audiences and different supplies of freaks. The shows had become more bizarre and the crowds more down-market. The stare had changed along with its object. By the end of the twentieth century, what remained was small. But it was not a mere remnant; it was very different from the sideshow of 1900. The aesthetic of freakiness has also shifted from the archaic and economically unsustainable setting of the circus and carnival to new settings: rock clubs and other boutique shows, but especially to film, TV, and even video games. This chapter will focus on the first part of this transformation—the fate of the traditional live freak show after 1930.

While, by the 1930s, the widening world of genteel (or, more broadly, middle class) culture was gradually delegitimizing the freak show, its performance gradually shifted from major circus and show routes to the county fair, small-time carnivals, and the skid road/bowery. Yet, the path was not all downhill. Freak appeals found a new home in the broad, largely middle-class, appeal of Ripley's "Believe It or Not" newspaper cartoon features and books, where oddities were enveloped in a veneer of boyish wonder at the bizarre and strange in the wider world. Elements of the traditional freak show survived in the carnival until the end of the twentieth century as promoted by showmen like Ward Hall and Chris Christ, even as the children of the gawkers at Coney Island moved to the suburbs and took the kids to Gettysburg to witness patriotic history. Yet, the freak show was obliged to change with new conditions and crowds. Show operators shifted away from physical/born-freaks to "working acts" of sideshow artists (like magicians and sword swallowers, but also more edgy blockheads and pincushions). Sideshows began to feature freaks who entertained audiences with song, dance, and comedy (suggesting a cuteification trend and attempts to attract to families). More common, however, were attractions appealing to the morbid (bottled fetuses, for example) and disgusting (geeks who devoured chicken's heads) with hints of the unserious or camp.

The Slide of the Sideshow

The freak show reached its peak in the golden age of the circus; and from the 1880s to about 1930 the circus was a premier site of American mass entertainment. The biggest shows were, of course, the Ringling Brothers (from 1884) and Barnum and Bailey (merged in 1881). In an age of corporate consolidation, Ringling and Barnum and Bailey combined corporately in 1907, and the two circuses merged in 1919. Known as one of the Sunday School circuses for its relative family-oriented fare (no "girly shows" or tricksters fleecing the rubes with rigged cards or shell games), it still offered the biggest sideshow of the dozens of touring circuses. As early as 1929, when competition from sound movies and radio made smaller circuses unviable, Ringling Brothers Barnum and Bailey (RBBB) bought out five medium-sized circuses (Sells-Floto, John Robinson, Hagenbeck Wallace, Sparks, and A.G. Barnes). Despite near bankruptcy (and the ouster of John Ringling in 1932), the "Greatest Show on Earth" survived with its three rings of animal and circus acts and large sideshow. By 1957, the RBBB was bought by Irvin Feld, a Texas music promoter, and this mammoth circus carried on for another sixty years.[1]

The Depression, however, took down many smaller circuses, reducing the number of sideshows. "Mud shows," circuses moving on trucks from town to town on back roads, relied on sponsorship from local fraternal organizations Often admission prices were kept as low as possible. Exotic animals and sideshows were often eliminated.[2] Smaller circuses survived the coming of TV in the 1950s, often with appeals to the "entire family," including nostalgic adults. Freak shows did not fit this image. Some like Roger Brothers tried to appeal to a new generation of boomer children by hiring movie and TV performers like the cowboys, Hopalong Cassidy (William Boyd) and Lash LaRue (famed for his use of the bullwhip). Circuses under the name of the Shriners still drew crowds. But small circuses were increasingly precarious as the towns they visited lost population and travel and production costs could no longer be covered by declining ticket sales.[3]

By 1955, even Ringling was in debt and the romance of the big top tent and sawdust was wearing thin in summer as audiences increasingly expected air conditioning. In 1956, RBBB abandoned the tents for cooled indoor arenas. The abandonment of the big top meant the end of the sideshow at RBBB for which there was no room in arenas. Increasingly circuses performed in auditoria, gyms, or even parking lots. Other pressures impacted the struggling circuses: From the 1980s, animal rights groups like PETA (People for the Ethical Treatment of Animals) attempted to ban circuses in major cities. Many circuses collapsed or closed early in the season by the 1990s. What had thrilled crowds for a century no longer drew them. And the freak show went away with the Big Top.[4]

Surviving circuses adapted in a variety of ways. Many drew on foreign talent, abandoned the large exotic animals (elephants and big cats) for trained dogs, horses, and monkeys, and dropped live bands for recorded or organ music. New circuses, free from ties to the old traditions, also responded by offering modern crowds spectacles that referenced contemporary popular culture. From the 1980s, the Cirque du Soleil from Montreal, succeeded with themed aerial and acrobatic acts, enhanced by dramatic lighting and music (rather than traditional animal acts). Instead of moving from small town to small town, these innovators offered crowds, who traveled to big cities and entertainment sites like Las Vegas, technologically sophisticated spectacles. Others appealed directly to children or offered traditional circus acts in new settings (like Renaissance Fairs).These innovative enterprises strove to attract a new generation and especially affluent city sophisticates who had, as circus historian Fred Pfening III notes, no memory of or interest in the "traditional sawdust troupes." No one thought of retaining a sideshow for this largely middle-class crowd.[5]

By the end of the twentieth century, traditional circuses were desperate. RBBB tried to win new audiences with more "interactive" experiences, including offering time before the show for families to meet the clowns and other circus figures. In 2006, it introduced a story-based show involving a father and daughter sharing "Dreams of the Circus," which replaced the usual array of circus acts in three rings. Crowds and critiques were not pleased. A reviewer in the *San Francisco Chronicle* found the one oval boring and admitted: "Maybe a fresh plotline is hard to come by after 158 years, but this one is especially lame." By May 2017, the RBBB gave up the ghost after years of conflict with animal rights groups and rising costs.[6]

With the decline of the circus came the transformation and eventual eclipse of the sideshow. As early as 1928, Joe Tracy in *Billboard* (the trade weekly) complained that sideshows had degenerated into "fire eaters, bladeboxes, and ten or twelve dilapidated rusty-looking illusions." Yet RBBB adapted to complaints that the sideshow was becoming old-fashioned by trying to make its show more spectacular and exotic. By the mid-1930s, Ringling featured a Parade of Freaks around the hippodrome tract after the Grand Entry of the circus acts. The Parade included celebrity figures like the Doll family of midgets and the giant Jack Earle. Other RBBB freaks included Clicko, the Bushman, Koo Koo, the bird girl (from *Freaks*), Al and Jeanie Tomaini (a giant and his legless wife), Eko and Iko, black albino twins, and even a popeye (who could extend his eyeballs from their sockets). Ringling sideshows in the mid-1930s also included a rubber-arm man, Betty Broadbent (a famed tattooed lady, said to be disowned by a wealthy family at sixteen years of age for her inkings), and even an Iron Tongue artist, Miss Jean.[7] Earlier in the 1930s, RBBB featured popular new exotic acts from well-publicized expeditions to central Africa (saucer-lipped Ubangi) and Burma (giraffe-necked women), the latter promoted as "The Last of the Unknown People of the Earth."[8] The old appeal of born-freaks and exotics from Africa still seemed to draw crowds.

The sideshow at RBBB changed in the 1940s, shifting somewhat toward body-invasive acts: In 1942, for example, this circus added a pincushion

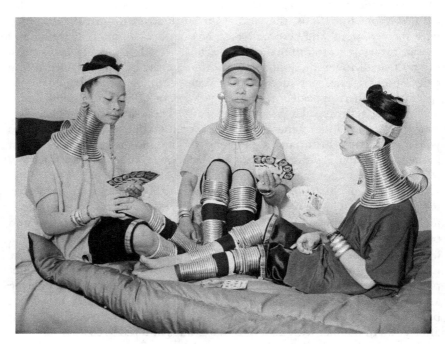

FIGURE 3.1 *"Giraffe Burmese Women" at leisure from their circus sideshow in London. Similar women toured with the Ringling Barnum and Bailey Circus sideshow, c.1935, Keystone/Getty Images.*

who practiced the art of piercing his flesh with pins. Still, RBBB kept up the celebrity freak show in the decade after the Second World War, occasionally featuring Frieda Pushnik, a woman without legs or arms, Sam Alexander, "the man with two faces," Sealo, the Seal Boy (with hands but not developed arms), Henry Pulley, the skeleton man, Baby Jane, the fat lady, and a popeye. What had disappeared were the saucer-lipped Ubangi, giraffe-necked Burmese women, and other foreign exotics with their imperialist/racist implications.[9]

Smaller circuses also tried to keep the sideshow going. In 1946, Cole Brothers still featured an armless woman and midget along with an escape artist and mind reader. A. G. Barnes offered a similar mix after the war: a fat boy, but mostly traditional acts, including a knife thrower, fire eater, puppeteer, and magician. Other circuses offered a geek, human ostrich, alligator skin man, elephant girl, and a pincushion that surely offended genteel sensibilities. Into the 1950s, Clyde Beatty's Circus still included a monkey boy, elephant girl, skeleton man, armless wonder, the man with two faces, seal boy, and even a "quarter boy" (with one limb).[10] There was still a demand for the old freak show, though, with the decline of the circus, the audience surely had become more "down-market."

For the small circuses, the problem was less customers than performers, as live freaks became harder to find and pay for. The Beers-Barnes Circus of 1938 had a sideshow consisting of leased elephants, horses, and monkeys along with a couple who did a snake and bladebox act, while a man faked a half-and-half (hermaphrodite) act for the blow-off. The Robbins Brothers Circus of 1949 still included a pinhead, but otherwise was free of born or exotic freaks. Instead it relied on a Punch and Judy puppet show, magician and sword swallower. These grab-bag shows reflect the small circus's diminished resources.[11]

The decline of the sideshow prompted self-reflection in the industry. In 1947, veteran showman Norman Carroll wrote in *Billboard* that the needs of the circus sideshow were changing: It required a "talker with a clear voice like that heard on radio with short snappy ballys and a peppy minstrel band, but no more than one or two freaks." Based on eight years of experience, he found that "parents with children are usually more than skeptical about allowing their children" to see freaks. Better to stick with magicians, marionettes, and "singing midgets." He continued: "Repulsive or malformed people usually play on the sympathy angle, which in my estimation is bad. The circus should be a happy merry occasion for all." Carroll was especially critical of the hermaphrodite act. The sideshow "should be for the entire audience, children included." For Carroll, the circus and its sideshow had to reach a family and largely middle-class audience, which was increasingly unsympathetic with the aesthetic of the old freak show.[12] This view was reflected in the shift toward "working acts" of fire eaters, knife throwers, the bladebox, and sword swallowers, often done by one person (and frequently a midget). Many circuses simply abandoned the sideshow entirely, anxious not to offend middle-class families or to reduce costs, keeping only a small menagerie or perhaps a magician.[13] All this confirms the gradual cultural shift away from the carnivalesque.

Ripley's Freak Show for the Middle Class

There were, however, settings where freak appeal survived the scientific and genteel assault—and yet remained acceptable to the mainstream. Robert Ripley (1893–1947) offered a new image of the oddity that was adaptable to a middle-class audience, especially of its youth. In 1919, Ripley, a young sports cartoonist for the *New York Globe*, was said to have run out of ideas during a winter slow spell in sports. To fill his allotted space in the newspaper, he drew cartoons and captions of amazing sports feats (a Babe Ruth home run that traveled 600 feet, for example). By 1922, he added other curiosities (like a man who could presumably revolve his head). His cartoons, given the catchy label of "Believe It or Not," gradually became a regular feature; by 1928, they were syndicated in about 100 hometown newspapers throughout the country. At its peak, 300 papers published his cartoon series, thanks to Ripley's connection to William Randolph Hearst's King Features. In December 1922, Ripley set off on a global tour gathering stories of oddities, especially in exotic places like India. Ripley took special interest in Hindu ascetics who, like the body-invasive freaks of the sideshow, submitted themselves to harrowing discomfort, pain, or mutilation (like the man who sat on a bed of nails for twelve years or a man who was buried alive for forty days). For Ripley, these "fakirs" were "the weirdest collection of humanity on the face of the earth—demented, delusioned, diseased, and devout." In this and his other highly publicized encounters with distant cultures and people, this "modern Marco Polo," as Ripley often was called, shared a common belief in white superiority (picturing himself frequently with the khaki shorts and pith helmet of a British colonist). But he also showed a certain fascination and often respect for these mysterious people. Cartoons of these and many other oddities were so popular that in 1929 Ripley authorized a book of his "Believe It or Not" cartoons along with some photos, many accompanied with short descriptions (published by the mainstream Simon and Schuster). In 1930, he appeared in a radio series on NBC and, in the following two years, in short movies produced by Warner Brothers. Ripley's radio show was often based on contributions from listeners who relished the brief moment of fame that came with sharing their strange feats. In 1933, Ripley lent his name to an oddity show at the Chicago World's Fair, which was produced by his friend, the publicist C. C. Pyle. Ripley's fame grew during the 1930s and 1940s, ending only with his unexpected death in 1947. Ripley brand and odditoria empire survived and continued to expand up to the present with Ripley museums in entertainment and tourist districts across the United States and elsewhere, along with many cartoon books. Several TV shows have been built on the Ripley franchise, including one during 1982–6 by actor Jack Palance and another in 2019 featuring Bruce Campbell.[14]

Much of the appeal of Ripley's cartoons came from the fact that they were basically about freaks and freakish behavior, but they were presented in ways starkly different from the sideshow. While often whimsical, they were seldom horrifying, disgusting, or grotesque as freak shows were increasingly becoming. Instead, "Believe It or Not" cartoons and captions evoked a sense of wonder and curiosity that was not only Ripley's stock in trade, but which he seemed to share with his readers. He was no ballyhoo talker, full of deception. Instead, as one writer notes, Ripley exhibited a "bottomless, off-kilter curiosity." And another declares, for Ripley "Everything was new to him." The *Public Ledger* of Philadelphia asserts that Ripley brought to his cartoons "the eye of the child," while the *New York World* claims, "He is not merely retailing empty wonders to make yokels gape. His research is for the very highest type of curiosity, the unbelievably true."[15]

FIGURE 3.2 *Drawings of Robert Ripley from Believe It or Not (1929), p. 19, show the range of Ripley's interest in curiosities,* © 2020 Ripley Entertainment Inc.

Unlike the ballyhoo on the midway, Ripley tried not to embellish his stories. In fact, he hired Norbert Pearlroth in 1923 to do research. Pearlroth (a studious immigrant from Poland) worked for Ripley and his organization for fifty-two years, conducting careful research in the New York Public Library to find and authenticate stories. Often Ripley's cartoons focused on faraway, alien people and places: cannibals and stories of "savages" from West Africa playing football with a human skull, or a horned-headed African "Kaffir." Readers encountered these oddities, not in the realism of a photograph, much less in a live encounter with an exotic at a freak show, but in a newspaper or book cartoon. They were anything but frightening. The main message was always "how weird and interesting." And he mixed these stories and images of exotic "freaks" with cartoons depicting ordinary people who had done extraordinary, but weird and sometimes, silly things: mothers at the age of eight and ninety; a man who caught the same fish twice; and a woman who crocheted a hat from her own hair. To this he added curious factoids that seemed to contradict conventional knowledge and common sense—a gallon of vinegar weighs more in the winter than summer, "there is no soda in soda water," and Charles Lindbergh was the sixty-seventh pilot to fly over the Atlantic, not the first (on a technical point). Ripley did all this in his cartoons as well as radio, film, and (briefly) TV appearances without a hint of disdain or noticeable condensation.[16]

Awkwardness in his mannerisms (slurred speech, flaying arms) and his buckteeth made him appear as anything but a Hollywood or radio star. Still, these everyman qualities made him seem what we would call today "authentic." His cartoons were inextricably bound with his public personality: a great adventurer, admired by ordinary Americans stuck in their hum drum lives, but also a "regular guy." He showed, as biographer Neal Thompson notes, "an appreciation for small-town America as well as genuine awe for those willing to spend years of concentrated effort carving a chain of matchsticks or building a violin entirely of sugar." He was the odd duck who attracted and related to other odd ducks. He appealed especially to young readers, mostly those middle-class boys who might have wandered into the freak show at the carnival, but whose mothers warned them to stay away. For the youth of twelve or fourteen, Ripley's newspaper cartoons were as regular a feature of their daily routine as checking out the box score of their favorite baseball team. And, though there are no statistics, many certainly bought the cheap paperback collections of Ripley's cartoons and stories. I got mine for thirty-five cents at the local drugstore in the late 1950s. These youth, no longer comfortable at the freak show, received something of the same thrill by identifying with Ripley's adventures and attraction to the oddity.[17]

The Chicago show of 1933–4 that featured Ripley's name modified and even threatened his image a bit. While the "Odditorium" was promoted as the product of Ripley, Pyle actually produced the show; and he featured traditional freak show characters—an armless knife thrower, ossified man, legless woman, alligator man, a mule-face woman, and Betty Williams with her parasitical twin sister with two feet attached. The Odditorium also featured body-invasive freaks including a human pincushion, a glass-eating "Ostrich man," and even a "swami" who skewered his tongue with a long needle. Though Ripley publicly rejected the term "freak" preferring "oddities" or even "queeriosities," the Chicago show and subsequent "odditoria" were really high-end freak shows.[18] Despite these edgy freaks, Ripley's image remained that of a middle-class boy-man whose adventures and irrepressible "curiosity" made his showmanship acceptable to a wide range of Americans, even as the freak show was increasingly being relegated to the gawking rube. As Thompson notes, "By celebrating weirdness, he made it mainstream."[19] This was accomplished because Ripley's weirdness wasn't found on the backlot of an increasingly tawdry carnival or in circus tent but in the stand-along "odditorium" or in the family newspaper or in cheap, but entirely respectable, books, found at the neighborhood drugstore.

Freaks Go Down-Market, 1930–60

Ripley's dive into the world of the "odd," even with its broad appeal hardly reversed the withdrawal of the middle class from the freak show and the drift of freakery into the grotesque. As Leslie Fiedler noted in 1976, the freak show "retreated from the center of our culture to its periphery . . . from Broadway to Skid Row" as well as the back corners of fairs and carnivals.[20]

Freaks found venues in increasingly down-market settings. We've encountered one site already, the world's fair, perhaps a curious one, given its "uplifting" and progressive reputation. Following the Columbia Exposition of 1893 in Chicago, subsequent expositions of technology and exhibits of national (and corporate) pride at Chicago (1933–4) and New York City (1939–40) also were sites of entertainment, even of the lowbrow variety. Competing with Ripley's Odditorium in Chicago's Depression-era fair was the "Darkest Africa" show of well-known showman Lou Dufour. It featured fake Africans "eating fire and walking through fire;" and as the blow-off, Dufour displayed a man said to have had his genitals cut off in Africa. At the Chicago fair, Dufour also opened the LIFE Museum that pretended to be an educational display of the stages of biological development with embryos of animals and humans along with revealing anatomical models designed to titillate and shock. A midget village (more in Chapter 4) was also featured in Chicago as was a "Crime Never Pays" spectacle reenacting the gangster massacre of St Valentine's Day of 1929 in Chicago. Not all of these were freak shows, but all shared a voyeuristic appeal for the abject and even bizarre that was at the heart of freakery. Many of these spectacles went on to the next big exhibition in San Diego. The New York fair of 1939–40 was more of the same: "Nature's Mistakes," featured animal freaks, including a cow with elephant feet and an eight-footed horse. A full complement of body-invasive freaks appeared in the "Strange as It Seems" show. Fairgoers could also witness thirty-model scenes of medieval torture in the "Crimes in the Tower." All of this suggests a trend toward the grotesque in the freak show after 1930 as compared, for example, to the famous Chicago exhibition of 1893.

Interestingly, by 1964, when New York had still another world's fair, the famous New York City planner Robert Moses rejected applications for a new midway of freak shows. Moses, long the voice of twentieth-century "rational recreation" and active opponent of the carnival culture of Coney Island, insisted that the American public no longer wanted "honky-tonk"

FIGURE 3.3 *The conjoined twins Violet and Daisy Hilton as young performers, postcard, c. 1914, Wellcome Collection, Attribution 4.0 International CC BY 4.0.*

and "catch penny" entertainment. He even demanded that the fair be closed at 11 p.m. rather than allowing revelers to indulge themselves until 2 a.m. as they had at the 1939–40 fair. According to Dufour, Moses bragged that he "made a clean-cut decision between strip teasers and Michelangelo."[21] Obviously showmen like Dufour vigorously dissented.[22]

The traditional and increasingly down-market freak show continued to find venues in urban settings after 1930. These were temporary storefronts in empty downtown stores or even short-lived shows like Dufour's "Congress of Freaks" at the New York Palace Theater in 1931. Novelty musical acts like the Hilton Sisters (conjoined twins talented in singing and instrument playing) worked the declining music hall circuit and other freaks appeared in movies. Moreover, permanent sites like the Baltimore Museum or Erber's Show of Living Wonders in St. Louis survived, as did freak shows at Coney Island, Niagara Falls, and even Hollywood. Many were gone by the 1940s, but, of course, Ripley's "Believe It or Not" and its rival Guinness World of Records Museum still flourish in the twenty-first century attracting casual crowds at the beach or big city.[23]

The most famous of these permanent sites was Hubert's Museum, located between seventh and eighth Avenue on 42nd Street in New York City. A holdover from the days of the dime museum but opened only in 1925, Hubert's survived until 1965. Through much of its history, Hubert's had an arcade on the main floor and a talker to get crowds to view the freaks in the basement. Many well-known born-freaks from RBBB and other circuses worked there in the winter months or when they tired of going out on the road in carnivals and sideshows (small rooms in the building were provided for them). At Hubert's Museum, acts that were no longer acceptable in other venues still found an audience. In the 1940s, Hubert's was the home to Professor Heckler's Famous Flea Circus, Serpentina the Snake Women (appearing to lack bones), Grace McDaniels, the Mule-Faced Woman, and Sealo the Seal Boy. Hubert's even featured Albert and Alberta, a hermaphrodite with exposed male and female breasts (a female impersonator) and Jack Dracula, a tattooed man with 306 pictures of horror film scenes inked on his body. For a time, Hubert's also included "posing shows" of women dressed as Pilgrims or French coquettes in provocative poses for men who brought their own cameras. Pretty tame, but that was the 1940s. Yet even Hubert's drew the line with geeks like the Great Waldo. An Austrian Jew, who fled Hitler in 1938, Waldo exhibited extraordinary muscle control, making a living by eating and regurgitating live mice. But he played at Hubert's only briefly. Despite lowering prices and the fame provided it by photographer Diane Arbus, Hubert's disappeared when 42nd Street became a center of pornography in the 1960s; and down-market, even slumming, crowds shunned this throwback entertainment site. But Hubert's survived for forty years after 1925, attracting the "honky-tonk" and slumming crowd that so peeved Moses.[24]

The carnival freak show and its showpeople perhaps best reveal the changing taste of the crowds that still could be lured by the bally pitch. From the late 1930s, freaks sometimes moved to the back lot of the carnival as opportunities in the circus declined. Sideshow performers had to adopt the often arduous life of moving from one caravan of mechanical rides, concessions, and spectacles to another, sometimes passing between circuses and carnivals, eking out precarious livings. Talkers lured the crowd (or from the performers' viewpoint, the "mark") into their tents with low-entry prices (often ten or twenty-five cents) for ten-in-one shows. Promoters hoped to "catch" more "pennies" from the penny-pinching crowd, when performers sold signed postcards or booklets about themselves or their skills (the art of sword swallowing, for example). Other sources of "inside money" included rigged card games, fortune telling, and extra fees for the blow-off (often a hermaphrodite or strip tease).[25]

But, even with the partial shift from the circus to the fairs and carnivals, freak shows were in decline. Costs, but also a changing aesthetic of the pleasurable stare, explain this change. Obviously, born-freaks were harder to employ. Parents were less willing to "sell" their unusual offspring to sideshow impresarios when such behavior became taboo and institutional alternatives became available. Medical treatments for endocrine disorders reduced the number of midgets and giants available; and surgical separation of conjoined and "parasitical" twins became successful by the 1950s. Some freaks, especially midgets, found alternative jobs. Despite the oft-heard observation of showmen like Ward Hall that some freaks earned good money, retired happily, and viewed their job like that of any other performer, other freaks (especially midgets and dwarfs) objected to their status and strove for dignity. Note the appearance of the Little People of America in 1957 that defended the economic rights of small people and rejected the term "midget." And the old guard was dying off. Famous freaks like Prince Randian (the human torso) died in 1934, and the half-man Johnny Eck retired in 1940. As we have seen above, other freaks replaced them (especially midgets, fat people, and bearded ladies) in the 1940s and, to a less extent, in the 1950s, but soon thereafter there were few replacements.[26]

Another change was the decline of sex shows, including hermaphrodites, reflecting both the increased scrutiny of local authorities and the increasing availability of porn. Hoochie-coochie dancers with sparse garments and even provocative strip shows had been a staple of carnival fare for decades. By contemporary standards, these shows were tame: Rare was frontal nudity (even when suggested by the talker to induce men to pay extra for entering the blow-off tent while their kids and wives went to see a puppet show). In the late 1940s, "farm boys" still gathered at the bally stage to see Velma shake her pelvis in preview of the Streets of Paris show as the talker, Harry Lewiston, suggested that the crowd "find out" if she has her red hair on "other places. Come on in, we won't tell." In another show, Lewiston claimed that his six female dancers came from the Shah of Persia's harem.

The mark's "imagination gave them the thrill they were after" even if the show was often a tease. In time, these traditional teases became too tame when uncensored X-rated movies and independent live nudie shows became available.[27]

More central to our topic was the decline of the hermaphrodite. Showman Ward Hall preferred a fake (male) half-and-half to real ones because the "gaffed" ones were better performers. From 1948 to 1961, his hermaphrodite was Diane D'Elgar (George Searles), who knew how to display "glamour" and was skilled at appearing to possess both sex organs. Though on the street, Hall claimed, D'Elgar looked like an effeminate man, in Hall's show D'Elgar dressed as a sexy woman with a six-foot-long ostrich feather. In the bally preview of his 1950s show, "she" was spotlighted on a runway surrounded by jugglers with torches, a snake charmer, a knife thrower, and a featured midget. Hall's pitch line was: "Diane is all man. Diane is all woman with full sex organs of both." He claimed that she could have legally married either a man or woman, but she had chosen to be a woman and had two children. Hall promised to show Diane's sex organs "without a G string" to those willing to pay the extra price for the blow-off. Throughout the 1950s, hermaphrodites continued to attract a voyeuristic crowd, presumably fascinated by sexual ambiguity and stimulated by the famous story of the 1952 surgical transformation of Christine Jorgensen from a man to a woman.[28]

Yet, already in the 1950s, these provocative shows faced both legal battles and a change in public taste: Not only did the Sunday School circuses reject them but the more down-market carnivals often had to pay off local officials to show them. Lewiston complained that already in the late 1930s he had to pay a fine of $200 under the "obnoxious person's" statute in Joliet, Illinois, for his male impersonating a hermaphrodite. Elsewhere, police simply demanded bribes. By the end of the 1950s, these sex shows were increasingly banned. Hall's Diane D'Elgar was obliged by 1961 to become the caretaker of his "pinheads" and to do a magic act. In any case, by then a "curious" crowd could see more in porn magazines and movies than ever was shown in the carnival or freak museum.[29]

Drifting toward the Bizarre

If the sex show was slowly withdrawn and the born-freaks became a rarity, the freak show continued long after 1940. It did so by increasingly drifting to illusion and especially the grotesque. As in any business, scarcity led to substitution as born-freaks were replaced with gaffes such as men claiming to be bearded ladies or "lion face" women appeared equipped with customized masks. Illusions like the "bladebox," where a pretty female enters a box through which knives were inserted, had long been featured in sideshows. Still, the illusion act seems to have expanded after the Second World War and they became more bizarre and freakish. A notorious trick was the "headless Olga," developed by a German refugee, "Doc" Heinemann, who introduced his illusion to an American sideshow in 1938. The "backstory" was that Olga was decapitated in a train accident, but was kept alive by a mad scientist, Dr. Landau (in reality, a physician who had lost his license but looked the part). Out of the headless body, seated on a dentist chair, came tubes and wires presumably to keep her alive while the arms and legs of a hidden live women flayed about.[30]

Expensive live acts could be replaced with cheap and grotesque spectacles, especially deformed human embryos in jars. These so-called pickled punks (sometimes replaced by fake rubber fetuses, amusingly called in the trade, "bouncers") appeared in carnivals as early as 1910. This spectacle became a featured part of the sideshow when, in 1927, the ever-resourceful Lou Dufour bought a fetus collection and called it "The Unborn." Soon he had placed pickled punk shows in Chicago amusement parks, Atlantic City, Revere Beach near Boston, and with a traveling carnival, charging twenty-five cents to see them. Most famously, he featured a "Two-Headed Baby" in his LIFE Museum at the Chicago fair of 1933. The baby was born live but had died in two months. In publicity, Dufour blamed the mother for overfeeding the two mouths for one stomach. Still, he tipped his hat to respectability by hiring a woman dressed as a nurse to present a scientific-sounding lecture about the specimen (perpetuating the "uplifting" tone of the Victorian freak show in a down-market setting). After the Second World War, the pickled punk attraction was picked up by many showmen, sometimes using this spectacle as the blow-off with various backstories and appeals. An example is Peter Hennen's Thalidomide Baby Show (drawing on publicity about the tragedy of pregnant women, who, after taking this drug, produced grotesque fetuses). Showman Howard Bone recalls how his pickled punk feature drew good crowds with his "hokum" about their origins and significance. Trying to be as vivid and mysterious as possible, he told the crowd, "these are acts of God. Medical science cannot explain them." This was an old line familiar to the Barnum-era freak show. But Bone also claimed that he tried to get people to "vomit or pass out," when viewing these grotesque fetuses in jars, making this part of the show. Another pickled punk show of the late 1960s featured a banner showing a nurse coddling a frog-faced baby and a two-headed baby playing with blocks, even though these fetuses were really fake fetuses (bouncers) in jars. The pitch referred to the recent film *Rosemary's Baby* that featured a woman giving birth to the devil.[31]The freak show was evolving into a horror show.

Other show people in the 1950s and 1960s drew on the fear of atomic radiation as in the Atomic Age freak, a two-headed pickled punk. In an attempt to evoke pity and fright, the pitch went, "the poor little creature was born only 23 miles from the Atomic Testing Ground in Los Alamos . . . See the horror we leave to the future. Make up your own mind: Can it happen here?" In 1969, Ward Hall obtained a real two-headed fetus (dating from

1893 that had floated around school displays for decades) along with additional embryos from a museum supply company and Wild's Curiosity Shop, collecting a total of about fourteen specimens. His pitch line: "Children of Forgotten Fathers. They did not ask to be born!" Hall added "Is the pill right? Is abortion the answer? You be the judge! But first see these children of forgotten fathers." Among these "children" were fetuses, informally named Cyclops, Frog Girl, and Elephant Nose Baby. These shows were cheap and graphic; And, especially in the 1960s and 1970s, the topical issues of abortion and the dangers of poorly tested drugs shaped audience response. These shows tapped into a deep anxiety of many—the still precarious and unpredictable nature of birth and the horrors of the "unnatural" body. Moreover, unlike the oddities of the Victorian sideshow, pickled punks were the unborn and never had a chance to tell their story or surmount their afflictions. There was only the disgusting horror; none of the redemption.[32]

Many of these showpeople also added another draw: grotesque animal acts. The Johnny Jones Exposition of 1936 featured "Giant Monsters Alive" (consisting mostly of snakes) for a credulous audience. Others went still cheaper with flea circuses where a showman played on the imagination of audiences to convince them that fleas equipped with tiny splinters and agitated with hot coals were "sword fighting." Animal freak attractions were sometimes embellished with horrific banners. For example, in the late 1940s a carnival banner showed a young blonde Second World War soldier eaten alive in a jungle pit by huge rats as villainous Japanese looked down. In country carnivals, animal freaks attracted crowds for decades. Al Moody's show in the 1970s featured farm animals with birth defects: eight-footed horses, and a cow with a bull's face. Even more recently, Rick West toured fairs with his two-headed turtles and cows. Once again, we see the trend toward the grotesque—on the cheap.[33]

Drawing on a deep and long fascination with death and pain and no longer restrained by genteel sensibilities were torture shows. Essentially grotesque extensions of the freak spectacle, these spectacles became common by the late 1930s in the more down-market carnivals. Wax exhibits, commonly featuring Chinese or Aztec figures, offered scenes of water torture or splinters under the nails. Also popular were portrayals of the medieval European use of the cat o' nine tails; And, as a talker informed his bally crowd, this nasty whip was "made famous by the Marquis de Sade, the master of human misery." Wax models of executions were sometimes accompanied by curiously sympathetic patter about the victim: "The case against capital punishment. See the hideous ritual of murder to avenge murder. . . . Come in, if you can stand it!" Likewise, appealing to this voyeuristic impulse were crime shows: The Johnny Jones Exposition of 1936 featured the former wife of gangster John Dillinger. Later, Howard Bone went a little further with his "The Man Who Can't Be Hung" show, where he asked two men in the audience to pull on opposite ends of rope wrapped around his neck, trying

FIGURE 3.4 *An example of the trend toward the grotesque in carnival sideshows is this "Giant Killer Rat" spectacle that appeared in the small Appalachian town of Abingdon, Virginia (1967). The "rat" was probably the harmless capybaras. Robert Alexander/Archive Photos/Getty Images.*

to "hang" him (all done with much drama). No longer being able to attend public executions (the last being held in 1936), carnival crowds could try to hang a showman.[34]

Calls from amusement industry elites for family entertainment meant that carnival shows, like the *World of Mirth* (1953) also featured attractions that were fun and exciting, but hardly freakish. This included motordromes (motor cyclists racing on a tilted circular course), Hawaiian revues, and even minor movie stars like Lash LaRue doing his lasso tricks. But many carnival shows moved further to the edge with a growing emphasis on body-invasive freakery and, more broadly, displays of the morose and creepy as the audience narrowed in culture. We've seen the popeye act already along with the pincushion, fire eater, sword swallower, and tattooed (as in the 1933 Chicago fair). But these spectacles, designed to astonish and even disgust, become ever more prominent by mid-century.[35]

The words of one of the leading impresarios of the interwar freak show, Harry Lewiston, makes clear what has happened. He claimed that when he set up his show in the late 1930s, he wanted a "family show," but realized soon that "acts that would make them sick" brought in the crowds. Lewiston, like others, introduced a popeye but also Waldo the geek and a pincushion who (as an Egyptian "fakir") pretended to be in a trance while he poked hot pins in his checks, breast, and legs. The audience was even invited to drive nails into his arm muscles. Al Renton featured a geek presumably from the Congo in a postwar show that lasted until 1961. Renton's geek pulled off the feathers of live chickens with his teeth and then bit off their heads. He also ate bugs. To excite the crowd, geeks sometimes smeared their faces with hot blood and viscera; they vomited fur, feathers, and gristle of the snakes, chickens, and mice that they devoured alive. Bone's geek shows sometimes had to pay off to the police when animal rights organizations complained. While Dan Boles, another carnival personality from the 1950s, noted that many carnival operators stopped booking geeks when locals banned them and because they were often unreliable drunks, less discriminating shows still featured them until the 1960s. Almost as grotesque were the freaks that lifted weights attached to their tongues or breast nipples.[36]

Lewiston's as-told-to autobiography makes clear his quest for disgust in his late 1930s freak show. His blow-off featured Grace McDaniels, the Mule-Faced Woman who suffered from a facial deformity. She wore a veil when introduced to the crowd: "When she takes off her veil, you will think how lucky you are that you are not like her," Lewiston recalls saying on stage. He describes McDaniels's face as "like red, raw meat; her huge chin was twisted at such a distorted angle, she could hardly move her jaw . . . [She had] huge mule-like lips, deep socketed eyes . . .[She was a] sickening, horrible sight." As for the audience, "some stared in fascination" while some fainted or "averted their eyes."[37] This was a long way from the gentle giants or fashionably dressed bearded ladies of the Victorian freak show.

New Show People and New Crowds

The acts reveal a lot; but to understand the evolving freak show crowd and its aesthetic, we need to consider the show operator: Who were they, what was their pitch to the crowd, and what did they believe the crowd was thinking and feeling? Ultimately, how were these show operators and crowds alike and different from Barnum and his marks?

It took a special person to run a freak show. It was a small-scale and volatile business with much coming and going between carnivals, fairs, storefront shows, and circuses. This life worked for adaptable impresarios, who possessed a keen eye for their crowds and how these audiences were changing. I will consider three representative sideshow operators in succession by age, whose careers spanned the twentieth century, and who tell us much about how these shows and their crowds changed.

Sam Gumpertz (1868–1952) began his entertainment career as a nine-year-old acrobat, moving quickly to child actor, cowboy in a Buffalo Bill show, and, by the age of twenty-one, a manager of an "opera house" and vaudeville theater. Beginning in the 1890s, he was a player in the nascent amusement park movement in St. Louis (even promoting Edison films and briefly managing the famous escape artist Harry Houdini). Notably, he produced the Lilliputia Village (1904), drawing together dozens of midgets

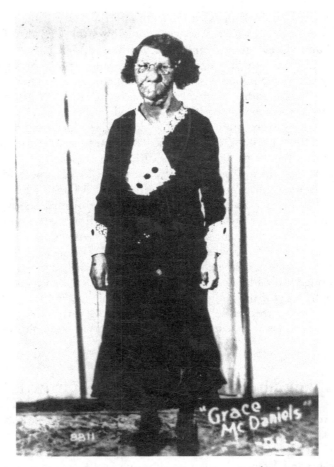

FIGURE 3.5 *Grace McDaniels (1888–1958), victim of elephantiasis of the lip, appeared in carnival shows for many years after 1935, Circus World Museum, Baraboo, Wisconsin.*

for the new Dreamland amusement park at Coney Island. In 1908, he produced a full-fledged freak show at Dreamland, and, after the amusement park burned down in 1911, he opened an independent freak show at Coney Island. Gumpertz hired the aging "Zip" ("The Missing Link") from Ringling and accumulated of a large assortment of exotics from abroad. Like others, he diversified, in 1916, purchasing the Eden (wax) Musée. By 1931, as Coney was in decline, Gumpertz sold his properties to his rival Sam Wagner; and, drawing on long-established financial links to RBBB (through his real estate dealings), he became in 1932 the circus's CEO. As we have seen, Gumpertz expanded the RBBB's sideshow (while others were scaling them back) until his retirement in 1937. Unable to give up the excitement of the midway, he took on Hamid's Million Dollar Pier at Atlantic City in the 1940s until his death in 1952. For his time, Gumpertz was a conventional entertainment promoter, cashing in on the freak show at its peak (as well as other profitable spectacles), both at Coney Island and with Ringling.[38]

Far different were Harry Lewiston (1900–65) and Ward Hall (1930–2018). They came into the business at young ages, but thirty years apart, illustrating the gradual transformation of the freak show and its crowd after 1930. Lewiston had experience in every phase of the business from 1914 until his youthful retirement in 1951. As a teen from a Jewish family in New York (birth name: Harry Jaffe), he ran away to join the circus. He was briefly a soldier in the First World War, returning to the circus as a candy butcher (seller) and expert at short-changing customers. Lewiston worked as a sideshow talker with the Christy Brothers Circus at twenty-two and three years later even managed a minstrel show; returning to the sideshow bally, he got fired for short changing customers. At twenty-six, he managed a hoochie-coochie show (promising the gullible rural women performers that his show would end in Hollywood). Unlike Gumpertz, he started out as a con man. But, Lewiston rose up the ranks of the sideshow business, first as the disciple of Lou Dufour, helping him to produce Darkest Africa and the LIFE Museum at the Chicago World's Fair in 1933–4, and, then, as the acolyte and assistant of Clyde Ingalls, managing the sideshow at RBBB in its glory days in the mid-1930s. By 1937, Lewiston broke from RBBB, taking some of the circus's best freaks with him for his own show, including the Mule-Faced Woman, Clicko, the Bushman, midgets, and four pinheads as well as snake charmers, a human balloon (who pumped air into his expanding stomach), and an anatomical wonder (who could pull in his belly so far crowds could see his backbone from the front), fortune tellers (including his wife Rose), blockheads, and even a girlie show. At first, Lewiston avoided geeks and pincushions, trying to uphold "class" acts. However, as noted above, after 1940, his show became more edgy than Gumpertz would have allowed, adding the Headless Woman and freak animals (a dog with only one foot) and a "swallower" who substituted a glowing neon tube for a sword. In 1941, Lewiston was actually jailed for six days for a "lewd show" in a county fair. In 1951, he retired to Los Angeles to run a hotel and employment agency for prison parolees.[39] Like so many showmen, he led a very unstable life, always looking for the "main chance" and a quick buck, sometimes skirting the law. But Lewiston knew his business and his marks. And he followed them into new territory with increasingly edgy acts.

Lewiston drew upon the crowd's imagination. He realized that audiences wanted not authenticity, but a story that conformed to their expectations and titillated: At first, his Darkest Africa show in Chicago had real Ashanti with tattooed faces, but they bored the crowd and were fired. Lewiston replaced them with "agitated American blacks" who danced and shouted as expected. Still, he avoided alienating his audience that still expected him never to be sarcastic or use "immoral words." Like others, Lewiston appealed to the "sympathy angle," asking for contributions for the care of the legless Freda Pushnik or pleaded with his audience to purchase cheap New Testament Bibles to aid the Mule-Faced Woman. Instead of extracting a maximum charge, he offered a low admission of twenty-five cents, expecting to get ultimately seventy cents after inducing customers to pay other small amounts for Bibles, fortune telling, and the blow-off (so that they would not notice the total price). He always tried to give his mark more than they expected, never mentioning the blow-off in local advertising or at the bally preview. He also realized that some shows played better to particular audiences: The animal freak show, he noted, appealed to farmers, but not to city people. African Americans in Detroit responded to the black popeye, Leonard Perry. And he realized that his audience was changing by the 1940s, becoming more rural and more minority. Ultimately, he found "what the public wanted most was to get sick and to see things that would make them nauseated." And they liked to "be fooled" as in his Headless Woman show. Lewiston's career marks the dramatic down-market shift in the sideshow that begins in the 1930s.[40]

Perhaps the most notable (and publicized) freak show impresario during its declining years was Ward Hall. Through his memoirs and interviews, Hall reveals an extraordinary career of adaptation and improvisation as he struggled to produce traditional freak shows in the face of increasing economic and cultural constraints and to find new thrills for a changing crowd. Like others, he literally ran away to join the circus, learning the arts of magic, clowning, juggling, eating fire, and playing the ventriloquist in small circuses. At eighteen, he was managing a sideshow and he owned one by twenty-one. In 1947, he teamed up with Harry Leonard, a knife thrower, in a partnership that lasted for sixteen years. After Leonard's death in 1964, Ward was joined by Chris Christ, a teen (very much like himself in the 40s), who learned knife throwing, sword swallowing, and fire eating before focusing on show management. This was a partnership that lasted from 1966 until Ward's death in 2018.[41]

Moving at a dizzying rate from one circus, carnival, or independent show to another, Hall nevertheless worked repeatedly with a wide range of traditional freaks: Best known were George Searles as Diane D'Elgar, the hermaphrodite, Peter Terhune (a midget who, for decades, played various roles including clown, juggler, snake handler, and "iron tongue"), and Dick Busten (the Penguin Boy, whose feet were attached directly to his torso). For shorter periods, Hall employed Tiny Hicks, a classic fat man (1964), Emmett Blackwelder, known as Turtleman, with stub arms and no legs (1969), and Barbara Bennett, the "World's Smallest Woman" (1976). At the same time, Hall offered curious crowds pickled punks (from 1951) and a giant rat show (1973), torture chambers (1977), a wax figure show, an illusion of a woman with a snake body (1978), and Dufour's old LIFE Museum (1979). He even tried a music and magic review (Wondercade in 1982). All this was in addition to the standard array of blockheads, snake charmers, albino girls, ostrich men, geeks, and giants that from 1950 were pulled together for his various shows. He produced indoor freak shows for RBBB in 1959, 1961, 1973, and 1974. He also did big freak shows for carnival chains like Goodings Million Dollar Midway in 1969 and 1972 as well as for a wide range of circuses (Beatty-Cole Brothers, Al Kelly and Miller Brothers, and Circus Vargas). At various times, he also did very small shows, including a simple "pit show" with his midget, Pete Terhune, placed in a cage with snakes (1956). Despite the decline in the freak show nationally, beginning in 1967, Hall, with Chris Christ, began to expand, buying other sideshows, including in 1972, the well-known show of Pete Kortes. Hall was at the center of it all, but his frenetic work life was like that of others.[42]

Rather than chronicle Hall's (and Christ's) full career, I will focus on two events that tell us much about them and the changing crowd. In 1950, when Hall was merely twenty years old, he made a deal with a small circus, agreeing to do a juggling act for the circus in exchange for the opportunity to exhibit on his own a two-headed fetus. Not having a real fetus, he did what others had done. He made a "bouncer" when he purchased two rubber dolls at a local store, glued the head of one doll on the other, placed his exhibit in a peanut butter jar with discolored water (to obscure the fakery), and sold the resulting pickled punk to the circus crowd with plenty of ballyhoo. In one small town where he exhibited his fake pickled punk, a customer pulled it out of the jar and the two-headed baby "said" Mama. The crowd, Hall claims, "didn't get mad," but instead laughed. Lewiston was right. They enjoyed being fooled. The next year, Hall had a two-headed baby professionally constructed, claiming to the crowd that the baby was from India. He asked for "donations" to support the poor mother of the fetus, a Mrs. Singh, who had twenty-one kids to care for. Hall knew that his show reached both those willing to see it as a con and those willing to buy into pitiful story, earning enough to purchase his first sideshow in 1951. The two-headed baby became a regular feature of Hall's shows; and, as we have seen, his pickled punks show was a major success in 1969 with his "Children of Forgotten Fathers," attracting crowds who found these bottled fetuses both fascinating and disgusting.[43]

However, in July 1977, Chris Christ was arrested in Lake County Illinois for his pickled punks show. A local coroner claimed that Christ illegally possessed and displayed human corpses. Hall and Christ believed that the coroner was seeking publicity for the higher office of sheriff; but they found themselves embroiled in a scandal that was publicized nationally by the Associated Press. In October, a judge ruled in their favor, noting that the punks had no birth or death certificates and thus could not be corpses. But the pair was accused of obtaining these ancient fetuses from "abortion mills." Bad publicity led Hall and Christ to bury the real punks in November 1977 and replace them bouncers the next year, but Ohio state officials banned these too from the state fair as fake. Soon the pair abandoned the "baby show" altogether.[44]

While Hall and Christ may well have been treated unfairly, pickled punk shows were already losing crowd appeal by 1977. Still, in a 1995 interview, Hall claimed that the punk show could sell "if presented in the right way." Hall always was convinced that he could find a hook to pull in a crowd. Hall and Christ were certain that the show was mostly in the pitch. Pickled punks, bouncers or not, were cheap substitutes for live freaks, but a good bally or pitch could draw in customers.[45]

These observations went beyond cynicism or a mocking of the naiveté of his mark. Hall took pride in creating illusions and finding a clever pitch that captured the imagination of the crowd. And, like Lewiston, Hall saw that many in that crowd enjoyed the deception, especially if it was playful. Hall and Christ merchandized whatever worked—throwing this or that on the wall, usually outrageous, but within limits, and saw what stuck—torture, two-headed babies, or even juggling midgets who always smiled. When I interviewed Hall and Christ in early 2018 at their retirement house in Gibsonton, Florida, a center for retired and off-season carnival people, I was struck at how unanalytical and instinctual they were about the changing crowd. Christ noted that he was too busy with managing the show and all its details to engage in this analysis, but he also claimed (as did Hall many times in his interviews) that he had to know his audiences, —their social and cultural backgrounds and what they responded to. As Hall summarized the talker's point of view, "You exaggerate, and they congregate."[46]

The Aesthetic of the Late Freak Show

While Gumpertz did not have to fret too much over what drew in crowds, Lewiston and Hall had to continually adapt in the decades between 1930 and 1980. And they responded by offering the crowd a wide and sometimes imaginative variety of experiences, even if these encounters were increasingly grotesque. Lewiston and Hall had to appeal to an increasingly unsophisticated crowd and crude thrill seekers. These people were sometimes willing to buy into the con (even as a joke); some were suckers for pity; others simply longed for any experience that was disgusting or horrifying and thus produced a shutter or a visceral reaction. And, though it is hard to measure, the freak show drew especially the young seeking a taboo experience (that was probably similar to what later attracted teens and youth to visceral horror movies).

It is easy (and common) to adopt a patronizing attitude toward these remnants of the old sideshow crowd. This image of the country rube listening to the ballyhoo at the county fair carnival in the late 1930s to 1941 was captured by photographers for the U.S. Farm Security Administration. One took a picture of farm families who gathered to hear a nurse claim that a black-and-white "twin" fetus in a jar was the "first in medical history"; another captured an image of a crowd gathered to watch "just one big fat family" tap dance and play musical instruments. Still another government photographer showed country people at a fair in Donaldsville, Louisiana, watching a black male geek presumably from the Congo pulling a snake from his mouth and teasing it. These photographers sought to reveal country rubes being conned by slick show people and capture this image in what they probably thought was the last gasp of a dying spectacle.[47]

Still, that rube continued to be drawn to the freak show long after the 1940s. Paul Ingrassia, a longtime activist in circus preservation movement who I met at the Ringling Museum Archives, recalled how Bob Snowden, a veteran showman, as late as the 1970s, could still draw crowds in the Bible Belt of Tennessee into his "free" "Last Supper Show." It consisted of wax figures that he carted from town to town in a semitrailer truck. Snowden earned money by obliging the crowd to enter the show through a narrow passage while Snowden blocked their way dressed in a white robe with hands folded as if in prayer, signaling a box in front of him for "offerings." The naïve long continued to fall victim to professional cheats with card and shell games. Many were simply shortchanged by ticket sellers from high ticket booths. Freak show historian Andrea Dennett claims that these spectacles were in decline from 1910; but they shifted gradually to the backwaters of rural America, especially the South, appealing to the naiveté of the inexperienced and the reflexive piety of the country church goer.[48]

However, there was another component of the crowd after 1950, be it rural or not: the customer that was attracted to the viscerally disgusting and shocking for its own sake. Reflecting on the success of his freak show at the Chicago World's Fair of 1933, Dufour insisted, "our unabashed appeal to the fascination with cruelty put the show over. "When a pair of women warned their friend not to attend: "you'll faint," that was "the strongest inducement to attend and their friend went right in."[49] And, as we shall see in Chapter 6, this impulse was hardly confined to the hick or unsophisticated lower class. That desire motivated college-educated middle-class youths attending *Night of the Living Dead*.

Still, is there more to what attracted crowds to the freak show? In a 1980 TV interview, Ward Hall claimed that he created "colorful, humorous word pictures" to lure a crowd. He appealed to the imagination—to be sure, often by drawing on old prejudices, current anxieties, and ignorance; and at times his words amounted to "gruesome seduction" as noted by his biographer, Tim O'Brien. But it wasn't all negative: Hall and other skilled talkers at the bally platform awakened curiosity, anticipation, and even a sense of urgency (by the oft-heard admonition of "see it while you still can").[50]

An English showman, Maurice Gorham, was especially insightful on this point in his memoir of 1951. He argues that fair goers, even hard-headed penny-pinchers, had a "sucker streak," a willingness to be conned by the showman. More than other memoir writers, he put a positive spin on this: His customers weren't stupid or masochists. On special occasions

FIGURE 3.6 *A "geek" performing at a fair in Donaldsonville, Louisiana, 1938. Library of Congress, LC-USF33- 011767.*

(in a sort of modern version of the saturnalian abandonment of cultural norms), Gorham insists that people give themselves over to the irrational belief that they can "win at the horses." They save and lose at the fair in a sort of sucker "fling." The showman must know when and how to let the crowd "make fools of themselves." This leap into irrationality was not simply some sort of rebellion against everyday common sense, much less a mark of the ignorance of the rube or even cynicism. Rather, it was based on "curiosity more than gullibility." And that curiosity was founded on a basic optimism—that the show would be as entertaining or thrilling as promised on the bally. And if it wasn't or if you were had, you never admitted it. And then you went to the next show hoping it will be good.[51]

Moreover, Gorham notes, what was enjoyed in the show was the sheer physicality of the experience (not realized in movies or TV). Seeing the giant up close, notes Gorham, "makes you see the world of the short person." Diane Arbus made this point larger in her "obituary" for Hubert's Museum in 1966: "We had our awe and our shame in one gulp. What if we couldn't always tell the trick from a miracle? If you've talked with someone with two heads you know they know something you don't." There was a willingness to stare and have the "other" stare back. And this exchange was what so spooked the modern cultured bourgeois and caused them to condemn the freak show. In fact, sometimes the freak show crowd was willing to face what moderns call a "disability" and the disgusting directly and personally. Is all of this gone today? Maybe so. Gorham in 1951 was already seeing a shift to rides at his fairgrounds.[52] Modern audiences increasingly preferred a visceral experience with a machine rather than an imaginative anticipation and a physical encounter with a person who didn't "fit" in the normative world.

The Final Decline

The end of the traditional freak show is a long and, for some, a sad, but revealing, tale. By the 1970s, even the carnival sideshow was in sharp decline. Often what was left were gross nudie shows and three-card monte at small town fairs. Banners for the Royal American Shows of 1979 screamed: "Jaws of Death, Most Feared of all Man-Eaters, Alive Crocodiles! Shocking!" Surviving acts were often cheap animal freak shows and cycle acts.[53]

But the story may best be told from a single lens in a brief recounting of the experience of Hall and Christ. In the mid-1970s, this pair may have been at their peak: They had purchased four sideshows over the previous decade (even though the fact of their consolidation indicates a decline in the profitability of freaks). Already in the late 1970s, Hall and Christ had increasingly relied on "grind shows" (a continuous presentation of acts often as crowds passed by) and wax works. By the end of 1980, they had closed their last ten-in-one show. The pair diversified in 1982 with a circus-type variety show, Wondercade with a band, chorus girls, aerialists, and illusions, but no freaks. This too failed at the box office. Returning to the old sideshow, the pair was unable to free themselves from debt and went into bankruptcy in 1985. Christ departed for circus work in South America, while Hall doggedly recreated a small show featuring the tiny Barbara Bennett, "The World's Smallest Mother" and a "museum" with oddities under glass. Later in the 1980s the pair returned briefly with animal freaks and old freak friends, especially Pete Terhune, with his snakes and fire eating, along with wax figures of celebrities.[54]

By the 1990s, the team had to compete with new age freak shows that featured "grotesque novelty acts," which replaced "human oddities," according to circus historian Fred Pfening (Chapter 5). By 2003, Hall had presumably retired, but in 2006, the team reorganized a World of Wonders show consisting of working acts (blockhead, glass dancer, contortionist, and, of course, Pete Terhune, fire eating). Tom Breen (a young college graduate in Cinematic Studies) in 2010 became manager and later bought the show.[55]

Perhaps not surprisingly, from the beginning of the decline of the freak show came nostalgia. Hall especially was able to exploit this. From the early 1960s, famed burlesque dancer, Sally Rand narrated a feature involving Hall for NBC. Interviews accumulated in the 1970s with appearances on various talk shows. In 1979 and 1980, Hall and Christ brought a bit of old Americana to the Smithsonian Institution's "Spring Celebration of American Popular Entertainment," with a sampling of their sideshow on the Washington Mall. Documentaries abounded—from Harry Rasky's film

Being Different of 1980 to the TV feature, *Sideshow* for The Learning Channel in 1997. Even RBBB, which had long ago abandoned the sideshow, reintroduced it briefly in 1998. It featured Michu (Mihaly Meszaros), the Hungarian midget who road into the arena in a carriage pulled by miniature horses, along with a strongman, fire eater, and snake charmer, all appealing to an increasingly nostalgic circus audience. Others attempted (largely unsuccessfully) to restore the old glory. An example is Jim Jajicek's 2002 collection of animal freaks and working acts under the slogan of reviving the "long, glorious bannerline."[56]

Todd Ray, a music producer with a fascination with the traditional freak show, formed his own small company at Venice Beach in Southern California in 2006. He even produced a short-lived reality TV show called *Freakshow* on AMC in 2013–14. This documentary featured "backstage" activities, often on nostalgic themes: For example, in one episode Ray throws a wedding for two little people who reenact the famous Tom Thumb Wedding. But along with bodybuilders and graffiti artists that had added "color" to Venice Beach, Ray's freak show disappeared in 2017. Rachel Adams nicely summarizes this nostalgia: "Sweltering heat, the smells of popcorn and animal dung, abusive exchanges between carnies, freaks, and customers—there are the freak show's Proustian mnemonics, capable of summoning back powerful recollections in those who once were there."[57] But nostalgia seldom is a revival. It often merely signals the passing of a culture and eventually of those who remember it romantically.

FIGURE 3.7 *Famed sideshow impresario Ward Hall (with the red top hat), shown in 2002 with cast members. Pete Terhune, longtime featured midget, stands in front of Hall. Olivier Chouchana/Getty Images.*

The author of a 2006 *New York Times* offers a patronizing, but revealing, description of one of Hall's latter-day show and his pitch:

> Poobah [Pete Terhune] is the attraction, the only physical oddity left. Poobah is the draw that gets the dupes standing out there in flip-flops, holding on to their plastic Spider-Man blowup dolls, to pay three bucks to go inside and see a man stick a screwdriver up his nose, a sword swallower with periodontal disease, an eight-foot woman made of foam. Her left foot is broken off, and she needs a dusting. Once inside, seeing they've been lied to, people get hostile.
>
> "Now, Poobah here is the king of the Pygmies," Mr. Hall yaps.
>
> The crowd comes closer. . .
>
> "Poobah is the last living munchkin from 'The Wizard of Oz.' "
>
> Poobah first saw the movie as a television rerun.
>
> "He is the star of 84 Hollywood pictures, 114 television shows and numerous Broadway musicals."
>
> Poobah couldn't sing to save his life. But Poobah says he doesn't mind. It's a living. He says he loves Mr. Hall. And it beats retirement.
>
> "Now, watch as Poobah eats the fire."
>
> Poobah does so for the umpteenth time today.[58]

This account makes it all seems so tired and we wonder why Hall, Christ, and Poobah kept at it, except to avoid the hot summers of retirement in Florida. But is this fair?

For Hall and other operators, freak shows died from a number of, if not a thousand, cuts: Of course, important factors were the decline of available human oddities and the willingness of crowds to view them or elites to allow them to be viewed. As Hall noted in a 2006 interview: "Nowadays, it's in the contracts: no freaks," lamenting that the do-gooders had put the oddities out of work at state fairs and carnivals. But he also admitted: "The fat man—Howard Huge—he wanted to come out with us. But I said, 'Howard, a fat man couldn't sell 10 cents' worth of fried chicken. Everybody in America's fat.' "Middle-class sensibilities had prevailed, while the old freak was no longer freakish.[59]

Yet, insiders mostly offered economic explanations for the decline: The introduction of single ticket or coupon tickets about 1977 reduced the possibility of piling on small costs at the freak show. And without cash transactions, there was no opportunity to short-change the sucker. Hall noted that carnivals came under pressure (from both consumers and suppliers) to buy increasingly more expensive mechanical rides, leaving less space for the shows. But, behind this claim was the fact that the visceral thrill of being spin or tossed for a couple of minutes was more attractive than personally engaging a strange body or behavior. And, there were also fewer opportunities to find employees—not just born-freaks but working acts. Who wanted to work seven days a week for a $100 and sleep under a show wagon? Moreover, by the 1990s, rising costs were leaving small towns without their annual carnival.[60] In a 1995 interview, Hall still insisted that the problem was not demand but supply: "A 20-30 foot [bannerline] with a well painted front might work today [and] if you could do a blackface minstrel show . . . or have a big girl review at fairs, these things still have a market . . . but it's just economically not feasible to operate them." Clearly, the traditional setting of the freak show no longer was cost efficient, and, despite Hall's insistence, they no longer drew enough customers.[61]

In the end, the more interesting point is less why the freak show died, but in its decline, how freakishness *changed* and attracted new audiences. This chapter shows how the freak show was marginalized, but not eliminated, at least, not for a long time. We have seen how the withdrawal of middle class from the culturally mixed spectacle in the twentieth century led to a freak show that was shorn of the Victorian veneer of "virtue" that had made the stare acceptable to middle America in the nineteenth century. With reduced "respectability" and increased costs, the freak show became even more of a "con" than before and certainly more grotesque. It even became creepy, with displays of two-headed fetuses, geeks, and simulated torture in wax. In time, especially with new competition in pornography and graphic horror movies, even these adaptations were insufficient to sustain the carnival freak show.

But that still didn't mean the "victory" of "family entertainment," much less a twentieth-century version of the Victorian ideal of "rational recreation" despite the wishes of Robert Moses of New York, the directors of natural history museums, or, as we shall see, the uplifting censors policing the movies with the Production Code. Working acts survived in spectacles like Tom Breen's World of Wonders sideshow. The freakish behavior of the sword swallower, blockhead, and strongwoman limped along at state and local fairs under the banner of "family entertainment."[62]

More important, the genteel/highbrow cultural complex failed to prevail in the United States as the reformers had hoped. In fact, the middle class never fully embraced this goal. Even the rejection of the freak within the middle class was never complete. If the "mystery" and moral and uplifting backstory of the Victorian freak large disappeared by the early twentieth century, middle-class Americans still found ways of engaging the extraordinary body. After all, the nineteenth-century oddity had both repulsed and attracted. The most obvious form of this, we have already explored in the tolerant, even boyish, enthusiasm of the globe-trotting adventurer, Robert Ripley. But there were other forms of this reintegration of the freak into modern middle-class culture that will be the focus of the following three chapters.

To begin, there was the domesticated freak in the form of the cuteified dwarfs of Disney, but also in the transformation of a key component in the old sideshow, the small person or midget. Just as the natural history museum learned that accurate displays of animal and plant life were insufficient to attract even the middlebrow crowd, spectacle makers sought to hold on and expand their audiences with promises of wonder, even as they abandoned the carnivalesque. One response to the middle-class quest for wonder was to cultivate the cuteified freak, often seen through the gaze of the cuteified child. Children of the respectable parents were admonished not to gawk at sideshow freaks and other extraordinary people. However, they still grew up in a sensually drenched consumer culture that invited them to gape continuously at new spectacles. As we shall see, by the early twentieth century, children and their parents were dazzled less often by people in sideshow pits, but they could take delight in *freakish* figures in new venues. This included midgets on the stage in musical spectacles and cuteified and humanized cartoon animals with extraordinary, but still delightful, bodies. Though rooted in the sideshow, the cuteified freak moved into a new world of *novelty* rather than the highly conventionalized and traditional setting of the bannerline.

But there were more edgy versions of this post-carnival return to the freak. The cute was not the only way to recover wonder in the freak. A new form of the stare emerged in the camp aesthetic, and it too came from the middle class, in a youthful consumer, who was amused but not captivated by freakish spectacle. Finally, in a rejection of the staid and sublime values of the genteel elite, many from middle America embraced the creepy, not only in the geek who devoured mice but flesh-eating zombies.

The rejection of classic genteel culture then took three forms—the cute, the camp, and the creepy and with this the irrepressible freak. The cute, easily adapted to a sensation-seeking (rather than highbrow) middle class, emerged fully in the 1930s. The camp and the creepy blossomed in the 1960s as part of youth counterculture. Thereafter the cute, the camp, and the creepy extended their boundaries, eventually contributing to important elements of contemporary popular culture. Let's begin with the cute.

Notes

1 "Robbins Brothers Circus Season, 1931," *White Tops*, November 12, 1958, 3; "Recollections of a Billposter," *White Tops*, January 2, 1954, 3–4; "Gentry Brothers Circus, 1929," *White Tops*, September 10, 1954, 3–4; "Experiences of a Circus Lawyer," *White Tops*, July 8, 1946, 17; "Floyd King: A Reminiscence," *Bandwagon*, January 2, 1997, 20–1.

2 Van Matre, "Going, Going Gone," *Bannerline*, August 1, 1966, 7; "Rogers Brothers Circus," *White Tops*, July 8, 1948, 13; "Sells and Gray Circus," *White Tops*, January 2, 1961, 7; Sells Circus," *White Top*, September 10, 1962, 17.

3 "Roger Brothers Circus," *White Tops*, September 10, 1949, 5; "On the Road with the Big Show in 1953-54," *Bandwagon*, July 8, 2008, 5; "Circus Year in Review," *Bandwagon*, March 4, 2009, 5. Circus fan and history magazines, including *Bandwagon* and *White Tops*, were supported by groups of nostalgic circus enthusiasts, especially the Circus Fans of America founded in 1925. These magazines sought to record and preserve circus heritage and regularly

chronicled the activities and fates of circuses in great detail, often with no author designation.

4   "1955 Tour of Ringling Brothers," *Bandwagon,* November 12, 1955, 10; "Highballing on the Moonlight Lady," *Bandwagon,* September 10, 2008, 9–17; "Barbara Miller Byrd," *Spectacle,* Fall 2000, 4; "Clyde Beatty-Cole Brothers Circus," *Circus Report,* May 22, 1989, 35; "Circus Year in Review," *Bandwagon,* January 2, 1991, 8, 11; "Circus Year in Review," *Bandwagon,* March 4, 1997, 4–23; "American Circus Seeks a United Stand in Its Defense of Animal Performers," *Spectacle,* Winter 2000, l; "Circus in Review, 2005 Season," *Bandwagon,* March 4, 2006, 26.

5   Circus Smirkus from Vermont (formed in 1987) grew out of an afterschool academy where youth learned the arts of acrobatics, juggling, and unicycling. An example of the Renaissance Fair show is the American Gypsy circus. It comprised eleven acts, a mix of costumed jugglers and acrobats as well as vestigial sideshow acts in the "Temple of the Bizarre," where "King Leonardo" laid on a bed of nails and had a concrete block broken on his chest. "Circus in Review," *Bandwagon,* March 4, 2006, 5; "The Sun Never Sets on the Cirque du Soleil," *Spectacle,* Fall 1987, 36–27; "Circus Smurkus," *Circus World,* July 31, 1989, 15; "Disney Channel Discovers Circus Smirkus," *Spectacle,* Summer, 1999, 8–10; "2005 Season," *Bandwagon,* March 4, 1006, 13, 23; "Scarborough Fair," *Circus Report,* July 10, 1981, 23; "Renaissance Fair," *Circus Report,* January 23, 1989, 2. "Fred Pfening, III, 'Circus Year in Review,'" *Bandwagon,* March 4, 1998, 5.

6   "Circus Report," *Spectacle,* Fall 1999, 20–1; "2006 Circus Year in Review," *Bandwagon,* March 4, 2007, 2–27; "A 2008 Season," *Bandwagon,* March 4, 2009, 5; "Shriner's Circus," *Bandwagon,* March 4, 2012, 21–2; Amy Wang, "Animal Activists Finally Have Something to Applaud at Ringling Bros. Circus: Its Closure," *Washington Post,* January 15, 2017, 1.

7   In 1936, Al Tomaini (1912–62) at seven feet, one inch met his future wife Jeanie (1916–99) while performing in a circus sideshow. She was born without legs, and was two feet, five inches in height. https://showmensmuseum.org/exhibits/strangest-couple-world/wppaspec/oc1/cv0/ab5/ptFred-Johnson-Sides how-Banner-Bearded-Lady-Brenda-Beatty; Circus Route Books, John and Mable Ringling Art Museum Archive (JMRMA): Gentry Brothers, 1923, 3; 1924, 3; 1926, 3; RBBB, 1936, 16; 1937, 17; 1939, 16. For more on Eko and Iko (George and Willie Muse), see Beth Macy, *Truevine: Two Brothers, a Kidnapping and a Mother's Quest: A True Story of the Jim Crow South* (New York: Little Brown, 2016). See also Neil Parsons, *Clicko: The Wild Dancing Bushman* (Chicago: University of Chicago Press, 2010).

8   *Saucerlips Ubangi Savages* (np, ca. 1932), Tibbals Circus Collection of Booklets, no. 14, JMRMA. This booklet reads like a *National Geographic,* with much detail about the origins and social/cultural practices of the Ubangi. It is written without disdainful humor. More information is found in A. W. Stencell, *Circus and Carnival Ballyhoo: Sideshow Freaks, Jabbers and Blade Box Queens* (Toronto: ECW Press, 2010), 121; Robert Bogdan, *Freak Show: Presenting Human Oddities for Amusement and Profit* (Chicago: University of Chicago Press, 1988), 115; Andrea Dennett, "The Dime Museum Freak Show

Reconfigured," in Rosemary Garland-Thomson, *Freakery* (New York: New York University Press, 1996), 318; "Whatever Happened to the Giraffe-Neck Women," *Bandwagon,* July 8, 2001, 12–15; "The Ubangis are Alive and Well," *Bandwagon,* May 6, 2005, 15–20.

9 Circus Route Book Collection, JMRMA: RBBB, 1940, 18; 1941, 18; 1942, 16; 1943, 18; 1946, 19; 1948, 16; 1949, 16; 1950, 18; 1951, 18; 1952, 18; 1954, 16; 1955, 7.

10 Clyde Beatty Circus Route Books: 1947, 14; 1951, 15; 1960, 9; 1961, 15, JMRMA; "Robbin Brothers Circus, Season of 1949," *Bandwagon,* May 6, 1998, 9; Route Book Collection, Robert L. Parkinson Library & Research Circus World Museum (hereafter cited as Circus World Museum): Cole Brothers, 1946, 51; 1947, 22; A. G. Barnes, 1947, 23; Mills Brothers, 1948, 12; 1949, 11.

11 "History of the Beers Barnes Circus," *Bandwagon,* November 12, 1994, 43; King Brothers Circus, Route Book, 1946 and 1947, np., JMRMA; "Capell Brothers Circus," *White Tops,* July 8, 1953, 21.

12 Norman Carroll, "Side Show—Knock or Boost," *Billboard,* July 12, 1947, 52.

13 Circus Route Books, Circus World Museum: Cole Brothers, 1949, np, Mills Brothers, 1960, np; "Circus World News," *Bannerline,* August 1, 1969, 7; "Carson and Barnes Circus, 1967," *Bannerline,* May 1, 1967, 12.

14 Neal Thompson, *A Curious Man: The Strange and Brilliant Life of "Believe it or Not" Robert Ripley* (New York: Three Rivers Press, 2013), 5, 68, 81, 86, 99, 132, 143, 370; Robert Ripley, *Believe It or Not!* (New York: Simon and Schuster, 1929), 8–9; Mark Sloan, Roger Manley, and Michelle Van Parys, *Dear Mr. Ripley: A Compendium of Curiosities from the Believe It or Not Archives* (Boston, MA: Little, Brown, 1993), 18–33. This book includes photographs of Ripley's collection of oddities, many physical, like a man pulling a car with his hair (1937) or even a man who held twenty-five quarters in his ear (1933), 83, 90, 143. A collection of postcards depicting acts Ripley shown at the expositions in the 1930s is in Tibbals Circus Collection of Postcards, Sideshows, JMRMA, including Betty Williams with a parasitic twin, blockheads, contortionists, elastic men, pincushions, and others. Note also PBS, "Ripley Believe it or Not" (American Experience episode, January 15, 2015).

15 Cited in Thompson, *A Curious Man,* 142, 155–6. Sources are difficult to identify but cited on pp. 389–92.

16 Thompson, *A Curious Man,* 131, Ripley, *Believe It or Not!,* 14, 16, 29, 39, 44, 63. 143.

17 Thompson, *A Curious Man,* 158, 180 (quotation), 181; Dorothy Gaiter, "Norbert Pearlroth, 89, Researcher for 52 Years for 'Believe it or Not,'" *New York Times,* April 15, 1983.

18 Andrea Dennett, *Weird and Wonderful: The Dime Museum in America* (New York: New York University Press, 1997), 129–31; Dennett, "The Dime Museum," 319. Ripley Odditorium Chicago World's Fair, 1933, postcard, Tibbals Circus Collection of Postcards, Sideshows, JMRMA; Thompson, *A Curious Man,* Chapter 15; Sloan et al. claim that Ripley toned down his

odditorium for the New York World's Fair of 1939: *Dear Mr. Ripley,* 25; *Century of Progress, Official Guidebook of the World's Fair of 1934* (Chicago: A Century of Progress, International Exposition, 1934).

19 Thompson, *A Curious Man,* 5.

20 Leslie Fiedler, *Freaks: Myths and Images of the Secret Self* (New York: Simon and Schuster, 1976), 284.

21 J. A. Liebling, "Masters of the Midway," *The New Yorker,* August 19, 1939, 23; Lou Dufour, *Fabulous Years: Carnival Life, World's Fairs, and Broadway* (New York: Vantage Press, 1977), 57–8, 71–5, 92–3, 120, 122, 126; Lew Dufour and Joe Rogers, *Darkest Africa at A Century of Progress 1933: Official Souvenir* (Chicago: Dufour & Rogers, 1933); Joe Nickell, *Secrets of the Sideshows* (Lexington: University of Kentucky Press, 2008), 321–2.

22 Dufour, *Fabulous Years,* 165.

23 *Souvenir and Life Story of San Antonio's Siamese Twins, Daisy and Violet Hilton* (San Antonio: Naylor Printing, 1930), 1–14; Dennett, *Weird and Wonderful,* 131–3; Durfour, *Fabulous Years,* 56–8; Ward Hall, *My Very Unusual Friends* (Sarasota, FL: Self-published, 1991), 39.

24 "Remembering Hubert's: Pat Bissonette Talks about Hubert's Museum," *Freaks* (a fanzine published by Chris Fellner, Ringling Museum Art Library), no. 11, November 1997, 2–7; Marc Hartzman, *American Sideshow: An Encyclopedia of History's Most Wondrous and Curiously Strange Performers* (New York: Tarcher/Penguin, 2005), 109–12, 164–5, 188; Jack Hunter, *Freak Babylon: An Illustrated History of Teratology and Freakshows* (New York: Creation, 2014), 106; "Hubert's Obituary: Text by Diane Arbus, 1966 unpublished," *Freaks,* no. 14 ½, August 1998, 22–3. Hall, *Unusual Friends,* 39.

25 Stencell, *Circus and Carnival,* 87, 143–4.

26 Hunter, *Freak Babylon,* 59, 65, 85–90; Fiedler, *Freaks,* 197; Hall, *Unusual Friends,* 49.

27 Jerry Holtman, *Freak Show Man: The Autobiography of Harry Lewiston* (Los Angeles: Holloway House, 1968), 7, 9; Howard Bone, *Side Show: My Life with Geeks, Freaks and Vagabonds in the Carney Trade* (Northville, MI: Sure Dog Press, 2001), 71–6.

28 "Is it a He or a She: Interview with Ward Hall," *Freaks,* no. 7, November 1996, 2–3; Hall, *Unusual Friends,* 47; Hartzman, *American Sideshow,* 135–6.

29 Stencell, *Circus and Carnival,* 66; Holtman, *Freak Show Man,* 7, 9, 253–4; "Is it a He or a She," 3.

30 "It Started with Barnum (Interview with Ward Hall)" and "Headless Olga," *Freaks,* no. 8, February 1998, 2, 7; Holtman, *Freak Show Man,* 271; Bone, *Side Show,* 33–4; Kevin Gerrone, *Peter G. Hennen's Hell's Bells* (np: Ballyhoo Press, 2017), 9, 19–20, 26; Dufour, *Fabulous Years,* 11, 60; A. W. Stencell, *Seeing Is Believing: America's Sideshows* (Toronto: ECW Press, 2002), 151–5; Bone, *Side Show,* xx, 29; Rick West, *Pickled Punks and Girlie Shows: A Life Spent on the Midways of America* (Atglen, PA: Schiffer Books, 2011), 135.

31 Dufour, *Fabulous Years,* 11, 47, 60; Stencell, *Seeing Is Believing,* 151–5; Bone, *Side Show,* 29; Don Boles, *Midway Showman* (Atlanta, GA: Pinchpenny Press,

1967), 57; "Goodman's Wonder Show, 1938, Circus World Museum, mss 65 (carnival file).

32 "Ward Hall: King of the Freakshow Men," *Freaks*, no. 1, August 1995, 3.

33 "Johnny J. Jones Exposition," 1936, np, Circus World Museum, mss 63 (carnival); Nickel, *Sideshows*, 306, 309–31; Stencell, *Seeing Is Believing*, 4, 7; Ricky Jay, *Jay's Journal of Anomalies* (New York: Farrar, Straus, & Giroux, 2001), 35–8; Fred Olen Ray, *Grind Shows: Weirdness as Entertainment* (American Entertainment Press, 1993), 25; Boles, *Midway Showman*, 36, 41, 47; Charles Meltzer, "Giant Rat Shows," *Bandwagon*, September 10, 1998, 17.

34 "Johnny J. Jones Exposition"; Boles, *Midway Showman*, 52–5; Stencell, *Seeing Is Believing*, 89–91; Bone, *Freak Show*, 65–9.

35 *World of Mirth Magazine*, 1954, 10–12 and other ephemera in Circus World Museum, Mss. 63 (carnival).

36 Stencell, *Seeing Is Believing*, 230–9; Bone, *Freak Show*, 23–4; Boles, *Midway Showman*, 29; James E. Strates Shows, 1949, np, Circus World Museum, mss. 63 (carnival).

37 Holtman, *Freak Show Man*, 11, 24–7, 269.

38 "Mr. Coney Island: The Amazing Life of Samuel W. Gumpertz," *Freaks*, no. 14, August 1998, 2–16; Edo McCullough, *Good Ol' Coney Island* (New York: Scribner's, 1957), 258–68.

39 Holtman, *Freak Show Man*, 28–9, 111–17, 186, 196, 219, 223–4.

40 Douglas Martin, "Frieda Pushnik Is Dead at 77; Turned Her Deformities Into a Career," *New York Times*, January 7, 2001, Sec. 1, 27; Holtman, *Freak Show Man*, 191, 237, 239, 243, 264, 281, 282.

41 "Ward Hall, King," 8–9; Ward Hall, *Struggles and Triumphs of a Modern Day Showman* (Sarasota, FL: Carnival Publication, 1981), 19; Hall, *Unusual Friends*, 42; Tim O'Brien, *Ward Hall: King of the Side Show* (Nashville: Casa Flamingo Literary Arts, 2014), 49.

42 "Ward Hall," *Freaks*, no. 1 August 1995, 10–12; Hall, *Struggles*, 27, 31–2, 42, 56–7, 98; O'Brien, *Ward Hall*, 20–6, 71–3, 122, 147–8; "Sideshow World: Little People on the Midway, Pete Terhune," http://www.sideshowworld.com /43-Little-Folks/2013/Chip/Pete.html; Hartzman, *American Sideshow*, 123–5, 222–3.

43 "Pickled Punks," *Freaks*, no. 3, November 1995: 2–3.

44 O'Brien, *Ward Hall*, 163, 166, 173; Hartzman, *American Sideshow*, 117–18. News of Christ's arrest and trail were widely publicized in 1977 in local papers such as the *Las Vegas Optic*, August 12, 1977, 8; *Dubuque Telegraph Herald*, August 22, 1977, 14; and *Jacksonville Courier* November 18, 1977, 32.

45 "Pickled Punks," *Freaks*, 4–5.

46 O'Brien, *Ward Hall* (quotation of Hall), 29.

47 Ronald Ostman, "Photography and Persuasion: Farm Security Administration Photographs of Circus and Carnival Sideshows, 1935-42," in *Freakery*, 121–38.

48 Paul Ingressia interview, Sarasota, February 5, 2019, JMRMA; Dennett, "Dime Museum," 315.

49 Dufour, *Fabulous Years,* 73.

50 O'Brien, *Ward Hall,* 30.

51 Maurice Gorman, *Showmen and Suckers* (London: Percival Marshall, 1951), 99, 100–2.

52 Gorman, *Showmen and Suckers*, 106; "Hubert's Obituary," 23; Michael Chemers, *Staging Stigma: A Critical Examination of the American Freak Show* (London: Palgrave, 2008), 19.

53 Arthur Lewis, *Carnival* (New York: Trident Press, 1970), 19, 74; "Humbug in Royal American Shows in 1979," *Carousel,* January 2001, 12.

54 Stencell, *Circus and Carnival*, 337, 339; O'Brien, *Ward Hall*, 176–207; Hartzman, *American Sideshow*, 119–20.

55 O'Brien, *Ward Hall,* 207–32; "Circus Year in Review, 1997," *Bandwagon,* March 4, 1998, 21; "Circus Year in Review, 2006," *Bandwagon,* March 4, 2007, 24.

56 O'Brien, *Ward Hall,* 101–3, 106–8, 171; Hall, *Unusual Friends,* 40; "Being Different," *Freaks,* no. 4, February 1996, 4; "Sideshow, The Learning Channel," *Freaks*, no. 8, February 1997, 37–9; "Notice," *Amusement Business,* June 15, 1988, 47 and May 2006, 6, 35; Hartzman, *American Sideshow*, 4.

57 Rachel Adams, *Sideshow U.S.A.: Freaks and the American Cultural Imagination* (Chicago: University of Chicago Press, 2001), 12.

58 Charlie Leduff, "Step Right Up, Ladies and Gents, to See the End of an Oddity," *New York Times,* November 30, 2006, https://www.nytimes.com/2006/11/13/us/step-right-up-ladies-and-gents-to-see-the-end-of-an-oddity.html?module=inline.

59 Leduff, "Step Right Up."

60 Among the many who have written on this are Stencell (who entered the sideshow business in 1967), *Circus and Carnival,* Chapter 10, especially 331–2; see also for Ward Hall's view, O'Brien, *Ward Hall*, 185–6, 191, 215; Hall, *Unusual Friends,* 49; and "Hall," *Freaks,* no. 1, August 1995, 16.

61 "Hall," *Freaks,* no. 1, August 1995, 18.

62 World of Wonders Show, https://worldofwondershow.weebly.com/.

4

The Cute

Domesticating the Freak

P. T. Barnum knew how to draw both the aspiring and respectable as well as recently urbanized immigrant peasants and hard-playing artisans to his dime museums, even to gawk at his freaks. Given the ideals of bourgeois civility, however, the genteel did not always embrace the carnivalesque practice of staring at a three-legged man, much less a geek—and, then only if that person was assimilated into a bourgeois world of standards and expectations.

But it was easy, even pleasurable, to gaze upon small people. Barnum and others of his day presented them as the respectable audience's vision of its own bourgeois perfection in miniature. Moreover, despite their age, small people reminded middle-class viewers of children—mostly innocent and in need of protection. Women, especially those who had imbibed the culture of domesticity and maternal nurturance that was becoming the bourgeois norm, were attracted to these special freaks. Small people like Tom Thumb and Lavinia Warren combined two bourgeois ideals: a diminutive expression of genteel cultivation and benevolence as well as the angelic child. The Victorian midget, even more than other freaks, had to remind viewers of their ideal selves and children to be successful, erasing the disturbing scene of a body far too small to be like them and too old to be their small offspring. Audiences gawked, but without shame, disgust, or anxiety.

By 1930, bodily difference was being reduced to a medical malady and even the moniker of respectability was insufficient to overcome bourgeois disdain for the freak. Small people might still wear top hats and be called "Counts," but this formality no longer necessarily carried prestige, as elites adopted more casual styles of self-presentation. Nevertheless, this diminutive curiosity remained desirable to the middle class, and became more attractive as the midget adapted to a major cultural shift—a new look and behavior based on whimsy, even with slightly roughish undertones—the cute.

The cute was an image and behavior increasingly associated with the child. And, because the performing small person was already associated with the child, the cute came naturally to the midget. By the end of the nineteenth century, the child was no longer seen as a fragile angel close to God who was often sent "early" to heaven. Rather, the child had become a wondrously vital creature (thanks, in part, to dramatic declines in infant and child mortality rates). With this change, the child began to remind adults less of heavenly than earthly delights. And this too was associated with the cute.

By 1900, the midget on display increasingly mirrored the cute child in delightfully cheerful troupes of small people, smiling as they sang and danced across the stage or performed in carnival shows. Their cheerful faces and amusing poses reminded audiences of cute children, even their own. While the midget of Barnum's day was dressed up as a general or proper lady (although they too sometimes sang and performed), the new mini-freaks looked more like the impish dolls or cartoon characters that children were increasingly given by parents. The midget had become part of a new sensual world of the cuteified child. While not all expressions of the cute were freakish, the cute made some freaks acceptable to the middle class.

At the heart of this change in the image of the small person was the common assumption that children and midgets shared qualities and a natural kinship. Parents let their little ones gaze at permanently little people who looked so much like children but still were different. Adults even wanted to share in their offspring's delight when their children identified with these childlike small people. Through these changes, however, the midget remained an extraordinary body and thus a freak.

Commentators on the cute phenomenon have usually emphasized the appeal of the midget's and child's dependence and unthreatening demeanor (especially if white); the cute are supposed to be affectionate but asexual, lively, but always harmless. Many writers agree that cuteness is at least in part new, created by modern culture. An oft-quoted statement by Daniel Harris makes a key point: "Cuteness . . . is not something we find in our children, but something we do to them." Since the end of the nineteenth century, Americans (and eventually much of the Western world and Japan) have taken pleasure in the dependence of the young. We reward the young who look and act vulnerable, but also cherish the moments when children imitate our "mothering" in their playthings, caring for their helpless miniatures. As the literary theorist Sianne Ngai notes, the cute is part of the "aestheticization of powerlessness." Sometimes people even find it adorable when the cute suffer (at least comically), even if that makes cuteness "ultimately dehumanizing." Over time, the cute become progressively ubiquitous. Dogs have been bred for juvenility, and even stuffed animals and cartoon characters have become rounder, more babylike, and more needy (though not always freakish).[1] The cute cult of the past century and a half or so seems to be part of a domestic culture of women and has been linked to an emerging feminized consumer culture—as cute objects have become major inducements to purchase and possess. As much, cute subjects (especially children) have become recipients of spending as adult "gifters" take delight in the child's delight.[2] More subtly still, the child, as the manifestation of the innocent wonder of the cute, offered adults a way of recovering wonder in their sometimes dull lives and as consumer satiation deprived them of delight.

The cute was more than the multifaceted delight in the dependent; it also gave expression to the vital, even the edgy. In fact, Victorian small persons were expected to show a bit of impishness—as were children, at least, if they came from middle-class households. This became even more a part of their identity in the age of the cute that emerged after 1880: A major element of the appeal of performing midgets was their exhibition of innocent exuberance, a trait that they shared with an emerging redefinition of the ideal child. But this liveliness could turn negative; it was and is frequently edgy. As a result, the cute could slide into its opposite, the cool that challenged adults or even the creepy that frightened them.

And there were still other planes of the cute. As Simon May notes, the cute is not "just about powerlessness and innocence; it also "plays with, mocks, ironizes the value we attach to power." Joshua Paul Dale also sees the cute as "an invitation to sociality," an encounter that makes us not merely feel superior to the dependent cute but less selfish and more open.[3] The cute has taken many forms, but its locus remains in the modern understanding of the child. And that understanding is reflected in the transformation of the midget and the middle class's continuing enchantment with the mini-freak.

We need to begin with a look at how the idealized image of both the midget and the child changed by the end of the nineteenth century. We could explore this (as I attempted some years ago) in the image of the child, but it occurred also in the look and behavior of the performing midget. Let's begin with benchmarking the image of the dime museum small person and how this look reflected the genteel self-understanding of the crowd and mirrored the ideal child of Victorian America. Our guide will be the pitch booklets and printed images of small people of the nineteenth and twentieth centuries.

Barnumesque Midgets 1840–80

The first thing to note about the small people of the dime museums and later sideshows is the obvious: Midgets[4] were extraordinarily small and the smaller the better (with many claims of being the "smallest in the world"); males often had high-pitched voices and were often said to be older than they were to hype their size. At twenty to thirty-three inches (about a third of the height of a typical adult), they looked like dressed-up toddlers, but often acted as adults, sometimes with aged faces (as midgets wrinkled early). This was both off-putting and attractive. They were proportionally identical to full-sized adults, not disturbing in the way that correctly labeled dwarfs were with their short limbs and relatively oversized heads, which gave them an awkward and misshaped appearance that was aesthetically unpleasing to Victorian viewers. While dwarfs were associated with the underworld and the grotesque, midgets were assimilated to the happy and carefree world of mythical fairies (and often so labeled) insofar as fairies had long been understood as miniature human beings. And, the proportionally correct mini-object (as in miniature furniture or figures) had long seemed to suggest the perfect in form as well as the possessable.[5] Moreover, audiences felt comfortable at being close to midgets physically, even touching them as they might fondle a small child, even though a stranger. The well-measured small person still presented an uncanny appearance—suggesting "normality," often with mature manners and fully developed talents, but in the form of a lively person the size and look of a toddler. But this was the uncanny that was pleasant, even comforting, not upsetting or disgusting as with other types of freaks.

In their presentation, performing midgets were far more than the small people of literature or fairy tales. Those figures (gnomes, elves, brownies, fairies, etc.) had been very young but also often old, but seldom the miniature in the form of the adult in the prime of life seen in dime museum shows. Think of Yoda in *Star Wars*. Medieval fairs had often paired small people comically with giants for the plebeian crowd to laugh at.[6] However, in their presentation to the middle-class crowd at Barnum's museum, small people were not mocked or humiliated, at least not in a boisterous way. When midgets were pictured with full-sized people, this was done primarily to illustrate size, not to make small people look foolish. Instead, in their presentation, dime museum small people conformed to mid-nineteenth-century ideas of the "perfect" man or women in miniature, but also, the "perfect" child. All this was part of the expectations of genteel America and especially the ideology of feminine domesticity.

Illustrative of these points are the life stories of small people. The biographies of males tended to stress their conventional family origins and morally upright and religious upbringings in an obvious effort to reduce the anxiety of viewers. The 1862 booklet describing the life of Charles Nestel ("Commodore Foote) begins oddly, not with a life story, but praise for "rational recreation" as essential for "republican government," a nod to uplifting (rather than carnivalesque) free time pursuits, which presumably included viewing midgets (odd in itself). The text goes on to normalize this behavior to a middle-class reader by noting the long history of admired figures engaging with giants and midgets (Herodotus, Gulliver), suggesting the viewer was partaking in a time-honored literary adventure. It is only halfway through the booklet that Charles Nestel, a twenty-five-year-old from Indiana who weighed merely twenty-three pounds and stood twenty-eight inches tall, was mentioned. Readers are told that his protective parents refused to display him as a child (rejecting the crass pursuit of gain) and that during the Civil War he tried to join the Union Army. It was only after

Admiral Dot,
Eighteen years old ; Twenty-five inches high.
Weighs only Twenty pounds.

FIGURE 4.1 *Admiral Dot, c. 1875, exhibited first by Barnum, was an exceptionally small midget, but, typical in his time, was dressed like a miniature ideal of bourgeois respectability. Tibbals Circus Collection of Cartes de Visite, John and Mable Ringling Museum of Art Archives.*

meeting Lincoln at the White House that he began to tour, sharing himself democratically with the whole world. The "American dwarf," Joseph Howard of 1853, was born into a family of farmers from Maine and had a grandfather who had fought in the French and Indian War, establishing his American heartland pedigree. Howard's story includes a recounting of his devotion to his mother and his living at home until thirty, only marrying a small woman at the mature age of thirty-eight when she was already thirty-three. Only on page 15 is there a hint of pity for his conditions but then in stolid middle-class form: "every disability in life . . . has something in it of a compensating character," noting that others have it harder. His fate was a result not of sin but a way to show "the power of God might be made manifest in him."[7]

These pious accounts were common in the origin stories of small freaks throughout the nineteenth century. In an 1861 booklet, General George W. M. Nutt, noted for being shorter than the famed Tom Thumb, was declared to be a divine gift. God "placed him among the small things of creation." Nutt's existence was a mystery, but it was no biological accident. He was born "for no vain purpose." Charles Decker (1868), dubbed the "smallest man in the world" in 1868, was portrayed as "evidence of the supremacy and sublimity of the Great Deity." The pattern scarcely changed through the 1880s and 1890s: The fate of Colonel Steere was a mystery that "cannot be accounted for by medical men." The Rossow midgets' condition was caused by a "mystic spell cast upon the[ir] house in past generations." Doctors, from their native Germany, could not alleviate their failure to grow for they had been "fashioned midgets by their creator."[8] It was only in twentieth century that these booklets acknowledged the medical origins of the size of these small people. Despite these attributions to divine intervention, nineteenth-century references to the ancient and medieval tradition of maternal marking or other miraculous or supernatural claims were rare. Instead midgets were presented with the conventionally comforting (and Protestant) claim that these creatures were part of God's plan. Otherwise, the small people were introduced as conventional Americans with whom all could identify.

Even more, the mini-freak at mid-century was presented as an exemplary, if miniature, version of the perfect bourgeois man. General Nutt was "a gentleman." You "will forget that he is a midget if you talk to him." Charles Nestel was not only shorter than either Tom Thump or Nutt but physically and mentally superior, boasted his pitch pamphlet. He knew three languages, was a Union man (impressive in 1862 to northern audiences), and interestingly "loves money as do we all," presumably accumulated to share with those "in misfortune." Charles Decker was portrayed as well educated, a "mechanical genius" and "shrewd" with a "fair share of business talent" but also witty, with many friends, generous, and courteous. Later in 1882, the three Rice "Lilliputians" of Germany were said to come from a wealthy family; and they were well educated and talented in music. Major Tot (1878), though never schooled, was said to love conversation and knew French. Perhaps even more impressive, he refused to talk to anyone who used profane language. As a young man, Major Winner (c. 1896) tried to go into business, operating a confectionary store, though he ended up in the circus. Still, he was of "spotless character," firmly in the camp of the temperance movement, and an opponent of tobacco. These small people were perfect, if miniature, representations of genteel manhood—cultivated, resourceful, sober, and benevolent.[9]

But character had also to be mirrored in physical appearance and bearing. And this came out in newspaper accounts and especially in the cartes de visite and postcards that were sold to customers at performances. A Boston newspaper gushed that Nutt was the "brightest manikin conceivable," while a Philadelphia paper found Charles Decker the "perfect specimen of the miniature man," far from the deformity of other freaks.[10] And these nineteenth-century miniatures were always displayed as bourgeois, dressed in contemporary suits and top hats, and often carried canes. They were sometimes pictured beside conventional furniture or some other prop (a rowboat or guitar) to show that the midget was indeed a wonder of smallness and even of childlikeness, not to be ridiculed.[11]

There was surprisingly little impulse to diminish them because of their diminutive size. Rather, the opposite: They were welcomed into salon society. There was no better exemplar of this than Charles Stratton (1838–83), long known as General Tom Thumb. The "aggrandizement" of Stratton as a "general" when he was still a child has often been noted, even as honorary title was used to heighten the contrast between size and claimed status. His audiences with European aristocracy, especially Queen Victoria in 1844, were widely trumpeted to enhance his status, as was his success in business and his comfortable estate. Presumably, he returned to the stage in 1868 only because of "ennui."[12]

But I would like to address another side of the display of the midget: the presentation of the miniature man as a living statue or even a one-person tableau (a posing of actors as in a living painting, a popular nineteenth-century salon attraction). The small person was more than a body; he was a performer in a miniature setting. In 1847, Barnum insisted that a description or even a picture of Stratton was insufficient to understand his wonderment. The physical encounter was essential. Tom Thumb was a package of refined manners and elegant clothing as well as a person with a fair complexion and a lively face and eyes, all of which was paired with captivating speech. "The only thing which seems childish about him is his voice," notes an 1849 account. His tableau of Cupid looks like he has "just been removed from an Italian Image Board." He did heroic re-enactments of Napoleon at St. Helena and of Samson as well as living statues of ancient heroes— the "Fighting Gladiator," Hercules, and Cincinnatus, all familiar scenes to a middling crowd.[13]

As Susan Stewart notes, an emerging bourgeoisie from the seventeenth century (especially the domesticated female) had created miniatures of their ideals, compressing the essence of what they valued in the representational form of doll houses and miniature paintings, for example. These objects focused the possessor's power in the confined, but refined space of domesticity. In time, these miniatures were passed on to descendants, offering the next generation objects to frame their understanding of the world. Some of the

FIGURE 4.2 *Tom Thumb, c. 1848, dressed to impress his genteel audience.*
Wikimedia Commons.

miniatures became toys for children. The performances of Stratton and
other midgets made these miniature images and constructions come to life.
For the middle-class adult, the small person became a living doll, animating
a miniature setting that told a moral tale. And for middle-class children, the
midget was even more: He or she was an animated toy.[14] While doubtless
amusing, Tom Thumb was more than a joke or a clown. But his presentation

was hardly cute in the modern sense of the word. Instead, his performances offered a reaffirmation of genteel values in a prized miniature form.

Not surprisingly, these midgets were also linked to a modern Romantic understanding of children as innocent, even angelic and otherworldly—close to God and (because of high infant and child mortality rates) seen as adjacent to heaven (death). Some of the pamphlet biographies emphasize the childhoods of midgets. Major Tot, a French-Canadian midget born in 1865, was portrayed as a fairy, who lay in his mother's hand and sat in his father's pocket as an infant. Another male midget, Joseph Huntler, was characterized as a bit impish (a "low comedian") but who always displayed good taste. Even when adult, small people could be childlike. Huntler's face (always a marker of character) was "happy and genial" with "playful folds and dancing dimples." His humor, "instead of being poured from a reservoir, gushes from a spring" so spontaneous and childlike was it. Huntler stood in contrast to "many people [who] look dried up." The pamphlet describing him was clearly designed for a female audience (containing recipes), women might well have delighted in the image of the midget as an idealized child. Tom Thumb was, again according to Barnum, beloved when he "kisses the ladies . . . especially when done roguishly or by stealth." Throughout his life, many still treated Stratton as a precious child. As Barnum biographer, Neil Harris, notes, Tom Thump's success was based on his "truly childlike benevolence."[15] Idealizing the innocent child as did the Victorian (especially female), the sight of a person who was perpetually that ideal child was not a sign of immaturity or arrested psychological development. Instead, that appearance was admirable precisely because the small person never grew up and thus never seemed to lose the virtues of childhood by coming "dried up." All this was in tune with Romantic ideas of timelessness welcomed in an ever-changing world. Such an ideal child made genteel Victorians feel close to the divine. That child (or midget) was by nature "redemptive and transformative" in a corrupt world.[16]

Some booklets seem to have been written for children themselves. For example, General Mite (1876) admits in his story that "sometimes wish I could grow up" like the "boys and girls who read this to do big things." Doubtless young readers enjoyed the tale of how Mite was saved from a ravenous wild pig by his 110-pound pet dog, Jeff, who also protected him from a "crazed" drunk (as drunks were almost always characterized according to temperance ideologues). Mite's rambling booklet goes on to tell a fantastic story of Mite's dream of meeting a little man astride an animal with the head and wings of a bird and a body and legs of a horse. Mite flies to a hill where he meets a gathering of small people led by a king. After giving a speech about the glories of the United States and the virtues of the president, Mite wakes up. This was a cheerful and positive story attuned to the late Victorian trend in children's fantasy fiction. In 1847, Barnum noted how "children are always delighted with [Tom Thumb] and little girls are his special favorites." Perhaps a third of his Museum audience were children.

Stories of Tom Thumb's wedding to Lavinia Warren and his life were part of the fantasy world of children. This famous event of 1863 during the Civil War was an expression of perfection, a model miniature.[17] Yet Mite, Tom Thumb, and other extraordinary people like them were more. They were freaks that parents felt comfortable sharing with their offspring. Children likely felt comfortable in the Lilliputian world of small people, especially when it was also a secret garden of fantasy.

The midget female was presented with parallel, but separate, traits, from males: She too had a familiar origin (respectable, even from a wealthy family), was divinely blessed ("the creator laughs at the effort of man to find [nature's] mysterious variety"), and exemplified the perfect genteel female (with modesty and delicacy).[18] Such was the description of Ellen Briggs, the "German Dwarf" (born in 1821), who grew up in New England, but found a home and marriage in Cincinnati. Not surprisingly, female midgets were even more modest than their male counterparts. Only at thirty-two years of age was Briggs persuaded to tour, but then with another woman (oddly a 764-pound lady). She, like other freaks of her time, was pointedly said to be not forced into the carnival life by greedy parents or profit-hungry managers. Described as a "fairy," she was "large enough to be a pet, fascinating enough to endanger the happiness of these young ladies who take their lovers" to see her.[19] Briggs was the perfect example of the domesticated and respectable woman, even though she did something normally very unlady-like, display her body to gawking crowds.

Lavinia Warren's pitch booklet emphasizes her privileged childhood, but also that her diminutive size was the result of "natural causes alone," not "mutilation," resulting in an "absolutely choice specimen of feminine humanity." Coming from a "pleasant home in the country," her mother, at first, rebuffed the advances of Charles Stratton because he had a mustache. Everything about Lavinia, apparently, was respectable.[20]

A variation on this story is found in the biography of Dollie Dutton (1852–90). Said to be only twenty-nine inches tall (and weighing merely fifteen pounds), Dollie toured the United States, presenting herself at numerous "levees" in public halls. Like others, she was compared favorably to Tom Thumb (at only one-third his weight), and yet perfect in form and feature. The booklet stresses that "her manners are free and easy" and even that she had a marked "phrenological development" with her head well formed, "requisite to constitute reason and intelligence." But the broader point, as one visitor notes, was that "she looks more like an angel than a human being." Her performances appealed especially to the sentimental taste of genteel women with the songs, "My Little Shroud" about a dead infant in "his tiny grave" and "Today, I'm Sixty-Two" about the loss of "friends of early youth." But a song for her, "To Dollie Dutton," affirms her angelic status:

We can but praise with wonder,
The God who made thee thus!
We leave thee in His keeping;

And when upon thy brow
He sets an angel-crown, thou' it be
More beautiful than now![21]

A quotation from a contemporary newspaper article about Dollie Dutton in 1860 rounds out this angelic image of the female midget: The author imagines "seeing her again in heaven when death shall remove her to her proper sphere among the other angels after she makes earth a paradise and life happy by her presence." It is easy to dismiss this rhetoric as Victorian sentimental drivel. But the author went on to note that Dollie Dutton reminded her of a dead child with her "marble" features and when she saw Dollie "we thought for a moment that we were in those celestial realms, and our own little lost pet was before us." This was a reference to an all-too-common experience of mid-nineteenth-century parents who lost infants and young children to sudden death and often photographed them for parlor display posterity. Dollie Dutton represented this and other images of the Victorian child. At the same time, she was welcomed for the viewing of children. For them, she was a "living doll" worth more than a "thousand wax dolls." Little girls delight in her, the booklet insists: "Is she alive? Can she talk?" they ask, as they listened to this talking and singing doll.[22]

Dollie Dutton had competition. Miss Belton (born in 1842) was an older version. By 1860, she modestly offered levees to neighbors who marveled at "what a beautiful modest little lady she is." On tour with Nutt, the "Fairy Queen," as Belton was dubbed, she sang sentimental (temperance) songs like "Song of the Drunkard's Daughter." Later female midgets like Miss Lucia Zarate (from Mexico) were displayed as perpetual children. Zarate was advertised as possessing a "miniature resemblance of all this is beautiful in childhood." In an 1883 carte de visite, she is posed on a pedestal next to a benevolent man. She looks like a shelf doll when eighteen.[23]

This, of course, is only part of the picture. All the small people noted above were white and were at least portrayed as coming from respectable middle-class families. There was another side of the miniature freak: the Aztec children, described in Chapter 2, for example, whose size contributed to their alien status. In dark skin, their diminutive state reinforced racial prejudice, especially when these small people were also microcephalic as was "What is it?" or later the albino African Americans, Eko and Iko, sometimes known the "sheepheaded Cannibals from Ecuador." Other black midgets, however, were portrayed in formal Victorian dress or military uniforms in the 1880s and 1890s, especially in Europe.[24]

The Cuteification of Small People

The midget as a bourgeois miniature persisted into the twentieth century. Though the booklet biographies of midgets became less common., the cartes de viste and later postcards that seemed to replace the pamphlets certainly confirmed this "look." Cartes de visite from mostly the 1880s and 1890s show no signs of the cutification of the midget; most appear in formal dress and frowning. Usually no information is provided about these small people but their height and weight. Typical was the card of "Gen. Mite" atop a small round table dressed in suit and with cane (1898). Other males were posed in military uniforms and the females were in formal dress, though sometimes looking more childlike. Given both the vaunted success of Tom Thumb and the conservative expectations of audiences, it is not surprising that there was a Tom Thumb Circus at Coney Island in 1907; and, a "Major Tom Thumb" midget strongman, and a "Turkish Tom Thumb" toured, it seems, in the 1930s. A famous band of small people, managed by Leo Singer, performed in music halls and vaudeville in Europe and the United States in the 1920s and 1930s, similarly dressed in top hats. Others continued the old practice of claiming aristocratic status like Princess Lorena, Princess Marguerite, and Duchess Leona, many of whom appeared at Coney Island in the early twentieth century. One of the most famous of these acts was that of the Canadian Count and Countess Philippe Nicol who, from 1906 until about 1930, toured the United States in formal dress. Their publicity stressed their business acumen and high culture.[25]

To be sure, it is hard to see just how viewers responded to these images or the degree to which they represented the midgets' presentations on stage.[26] But these postcard portrayals do point to the persistence of a traditional look of the small freak as miniatures of the respectably elite with hardly a hint of the modern cute in pose or appearance, even as they sang and danced in sideshows and increasingly in vaudeville. This may not be surprising, given the conservative expectations of crowds and stylized acts of performers at these venues.

Nevertheless, the look and setting of the small person was changing. After 1880, midget performers began to adapt to new expectations of consumers for the jolly and even zany in popular theaters and music halls. Before the Civil War, the American urban middle classes embraced sentimental fare in theaters (similar to the levees of the midgets), even if these middle class shows often included farce and even minstrelsy. Barnum himself was a strong proponent of sentimental theater in the 1840s and 1850s. After 1865, however, audiences broadened to include skilled workers. This encouraged variety programs, which included trained animals, acrobats, comedians, song and dance features, and even freaks. These shows were preferred by male-dominated crowds at barrooms (concert saloons) in the 1860s. Gradually, variety moved to theaters that catered also to women and even children. This became vaudeville. As promoted by Tony Pastor from the 1870s, the new entertainment supplanted sentiment with lighter fare that featured glamour, escapist fun, and even satire. But in order to accommodate female and even juvenile viewers, vaudeville abandoned earlier bawdiness and a toleration for prostitutes at the theater door; theater owners offered matinees and demanded orderly crowds at their programs of "family" entertainment. This included even child acts (often comically impersonating adult foibles).[27] In this environment, troupes of singing and dancing midgets found enthusiastic crowds. No longer were they portrayed sentimentally as angels or miniatures of bourgeois propriety, but simply as promoters of fun and delight.

Midgets reflected another closely related aesthetic trend: the "cute." It can be defined as a look and behavioral pattern that adults associated with, even imposed, on children and found amusing, attractive, and especially endearing. The cute suggested dependency, vulnerability, and even ridiculousness at times. The cute evoked nostalgia or even a sense of timelessness. But the cute also meant the naively willful and sensuously desiring, even impish, spunky, and coquettish. These traits (more later), associated with children by 1900, were inevitably attached also to small people, often with another layer of irony and eeriness.

Elements of all this appear with Tom Thumb and other Barnumesque little people, but these flashes of cuteness were secondary to the older image and behavior of the miniature Victorian adult and child. The Burdett Twins (1881), a brother and sister act anticipated what was to come. These midget twins had been touring with circuses since they were thirteen. Their impish ways were emphasized in printed tales of the brother's hatred of school and his love of playing of tricks on his sister. Though by 1881, the sister, Fanny, had become "a fine woman" and the brother a Major and "a man with a moustache," they were still a great "source of amusement to the little folks" who crowded around the stage they performed on. As midget twins, they were not only perpetual children but appealed to children. [28]

By the late 1880s, twin acts had become common in vaudeville. The image became ubiquitous when childlike twins had appeared regularly in product trademarks (e.g., Gold Dust Twins of black children for washing powder from 1892 and Campbell Kids for soup from 1905). All this was consistent with the fun-loving bad boy theme of American male childhood—Mark Twain's *Tom Sawyer* and George Peck's numerous stories of his youth as a "bad boy," for example.[29] The change, compared with the small people of Tom Thumb's day, was subtle and gradual: while the Burdett Twins made no pretense to bourgeois aggrandizement, other midgets like Ike and Mike and Major Mite continued to be dressed formally in tuxedos, spats, top hat, and cane through the 1920s.[30]

But the trend was clear. Small people were becoming cuteified. Shortly after 1910, the best-known exemplars of this were the Doll family of midgets, who appeared on stage, in circus sideshows, and film (as in *Freaks*) through the 1950s. Born in Germany, Kurt Schneider (1902) and sister Grace (1898) played Hansel and Gretel in amusement parks in the 1910s; they were joined by their younger sisters, Daisy (b .1907) and Tiny (b. 1914) in the 1920s under the surname of their manager Burt Earles. After his death and when they toured with RBBB, they became the Doll Family, adopting a stage name appropriate for their appearance. One of many postcards of

FIGURE 4.3 *"Lady Little, The Doll Lady,"* c. 1911, at 9 years old, weighing 10.5 *pounds, epitomizes the transition to the "cute" in her coy demeanor despite her formal dress. Postcard, author's collection.*

the siblings featured Grace dressed in exotic a Spanish gown and Daisy as a 1920s flapper dancing cheek to cheek with Harry. The Hungarian twin midgets, Ike and Mike (aka Little Speck and Small Speck), toured the world as tiny children while being tossed from one manager to another, continuing on the stage as adults, still being cute and childlike. This "game little bunch" performed in a tiny car, according to their pitch booklet of 1931. When it crashed, Mike flew out and was caught by a man who said, "I have the baby safe in my arms." Their postcards featured them in baby clothes or staged incredulously in boxing matches, a common theme in midget acts by the 1920s.[31]

Twin midget (especially brother/sister) acts evoked childlike themes of sibling rivalry and affection (even innocent sexuality)—again far from the nineteenth-century ideals of miniature "perfection" or even angelic innocence. Still, other signs of creeping cuteness were more subtle in other images of small people. Postcards gradually dispensed with the formal and bourgeois dress, introducing, for example, an innocent, but impish, "tramp" look on Princess Victoria's 1911 card with her peasant's cap and bag over her shoulder (an endearing theme picked up by Charles Chaplin, especially in his famous film *The Kid* of 1921 using the urchin child, Jackie Coogan, as the cute extension). Anita, "The Living Doll," is shown beside a large chair to emphasize her size; but though dressed as a fine lady with pearls, she appears, as if a child, coyly standing slightly behind the chair as if playing peek-a-boo. By the 1910s, the Glassenee's midgets used teddy bears as props. Teddy bears, invented in 1906 and thereafter used as an accessory of delighted and delightful child, were quintessential symbols of the cute. Other postcards simply had their small people strike childlike poses with parental adults looking on in bemusement. A midget couple called Hans and Gretel (about twenty-two years old) was pictured dancing the Tango in formal dress, while three full-grown adults looked benevolently down on them as if they were children. A postcard of Zeynard's Liliput Speciality Troupe

FIGURE 4.4 *Three of the "Doll family," c. 1924, performing in formal dress but in childlike endearing poses on the theater stage, a clear break from the levees and sideshow appearances of midgets in the past, Tibbals Circus Collection of Postcards, Midgets, John and Mable Ringling Museum of Art Archives.*

of 1916 showed a line of male midgets in long military coats comically saluting, while another from 1912 features a midget weightlifter in leopard skin looking like a toddler posed ridiculously by bemused parents. And the postcard of the French Le Lilliputian Célébre Show simply, but tellingly, features three midgets sitting on a bench like kids teasing one another.[32] Over and over, the small person delighted audiences as surrogate children, displaying the cute in all of its forms.

Beyond the cute and childlike poses, early twentieth-century midgets were sometimes placed in fairy-tale settings. A troupe that played at the Casino de Paris was dressed as toy soldiers with a drummer and a sword-wielding leader. These were like the Victorian images of General Tom Thump, but in groups they appeared more like kids playing dress-up rather than miniature military officers. Instead of posing these midgets in scenes of classical heroism (as Hercules or Samson, for example), Scheuer's troupe of midgets from Germany were featured as the seven dwarfs with Snow White, a children's tale (1910). Later, in the 1920s and 1930s Schaeffer's "Märchenstadt" (fairy-tale town) from Lubeck included thirty-two small people variously dressed in exaggerated aristocratic, medieval, Chinese, and Russian costumes, often doing acrobatic feats. They toured Europe, offering playful, but essentially nostalgic, performances. Schaeffer's midgets evoked memories of childhood stories that were popular on both sides of the Atlantic.[33]

A variant of the cuteified small person was the impish midget, often incredulously appearing as a letch. For example, Andy Potato Chips appeared in the Ziegfeld Follies with (Ole) Olsen and (Chic) Johnson as well as at Hubert's Museum as late as 1958. He is portrayed smiling while strolling hand in hand with a shapely and leggy woman in a swimsuit in an undated postcard. Similar is the look and behavior of the midget, Billy Barty, who famously appears in a dancing spectacle of Busby Berkley's *Golddiggers of 1933*. First appearing as a baby in a stroller, Barty impishly hits a policeman with a peashooter and lecherously goggles at pretty, scantily clad women in a dance act.[34]

Tiny Towns and Midgets on the Screen

These playful reimaginations of the small freak seem to have attracted a broad theater audience, even as the monstrosities of the sideshow were being relegated to the remaining gawking crowd. As troupes of performing midgets, the small person was repositioned in a world of jollification. Their origins, respectable or not, were no longer important; and their "personalities" were reduced to stereotypical comically miniature versions of conventional music hall or vaudeville acts, often suggesting the impish youngster.

This trend was fully represented in the flowering of the "tiny town" or midget village. The idea of a troupe of young midgets was featured as early as

ANITA "THE LIVING DOLL"
Smallest Adult Human Being the World has ever seen
Age 31 Years on Dec 27ᵗʰ 1913 — Height 26 inches.
PERFECT IN FIGURE, FACE, FORM & INTELLECT.

FIGURE 4.5 *Anita "The Living Doll," 1910 appeared in Europe, South America, and the United States. Though thirty years of age and dressed as a "lady" in this postcard, she looks like a toddler playing peek-a-boo with a parent, quintessentially cute. Tibbals Circus Collection of Postcards, Midgets, John and Mable Ringling Museum of Art Archives.*

1886 by the Hungarian S. Horvath, who toured American stages and circuses with a varied program of light opera, dance, magic, and pantomime. The interaction of small people amused audiences, setting the stage for groups of small people of various ages and roles set in their "own" communities through which audiences walked and observed. While Peter the Great is said to have built a midget village on the Neva River in 1710 for his and his friend's amusement, the full-fledged midget village for the masses appeared in the United States in 1904. As we have seen, Samuel Gumpertz's Lilliputia (aka Midget City) became a sensation at the newly opened amusement park of Dreamland. Gumpertz invited as many as 300 midgets, mostly from European fairs and circus sideshows to join this scaled down community that was supposed to resemble a romantic version of medieval Nuremberg Germany. In addition to performing troupes at the Opera House and Tom Thumb Circus, the small people at Lilliputia had their own "fire department" that amused visitors when a team of midgets scrambled hourly to false alarm fires. After Dreamland was burned in May 1911, Gumpertz relocated his tiny town to the Dreamland Circus Sideshow that he ran until 1929. [35]

Tiny towns shared a common whimsical quality, fairy-tale-like where neither real work took place nor power-relations were visible. Essentially, they were blowups of children's doll houses and playsets that parents and their kids could walk through. And like doll houses, they evoked feelings of nostalgia and material comfort, suggesting a sort of timelessness. This anticipates later theme park attractions like Knott's Berry Farm or Disneyland where romantic miniatures of the pioneer West or cartoon villages became live, walkthrough fantasies. [36]

There were numerous other tiny towns that found homes especially at international fairs across Europe and the United States in the first forty years of the twentieth century. A Village des Naines drew crowds at the Brussels Exhibition of 1910, and Leo Singer set up a midget village in Vienna in 1913 with a claimed troupe of 125 performers, some of whom later toured the United States on the Marcus Loew vaudeville circuit. Tiny towns also appeared in London, Blackpool (a seaside town on the west coast of England), and again in Vienna in the 1930s, combining the mystique of the "realistic" village of little people with featured musical and acrobatic performers such as one would see in music halls or vaudeville. [37]

Among the best-known midget villages appeared at the Chicago "Century of Progress" exposition (1933–34) and the New York World's fair of 1939–40. Drawing on a conventional fantasy, the Chicago village was a "reproduction" of the medieval Bavarian city of Dinkelspühl. Managed by Stanley Graham, it included forty-six buildings, with a church, school, fire department, and town hall (as well, of course, a souvenir shop and children's sandwich shop) and claimed to house 115 small people from Europe and the United States. The "mayor" was Major Doyle (tall at 33 inches) and the village even included the eighty-three-year-old Jennie Quigley from the old dime museum era. Some of the troupe went on to a smaller exhibition in San Diego in 1935 and joined Stanley Graham's International Midget Circus in 1937. A portion of the midget gang was recruited for the Munchkin scenes in *The Wizard of Oz*. The Chicago midget village of 1933 was one of several nostalgic villages, based on common stereotypes of exotic places and times (Irish Village, Merrie England, and Black Forest Village), which were popularized on the Midway at the Chicago fair of 1893. The postcard of the midget village looks like a playset. [38]

At the 1939 New York World's Fair, Morris Gest, a veteran producer of spectacles and theater, produced the Little Miracle Town with sixty-five little people mostly from Europe, again with a romantic German theme, including sixty-five buildings, three orchestras, and numerous comedians, magicians, aerialists, and ballet dancers. Gest's Midget Town Theatre offered the Red Knights, a revue of small people dressed as medieval knights, a parade of "Wooden Soldiers," the Dresden Dancers in eighteenth-century aristocratic costumes, a Chinese ballet, and even a "Flea Weight" boxing contest. Against the seriousness of the fair and looming war, Gest promised "fun" on a "Platform of Peace." Other midget villages at the New York fair offered more contemporary themes, including Singer's troupe doing Hawaiian dancing (among much else) and Rose's Midget Follies, featuring modern themes of a swing band and rumba ensemble.[39] The evocation of timeless romance could be shifted to the amusing posture of miniature modernity. Whatever the pitch, all were cute.

The goings-on in "villages" were repeatedly filmed as comic relief in the "newsreel" shorts that preceded feature movies in the 1930s. In two short films, the English Pathé company offered bemused patter about midget villages on the Vienna fairgrounds of 1934 and at the exposition of Paris in 1937. In the Viennese village, the scene of seemingly ordinary people sitting at cafes or buying perfume or beer from stalls is broken by the sight of a regular-sized woman having her fortune told by a female midget and a jazz band of midgets playing and singing in high-pitched voices. The Paris film focuses on another contrast: a midget policeman shaking the hand of a full-sized gendarme while another small person steals salami (like an errant boy) to give to his girlfriend while midget couples smooch in doorways. Each of these scenes suggests the absurdity of these childlike people "pretending" to act like "real adults" in cute ways.[40] The perpetual contradiction between the childlike look and adult behavior suggested the amusement that audiences found in children impersonating adults.

While the midget village was popular through the 1930s, many midget shows were part of revues, either in single acts in vaudeville or in featured midget shows. Often, they were managed by a full-sized man, like Fred Roper, who sometimes also appeared in the act as a foil to the small people. From 1929, Roper's troupe of ten to twenty-two midgets performed acrobatic and music acts in Britain, offering a variety of postcards with the tall Roper posing benevolently along a line of small people dressed as toy soldiers or playfully dressed in swimming suits on a diving board. Roper published a new-style pamphlet, *All About Midgets* (1935), describing his troupe. Unlike its Victorian equivalents, his booklet doesn't feature the biography of any of his performers, and certainly promised nothing uplifting in their tales. Rather, it treats his midgets as a group, a tribe apart, that "look like little children." It features images of the "Merry Moments with Happy Midgets" who, nevertheless, we are told, have difficulties like in buying cigarettes because storekeepers think they are children. No longer are these small freaks treated as mysterious gifts of God. Instead Roper's booklet calls them victims of small thyroids or dysfunctional pituitary glands in an obvious nod to advancing science. Still, they are otherwise characterized as normal, even smarter than the average person. But Roper could not resist displaying their exceptional love of sunbathing (a 1930s British fad), with photos of them appearing nude (looking eerily like a cross between innocent naked toddlers and adult body builders).[41]

Similar was Bob Hermines's midget troupe of wire-walkers, trapeze artists, military band musicians, and even minuet dancers that was active in the late 1930s and 1940s. It even included a group of midget bathing beauties that appeared at Atlantic City. *Bob Hermines Magazine of Midgets* was subtitled *A Fairy Tale Comes True*. It seems to have been directed toward young readers with a "Believe It or Not" style of presenting the history of midgets and suggesting that readers "imagine" being a small person coping with oversized furniture. Like confessional magazines of its time and contemporary accounts of the real lives of freaks (such as the lives of the Hilton conjoined twins), this "magazine" asks readers to identify with the personal life of the freak, especially the limits and frustration of having to deal with normal-sized objects and human relationships (marriage, childbirth, etc.). [42] No longer is the freak idealized as a "fairy" or "angel" or treated as a living miniature hero. The midget is a comical character and an object lesson for children. It has also become cute.[43]

FIGURE 4.6 *Schaefer's Fairy Tale Town, 1933, in Lubeck, Germany. Similar groups had been appearing since about 1907 in various German cities. Tibbals Circus Postcard Collection, Midgets, John and Mable Ringling Museum of Art Archives.*

Inevitably as entertainment shifted from the stage to the screen, midgets too made the migration. While Harry Doll plays a role as a robber who could climb through door transom in the silent crime thriller *The Unholy Three* of 1925, most of the movie midgets play ironic children—as the ambiguity of age becomes the most pronounced characteristic of the small person's presentation. Even Harry Doll in *Freaks* expresses a pathetic insistence of his character, Hans, saying, "I'm a man" when his forlorn love interest Cleopatra kisses him on the cheek like a dependent toddler. Publicity posters for the film asked the question: "Can a full-grown woman truly love a midget?" Obviously not. By the 1930s, to most viewers, small people had become simply children in arrested development, no longer miniatures of ideal men and women. Once again this reflects the modern obsession with childhood and generation. [44]

And this take on the midget became very pronounced in the famous Munchkin scenes in *The Wizard of Oz*. This noted ensemble included many celebrated midgets of the era, especially Harry Doll. In the movie, Munchkins sang and danced as members of a midget village (much like those in the fairs of the 1930s), but here liberated from an oppressive wicked witch by the accidental arrival of the early teen Judy. Significantly, these professionals off the screen acquired a reputation for drunkenness and lechery while in Hollywood. This image was fostered by Judy Garland's TV interview on the *Jack Parr Show* in 1967, where she claimed that the Munchkins were "little drunks" not "little children" as they appeared on screen. Much later, a movie, *Under the Rainbow*, mocks the making of *Oz*, portraying the midgets as swinging from chandeliers. At least, this suggests still another side of the cute—the edgy, disruptive, and sexual—despite their size and seeming innocence. Surviving Munchkins denied these charges, but the story fit the image of little people as small in size but big on libido. [45]

A much less celebrated film featuring freaks is the "B" western *Terror of Tiny Town* of 1938 in which appeared many of the same small people who a year later became Munchkins. The plot was conventional: two warring families fighting over stolen steers with a Romeo and Juliet subplot and a conniving third party trying to exploit the conflict. At times, *Tiny Town* seems like just another quickie western and was panned for this. The actors look a bit like children. The makers of *Tiny Town* couldn't refrain from seeking the cheap laugh by showing the midget stars walking under hitching posts for their Shetland ponies. And incredulously, the film's plot is repeatedly interrupted by the singing and dancing of midget ensembles. However, this should not be surprising once you realize that many of the players came from Leo Singer's vaudeville troupe. But the film remains uncannily cute as we move back and forth from the familiar western to the midget variety show. [46] Finally, Angelo Rossitto, a thirty-five-inch-tall midget, was a regular in the 1930s and the 1940s screen, mostly in "B" features like *Spooks Run Wild* and *Mr. Wong in Chinatown*. In his postcard he is featured not as a circus freak but as a serious movie star appearing with famous actors like John Barrymore, Dolores Costello as well as horror players like Boris Karloff and Bela Lugosi. Who could blame him for not stressing his cuteified roles?[47]

Though midgets were not welcome into the Screen Actors' Guild until 1970 (allowed to perform on a waiver but dependent on agents), they found favor as icons of name-brand goods. Babies and children had been featured on consumer products, especially from the beginning of the twentieth century (Morton's Salt, Fairy Soap, Uneeda Crackers, Fisk Tires, Cracker Jacks, Dutch Boy Paints, and Skippy Peanut Butter, for example).[48] Often midgets were substituted for real children (in part because they were better actors), especially for "live" promotions. The use of these cute characters to sell such a wide range of goods clearly had nothing specific to do with the products themselves; but they provided an attractive association of their look of the dependent and needy but often delightful with whatever was being sold. The advertising principle was simple: The cute sells. Customers wanted to hug and possess the cute person and that made them want to buy the product associated with the cute (or, at least, that is what merchandisers thought). And their impishness seemed to prompt consumers to want to desire what the cute child wanted. It lowered "consumer resistance." The best example of this is the Buster Brown Shoe Company, maker of children's footwear. This manufacturer licensed a comic strip character by that name (1902) for its brand. Featured in newspaper comics, Buster was the iconic impish boy from a respectable family. Though appearing wholesome in his Little Lord Fauntleroy suit and haircut with his loyal bulldog Tige, Buster was, in fact, always innocently testing the limits of his mother, a theme that delighted early twentieth-century Americans. The impish midget gave consumers permission to indulge. In the 1920s, the midget Johnny Clifton played Buster with his red beret, blond wig and dog, entertaining children, while hyping shoes. Even more famous was Johnny Roventini, a forty-seven-inch person, who from 1932 played a bellboy on radio and print ads. Like other bellboys, he called hotel customers with messages on the phone. And so, his job consisted simply of shouting "Call for Phillip Mor--is" promoting the cigarette company by that name. The cute in midget form sold stuff just as it offered an endless variety of fantasy.[49]

The Wider Context of the Cute

After all this, it may be time to reflect a little more on why the cute attracted twentieth-century Americans and how it ultimately shaped new forms of freakishness. In biological and anthropological circles, there has long been the assumption that the attraction to the childlike look and behavior is built into our human (even mammal) evolution. As an historian, perhaps inevitably, I am biased in favor of a cultural explanation—that the attraction of the cute is a product of multivariate historical (more than biological) change. Images and performances that can be clearly identified as cute appear only toward the end of the nineteenth century, and this was mirrored in the cuteification of the midget. Still the question persists: Is the *response* to the cute look and behavior biological or cultural? The biological argument was famously advanced in 1943 by Konrad Lorenz. He claimed (backed up by recent research) that we are hardwired to respond positively and preconsciously to traits that naturally appear in small children (and other animals). These traits include an oversized head, large eyes, rounded body, short limbs, body surfaces pleasurable to touch, and a measure of clumsiness in movement (all features commonly associated with the cute). This positive response to these traits is a product of evolution insofar as this reaction can produce nurturance and thus promote the survival of the species. These traits, even when they appear in animals or artificial beings (like dolls, stuffed animals, or cartoons), continue to induce the same nurturing response. This may explain part of the "affection" shown midgets who evince these traits while other similarly "helpless" freaks like three-legged men evoke feelings of horror and disgust.[50]

The question remains, however, to what extent is this response a biological reflex or a cultural invention. Dale suggests a nuanced answer when he says that a nurturing reaction to the cute is "a potential, rather than instinctive or reflexive, human response." We may be biologically programmed to take note of the "cute," but, for cultural or personal reasons, may not follow through. Certainly, that "potential" has been cultivated only in recent history. As art historian Anne Higonnet notes, the image of the innocent child (and, at that, merely a portion of the modern cute) appeared only sporadically in Western art until the mid-seventeenth century (in, for example, Jan Steen's *Eve of Saint Nicholas* showing the glee of children receiving gifts as well as the horror of a bad boy receiving the birch rod). The image of the delighted child increasingly delighted adults thereafter. In the eighteenth century, Thomas Gainsborough and Joshua Reynolds offered images of youngsters playing with kittens and bringing joy in informal family settings. The young display looks of wonder and affection. This was a major departure: These painters abandoned the old tradition of portraying children as small adults or picturing them only in allegorical roles as angels, mythological figures, or the baby Jesus. Nineteenth-century artists celebrated children laughing and blowing bubbles.[51] In large part, however, these images reflect a mid-nineteenth century idea of childhood innocence: the romantic idea of the small person as a gift of God in need of protection, but also giver of redemption.

In *The Cute and the Cool*,[52] I try to show a shift in the late nineteenth century to a cultural recognition of something somewhat different—the cute child. I trace how middle-class adults abandoned a romantic idea of protected and sanctified childhood for a recognition of children as delightfully willful and even innocently naughty. Images of angelic children with kittens slide in the twentieth century into portrayals of youngsters defying adults: Boys are shown on magazine covers "skinny dipping" at forbidden swimming holes and comic strips portray naughty "Katzenjammer Kids" tricking adults, while stealing pies. Significantly, adults found these "brats" charming.

Recent commentators on the cute like Dale and Simon May confirm that the "natural response" to the cute in caring for the next generation of the species is only part of the story. Dale argues that the cute is as likely to evoke childlike behavior (playfulness) in adults as nurturance. May adds that further down on the "spectrum" of cuteness are distortions of sweetness, expressed in the "uncanny cute," an indeterminate, eerie, and even menacing look. This was frequently part of the presentation of cute midgets on stage and screen. Recall the babylike look of Billy Barty in *The Golddiggers of 1933*, who, appearing in a baby carriage, suddenly becomes lecherous as he chases dancing females.[53] The "uncannily cute" gives power to the cute figure despite its seeming dependency. The "dark side" of the cute may sometimes originate in a negative response to the infantile that Lorenz missed: The caregiver may resent the cute and the cute may resent the caregiver. We should not forget that the word "cute" is a short form of "acute," meaning sharp or smart, not primarily adorable. The original meaning of the "cute" is conniving or manipulative, recalled by many of us when our mothers scolded us with, "Don't be cute" when we were "smarting off." The cute remains edgy and willful.[54]

However, around the turn of the twentieth century, the cute in all this complexity began to be tolerated in children. This historic acceptance occurred because adults—especially in the middle class—saw the cute also as an expression of naïve wonder. What had been punished or ignored in children came to be tolerated, even celebrated—if it was innocent and ultimately unthreatening. This response was more than permissiveness. It was the embrace in the cute of "wondrous innocence." Adults begin to see kids not as innocents requiring sheltering or as bestowers of benevolence as in nineteenth century, but as vital bringers of delight, naturally desiring and curious, neither angels nor urchins, but cute, perhaps naughty but also nice.[55] The cute served many purposes, one of which was to redeem a portion of the freak show.

So why did this transformation happen toward the end of the nineteenth century? Viviana Zelizer famously argues that around this time Americans were no longer willing to tolerate parents "using" their children for wage labor and instead sought to shelter the young from life's dangers in many ways. This sacralization of the child, however, went further than making the child "priceless" as Zelizer argues.[56] It provided room for a more tolerant and delighted form of childrearing that was expressed in the cute. The decline in infant mortality rates at this time did the same. We see this graphically in the shift around 1900 from the stylized and professional mortuary photograph of the dead child (so common in homes of even the rich in the nineteenth century) to the spontaneous snapshots of frolicking and healthy children taken by the indulgent mother with her Kodak.[57] Other factors were certainly in evidence: The beginning of a new childrearing theory based on Freud and other psychologists that rejected old patterns of excessive moralizing played a role. Even more influential may have been new advertisement-driven consumer culture. From 1900, merchandisers were incessantly seeking to create desire for new products through ads that featured the child who "naturally" craves consumer goods, making that desire not only acceptable to wary parents but a duty to fulfill. Other even more subtle factors may have come into play. Adults seemed to desire to regain a "lost" wondrous innocence in their own lives as they vicariously enjoyed their children's delight when they showered their offspring with Christmas or birthday gifts. All this puts the cuteified midget in sharper light.[58]

The cuteified midget on stage and screen or even in the freak show has much in common with other changes in the popular culture beginning around the turn of the twentieth century. One obvious context is the peculiar phenomenon of the emerging cult of the baby and its association with the freak show. American women had long gathered for baby shows at county and state fairs. Competitions of mothers displaying their offspring was a variation of contests for the best calf or largest potato. As they emerged in the mid-nineteenth century, these competitions were celebrations of the healthy and happy child, a recognition that culminated a generation later with the cult of the cute.

Stranger was the appeal of Martin Couney's baby incubators, containing premature babies, especially when they appeared on Coney Island's string of sideshow attractions. Couney's attraction was in fact among the longest-lasting of these shows (from 1903 to 1943). To be sure, it was free of the exaggerated bally of the freak show and had some real claim of scientific legitimacy. Still, Couney's actual training as a doctor and expertise in postnatal care was something of a mystery. He came to the United States from Paris, where he learned from Pierre Budin the use of the incubator for enabling babies born prematurely to survive. Couney made these machines and their processes for saving "preemies" into a personal crusade. Hospitals, he later claimed, were disinterested. Instead, he set up shop at world's fairs and exhibitions in London, Omaha, and Buffalo, charging admission to the curious to view these helpless creatures until they could live on their own. After winning favorable publicity at the fair in Buffalo, he settled at Coney Island in 1903 (as had other temporary spectacles at world's fairs). He charged twenty-five cents (not cheap at the time), attracting mostly women (some observers said especially older unmarried females) to view the progression of these vulnerable infants from wrinkled preemies to bouncing babies. As A. J. Liebling notes in a 1939 *New Yorker* article, "The backbone of Dr. Couney's business is supplied by the repeaters. A repeater becomes interested in one baby and returns at intervals of a week or less to note its growth . . . After a preemie graduates, a chronic repeater picks out another one and starts watching it."[59] Couney took pride in the cleanliness of his facilities and the good hygiene of his wet nurses (no Coney food allowed). Lecturers had to keep to scientific explanations (no jokes). Employees were dressed as nurses or doctors, and visitors filed respectfully pass babies displayed in incubator boxes fed by oxygen from pipes. Couney took pride in his success rate (claiming to have saved about 6,500 of the 8,000 babies that his incubators cared for). Even so, Couney was treated with suspicion by the medical establishment and the press, and repeatedly was accused of exploiting his preemies for his Coney Island show.[60]

While most writing on this subject focus on Couney's life and motives, what should interest us here it the gaze of the visitors, especially the "repeaters." Obviously, there was something very captivating about viewing these helpless and pitiful infant freaks through glass, drawing women to watch their precarious lives emerge and often turn into vital and cute babies. It's not by accident that Couney's display coincides with the rapid decline in infant mortality in America and elsewhere. It was a perfect expression of the emerging cult of the cute. Here the freakish preemie is transformed into the cute baby, a victory over the fate of the pickled punk.

Still another form of cuteness took shape over a far longer period, the domestication and cuteification of the pet animal. Dogs had undergone thousands of years of diverging from their origins as wolves (beginning about 40,000 years ago, but clearly domesticated about 14,000 or 15,000 years ago). Similarly, the African wild cat was domesticated, but more recently (roughly about 10,000 to 12,000 years ago). This taming only gradually made dogs and cats into pets. To be a pet, the animal not only had to be brought into or near the household but named, and not eaten. There is at least some evidence that small dogs were associated with aristocratic women from the Renaissance (the same time that midgets were "kept" by aristocrats and kings—and for many of the same reasons, as objects of subordinate affection and display). Moreover, pet keeping, especially from the eighteenth century, coincided with changes in childrearing and images of the child. Part of this linkage was the emerging cult of kindness to the weak (both shown toward children and expected of children in their treatment of pets). Such kindness was supposed to lead to a civilized behavior as an adult. Not surprisingly, images of the innocent child and the pet, especially puppies and kittens became a major theme of nineteenth-century sentimental illustration (as on trade cards). The evolution of the pet follows the transformation of the image of the child.[61]

Unsurprisingly, by the end of nineteenth century, the impact of the cult of the cute began to shape pet practices. Dogs with little or no practical value like the pug had long been preferred by the aristocracy (bred 2000 years ago in China and brought to the Netherlands and England in the sixteenth century and the United States in the nineteenth century). However, only after 1860, not long before the emergence of the cute as an ideal in children, pugs began to take on their modern form with short legs and smashed nose (both with babylike associations). Interestingly, one of the first animals referred to as "cute" was the pug. A similar transformation toward neoteny occurred in other breeds with a shortening of legs, bigger eyes, but especially miniaturization. The "toy" dog was a permanent puppy (as in the bichon with roots in Renaissance France). Today some of these cuteified dogs have become, in effect, living stuffed animals. They are not necessarily freaks in the common understanding of the term but expressions of the power of the cute.[62]

However, there was not always an unqualified swing from the old idea of sacred and sheltered innocence to cuteified wondrous innocence in pets or children. A great example of this ambiguity takes place at the height of the midget village in the 1930s with Shirley Temple. Born in 1928, by the time she was four, Temple was in movies, and from six she was the star in a series of nineteen features. She was portrayed often as an orphan who by her natural goodness softened the hard hearts of the adults around her and reconciled bitter foes as she sang sweet songs and daintily danced. In this Temple, followed a long line of child actors on vaudeville and on film that (following Frances Hodgson Burnett's *Little Lord Fauntleroy* of 1886) reflected the Victorian image of the "sacralized child."[63] She was a temporary midget in the tradition of Victorian small people like Dollie Dutton.

Yet Temple began her career in a famous series of Baby Burlesks and Kiddie Kabarets where toddlers were portrayed in unsentimental, even slightly edgy roles, playing adults often in satires of famous movies of the era. Adults found this age ambivalence in the Baby Burlesks amusing, perhaps especially so, when these small children were playing sexualized roles (like Shirley did, doing an imitation of the famous female sex symbol of the time, Marlene Dietrich). It has become common to interpret Shirley Temple's short dresses and frequent associations with single men, as signs of at least latent pedophilia (as claimed at the time by novelist Graham Green). However, recent historians, including John Kasson and Kristen Hatch, have gone back to how audiences in the 1930s actually responded to Temple's scenes. They found that it was common for child performers to mimic adult sexuality and adult men to lavish loving praise on young female children with no pedophiliac impulse. The bigger point was that Shirley always retained that nineteenth-century idea of sacred innocence that was both incapable of corruption and skilled in transforming the "fallen man."[64]

Yet Shirley was always more than a vulnerable angel. She went beyond the Victorian script. What sold Shirley was also her cuteness, combining the "pert and powerless" that brought forth both "moral protection and possessive desire," in adults. She had the "cute" look: large head, short and thick legs, and short nose as in the bodies of infant mammals; and her bosses at Fox insisted that she wear those toddler short dresses even as she approached eleven. Like the small person in the sideshow, she was often paired with especially tall men. Whatever it took to keep that babyish and cute look. Shirley Temple preserved an "enchanting, toylike character" sharing with midgets the skills of highlighting "the boundaries—and ambiguities—between childhood and adulthood." It was also Shirley's job to show a spontaneity, the naturalism of the untrained child. In a gentle way, free of guile or resentment, she displayed an innocent disregard for propriety as revealed in her numerous conflicts with old maids and other stuffy characters. She embodied the edginess of the cute just as did many performing midgets.[65]

Surrogate Midgets Cuteified for Kids

If the cute slides between preemies, pugs, kids, and midgets, it could easily take still other forms—even as toys and dolls, comic strips, and animated cartoons. Some, but not all, of these modern creations took the form of freaks. These commercialized expressions of the cute could be extended, even exaggerated, creating the full "spectrum" of the cute potential. Just as the cute became what children were supposed to display (as Shirley Temple's mother constantly admonished here, "Sparkle, Shirley, Sparkle!"), the cute was supposed to be the object of children's delight. As the child was cuteified in the eyes of adults, the world of the child was extended to fantasies and projections of the cute. Kids were brought to the cute to experience wonder and to accentuate their own cuteness. Thus, not only were kids invited to the midget villages, they were given their own midget icons in toys, dolls, and stuffed animals and cartoons. And some of these objects made freakery acceptable to children and parents—especially in the middle class.

Again, all this developed fully around 1900. Girls dolls were transformed from miniatures of adults (often hardly playable shelf dolls that easily were broken) or practical effigies that were supposed to train girls in the arts of sewing into huggable miniatures of themselves. These new dolls were epitomes of cuteness, inviting little girls to stay cute for as long as possible, not to anticipate adulthood as earlier dolls were intended to do. Still, the most obvious example of all this is the Teddy Bear that appeared in 1906. Teddy transformed the hard and often frightening toy bear into a child's fetish, itself cute and cuteifying the child hugging it. This anyone knows who has ever seen a staged or spontaneous photo of a toddler clutching a stuffed bear or toy animal.[66]

By the 1930s, the cute animal was animated in the cuteified mouse. In everyday life, mice are dirty pests deserving of no more than a broken spine in a trap. Instead, Disney magically converted the rodent into Mickey Mouse, who reminded all of the ever-so-cute boy next door with his own dog. However, he first appears in 1928 as a rather nasty fellow in Disney's cartoon *Steamboat Willie*. Mickey abuses other animals as he turns a goat into a hurdy-gurdy and a cow's teeth into a xylophone. And he looks like a mouse, with a longish nose and face. But, within four years, Disney had changed both Mickey's appearance and his character. By 1934, Mickey had become rounder and shorter, his mouse-like nose reduced to a snub, with an enlarged head, hands, and feet that made him look more like a child. Many commented on Mickey's massive appeal: his echoing the Charlie Chaplin–like everyman or ability to bring adults back to their childhood. Yet what was most notable about Mickey was that he had the "feeling of cuteness and boyishness" as noted by Les Clark of Disney studios. The naturalist Jay Gould famously claimed that Mickey's juvenilization confirms Lorenz's theory that Mickey's new childlike look instinctually prompts feelings of caring from audiences. This was an "unconscious discovery of this biological principle by Disney and his artists." Mickey's mate Minny was never so prominent, but like Mickey, she too was turned into a cute child, who played at being coquettish with a coy look and frequently revealed lace panties. [67] All this may explain some of Mickey's popularity in the 1930s that reached across the globe; but it does not account for why it occurred at that time. While I do not entirely discount Gould's and Lorenz's biological/evolutionary argument, I believe that the appeal of the childlike Mickey is rooted in a cultural moment: an emerging popular longing for the cute expressed in changing attitudes toward children that was given special form in the talking and animated movies of the 1930s. In this, Mickey shared much with the Doll Family. Although many might not see him as a freak, he was in his cuteness a classic form of freakishness in being the hybrid human/animal.[68]

While Mickey had become popular with his "impish subversiveness," in his early years, Walt Disney felt that he could widen and maintain that success only if Mickey became unoffensive. This meant accentuating the adorable little boy in Mickey, the soft side of the cute. This displeased many who longed for the impish Mickey of his earliest cartoons. Unsurprisingly, in 1934, the studio came up with a foil in Donald Duck. This new cartoon character illustrated in effect the more edgy side of the cute. Donald was always the out-of-control character, first with a long beak and other ducky features. However, by 1936, like Mickey, Donald too was humanized and juvenilized to make him more cute. Still, marked by a hot temper, vanity, and self-indulgence, Donald became even more popular than the increasingly saccharine Mickey. This was especially true with children who immediately recognized that Donald was even more unrestrained than they (or their baby brothers) were sometimes. This made the child feel superior. Warner Brothers played with a similar transformation, turning the tables on the "normal" battle between man and the garden rabbit, producing a less "innocent," but still lovable and thus cute, Bugs Bunny.[69]

Toying with the animal as human may have had a long history (e.g., Aesop's Fables), but in the modern context it displaced the "normal" subordination of the child to the adult in a fantasy world free of parents (and siblings). In the process, the humanized cartoon animal made the small big. These anthropomorphized and cuteified cartoon animals provided characters with which children could identify, made more effective because they were not too closely patterned after the child's real social world (with the notable absence of parental figures). In fact, these anthropomorphic characters were sometimes fantasy freaks (especially when their bodies or behavior was made extraordinary), but they were seldom horrifying or even pitiful. And, when children cheered Donald's nephews for pummeling their uncle in a snowball fight in one well-known Disney cartoon (every little kid's dream), adults did not see this as a challenge to adult authority, but cute. The cartoon character shared much with the traditional oddity, especially the midget in its cuteness. But it gave the freak new forms, often extraordinary fantasy shapes and colors and personalities as the human freak disappeared from the scene. Just think of the Muppets (Big Bird, Oscar, and Animal, for example).

The cute accompanied, even preceded, the decline of gawking at the extraordinary body. Indeed, the cute extended the "life" of at least one form of freakish display—small people and their fantastic surrogates—even as other forms of freakishness were marginalized and in decline. The cute has roots at the end of the nineteenth century. The aesthetic of cuteness reached into midget acts on the musical theater or vaudeville stage from the 1880s, shaped the performances of small people in sideshows, and then went on to the movies. From the 1930s, the cute was wrapped in a wide range of media characters and stories that toyed with and challenged expectations about body size and behavior. The cuteified small person and these commercial surrogates were the one form of the Barnumesque world of the side show to which the middle-class culture remained loyal.

At the time of Barnum, the small person was the embodiment in miniature of bourgeois ideals in ways that Siamese twins and fat ladies could not easily be. Their bodily distortion was only in size, while proportionally they were identical to "regular" people. Their size made them uncanny representatives of normality. Even more, in a culture that valued the miniature in art and display, the midget could be treasured and not simply pitied, seldom seen as creepy or frightening. Moreover, because of their size, the midget reminded audiences, especially women, of children. And by the mid-nineteenth century, the child had been sacralized, in need of protection from profanity, but also the vehicle (ideally) for redeeming a fallen world. And this attachment of the midget to the image of the child made the midget an acceptable object of children's viewing.

As the image of the child gradually shifted from the sheltered/sacred innocent to the active/wondrous innocent (the cute) around 1900, the midget performer was freed from the gaze of the salon or dime museum and moved to the comedy and fun of vaudeville and film. As important, the cuteified small person as the redeemable freak had a child audience. Kids both became cute and were brought to the cutefied freak to experience wonder and to accentuate the child's cuteness. The cuteified small person was delivered to children at midget villages, in amusement parks, and world's fairs. Imperceptibly, perhaps, children became part of a new playful crowd. At these sites, kids expressed wonder in a family setting at the very moment when middle-class parents were abandoning wonder in crowds as at the old freak show (and other carnival entertainments). Coney Island's fate is an interesting illustration of this: By the 1920s, this vast expanse of entertainments wherein the freak show played a major role was in decline, as was the circus sideshow. Disneyland, of course, from 1955 provided the new family setting for cuteness.

When middle-class sensibilities sidetracked the sideshow, "middlebrows" did not abandon wonder for a rational/scientific gaze (however much natural museum curators and other educated minorities might have wished this to be the case). It is here that the middle class broke from the highbrow elite that might have sought the sublime, the intellectually complex, or even what just wasn't middlebrow or kitsch. Instead the middle class found wonder in the vast expanse and ever-changing world of mass entertainment. And part of that realm was the delight of the cuteified midget and its surrogates. Wonder was all the more enticing to the middle class when it was seen in the faces of children around whom adults gathered.

This wonder was perhaps first encountered in midget villages, but far more often wonder was found in a vast array of art-designed forms—toys, dolls, and cartoons, all of which offered the complex allure of a Mickey Mouse and the many cuteified composites of animal and human, small and large, clever and naïve that made the fantasy world of children so "adorable." Perhaps, not all, but many of these were freakish.

No organization knew better how to exploit the cute and to create settings for family wonder in the cute than Disney, in its cartoon features and in its theme parks, Disneyland (1955) and Walt Disney World (1971). And like the midget villages of the early twentieth century, Disney's Lands offered a fantasy setting for its wondrous but cute monsters, with walking and sometimes talking Mickeys and Minnies for the kids to meet. Baseball teams do the same with cuteified animals that greet the small fry in the stands. Others have considered the full ramifications of this phenomenon, especially recently, particularly as it has been manifested by the Japanese.[70] What we shouldn't forget is that, despite their cuteification, these composites were and still are often freaks.

Still, the introduction of the cute wasn't always a bowdlerization. It was frequently edgy and even slid into its opposite, the cool or even the creepy. The cute freak, be he/she a midget or otherwise, could be impish, a trickster, or deceiver, even a letch if male; and the cute child could be the same, become coquettish if female, impish and disruptive, if male. But what made the edgy cute acceptable in midgets, cartoon characters, and children was that it was "innocent," partly because it came in an unthreatening size, but also because it wasn't intentionally seductive or malevolent.

However, as we shall see, that innocence was not so easily preserved. As I argue elsewhere, children were not content with becoming the cute or in being entertained by the cute. As they grew up, they became cool—adopting an attitude and posture of indifference to the adoring parental gaze and of longing for independence, even rebellion. The young looked to displays of the cool in their media in the edgy character and story.[71] This took many forms. But for us youth rebellion entailed a reconsideration of the freak show that their parents had rejected—in camp and the creepy. This rebellion most clearly appeared in the counterculture of middle-class youth in the late 1960s. These will be my topics that follow.

Notes

1 Daniel Harris, *Cute, Quaint, Hungry and Romantic* (New York: Basic, 2000), 5–10; Sianne Ngai, *Our Aesthetic Categories: Zany, Cute, Interesting* (Cambridge, MA: Harvard University Press, 2012), 3, 64, Chapter 2.

2 Lori Merish, "Cuteness and Commodity Aesthetics: Tom Thumb and Shirley Temple," in *Freakery: Cultural Spectacles of the Extraordinary Body*, Rosemarie Thomson-Garland, ed. (New York: New York University Press, 1996), 185–203.

3 Simon May, *The Power of Cute* (Princeton, NJ: Princeton University Press, 2019), 2, 127; Joshua Dale et al., eds., *The Aesthetics and Affects of Cuteness* (New York: Routledge, 2017), 52.

4 Throughout I use the word "midget" (even though small people today sometimes object) to distinguish these proportional but miniature people from dwarfs (even though in the nineteenth-century midgets were sometimes called "dwarfs") and because it is the commonly used term.

5 Susan Stewart, *On Longing: Narratives of the Miniature, the Gigantic, the Souvenir, the Collection* (Durham, NC: Duke University Press, 1993), 111.

6 Leslie Fiedler, *Freaks: Myths and Images of the Secret Self* (New York: Simon and Schuster, 1976), Chapter 1; Hy Roth and Robert Cromie, *Little People* (New York: Everest House, 1980), 7–10, 75.

7 *History of Charles Nestel and Joseph Huntler, The Two Smallest Men Living* (New York: Torry Bros., 1862); *Life of Joseph Howard, An American Dwarf* (Bangor, MA: Smith and Sayware, 1853), Tibbals Circus Collection of Booklets, no. 13, The John and Mable Ringling Museum of Art Archive (hereafter cited as JMRMA).

8 *Biographical Sketch of Gen. Geo. W.M. Nutt and the Little Fairy Queen, Miss Belton* (Buffalo, NY: Commercial Advertiser, 1861); *A Sketch of the Life of Chas. R. Decker, The Smallest Man in the World* (St. Louis: Jnot and E. T Ustick, 1868); *Biography of Col. Steere and His Wife* (New York: Popular Publ., 1882); *History of the Rice Lilliputians* (New York: Popular Publ., 1882); *Biography of the World Famed Rossow's Midgets* (Milwaukee: Riverside, 1896); *Sketch of the Life of Maj. Samuel E. Houghton* (np, nd, *c.* 1870), Tibbals Circus Collection of Booklets, no. 12, and 13, JMRMA.

9 *Biographical Sketch…Nutt; History of Charles Nestel; Chas. Decker; Rice Lilliputians; Biographical Sketch of the Life of Major Tot: The Prince Lilliputian* (Buffalo: Literary Messenger Press, 1878); *A History of the World's*

Greatest Midgets, Major N.G.W. Winner and Wife (Montcello, IW, ca 1896); Tibbals Circus Collection of Booklets, no. 12 and 13, JMRMA "Gen. C.R. Decker," Tibbals Collection of Cartes de Visite, nd, Midgets, JMRMA.

10 *Biographical Sketch of Gen. Geo. W.M. Nutt,* 9; *Life of Chas. R. Decker,* 8, Tibbals Circus Collection of Booklets, 12, JMRMA.

11 Tibbals Circus Collection of Cartes de Visite, JMRMA: "General Mite," 1898; Admiral Dot, nd., Brothers Littlefinger, nd, and similar male midgets.

12 *Sketch of the Life, Person, Appearance, Character and Manners of Charles A. Stratton and his Wife Lavinia Warren Stratton* (New York: Wynkoop and Hallenbeck, 1868), 1–6; Robert Bogdan, *Freak Show* (Chicago: University of Chicago Press, 1988), Chapter 6.

13 *Sketch of Stratton,* 1–6; P. T. Barnum, *The Life of Barnum, The World-Renowned Showman* (Chicago: L.P. Miller, 1892), 103–23, 288–303; Michael Chemers, "Jumpin' Tom Thumb: Charles Stratton Onstage at the American Museum," *Nineteenth Century Theatre and Film,* 31, 2 (2002): 16–27; Tom Thumb, *Life and Travels of Tom Thumb* (Philadelphia: Linsay, 1849), 13; James Cook, ed., *The Colossal P.T. Barnum Reader* (Urbana: University of Illinois Press, 2005), 118–200; Robert M. Lewis, ed., *From Traveling Show to Vaudeville,* (Baltimore, MD: Johns Hopkins University Press, 2003), 39.

14 Stewart, *On Longing,* xii, 43, 48, 55–6, 112.

15 *Life of Major Tot,* 3; *History of Charles Nestel and Joseph Huntler,* 15–6; Cook, *The Colossal P.T. Barnum,* 220; Bodgan, *Freak Show,* 151; Neil Harris, *Humbug: The Art of P.T. Barnum* (New York: Little Brown, 1973), 51.

16 Gary Cross, *The Cute and the Cool* (New York: Oxford University Press, 2004), Chapter 2; Kristen Hatch, *Shirley Temple: The Performance of Girlhood* (New Brunswick, NJ: Rutgers University Press, 2015), 11.

17 *Life of General Mite* (Philadelphia, PA: Exchange Printing, 1876), 9, Tibbals Circus Collection of Booklets, no. 13, JMRMA; "Commodore Foot, Midget," Tibbals Circus Collection of Cartes de Visite, Sideshow, JMRMA; *Sketch of . . . Stratton,* 10; "General Tom Thumb," *Frank Leslie's Ladies' Magazine,* 12 (1863): 263–71; Cook, *The Colossal P.T. Barnum,* 220; Stewart, *On Longing,* 117–23. Lavinia Magri, A. H Saxon, and Sylvester Bleeker, *The Autobiography of Mrs. Tom Thumb: (Some of My Life Experiences)* (Hamden, CT: Archon Books, 1979). For cabinet cards depicting Count Magri see Tibbals Circus Collection of Photographs, Midgets, JMRMA.

18 A very early example is *History and Travels of the Little Nanette Stocker and John Hauptmann* (1814) that features Nannette, born in 1781 in Austria, a "prodigy" exhibited by a guardian when she was sixteen and her mother died. The booklet assures us that she didn't go to "places of public amusement" because she was shy and wished to avoid the "lively demonstrative pleasures which are contrary to good breeding," but eventually appeared in theaters, 3. Tibbals Circus Collection of Booklets, no. 13, JMRMA.

19 *Life of Mrs. Ellen Briggs, The German Dwarf* (Cincinnati, self-published. 1856), 5–6, Tibbals Circus Collection of Booklets, no. 14, JMRMA.

20 *Sketch of Stratton,* 10–11.

21 "Dutton," *The Caledonian*, March 14, 1862, http://childperformers.ca/dire
ctory/dutton-dollie-27; Anthony Sansonetti, "Dollie Dutton," http://childper
formers.ca/dollie-dutton/; *History of the Little Fairy, Miss Dollie Dutton:
Also Containing the Songs She Sings* (Buffalo: Buffalo Commercial Advertiser,
1859), 1–3, 11 for quotation, Robert L. Parkinson Library & Research, Circus
World Museum (hereafter Circus World Museum), Small Collection.

22 *History of the Little Fairy*, 11, 15.

23 *W.M. Nutt and the Little Fairy Queen, Miss Belton*, 14; *Uffner's Royal
American Midgets: Miss Lucia Zarate* (1880), Tibbals Circus Collection of
Booklets, no. 14, JMRMA. Note also "Miss Jeanie Quigley" (1884); "Anita,
The Living Doll" (*c.* 1913); "Miss Millie Edwards," (1884); "Madame Shaw"
(*c.* 1889, an unusual forty-two-year-old female midget with a normal young
daughter that doesn't emphasize the childlike), Tibbals Circus Collection of
Cartes de Visite, Midgets, JMRMA.

24 For images of black midgets, see Tibbals Circus Collection of Cartes de
Visite, Midgets, JMRMA; Tibbals Circus Collection of Postcards, Sideshows,
JMRMA; Robin Bernstein, *Racial Innocence: Performing American Childhood
from Slavery to Civil Rights* (New York: New York University Press, 2012).

25 For images of late nineteenth- and early twentieth-century midgets, see Tibbals
Circus Collection of Postcards, Midgets, JMRMA; Tibbals Collection of
Cartes de Visite, Oddities; *Biographical Sketches of the Count and Countess
Philippe Nicole* (Montreal: nd, 1930?), Tibbals Circus Collection of Booklets,
no. 14.

26 For example, on one postcard of the Chinese midget Che Mah (from 1908),
the sender simply wrote on the back to a friend: "I guess while you were here
[in Parker, Indiana] you got to see this little fellow did you not? He is a dandy.
Ha Ha." I suspect that Che Mah was a casual novelty that amused, rather than
upset, viewers. Tibbals Circus Collection of Photographs, Sideshows.

27 David Monod, *The Soul of Pleasure: Sentiment and Sensation in Nineteenth-
Century American Mass Entertainment* (Ithaca, NY: Cornell University Press,
2016), 1–13; Chapters 3 and 6; Richard Butsch, *The Making of American
Audiences: From Stage to Television, 1750-1990* (New York: Cambridge
University Press, 2000), Chapter 5.

28 *History of the Burdett Twins* (New York: Popular Press, 1881); Tibbals Circus
Collection of Booklets, no. 13, JMRMA.

29 Lewis Erenberg, *Steppin' Out: New York Night Life and the Transformation
of American Culture* (Chicago: University of Chicago Press, 1981), 67–8;
Merish, "Cuteness and Commodity Aesthetics," 195.

30 For images of the Burdett Twins and other midgets, see Tibbals Circus
Collection of Postcards, Midgets, JMRMA. For a wide ranging digital
collection of midgets see, "Sideshow World: Little Folks on the Midway," http:
//www.sideshowworld.com/43-Little-Folks/BL-History-SSW-Little-Folks.html.

31 "Doll Family Midgets," Tibbals Circus Collection of Postcards, Midgets,
JMRMA. A similar look is captured in the midget postcards of Johnny Jones
Expositions, Tibbals Circus Collection of Postcards, Sideshow, JMRMA;
"Three Members of the Doll Midgets," Tibbals Circus Collection of

Photographs, Sideshow, JMRMA; "Don't Cry Hans! The Life and Career of
Harry Doll," *Freaks*, no. 9 (May 1997): 14–16; *Ike and Mike Midget Twins*
(Leavittsburg Ohio: Doc Angel, 1931), Tibbals Collection of Booklets, no. 14,
JMRMA; Roth and Cromie, *Little People,* 97.

32 Various postcards, Tibbals Circus Collection of Postcards, Midgets, JMRMA.

33 Various Postcards, Tibbals Circus Collection of Postcards, Midgets, JMRMA.

34 Various Postcards, Tibbals Circus Collection of Postcards, Midgets, JMRMA.

35 Edo McCullough, *Good Old Coney Island* (New York: Scribner's Sons,
1957), 258, 267–8; various postcards, Tibbals Circus Collection of Postcards,
Midgets, JMRMA; Roth and Cromie, *Little People,* 22–4, 95; Frederick
Drimmer, *Very Special People* (New York: Bell Publishing, 1985), 205, Andrea
Dennett, *Weird and Wonderful: The Dime Museum in America* (New York:
New York University Press, 1997), 319; Warren's Coney Island story is
summarized in Walker Bodin and Burnet Hershey, *It's a Small World* (New
York: Coward-McCann, 1934), 250–3.

36 Gary Cross, "Knott's Berry Farm: The Improbable Amusement Park in the
Shadow of Disneyland," in *The Amusement Park*, Jason Wood, ed. (New York:
Routledge, 2017), 120–37; John Hench, *Designing Disney: Imagineering and
the Art of the Show* (New York: Disney Editions, 2003), 2, 67, 56; Stewart,
On Longing, 60–9.

37 Bodin and Hershey, *Small World,* 283; Drimmer, *Very Special People,* 206;
Anthony Slide, *Encyclopedia of Vaudeville* (Jackson: University of Mississippi
Press, 2012), 295–6; *Bob Hermines Magazine of Midgets* (Flushing, NY:
np, 1947); Tibbals Circus Collection of Booklets, no. 12; various postcards,
Tibbals Circus Collection of Postcards, Midgets; both in JMRMA.

38 *Century of Progress, Official Guidebook of the World's Fair of 1934* (Chicago:
A Century of Progress, International Exposition, 1934), 118–19; Roth and
Cromie, *Little People*, 122–5. F. D. Pfenig Jr., "Stanley Graham's International
Midget Circus," *Bandwagon*, June 1994, 23–5; various postcards, Tibbals
Circus Postcard Collection, Midgets, JMRMA.

39 Various postcards, Tibbals Circus Collection of Postcards, Midgets, JMRMA;
Drimmer, *Very Special People,* 207; Roth and Cromie, *Little People*, 135;
Morris Gest's Midget Town with the World's Greatest Midget Artists
(New York: New York World's Fair, 1939), 23–8.

40 "*Lilliput Town!*" British Pathé, 1934, https://www.britishpathe.com/video/
lilliput-town/query/midgets; *Cineviews In Brief,* no. 53, British Pathé, 1937,
https://www.britishpathe.com/video/cineviews-in-brief-no-53/query/cows+with
+boots; various postcards, Tibbals Circus Collection of Postcards, Midgets,
JMRMA.

41 Fred Roper, *All About Midgets* (London?, ca., 1935), 21–2, 28, Tibbals Circus
Collection of Booklets, no. 12, JMRMA; various postcards, Tibbals Circus
Collection of Postcards, Midgets, JMDMA. After about 1930, booklets on
freaks seem increasingly to recognize the biological causes and variations
on the midgets. Note also *Nate Eagle Presents His Internationally Famous
Midgets* (Sarasota, FL: np, 1950?), Tibbals Circus Collection of Booklets,
no. 13, JMRMA.

42 *Bob Hermines Magazine of Midgets.* Similar was Rose's Midget Revue of twelve performers, males in a band, females in dance dress (1945) and Henry Kramer's "Midget Starlets," (1942) pictured in revue with Maracas, Tibbals Circus Collection of Postcards, Midgets, JMRMA.

43 Bodin and Hershey, *Small World,* 282, 291.

44 Jack Hunter, *Freak Babylon: An Illustrated History of Teratology and Freakshows* (New York: Creation, 2014), 143.

45 Stephen Cox, *The Munchkins Remember* (New York: Plume, 1989), 6–12; "Teenage Judy Garland Was Repeatedly Molested by Munchkins on Set of Wizard of Oz, According to Her Ex-Husband," *USA Today*, February 7, 2017, https://people.com/celebrity/teenage-judy-garland-was-repeatedly-molested-by-munchkins-on-set-of-wizard-of-oz-says-her-ex-husband/; Roth and Cromie, *Little People,* 133; "Harry Doll," *Freaks,* 9, 21–2; Boden and Hershey, *Small World,* 97.

46 *Terror of Tiny Town* (Jed Buell Productions, 1938); "Terror of Tiny Town," *Freaks*, 9 (May 1997): 35.

47 Angelo Rossitto postcard, Tibbals Circus Collection of Postcards, Midgets, JMRMA.

48 1880s Trade cards, Ann White Collection, Box 134; American Trade Card Collection, Box 7, Winterthur Museum Library; Miriam Formanek-Brunell, *Made to Play House: Dolls and the Commercialization of American Girlhood, 1830-1930* (New Haven, CT: Yale University Press, 1993), 90–2, 109–16; Cross, *The Cute and the Cool*, Chapter 3.

49 Drimmer, *Very Special People,* 210, Roper, *All About Midgets,* 3–4.

50 Konrad Lorenz, "Part and Parcel in Animal and Human Societies," in *Studies in Animal and Human Behavior* (Cambridge, MA: Harvard University Press, 1971, 1950 original), 154–62; Stephen Jay Gould, "A Biological Homage to Mickey Mouse," in his *The Panda's Thumb: More Reflections in Natural History* (New York: Norton, 1980), 95–107; May, *Power of Cute*, 50–1; For a thorough review of the literature concerning Lorenz's biological argument, see Joshua Dale, "The Appeal of the Cute Object," in *Aesthetics and Affects of Cuteness*, 25–53. An accessible survey of the science behind this biological response to the cute is found in Gemma Tarlach, "Why Babies are so Cute—and Why We React the Way We Do," *Discover Magazine,* November 13, 2019, https://www.discovermagazine.com/mind/why-babies-are-so-cute-and-why-we-react-the-way-we-do.

51 Dale, "Appeal of the Cute," 33; Anne Higonnet, *Pictures of Innocence: The History and Crisis of Ideal Childhood* (London: Thames and Hudson, 1998), 31, 32, 51.

52 Cross, *Cute and the Cool,* Chapters 2 and 3.

53 Dale, "Appeal of the Cute," 35; May, *Power of Cute,* 20–7, 40–1.

54 Dale, "Appeal of the Cute," 35; May, *Power of Cute,* 20–7, 40–1.
    The classic discussion is in Sigmund Freud, "The Uncanny," in *The Standard Edition of the Complete Psychological Works of Sigmund Freud,* James Strachey, ed. (London: Hogarth, 1955), Vol 17, 218–56. May, *Power of Cute,* Chapters 3 and 7, Harris, *Cute, Quaint,* 5–10 and Ngai, *Our Aesthetic*

Categories, 65, 85–7, 108, similarly note the freakish and contradictory elements in the cute, especially between the response of tenderness and cruelty; Cross, *Cute and the Cool,* Chapter 3.

55 May sees my concept of "wondrous innocence" as a "flight," essentially an expression of "escapism." This misses the dynamic of the shift in the meaning of innocence (from sheltered and sacred) to the vital and willful, essential to the modern understanding of the cute in children or freaks, part of May's "celebration of childhood in all its complexity." May, *Power of Cute,* 138, 149.

56 Viviana Zelizer, *Pricing the Priceless Child* (Princeton, NJ: Princeton University Press, 1985).

57 Nancy West, *Kodak and the Lens of Nostalgia* (Charlottesville: University Press of Virginia, 2000).

58 Cross, *Cute and the Cool,* Chapter 3.

59 A. J. Liebling, "A Patron of the Preemies," *The New Yorker,* June 3, 1939, 20–4.

60 McCullough, *Good Old Coney Island,* 276–8; Dawn Raffel, *The Strange Case of Dr. Couney* (New York: Blue Rider Press, 2018), 64–6; William Silverman, "Incubator-Baby Side Shows," *California Pediatrics,* 64, 2: 127–41, August 1979; Claire Prentice, "The Man Who Ran a Carnival Attraction That Saved Thousands of Premature Babies Wasn't a Doctor at All," *Smithsonian Magazine,* August 19, 2016, https://www.smithsonianmag.com/history/man-who-pretended-be-doctor-ran-worlds-fair-attraction-saved-lives-thousands-premature-babies-180960200/#y2vDQKSWI1ZM0ukC.99.

61 In the West, the separation of pets from other domesticated animals took place between 1400 and 1800. Many varieties of dogs were bred for outdoor functions (hunting, shepherding, etc.), but some dogs were designed for the indoors and many of these domesticated dogs retained the traits of the juvenile look and behavior (neoteny) of wolves: floppy ears, upward curving tails, and a proclivity to bark. Katherine Grier, *Pets in America: A History* (Chapel Hill: University of North Carolina Press, 2006), 7, 13, 59, 131, 133, 137–9; Mary Thurston, *The Lost History of the Canine Race* (Kansas City: Andrews and McMeel, 1996), 37; Keith Thomas, *Man and the Natural World* (New York: Oxford University Press, 1983), Chapter 3.

62 American Kennel Club, "Pug History," *American Kennel Club – Pug,* https://www.akc.org/dog-breeds/pug/#timeline; Thurston, *Lost History,* 70, 77; Grier, *Pets in American,* 33. Further discussion of pets and breeding can be found in Katherine Grier's blog, https://thepethistorian.com/; Jake Page, *Dogs, A Natural History* (Washington: Smithsonian Books, 2007); David Grimm, *Citizen Canine: Our Evolving Relationship with Cats and Dogs* (Washington: Public Affairs, 2015).

63 Hatch, *Shirley Temple,* 25–54; John F. Kasson, *The Little Girl Who Fought the Great Depression: Shirley Temple and the 1930s* (New York: Norton, 2014), 46–86.

64 Hatch, *Shirley Temple,* 3–11; Kasson, *The Little Girl,* 48–50, 81.

65 In her first feature-film role in *Stand Up and Cheer,* Temple famously transforming a scene of female sexuality into the cute when she innocently,

but flirtatiously, appeared between the legs of her formally dressed father surrounded by chorus girls. "Eroticism has been supplanted by cuteness," notes Kasson. Hatch argues that Temple represents a transition from the ideal of the innocent child who redeems the adult to the cute child who exuded a vitality and coquettishness appealing to the "full of life" modernist. Kasson, *The Little Girl*, 83–4 (for quotation), 156–9, 162–3; Hatch, *Shirley Temple*, 48, 72.

66   Gary Cross, *Kids' Stuff: Toys and the Changing World of American Childhood* (Cambridge, MA: Harvard University Press, 1997), 92–7; Cross, *Cute and the Cool*, 54–5.

67   Neal Gabler, *Walt Disney: The Triumph of the American Imagination* (New York: Vintage, 2006), 120, 127; Christopher Finch, *The Art of Walt Disney* (New York: Abrams, 2004), 208; Gould, "A Biological Homage," 104.

68   Cross, *Cute and the Cool*, Chapter 3. For a different perspective, see May, *Power of Cute*, 56–7.

69   Gabler, *Walt Disney*, 201–3; Cross, *Cute and the Cool*, 55–6; Norman Kline, *Seven Minutes: The Life and Death of the American Animated Cartoon* (London: Verso, 1993), 35–40, 43.

70   Brian McVeigh, "How Hello Kitty Commodifies the Cute, Cool and Camp: 'Consumutopia' versus 'Control' in Japan," *Journal of Material Culture*, 5 (2000): 225–45; Frances Richard, "Fifteen Theses on Cute," *Cabinet*, 4 (Fall 2001), http://cabinetmagazine.org/issues/4/cute.php; John Sanders, "On 'Cuteness,'" *British Journal of Aesthetics*, 32, 2 (1992): 162–5; Anne Allison, *Millennial Monsters: Japanese Toys and the Global Imagination* (Berkeley: University of California Press, 2006); Christine Yano, *Pink Globalization* (Durham, NC: Duke University Press, 2013). Note also Dale et al., *Aesthetics and Affects of Cuteness*; Ngai, *Our Aesthetic Categories*; May, *Power of Cute*.

71   Cross, *The Cute and the Cool*.

5

Countercultures of the Freakishly Camp

Camp, like the cute, adapted the freak to evolving middle-class sensibilities. While the cute made acceptable the oddity that could conform to a modern middle-class adult fixation on childlike wonder, camp embraced the full range of freakiness, often as an act of youthful, but still basically middle-class, rebellion from a genteel culture of constraint and even from the cute. Yet far from returning to the open-mouthed wonder of the rube at the sideshow, these rebels gazed at the bizarre from a bemused and even mocking distance that often pretended to be shocked (or used bemusement to evade terror). Like the cute, camp had origins in the nineteenth century (perhaps earlier) in the freak show itself and in the self-alienating posturing of a middle-class minority. Yet, again, like the cute, modern campish aesthetics emerged within a middle class (set in modern consumer culture) that challenged its genteel roots; and, this rebellion emerged in full force in the twentieth century. While the cute took on many of its contemporary features in the 1930s, camp did the same in the 1960s. If the cute brought children to the show and produced an amazing array of freak surrogates, camp brought freakishness into new venues. These settings were as varied as participatory viewings of "bad" movies, outrageous TV talk shows, and new age freak shows. While the cute enlivened middle-class culture with childlike wonder and attempted to create bonds between old and young, for a new generation emerging fully in the 1960s, camp challenged both the middlebrow and high modernism (highbrow) of the older generation with defiant combinations of outrageousness and indifference.

Camp was the embrace of otherness with bemused distance. Its roots in the sophisticated world of modernist elites has often been noted, but it took decisive form in the youth counterculture of the 1960s in the form of the hippie as "freak" as in the cartoons of Robert Crumb. It was especially notable in crowds that attended midnight movies (including the revival of Browning's *Freaks* in 1970) whose oddities were seen no longer as horror but with distance as a kind of joke, appreciated for their outlandishness. Camp was central to the displays of otherness in the psychological freaks on Jerry Springer and other shock talk shows who were campishly cheered (and jeered) by the TV studio audiences. This adoption of the campish freak later appeared as a new type of freak show in the tattooed and pierced dropouts of Jim Rose's "Circus Sideshow" and others that appeared at rock clubs. Camp celebrated the outrageous and the act of playfully putting on both the rube and the freak as a not-too-serious rejection of uptight, scripted, and sanctimonious genteel (and kitsch) culture.

Camp Theory

In order to understand camp, we need to situate it in theory and history. Unlike others who stress its purely aesthetic qualities, I find camp within a social context, especially in youth and generational rebellion rather than primarily in sexual nonconformity (though this certainly had a major role to play). Further, rather than seeking to identify the essentials of camp performance (and distinguish it from other presentations), I will stress the origins and development of campish reception and audience behavior.

Most thinking about camp begins with Susan Sontag's famous "Notes on Camp" essay of 1964. Critically situated at the beginning of the "cultural 60s" that extended into the chronological 70s, Sontag, the quintessential commentator on the New York *avant-garde* scene, offered an accessible, if unsystematic, set of "notes" about an emerging cultural phenomenon. As the celebrity of anti-intellectual intellectualism, Sontag found camp in the easily bored tribe of artsy New Yorkers (and their counterparts in other big cities) who then and later attended cheeky revivals of over-the-top dance shows like *No No Nanette* and the films and performances of Andy Warhol. As Sontag writes, camp "is part of the history of snob taste."[1]

Rather than seeing it as a break from past ideas or art forms, for Sontag, camp is an attitude, a "style" emphasizing "irony over tragedy," relishing exaggeration, not the natural. At the same time, camp is "disengaged," essentially unserious, and thus can embrace both the popular and kitsch as jokes. Among her many illustrations of camp is "old stag movies seen without lust." This distancing means also the abandonment of old aesthetic standards, the embrace of the "good taste of bad taste." Camp is not scolding like the high modernist critics of kitsch and pop culture, but "generous"; it "relishes, rather than judges." It rejects the moralistic tone of traditional high culture along with the emotionalism of the *avant-garde*, for a sensibility that is "wholly aesthetic."[2]

This distancing in the camp consumer goes beyond amorality and aestheticism. It means a partiality to the past, based on the realization that one is "better able to enjoy a fantasy as fantasy when it is not your own" and "when we become less involved." As Sontag notes, "time liberates the work of art from moral relevance, delivering it over to the camp sensibility," sometimes even turning the banal into the fantastic. This may explain the campish delight some people take in the kitsch of their (or their elders') youth such as in the modern fascination with mid-century modern furnishings or 1970s "mod" fashion. Camp is sometimes an appreciation of what elites have labeled "bad" in the past, especially in popular culture (such as kitsch) with a new sort of knowing distance, but also with a rejection of the highbrow's rejection. Thus, film scholar Ken Feil observes, "camp involves the ironic appreciation of low, failed culture, and the parody of taste codes that rank cultural works as 'high' or 'low.'" All this, of course, explains the 1960s fascination with 1930s popular movies such as the Marx Brothers, Three Stooges, and, of course, cautionary tales like *Reefer Madness* viewed by college students in the 1970s while high on marijuana.[3]

The camp aesthetic did not appear suddenly in the 1960s, of course. As Sontag and others note, it had roots in the dandyism of the late nineteenth-century aesthete, most notably Charles Baudelaire and Oscar Wilde who mocked bourgeois social convention. For Sontag, modern camp is dandyism with a new-found appreciation for the "art of the masses," even its "vulgarity," rather than Wilde's elitist detachment and search for rare sensations. The best camp, Sontag insists, is "naïve," art that isn't trying to be camp but later is appreciated as camp (Liberace and his piano with the candelabra, for example).[4]

Others have offered somewhat different definitions and explanations of camp, without, however, breaking from Sontag's elite literati perspective. Mark Booth (1983) boldly claims that camp is a posture of the performer, presenting "oneself as being committed to the marginal with a commitment greater than the marginal merits." While Booth may not totally agree with the 1909 dictionary definition of camp as "acts and gestures of an exaggerated emphasis . . . used chiefly by persons of exceptional want of character," he adopts a negative tone. For Booth (like Fiedler, Bell, and Sontag and others) the 1960s introduced camp to an urban cultured elite, for good or ill, challenging the standards of genteel cultivation, restraint, and responsibility. Likewise, Marxists like Frederic Jameson and Andrew Ross claim that camp intellectuals abandoned the classic role of bourgeois thinkers in legitimizing the power of the ruling class. Instead they expressed their impotence by distancing themselves "from the conventional morality and taste of the growing middle class." Many of these intellectuals became part of the mass entertainment industry, especially with the emergence of pop camp in the 1960s.[5]

Booth, like others, tries to distinguish camp from other related phenomenon: the popular, kitsch, gay aesthetics, and dandyism.[6] All this may be helpful, but this procedure assumes some essential essence to camp, and, more important, neglects the historical context in which camp appears. For Booth, camp is the perspective of lonely people, "knocked off balance in childhood." It even demonstrates "a refusal to grow up." Camp is "basically exhibitionism" and "superficially garish." While Booth concedes that camp challenges a common "bogus decorum of maturity," and even makes life "lighter, brighter, more carefree," practitioners of camp seldom offer anything creative.[7]

Proponents of camp (be they cult movie makers or fans of trash talk TV) might dismiss Booth and other critics of camp as unreflective defenders of a stale and scolding high culture. Moreover, as Humberto Eco notes, Sontag's list of what is camp and what's not reflect personal taste (Mozart and Pope are camp, but Swift isn't?). Her views may also represent the taste of New York intellectuals in the 1960s.[8] Booth is not so cavalier as Sontag, but he certainly does not get beyond her urbane elitism. Still, we do not have enter this debate to find Booth's and Sontag's approach problematic.

I think that there are sources of camp that are unrelated to the dilemmas of high modernism or urban life, in fact, that ultimately get us back to the freak show. Camp had more popular origins. The campish response of the crowd is at least as important as the "exhibitionist" on the stage. Moreover, there is often a symbiotic relationship between the producer and consumer of camp (especially when show people and moviemakers discovered the appeal of *intentional* camp in their productions). A final problem is why camp seems to go mainstream in the 1960s. And does that appeal go beyond Sontag's "snobs"?

Briefly, let me first offer a couple of thoughts about what is missing in these standard interpretations. By focusing on camp as an audience reaction, not just or even primarily as a performance, we can see that the camp crowd emerged from diverse social and cultural milieu and at different times and contexts. Paralleling the campish dandies of the late nineteenth century were individuals at freak shows who adopted a camp response as a popular alternative to the gawking and gullible majority in the audience. Historians of those Victorian freak show have often noted the "aggrandizing" presentation of oddities but also their encounters with the sometimes cynical, even "knowing," members of the crowd. As Rachel Adams observes, "If freaks could misbehave in unpredictable ways, customers also frequently caused disruption by attempting to unmask the fraudulence of human exhibits. Born in the era of humbug and confidence men, freak shows promised to shock and amaze, but also encouraged their audiences to question what they saw ..."[9] As bemused observers, these members of the Victorian dime-museum crowd were precursors of modern camp audiences. This mock response to humbug in the golden years of the freak show reveals that a working-class crowd was as capable of camp as were elites.

More important here, from the 1960s, in addition to Sontag's glitterati/literati, another group embraced camp—a portion of middle-class youth. In an emerging counterculture, this rising generation rejected the values and aesthetic of their middle-class (sometimes highbrow) parents. One form of that rejection was youth's denial of their parent's imposition of the cute on them when they were children for an embrace of the cool. One form of the cool was a distancing from parental values in a rebellious adoption of the "freak." As camp, this response involved a rejection of *both* middle-class disgust and lower-class gawking at the extraordinary bodies and behaviors in the traditional freak show. Identifying with, rather than abhorring, the freak was part of a usually temporary dismissal of the middle-class values (material accumulation and conformist comfort).[10] But this young audience for camp was also alienated from the folk culture of the past. They found traditional beliefs laughable, but also intriguing, making the freak fascinating, but in a distinctly campish way. Camp has origins not just in the dandy or 1960s New York intellectuals, but also in rebellious youth of the 1960s that situated itself between the "hang-ups" of their middle-class parents and the naiveté of an alien folk culture.

The camp response of the youth counterculture was especially directed toward freakery, but often in its relatively new forms: cartoons, cinematic monsters, oddballs on TV, and even outlandish performances of the pierced and tattooed at rock clubs. Freaks were no longer beyond the pale to these camp crowds; instead, these modern freaks were often objects of personal identification because they were symbols of disdain for the "normal." The crowd as well as the performers welcomed being called freaks. Camp was also a rejection of the manipulation of the impresario; it was about not being taken in by the ballyhoo in whatever form, and thus part of a broad culture of cynical disengagement—ultimately expressed in the "whatever" of modern jaded youth. However, if the audience could no longer be "taken in" by the bally fantasy in a modern secular age, it was sometimes willing to "put on" the rube, experiencing the wonder of the naïve carnival or circus goer, by engaging in a form of play that was "knowing," but that also suspended disbelief. The camp crowd became in imagination the gawking crowd of the past. The self-declared "freaks" of the cultural 60s have largely disappeared (though later generations of tattooed and pierced youth at least channel that ethos). Still, in campish encounters with the extraordinary body/behavior, they live on.

Campish Characters as Freaks in the 1960s

An oft-noted characteristic of the 1960s *avant garde* was a very particular rediscovery of the carnival. Camp emerges, as Sontag and Booth note, as part of an elite rejection of elite values. One form of that rejection was the embrace of the freak. Note the famous case of Diane Arbus, who began her career as a New York fashion photographer for her father's upscale department store, but in the early 1960s she became enchanted with the freaks and other outcastes on 42nd Street, especially the oddities at Hubert's Museum. Their fate of being born with the traumas that others feared made them "aristocrats" in her eyes. Without voyeurism or condescension, she photographed freaks in settings and natural poses that challenged the look of their public display; thus "freakish comes to seem normal and vice versa." One reviewer of her photos saw a "guileful mixture of exhibitionism and concealment." Though Arbus committed suicide in 1971 at forty-eight, her photographs entered the elite world of the Museum of Modern Art in a special showing the next year. Sympathetic literary treatments of freaks appear also in Carson McCullers's novels (*Member of the Wedding,* 1946 and *Clock without Hands,* 1961) and Katherine Dunn's *Geek Love* (1989). Joel-Peter Wiktin included images of freaks (as well as corpses and nudity) in his book of photos (*Gods of Earth and Heaven,* 1988).[11] These presentations of the freak were not purposively camp, in fact quite the opposite, but they set the stage for a new generation's largely playful embrace of the freak.

In the late 1960s, a segment of the rising generation of middle-class (mostly) whites followed Arbus and company with a new fascination with the freak, even calling themselves freaks. Usually identified with the counterculture, this attraction to the conventionally abject has been attributed to a broad rejection of middle-class culture and its acceptance of authority, self-denial, and deferred gratification as the price of present and future consumption. A media-drenched and increasingly jaded upbringing in a generation of affluence made this trade-off seem silly by the late 1960s. Moreover, the lifting of the 1950s Cold War culture of fear and anxiety led these youth to mock the obsessive concern with the threat of nuclear war and of the Soviet Union (satirized famously in *Dr. Strangelove* in 1964). Along with a rejection of the old siege mentality came a gleeful denial of markers of middle-class civilization. A small-but-influential cohort of youth expressed this dissent by identifying with the "freak"—not literally the born freak but the individual alienated from the world of "repressive" consumption and bureaucratic work. These would-be "freaks" demanded not only unrestrained individuality and immediacy of experience but, as Daniel Foss wrote in 1972, the "right of total control over their physical appearance and outward behavior." They insisted on looking and behaving freaky.[12]

Yet, as was often noted at the time, there was something curious about countercultural identification with "freaks." The word conventionally meant "physiologically deviant human beings" who were involuntarily rejected by society; but in the context of the late 1960s it meant also a "choice," a mark of estrangement, but also an "honorific title by the . . . physiologically normal but dissident young people who use hallucinogenic drugs and otherwise are known as 'hippies.'"[13] How to explain this curious shift in meaning? Michael Chemers finds the freak show to be a "staging of stigma," the display of difference recognized by the audience as abnormal and thus a means of defining the normal. Audiences and performers respond to this stigma in varied ways, but the point here is that counterculturalists claimed this "abnormality" as their own in rejecting normality (at least in theory). They turned themselves into freaks in body and behavior, or, at least, claimed to. Thus, rocker Frank Zappa in his "Freak-Out" album of 1965–66, in curiously academic language, claims "Freaking Out is a process whereby an individual casts off outmoded and restricting standards of thinking, dress, and social etiquette in order to express CREATIVELY his relationship to his immediate environment and the social structure as a whole." Becoming a countercultural freak meant discarding conventional normality for individuality, but it also implied accepting being stigmatized along with the carnival freak, presumably adopting the perspective of the gawked at. Yet countercultural "freaks" were far from the staged stigmatized in the traditional freak show; they were neither pitied nor mysterious in the way that carnival freaks were. As in camp, their freakishness was often exaggerated. Sometimes the word and its associates meant to be out of control or even to be obsessive. The countercultural freak, however, was mostly about a voluntary break from and often an intentional disruption of the norms of constraint and compromise. And this was another step toward camp because it often was a put on.[14]

A couple of examples of late 1960s freakery (and, with it, subtle links to camp) will suffice. One of many is Robert Crumb and his pivotal role in the "underground" comics movement (his *Zap Comix*, for example and later his *Keep on Truckin'* comic strip). His account of his early success in the 1960s is a classic story of the artist as "freak." Ever disdainful of his middle-class Catholic upbringing in Cleveland, he repeatedly abandoned his young wife as he wandered from New York to Chicago, and San Francisco. He claimed to break the boundary between the conscious and subconscious in a period when he drew a "tawdry carnival of disassociated images," which gave birth (with the aid of LSD) to ten years of characters for his cartoons. His countercultural anti-conventionality led to his ostracism for his brutal portrayals of the beheading of Catholics, degrading images of women, and for his (1993) tongue-in-cheek, but outrageous, comic book that freely used the taboo "n-word." Still, he refused to "repress" anything, even misogyny or racist stereotypes from his childhood. So outrageous were his cartoons that it was impossible to take them seriously, to see them as anything but camp. Like Arbus, Crumb was embraced by the cultural *avant-garde* in art shows by 1972, even as he continued to appeal to the rebel in ways that Booth would recognize as essentially juvenile. For example, in his cartoon the "City of the Future," he draws a place where everyone can be Jesus Christ or "blow up the world."[15]

While baby boomers were amused by Crumb's anarchistic cartoons of out-of-control characters on the edge of hippie culture, Ed "Big Daddy" Roth (1932–2001), epitomized campish excess from the perspective of the Los Angeles hot rodder. Roth was closer to the working-class "greaser" who rejected the psychedelic middle-class hippie than Crumb's counterculture. But, by the late 1960s, Roth had become for Tom Wolfe in his famous essay on California hot-rod scene, the "Salvador Dali of the movement—a surrealist in his designs, a showman by temperament, a prankster."[16] Like many who grew up with the hot-rod movement of the late 1940s, Roth hoped to make the obsession of his youth a profession.

FIGURE 5.1 *Ed "Big Daddy" Roth's Beatnik Bandit customized car, 1960. It was built from a 1949 Oldsmobile, but drastically changed to make it a caricature of a classic hot rod. Wikimedia Commons, Creative Commons Attribution 2.0.*

By the late 1950s, he had succeeded, constructing what could be called caricatures of the customized hot rod, including the bubble-topped Beatnik Bandit. Made out of junk parts and fiberglass, this "car" was utterly impractical; yet it was rebelliously cool. Even more notable was Roth's "trademark" image of Rat Fink, an anti–Mickey Mouse, the very opposite of cuteness with bulging, bloodshot eyes, and a pot belly. On T-shirts, it appealed to "gear heads" in playful rebellion against both GM and Disney. Later in the 1980s, his Rat Fink image was adapted by surf musicians and edgy rock bands. Roth had much in common with the punk bands of the 1970s like the Clash, the Ramones, and the Sex Pistols, each of which tried to outdo one another in outrageousness in hair, dress, and behavior. Their raw, unsophisticated rock, combined with anarchic, anti-politically correct posturing, may not have been taken as camp by many fans, but in its rejection of conventional morality and religion as well as its extremism, it certainly fit Sontag's description.[17]

As long noted, the countercultural freak's embrace of what bourgeois elders rejected was short-lived, vanishing as that generation's youth passed with marriage, family, and career as well as other internal contradictions that need not delay us here.[18] But much of the spirit of the countercultural freak survived the 1960s in somewhat truncated and confined form in camp. This was not generally a daily lifestyle but often merely a way of viewing and presenting popular culture, mostly restricted to the weekend.

Midnight Movies and Camp Crowds

While Robert Crumb and Frank Zappa were "freaking out," in 1970 Todd Browning's *Freaks* was returning to popular movie houses like the Elgin in New York City, patronized in large part by young want-to-be "freaks." As we have seen, Browning's mixed message in his 1932 feature—both offering a troupe of circus oddities to sympathize with but also presenting horrifying monsters taking vengeance on a "normal" couple—was too daring and confusing for the insecure audiences of Depression-era America. Few viewers could see anything more than horror (or pity) in the freaks. Movies then mostly featured "beautiful people," not the lowest of the low, the freak. *Freaks* survived in the 1940s and 1950s on the grindhouse circuit where it offered a down-market crowd a voyeuristic taste of the grotesque wrapped in a thin veneer of moralism. In 1962, however, an elite crowd rediscovered *Freaks* at the Venice Film Festival, winning eventually the applause of famed film critic Vincent Canby. The unearthing of this "oddity" by a high modernist clique might have been expected. *Freaks* challenged the predictable Hollywood fare of the time and offered an intriguing glimpse of the Other. Yet the most telling feature of the *Freaks* revival was its introduction to youth on the midnight movie circuit in 1970. This crowd identified with the freaks and cheered them on as they attacked their "normal" tormenters, but the applause was pure camp. *Freaks* became one of many cult films, a genre, as film critic James Monaco says (1979), that attracted mostly the "privileged child of the middle class."[19]

If this was the crowd of camp, let's consider a significant setting of this crowd, the midnight movie. Everything about it was unconventional: Offered at the ungodly hour of 12 am, often far from the first-run theaters, these movies were usually unadvertised, attracting nevertheless throngs of hip young people through word of mouth. Moreover, unlike "regular" films, these midnight movies (often shown on weekends only) sometimes ran for weeks or months on end as a sort of ritual for repeated viewers. In New York, *Rocky Horror Picture Show* played for ninety-six weeks from its opening in 1976, drawing crowds that sometimes lining up for hours. The absence of promotion enhanced the cult value of the showing. Carrying on the spirit of the midnight movie houses in the 1970s and early 1980s were several hundred college film societies that showed cult films in college auditoria.[20]

While some of these films were *avant-garde* films by Luis Brunel or even Andy Warhol as might have once attracted cult film goers to art houses, many were camp at least in the viewing of the young crowds. As film historian Harry Benshoff notes, the midnight movie theaters created a "space" for "camp receptive practices," with homogeneous crowds of the young out on a lark. The midnight movie circuit included a wide range of films—from horror features (*Eraserhead* and *Night of the Living Dead*) and campish oddities

(*Planet Nine from Outer Space*) to the quirky but sentimental *Harold and Maude*. Included were revivals of 1930s comedies and even horror like *King Kong* and *The Invisible Man* that young people had viewed as children on the TV late show. They came to the theater to see them again as crowds of "knowing" youth, sharing their own space and time. This audience saw the popular culture of the past as camp (as Sontag notes)—not as horror or melodrama, but as corny and amusing. Midnight movies also offered a contrast to the aesthetic of parents, be it either expressed in middlebrow delight for the romantic comedies of Doris Day or the sublimity of the highbrow art films of Ingmar Bergman. Their parents may have rebuffed "low class" and tasteless movies; but these youthful crowds sought out cheaply made Japanese science fiction and American B-movies that blended horror and sexuality (e.g., *Ghost in the Invisible Bikini*), viewing each as camp, even if their producers had not intended them to be so understood.[21]

New movies also appeared in these midnight gatherings of self-declared freaks that might not strike one immediately as campy. Most famous was *El Topo* that hit the midnight circuit in 1970. Produced by Alejandro Jodorovsky, *El Topo* sold out every show for nine months when it appeared at the Elgin. A low-budget western, distinguished by gratuitous gore, with a veneer of "spirituality," *El Topo* became a surprise cult hit. Among its admirers was John Lennon, who bought the film to show in a regular movie house setting (with disastrous results). The midnight cult setting of the movie is what made it attractive. But its unrelenting violence gathered bemused crowds of counterculturists in what Eco called a "spirit of a cheerful playfulness." Its exaggerated gore made it camp. Moreover, *El Topo* "belonged" to the kids; it wasn't a Hollywood retread of *Dracula*. And there was precedence for this generation brought up on the horror comics of the early 1950s and even the demystifying and sometimes whimsical take on horror in the preteen comic book *Famous Monsters of Filmland* (1958–83). In this context (more in Chapter 6), the gore of *Texas Chainsaw Massacre* (1974) offered, complained the *New York Times*, "kinky humor" for the young "generation raised on excitement." This bloody thriller attracted an upcoming generation looking for an "event" that suggested "something missed in the 60s."[22]

An even more definitive cultural and generational break came with the outrageous films of John Waters, which prompted an elder from the *Chicago Tribune* to lament that youth no longer went to the movies for "making out," but rather for "grossing out," while watching the obese transvestite "Devine" eat dog manure in *Pink Flamingos*. This lament from a member of a generation nostalgic for the era of the romantic "date" suggests a broader change that accompanied the midnight movie—a new form of audience interaction. And this became most obvious in the most successful midnight movies like *Rocky Horror Picture Show*, where audiences were as much participants as viewers. The midnight movie's heyday was in the 1970s. It was superseded in the 1980s as camp and cult went mainstream and was de-collectivized by home-viewing on VCRs and later DVD players and streaming. Even so, *Rocky*'s frequent revivals with new generations of youth and the association of youth and camp in the movies lived on, even becoming more pronounced.[23]

Camp, of course, preceded the midnight movie, as did the peculiarly lowbrow form that it often took. A look back at these precedents will not only clarify this shift in taste cultures of youth from the late 1960s but link the midnight movie to our broader topic—the irrepressible freak. Countercultural camp ultimately derives from the carnival culture of grindhouse theater and is unconventional movies, especially of the 1930s and 1940s. The most obvious example is *Reefer Madness* (1936), a cautionary tale of how degradation and suicide attend marihuana use. With its trite dialogue, and the strained sermons, Eric Schaefer notes, it became for the students of the 1960s "the essence of camp."[24]

Separated from major studios and their distribution system in the 1920s, grindhouse cinema was made and circulated by independent producers who specialized in exploiting themes rejected by the major studios. It attracted primarily a down-market crowd (much as did the traveling carnival freak show of this era). These films were cheaply made and distributed often in independent and seedy theaters in the "bad" part of town that played movies continuously (thus grindhouses). Most important, their makers did not subscribe to the various voluntary codes of censorship that the major studios adhered to and thus could focus on forbidden topics (sex, venereal disease, drug addiction, prostitution, etc.). Their advertising on garish posters particularly suggests parallels with the bannerlines of sideshows, titillating prospective audiences. The poster promoting *The Desperate Women* (1954), for example, suggests the movie's theme of abortion with images of women in illicit embrace but also with looks of shame and fear, capped by the provocative question, "Are You Next?" Neither pornographic nor graphically violent, grindhouse films were suggestive, but often "covered" in a gloss of a moral pretense (sometimes viewings included lectures on sexual hygiene presented by "nurses"). Brief and limited nudity was justified with the "educational" claim that the film's subject was the exploration of distant and exotic cultures. This protected exhibitors from local censors and mollified the scruples of some viewers. Dwain Esper, along with his screenwriting wife Hildegarde Esper, was the most famous of the exploitation film makers in the 1930s and 1940s (noted for distributing *Freaks*).[25]

Grindhouse had clear links to the carnival culture of the traditional freak show. As film historian David Church notes, not only did grindhouse and the freak show attract a similar crowd from the "lower cultural stratum" but the "body-as-cinematic-spectacle" in grindhouse cinema paralleled the freak show's stress on the extraordinary body, meeting similar crowd needs.[26] It should be no surprise that the appearance of *Freaks* on the grindhouse circuit sometimes was accompanied with a troupe of real circus freaks. Famed conjoined twins Daisy and Violet Hilton made public appearances promoting the exploitation film *Marihuana* in the 1930s and starred in their own exploitation film, *Chained for Life* (1950), a sad tale of the twins being tried for murder when one kills the jilting lover of the other. Advertising for *Chained for Life* drew on a common query of freakshow crowds: Could women who were forever joined find the love of a man (or be held jointly responsible if one of them is a murderer)? Grindhouse films shared also with freak shows a common effort to cover the exploitation with an educational or moral message. Finally, at the same time as the freak lost its gloss of middle-class respectability, human oddities appeared in exploitation and cult films as icons of transgressiveness, and this carried into the age of the

FIGURE 5.2 *Classic poster from the grindhouse cinema, featuring garish images and provocative words for a cautionary tale in the midst of a crusade against marijuana, 1936. Wikimedia Commons, personal collection.*

midnight movie. In Jodorowsky's *El Topo*, for example, an armless man and legless man join forces as one gunfighter.[27]

The increasingly grotesque character of carnival sideshows was also mirrored in another variation of the grindhouse circuit—the midnight ghost (or spook) shows. These "spookers" were magic shows that appeared after movie programs, becoming common in the 1940s. While early shows featured séances, later programs became more edgy with mock decapitations and buzz-saw mutilations, often ending with a blackout and ghostly images being projected on the walls. Ghosts shows became haunts of youth, whose unruliness, especially by the early 1950s, contributed to their decline. Still, they laid the foundation for the crowd participation of the midnight movies a generation later. And, while the spookers might have been taken seriously by some, they were camp for many others, just as was *Rocky* in the 1970s. More broadly, grindhouse also contained elements of naïve camp (for some of its first audience and then much more when seen again by the countercultural youth in the 1960s and 1970s).[28]

Gradually grindhouse (like the carnival freak show) lost its audience. After about 1959, these mostly merely suggestive exploitation films were replaced by the more explicit "sexploitation movies" that abandoned the educational pretense, though still were far from "hardcore" porn.[29] Even more as censorship rules were loosened with the rating system in 1968, the muted violence and mere titillation of grindhouse was replaced with gore and porn. But grindhouse features were sometimes revived, becoming cult features of the midnight movie and, with it, a camp aesthetic that sardonically embraced the "bad taste" of grindhouse.[30]

B-movie makers like Roger Corman at American International Pictures (AIP) also fed into the emerging culture of camp. From the mid-1950s, Corman specialized in car, motorcycle, and monster films (sometimes produced over a weekend) like the original *Fast and Furious* and *The Day the Earth Ended*. These movies were often seen in double features at drive-ins. In part, because the acting and special effects were so bad, Corman's early films were treated as "naïve camp" by "knowing" viewers as were the sexploitation movies of Russ Meyers. AIP progressively shifted to "intentional camp" in films that offered exaggerations of established genre (like Corman's *Wild Angels* of 1966, featuring a motorcycle gang of low lifes, with advertising that encouraged a camp response ("Their creed is violence . . . their bond is hate"). Other campy B-movies combined genre, featuring cinematic clichés, like the sex and horror themes (*Attack of the Fifty Foot Woman,* and *I Married a Monster from Outer Space*) that were intentionally and playfully "ridiculous or tawdry." Samuel Arhoff of AIP understood that "pseudo intellectuals" went to see his films "on the basis that they're campy, but also others go who take them seriously."[31]

What made the midnight cult movie somewhat different from Arhoff's drive-in feature was that the midnight movie attracted primarily a youth in rebellion from middle-class conformity and respectability. That culture was distinct from, but shared some attitudes with, the working-class audience of exploitation films. Midnight movie audiences were primarily white, educated, at least fairly affluent, mostly male, and predominately under thirty. As such, that crowd was probably more aware of the tongue-in-cheek messages of cult films, sharing some of the cultural background with older art film audiences, but still rejecting the elitist aesthetics of their elders. In its campish celebration of lowbrow, this audience claimed a unique identity as "freaks" distinct from the conformist herd. Yet, in their engagement with the grotesque and disgusting, they maintained a campish distance that separated them from the voyeurism of the carnival rube.[32]

Waters, Rocky Horror, and Camp Participation

This marriage of youth counterculture and camp took many forms. One of the most notable was the short-lived TV series *Batman* (1966–68), a spoof on action comics that many youths in the 1960s had grown up with. Famed for its cartoonish fight scenes with word bubbles shouting "Bang," *Batman* featured famous has-been actors like Burgess Meredith, Cesar Romero, Vincent Price, and Van Johnson that many young viewers had seen on the late show but now were portrayed in freakish and exaggerated roles.[33]

But camp (at least the intentional variety) was rare on television in the 1960s and 1970s. It remained best expressed in movies, especially cult films and their audiences of countercultural youth (often, but not always, seen at midnight). Obvious examples of camp are the films of John Waters and the apparently timeless *Rocky Horror Picture Show*. Waters's *Pink Flamingos* (1972), described by Waters himself as an "exercise in bad taste," is a feature-length display of the voluntary freak. Waters has no personal story of hardship or exotic upbringing. Unlike Ward Hall and so many other sideshow impresarios, he never ran away to the exotic (and traditional) world of the circus. Instead he grew up in the Baltimore suburbs and prided himself on including his neighborhood friends in his films. Yet, his movies are a mockery of that normality. He took his clue from seeing soft-core skin flicks of Russ Meyer at the drive-in. A central theme in *Pink Flamingos* is the story of Divine, who, with a son who sodomizes chickens, is challenged by a bizarre couple for the title of the "Filthiest person in the world." This couple kidnap teen girls, have them raped by a sadistic servant, and then sell the resulting babies to a lesbian couple in order to finance a heroin ring preying on preteen students. Absurdly campy. Divine (really Glen Milstead, a hairdresser) appears in Waters's films as an obese, middle-aged woman with a bouffant and arched eyebrows. In an interview in *Gay News* in 1977, Milstead admits to having no acting skills or even ambition to be a drag queen: "I may be a freak but at least I ain't dreary," he said. In this and a series of films culminating in a suburban spoof, *Polyester*, Waters played out his camp aesthetic on the screen. He was imitated by a wide variety of

FIGURE 5.3 *Poster for* The Screaming Skull *(1958). This is an example of the carnivalesque posters that advertised inexpensive horror films that AIP distributed. Note the promise to bury any viewers who died of fright seeing this movie. Employee(s) of National Screen Service Corp., Wikimedia Commons.*

B-movie makers who offered a wild mix of camp horror, action, comedy, suspense, sexploitation, and blaxploitation for theater audiences and after 1980 with the coming of VCR and later DVD for the home-viewing of weekend gatherings of bemused fans.[34]

While camp was embedded in the outrageous plots and characters in Waters's films, it was more clearly displayed in the behavior of the crowds at *The Rocky Horror Picture Show* (1975). It appeared on April Fool's Day in 1976 at the Waverly Theater in New York's Greenwich Village. *Rocky* soon gained a cult following playing continuously through the year. The story was certainly campy enough: A conventional white suburban couple, Brad and Janet, who are engaged to be married, find themselves seeking help in a mysterious castle after their car breaks down, only to be drawn into the convention-defying world of the transvestite Frank-N-Furter, leader of a band of aliens who are creating the perfect male, Rocky Horror, an updated freak show. Cheaply produced with a chaotic plot (including the seduction of the couple, Janet having sex with Rocky, and ending with the destruction of Frank and the castle, leaving Brad and Janet in the rubble).[35]

In classic camp form, the story was secondary to moments of recognition by a "knowing" crowd. For the sophisticated film buff (especially after seeing the movie multiple times), there were the real or imaged allusions to film classics. Film scholar Liz Locke found references to "Mae West and Elvis Presley movies, Roger Corman's biker flicks, gothic romances, Kubrick's Dr. Strangelove, strip-tease and cabaret shows, the Roman myth of Psyche and Amor, 1960's-style happenings, and daytime soap operas."[36]

Still, what brought in the crowds was the crowd itself. The movie had a lot of rock music and sexuality, but also plenty of opportunity for audience participation. By Halloween 1976, a crowd of regulars attended, dressed up in corsets and fishnets, fright wigs, and sequined jackets. Ardent fans formed a club and eventually held a fan convention. One survey of the audience found two-thirds had attended multiple viewings of the movie and half of these dressed in costume. Many came as a group. Movie goers brought props, lip-synced the dialog, or shouted obscenities at the characters on the screen (participating in "cosplay," costumed play acting). Some flooded the screen with flashlights to "help" Brad and Janet find their way in the dark and showered each other with water pistols (during a rain scene) and rice (at a wedding scene). As Liz Locke describes the process: The audience utilizes "intertextuality" to create "inter-performance." As she notes, fans

> gather up their props, put on stage make-up, outfit themselves (often in drag) and attend a film at which they shout instructions, comments, requests, mockeries, rhetorical questions, and appreciative catcalls . . . Many of the showings are prefaced by "pre-shows," usually involving the initiation of "virgins," and frequently involving costume competitions, trivia bowls, parodies of beauty contests, or skits incorporating material from other movie cults.[37]

Molly McCourt has characterized *The Rocky Horror Picture Show* as a revival of the medieval carnival. According to Sarah Cleary, the "immersion of mind and body" in the costumed audience's performance created moments of escape from the humdrum of daily life and the inversion of roles (as in carnival). Men could dress in corsets and everyone could gleefully parade in their underwear without anyone judging them and often joining in. Just like centuries-old carnival revelers' mocking traditional roles, contemporary cosplay released tension and repression.[38]

The difference is that the traditional carnival was infrequent, once or a few times a year, followed by the austerity of Lent and the constraints of a world confined by master–servant relations and routine. The modern-day carnival of *Rocky* spectacles is hardly rare. It is repeated in daily encounters with the carnivalesque in rule-breaking entertainment, perhaps on the weekend or the occasional visit to Las Vegas, but also on streaming TV. Another difference is that *Rocky* cosplay is camp, the crowd just pretending to be carnival revelers. The audience in the theater simultaneously treat the movie as a "sacred" text but also as a joke, the essence of the contemporary aesthetic of camp.

Of course, not all attendees at midnight movies and cult films saw them as camp. Yet the invitation to respond with bemused distance and to "put on the rube" permeated these movies. Camp challenged both the "taste" and taboos of the middle class as well as mocked the gawking voyeurism of the lower class. Disdain for both has continued to shape cultural rebellion to the present day. The embrace of camp expressed generational (and class) rejections of high modernism and sentimental populism; but it was also an attempt of a cohort of youth to bond around a unique identity.

Still, that bonding was usually from a distance and in a mock embrace. As David Church notes, the camp identification with the freak in *Freaks*, *Pink Flamingos*, or *Rocky Horror Picture Show* was always "temporary," a gesture, a "put on" that was limited to the brief years of youth or on Saturday night, not for the workweek, much less for life. And the very unseriousness of camp meant that there was no meaningful encounter with or challenge to the inequalities or the ostracism faced by the real freak or disabled. Jeffrey Sconce sees camp readings of freakery as a way for cultists to separate themselves from their "normal" backgrounds. These fans see freakery as a shorthand for weirdness and championing freaks allows them to transgress middle-class conformity. However, this game in the end reinforces that strangeness and abnormality imputed to real freaks rather than reduces their alienation, doing nothing to recognize the humanity of the disabled and outcaste.[39]

Trash TV and Camp Studio Audiences

While freakish movies became the quintessential site of the modern camp aesthetic, there was still another setting for the display of the oddity, which garnered a camp response—trash talk TV. While the midnight movie had its roots in the carnivalesque world of grindhouse and was adopted by countercultural youth, trash TV had its origins in the videoized homemaker magazine, a middle-class, mostly female, weekday afternoon venue set in the secure environs of the home. This was a far cry from the midnight movie— and the freak show. However, the wide-ranging influence of the freak and of its campish adaptation is revealed when this conventionally middle-class

FIGURE 5.4 *A gathering of costumed fans for the final viewing of* Rocky Horror Picture Show *at the Roxy Theater in Toronto (May 8, 1983). The movie had been playing for seven years. Frank Lennon/Toronto Star via Getty Images.*

programming was transformed in the mid-1990s into trash talk TV. The formula was simple: daily confessionals of psychological freaks, hosted by a cool, but enabling talker with plenty of reaction from a mock serious studio audience.

First, a few words about origins. Talk TV started out featuring a presumably unscripted conversation between host and guest, usually in front of a live audience. Phil Donahue fully developed it for the afternoon audience in 1967 on a Dayton Ohio TV station (syndicated nationally in 1970). Donahue cultivated a persona as a sensitive and tolerant male that reached mostly a homemaker audience. In contrast to the interview/entertainment programming of early talk TV, he opened his program to discussions of social and personal issues of interest to women (health and beauty topics), but also culturally controversial topics (birth control, abortion, atheism, and homosexuality), gradually introducing audience comments. In 1986, Donahue faced national competition from Oprah Winfrey (syndicated out of Chicago until 2011). Her story as an African American climbing up from poverty in Mississippi brought a more self-revelatory style. By 1994, Winfrey was outperforming Donahue in ratings (leading to his retirement in 1995). Others joined her, including Sally Jessy Raphael (1984–97), Geraldo Rivera (1987–98), and Ricki Lake (1993–2004), each offering increasingly more sensational programs that often appealed to a younger and more down-market crowd. Especially significant were the arrival of Jenny Jones (1991–2003) and Jerry Springer (1991–2018) who tipped the genre of talk TV into "trash" talk. They not only featured "fringe" guests (prostitutes, bigots, Satanists, and transgenders, for example) but also encouraged confrontations between guests (especially focusing on relationship betrayals, like setting a male porn star against his wife who was having a lesbian affair). By the mid-1990s there were fifteen such shows on national American TV. Before retiring, Donahue was forced to drop his relatively genteel programming for shock themes (announcing his plans to televise an execution of a criminal and wearing a skirt in a show devoted to cross-dressing).[40]

For their many critics, competition between the talk shows (increasingly called tabloid TV) produced a race to the bottom as increasingly tawdry and controversial guests were recruited to "excite" the audience and promote conflict. Donahue and Rivera claimed that they were only presenting the world as it is, rather than as the traditional tastemakers would have it. Springer, though an offspring of a respectable Jewish family, a law school graduate, and once mayor of Cincinnati (1977–84), even called himself a "ringmaster" in his autobiography (1990). Springer always kept his early commitment to liberal Democratic Party politics, but he readily admitted that his show was entertainment, a circus (but really a freak show). His guests often contacted the show for an opportunity to display their "bizarre or unusual lifestyles," creating an air of exhibitionism. Though certainly his producers set up the general theme of each show and directed its trajectory, there was no script; Springer claimed that he knew little about the guests before interviewing them (to be able to share the response of the audience). Springer famously always maintained a calm and collected manner, letting the guests shout at each other and the audience to take sides. Springer often finished the show with a prosocial speech: usually a salute to tolerance and humanity. He discouraged more than boos and cheers from the audience and, with the help of beefy security, he never let fist fly to excess between warring guests.[41]

Nevertheless, politicians (like conservative culture pundit William Bennett and two Democrats, Senator Joseph Lieberman and Secretary of Health and Human Services Donna Shalala) attacked tabloid TV as an affront to civility because these shows tolerated the use of crude language and aggression and for foregrounding formerly taboo themes. Academics Vicky Abt and Leonard Mustazza joined the choir, denouncing these programs as freak shows full of "disgusting talk, misinformation, hate talk (racism, anti-Semitism, sexism), poor English."[42]

Other academics rejected this critique and emphasized the diversity of voices on trash talk TV. They argued that these shows were really daily morality tales that featured genuine contemporary conflicts over behavior and lifestyle, often allowing the audience to defend their moral standards. While these programs sometimes were designed to shock audiences with boundary-breaking guests, many featured victims stating their grievances followed by a victimizer who is shamed by the audience.[43]

But here we need to look a little deeper to see how the trash talk show relates to our narrative about the irresistible freak: Was it a modern freak show? How did it introduce another form of camp? And ultimately how did trash talk present a new form of encountering the extraordinary body/ behavior?

It isn't surprising that Abt and Mustazza called *Springer* and other tabloid programs freak shows. Occasionally, these programs even featured carnival prodigy, including conjoined twins (the Gaylon brothers, the Jones sisters, and Lori and Dori Schappell, the second of which identified as a transgender). Other guests included bearded women and fat ladies—sometimes presented under humiliating program themes as in Richard Bey's 1999 show, "You're Too Fat for the Beach" or Ricki Lake's 1995 program "Mom, I Don't Want to Be Fat Like You." Professional freaks from Gibsonton, Florida also appeared on these programs. Talk TV often featured an insiders' view of the freaks' real lives and abandoned the traditional sideshow characterization of the fat lady as "jolly," for the cautionary or confrontational theme of women's and trash talk TV. Still the freaks on trash TV remained the fascinating but repulsive Other.[44]

More common on these shows were psychological freaks—whose unconventional behavior or lifestyle (sexual nonconformity or rare addictions especially) became the topic of self-disclosure and audience judgment in patter that mirrored the bally of the carnival. But things had changed. By the 1990s, gawking at people with birth defects or glandular or eating disorders no longer had much appeal. Even the *Schadenfreude* of knowing that at least you weren't like them was less attractive in an age when the anxiety of irregular birth and childhood development had declined. Instead, guests who had undergone "gender reassignment" or were "sexaholics" kept audiences glued to their TV sets. In the 1990s, such conditions were unusual enough, but still imaginable fates of ordinary viewers. Trash TV freaks (like the geeks on the midway) sometimes made a point of "pushing people's buttons," deliberately grossing out audiences as when a male in drag ostentatiously kissed another man on stage.[45]

Springer and the other hosts of talk TV drew on a growing distrust in mainstream media and appealed to Americans who might believe that Elvis had actually sang from the grave at Graceland. As Kevin Glynn notes, such programming indulged in "short-circuiting reason through excessive emotionality." These shows attracted viewers who were alienated from mainstream news programs where reporters used big words and made claims of "objectivity, detachment, and critical distance." All this gave voice to the bizarre and deviant, and to the priority of story over facts, prefiguring the sensationalism of many internet websites a few years later. This tabloidization in talk TV made it a new form of freak show.[46]

Tabloid talk TV shared still another trait with the traditional freak show—at least an occasional interjection of genteel and middle-class values if only as a respectable cover or to foster a clash of cultures. Like the old freak shows, talk hosts sometimes lent their voyeuristic programming a measure of traditional legitimacy by inviting willing medical and psychological experts to "explain" the behavior or condition of the guest. Middle-class values and judgments frequently entered the story line. Joshua Gamson notes a common strategy of programmers: "freakify [performing guests] to get viewers in the door," which the shows then "humanize to keep them there." And, remember Springer's habitual little "final thoughts" at the end of his often-wild shows. Typical was his comment after a show focused on strippers: "It's not bad money for just stripping oneself of one's clothes, but when you strip yourself of your dignity, is any amount worth it?"[47]

So, if trash talk shared much with the freak show, did it also become camp as did the grindhouse movie when it appeared at midnight theaters? Maybe not. Springer's producers found his over-the-top programming "exciting," not camp. Others simply found it real or simply entertaining— "both pleasurable and empowering," Gynn says that these shows denied the "reigning sense of normality." Julie Manga finds that Springer's viewers are "pulled in" as the sheer outrage and excitement "grabs their attention" with an "ecstatic haunting," freeing them from the dullness of their daily routines.[48] Not much sign of camp in this.

But there was more. First, there was a lot of camp in the presentation of tabloid TV hosts: Ricki Lake before launching her TV show appeared in John Water's films. Later, on TV, she mocked the pretension and puritanism of Oprah and Donahue. While Springer was always the voice of tolerance and gentle morality, his very position standing in the middle of the frequent chaos revealed a distancing and even suggested a lack of seriousness. For him, his show was a twenty-seven-year joke.

More important, the audience for tabloid TV extended beyond the modern-day rube, distrustful of elites. These shows appealed also to the young and probably more educated, who encountered the psychological freak less with a thrill than with bemusement. Popular writer Neal Gabler got it right when he argued in 1995 that the studio audience, not the guests (or host), were the real stars of the program. The out-of-control guest on the stage "creates a continuing sense of degeneracy for the viewing without implicating the viewer in it. The degeneracy is always kept at arm's length— the viewer's arm." The "freaks" on stage were "daily sacrificed to the larger middle-class good" embodied in the stage audience. And that "good" was the audience's amusement. Frequently, commentators noted that this audience was dominated by college students or the middle class, often in sharp contrast to the "trailer trash" on display. To some degree, the studio audience was the same crowd who performed at showings of *Rocky Horror Picture Show.* From a bemused distance, they appropriated the freak, simultaneously mocking the propriety and taste of their genteel predecessors and playing at being the rube gawking at the freak. In contrast to Donahue, Springer was less concerned about issues of discrimination and individual rights. Rather his guests were expected to "revel in their differences" and in the outrage of their often-overwrought conflicts (much as in professional wrestling). Seriousness disappeared with mock fights and deliberate attempts to outrage uptight America. Springer offered pleasure for the déclassé (as many note), but also campish amusement for "modern ironists to celebrate transgression for its own sake," as Louis Gates observes (1995).[49]

In many ways, the evolution of talk TV in the 1990s and early 2000s seems to reflect a broader trend: a shift from a middle-class (largely female) to déclassé audience as talk TV becomes a freak show. That was certainly the conclusion of moralistic critics like Bennett in the 1990s. Yet this thinking misses a step, the return of the middle class (or at least a rebellious, usually young part of it) to TV's new freak show—in the studio audience.

Moreover, TV added a new set of players—the audience in front of the set. Unlike the studio audience, these viewers were largely passive and somewhat bemused by the goings-on (according to Manga's research). This added a second layer of detachment and another way of appropriating the freak. This new crowd encountered TV freaks, not in festival (or annual carnival) time, but in daily, deracinated engagements that made for less mystery and wonder and with none of the crowd excitement and interaction experienced at the county fair. No longer was there a "need for dark spectacle" in the tawdry corners of "rickety" carnivals, notes journalist Charles Oliver, but the "dark, sleazy and the tawdry" could be seen "without leaving the safety of their homes." TV viewers experienced a superficial affect in ever-changing daily scenes as they switched channels to casually engage in several similar shows at once, much as is done today in channel surfing. Viewers gained access and privacy, but lost community, even if watching may have been a way of looking for that community. No longer was the transgressive contained in time and place, but accessed whenever and wherever, even as it lost its emotive force and meaning. While this genre has largely run its course, trash talk TV was the culmination of campified freak show and reappears in new forms with YouTube streaming and the internet.[50]

New Age Freak Shows

While the irrepressible freak appeared in the decades after 1960 across a wide range of media—from midnight movies to late afternoon talk—these encounters with the Other did not require face-to-face encounters with what an increasingly dominant middle America found disgusting and repulsive. However, the new age freak show that emerged in the 1990s offered paying crowds personal contact with the abject, but, in so doing, proved again the power of camp. Appearing as an offshoot of punk rock, a new generation of freaks met the "raw desire to subvert the drudgery of the ordinary order" according to J. Dee Hill, a sympathetic chronicler of the new age freak show. Although clearly imitating the acts and looks of the traditional freak show (tattooing, fire eating, and skin piercing, for example), the new freak performers were closer to grunge rockers than Ward Hall's band of carnival characters. Hill insists that the object was not to duplicate a largely traditional ensemble of oddities, but "to elevate play to a sort of guiding principle." These performers were young, with scarcely any ties to the old freak show. They did not learn their acts from sideshow veterans, but from books and each other. Many had middle-class backgrounds (even PhDs) and careers before they joined the alternative freak show. Hill claims that the new freaks engage in "explorations of subconscious, subterranean, and occasionally dark imaging" (whatever this means).[51] But all of this would make sense to Frank Zappa or R Crumb. And it shades into camp as a young generation recovered in unserious delight what their elders had abhorred.

Just as the traditional freak show was disappearing, out of a generation with few personal ties to the carnival and circus came a curious nostalgia for some elements of that tradition. This pattern of longing for an elder generation's memories is quite common (as when, beginning in the 1980s, young fans of the long-forgotten 1950s pin-up and bondage model Bettie Page made her a pop culture icon). Chris Fellner's "fanzine," home published on a mimeographed machine from 1995 to 1998, offered fellow "freakophiles" detailed and knowledgeable features on all aspects of the history of the freak show. Fellner's magazine shares much with other publications of amateur nostalgiacs—an antiquarian quest for recovering a lost world of commercial ephemera with an enthusiasm for mastering the last detail.[52] James Taylor's *Shocked and Amazed on and off the Midway* (2002) takes the point of view of the rube's excitement at the carnival. Taylor became well known for his "American Dime Museum," a small and short-lived effort to restore some of the glory of P. T. Barnum in Baltimore and then Washington DC storefronts. His museums included pickled punks, a mummified hand, and a stuffed five-legged cow. Similarly, Ricky Jay published a *Journal of Anomalies* (2003) that reprised the history of freaks from the eighteenth century. Both Taylor and Jay received much attention from the media. The press enjoyed "camping up" their reviews of Jay's catalog of oddities: The *Los Angeles Times* found it "perfectly pitched in luxuriant bombast" that allowed the "reader to ramble in his delicious overgrowth of detail and adjectives for surprises, conjunctures, possibilities"[53] Typical of camp, these efforts to introduce a new generation to the freak show were expressions of a playful and distant nostalgia for what has been judged as "bad taste" in the past, a rejection of "political correctness" and the dull rationality of the middle-American.

So, it isn't surprising that a group of young people with no personal contact with the historic freak show would try to revive it for real—after a fashion—as a campy demonstration of countercultural values in the new age freak show. Perhaps most notable is Jim Rose's Circus Sideshow that for twenty-five years toured the United States and the wider world. At various times it featured The Amazing Mister Lifto (Joe Hermann), who hung cinder blocks and beer kegs from his pierced nipples and genitalia, Bebe the Circus Queen (Beatrice Aschard, Rose's partner), who laid on a bed of nails while weights were placed on her chest, and The Tube (Matt Crowley) who had beer pumped down his throat, which he then regurgitated. Rose's freak show also included The Enigma (Paul Lawrence), notable for his body being

FIGURE 5.5 *"The Enigma," combining extreme tattooing with the classic act of sword swallowing, in a performance with Jim Rose's sideshow (1995). Joe McNally /Hulton Archive/Getty Images.*

completely tattooed in blue jigsaw puzzle pieces. In addition, he swallowed bugs and swords in classic "geek" fashion. Zamora the Torture King (Tim Cridland) combined the classic sword ladder and pincushion act with consuming broken lightbulbs and electrifying himself by touching a live wire, which illuminated a fluorescent light that he held in the other hand. Rose himself put his face in glass and lay on a bed of nails and asked the audience to stand on him. Like the others, he was no one-trick pony, serving also as a human "dart board" and conducting a blockhead routine. In a 1993 video, he promised entertainment that was not slick and contrived, but "live, real, raw, and dangerous."[54]

Many of these were standard sideshow acts (especially in the later carnival shows), though the performers were almost entirely made, rather than born, freaks. More important, they performed and were received in ways rather different from the traditional troupe of performers and rube audiences. Rose's story makes this clear. First, while Jim Rose worked in

Arizona fair carnivals as a teen, his side show training (first, as a fire eater) came from young street performers in Venice Beach in Los Angeles. Having a knack for commercial promotion, he and his wife Bebe moved to Seattle in 1989 to perform before the "tattooed, pierced eyebrows, studded-tongue crowd." Clearly aiming at participants in the "grunge" movement, Rose, at first, found it difficult to compete with the heavy metal band, Gwar, that "squirted fake blood on the crowd." However, in 1991, he found a venue at a cheap Middle Eastern restaurant, scoring a success with a crowd of "downtown hipsters . . . who'd never seen sideshows." Rose admits that his show was little more than a "campy version of the Venice Beach show," dressed up with a lot of swear words. However, his act got ever edgier. Rose ate not only fire but razor blades and his early associate, The Tube (Crowley), thrilled the grunge crowd by putting a condom in his mouth and blowing it out his nose. By 1992, Rose added the tattooed Enigma. He was not merely an exotic body, but later had horns implanted on his skull.[55] Rose moved up to rock clubs and auditorium venues and hired a juggler, magician, contortionist, and even a midget (a veteran from the Mills Circus). Then, his show went on a tour in the spring of 1992 in Canada, the Northeast United States, and even England, France, and Australia, playing mostly at rock clubs and on college stages. Rose's sideshow offered young crowds a "revolving door of performances, a kaleidoscope of wonderment so that audiences would never know what to expect." In July 1992, Rose's show gained fame when it appeared at the traveling music festival "Lollapalooza" that featured Red Hot Chili Peppers, Pearl, and other hot rock groups of the era. Soon Rose was noticed in *Rolling Stone* and the mainstream press. His show even appeared on tabloid talk TV (*Sally Jessy Raphael*) and was featured on various other TV shows, including an episode of the cartoon sitcom *The Simpsons*. In a 1993 interview, Rose called his show "the most popular, vulgar display since they outlawed public hanging."[56]

Other new age freak shows appeared in the 1990s. The most successful was probably the Bindlestiff Family Cirkus, famous not as family entertainment but as a "family" of countercultural freaks carrying on traditional sideshow and circus acts with a gender bending and otherwise transgressive playfulness. Bindlestiff was the 1995 creation of Keith Nelson, a college-educated street performer, and Stephanie Monseu, who had previously worked with Nelson in a sex-tinged act at East Village clubs. Nelson appeared as Mr. Pennygaff with a pierced tongue doing the blockhead and sword-swallowing acts. He also performed as Kinko (and sometimes as Kinkette), the down-and-out clown. Monseu appeared as a man in the role of Philomena Bindlestiff, the Cirkus's whip-snapping ringmaster, wearing a beat-up top hat and fake mustache. Monseu announced acts with much banter, but she also ate fire, swung on a trapeze, and spun plates on stilts. Adding to the mix was "Scotty Grabell, the gay Blue Bunny who did a campy juggling act and fire eating, a bearded lady who danced, joked, juggled, and ate lightbulbs, and a contortionist who slithered through a tennis racket. The Bindlestiff Family

Cirkus (in reference to the backpack of a hobo) combined the "lost" arts of vaudeville, the circus, and the sideshow, playing in a wide variety of settings (clubs, but also live theaters, college stages, and music festivals). In 1999, the group was incorporated as a nonprofit with a mission to teach circus acts to youth (among other things). The Cirkus has played at upscale venues like Avery Fisher Hall, the Burning Man Festival in Utah, and even Caribbean cruises. In 2018, Monseu joined the relatively traditional Big Apple Circus as ringmaster.[57] While the Cirkus went somewhat upscale and far afield after 2000, its roots were clearly in the punk world of New York clubs. Obviously kinky, but hardly serious, the Cirkus was received by the crowd as camp—a mockery of a circus tradition that long before had become a site of childhood and nostalgia.[58]

There were others: Circus Redickuless, Circus Contraption, Bros. Grim Circus Sideshow, and Circus Amok. As recently as 2018, the Hellzapoppin Circus Sideshow featured Shorty E. Dangerously, a legless man who walked on glass with his bare hands, the Lizard Man boasting tattooed scales, sharpened teeth, split tongue, and green ink lips, but who also did the blockhead and fire-eating acts, and the Illustrated Penguin, a reprise of a featured born-freak act, but with the added feature of being tattooed over his entire thirty-nine-inch-tall body.[59]

Rather different was the Coney Island Sideshow founded by Dick Zigun in 1985. With a master's degree from the Yale Drama School and a fixture at Coney Island since 1980, Zigun organized programs promoting Coney Island (the Mermaid Parade, for example). For decades, he served as a spokesperson for Coney and lectured student and community groups about its culture and history. Unlike other new age sideshows, Zigun long insisted that his ten-in-one revival was about skilled performance and appreciative audiences, not spectacle and gawking. At various times, the Coney Island Circus Sideshow has been supported by humanities grants from the national government and New York City's Department of Cultural Affairs. Most of its ever-changing acts have been traditional, but self-made, freaks: snake-handlers, contortionists, and illusionists, but also blade walkers and worm eaters. The Sideshow occasionally included born-freaks, such as Koko the dwarf clown or Jennifer Miller the bearded lady. Visitors to the Sideshow over the years have noted, however, that the crowd is hardly the same as that of the traditional freak show. One described it as "mixed group of heckling teenagers, punk couples on dates, bemused family groups." And in my two visits to the show, I found that, while the acts were hardly as outlandish as those of Rose or the Bindlestiff Family, the "talker" adopted a clearly campy tone in his over-the-top presentation, to which the audience (of teens, hipsters, and a few "hip" families) responded as if they were dumbfounded country rubes embracing the show as wonder.[60]

The new freak show has a curious relationship with the past. Its proponents like Rose and Katherine Dunne (author of *Geek Love*) have criticized the traditional freak show for its greedy operators, who were essentially fakes.

Rose saw the born freak of the traditional spectacle as outdated, retired to "Florida Trailer parks or institutional moldering." By contrast, Rose's troupe were artists "exploring the limits of physical possibility" in their body-invasive performances. Rose admitted that he learned from Ripley, Barnum, and Houdini. But he also learned from his contemporaries, Howard Stern, Evel Knievel, and Don King, all playful promoters of outrage in defiance of respectability. Rose toured rock clubs and college venues, not the sideshow of circus acts and carnival rides, but sites of youthful rebellion, drugs, and transgressive music.[61]

Like the 1960s countercultural freaks, Rose claimed that his troupe were refugees from "a larger community in which the individual is shunned . . . for his or her peculiarities." However, in the show they formed a "smaller community in which those peculiarities are embraced. It's about relationships, not just physical anomalies." The troupe of circus or carnival freaks might have said something similar about their "community," but most of them were born outcastes, not adult volunteers for freakdom as were Rose's team. Moreover, Rose's family of performers presumably shared that feeling of alienation with the "latent freaks" in the crowd. The gawking throng at the country carnival had nothing in common with the geek in the pit (or so Rose thought). In 1992, Rose claimed that his show was "by freaks for freaks" a far cry from the language of the traditional showman with his characterization of the crowd as a "mark." Finally, new age audience were mostly pretending to be outcastes, but, in reality, were often economically secure and decidedly weekend freaks. Many paid large admissions, not only at rock clubs but at events like Rainbow Family Gatherings (rural summer meetings of peace-promoting hippies and their descendants) or even the Burning Man Festival (somewhat more upscale) to see Rose's sideshow. Few shared much with the country rube who paid twenty-five cents to see a geek eat mice at the country fair fifty years ago.[62]

This brings us back to the essential campishness of the new age freak show. Though obviously commercial, Rose and his associates talked the language of anti-commercialism. They claimed to be doing what they wanted rather than to please the audience. This tone replaced the pretense of moral uplift or education. Everyone knew that the moral cover was phony. Rose instead promised authenticity as well as wonder in his self-assumed anti-commercial program. But, in fact, the whole show was an extended campish joke. Like the traditional bally, the pitch of the "ringmaster" was hyperbolic, but in the new version, it was often excessive and mocking: Rose claimed that his troupe were "performing mind boggling physical miracles that make audiences eyes pop out or roll back in a dead faint." Even their oft-stated objective of "grossing out" the crowd was something of a put-on. Rose claimed that "The Tube" was triumphant when he regurgitated beer accompanied with "moans and groans" from the first row of the audience. For Rose, fainters and "hurlers" (who vomited) were part of the act. At the end of the show when Rose placed his body on cut glass, there was seldom

FIGURE 5.6 *Latter-day Coney Island freak show (2006) appealing to the nostalgic and camp crowd. David Shankbone, Wikimedia, Creative Commons Attribution 2.5.*

a shortage of volunteers to join in the fun of stomping on Rose's face in glass. But it was a game, a campish collective shout of crudity and bad taste/ behavior. The performing audience found that the show let them abandon temporarily their "repressed" civil behavior, but none of it was serious.[63]

Both the cute and camp challenged bourgeois culture and its rejection of the carnival freak, the cute largely from within the bounds of middle-class respectability and the camp from a claim of being outside those walls. Yet neither the cute nor the camp ultimately broke from middle-class expectations. Both offered relief from the limits and disappointments of middle-class culture and a way back to the carnivalesque. The cute found that escape in the miniature, a flight from the disappointments of work and consumption even while never abandoning either. Camp instead offered those who rejected and were rejected by middle-class respectability (especially the young) an alternative to the cute: an escape from consumer conformity through a flight back to the carnival. However, this was temporary, and the practitioners of camp came to the carnival not as "pitiful" freaks or gawking rubes, but as simply play-acting them.

Both solutions emerged from the satiation produced by modern consumption: The cute offered desire and delight renewed in the form of the midget and later media surrogates, often accompanied with a gazing child. Camp refurbished desire in commercialized "hits" of disdainful distancing pleasure that sometimes included a put on of both the freak and the rube. Like the cute, the camp mode was easily coopted by commercial entertainment, even if that pleasure took a mock rebellious form in freakdom.

Finally, there was yet another way in which the freak proved to be irrepressible; and this too was part of a culture of jaded consumerism—a return to still another feature of the freak culture of the past—the creepy. And this took the form of ratcheting up the visceral response to the freak, turning the disgust at the sight of *Freaks* from 1932 into the thrill of confronting the zombie in *Night of the Living Dead* in 1968.

Notes

1 Louis Rubin, "Susan Sontag and the Camp Followers," *Sewanee Review*, 82, 3 (Summer 1974): 503–10; Mark Booth, *Camp* (London: Quartet Books, 1983), 2, 11; Susan Sontag, "Notes on Camp," in *Susan Sontag Reader*, Susan Sontag, ed. (New York: Vintage, 1983), 117; Humberto Eco, *On Ugliness* (London: Rizzoli, 2011), Chapter 13.

2 Sontag, "Notes on Camp," 115, 107–8, 114–19; Juliane Rebentisch, "Camp Modernism," *Criticism*, 56, 2 (Spring 2014): 235–48; Anna Malinowska, "Bad Romance: Pop and Camp in Light of Evolutionary Confusion," in *Redefining Kitsch and Camp in Literature and Culture*, Justyna Stepien, ed. (Newcastle: Cambridge Scholars, 2014), 12.

3 Sontag, "Notes on Camp," 113–14; Eco, *On Ugliness*, 417; Ken Feil, *Dying for a Laugh: Disaster Movies and the Camp Imagination* (Middletown, CT: Wesleyan University Press, 2005), xiv.

4 Of course, camp creations have often been associated with the gay and Jewish experience. Sontag attributes this to the affinity for sensibility in these groups that allows them to enter mainstream society; and for gays the desire to perpetuate youth. Sontag, "Notes on Camp," 109, 110, 117–18; Eco, *On Ugliness*, 411. Booth, *Camp*, 29–32. The links between gay and camp culture are analyzed in Moe Meyer, ed. *Politics and Poetics of Camp* (London: Routledge, 1994); Fabio Cleto, ed., *Camp: Queer Aesthetics and the Performing Subject* (Ann Arbor: University of Michigan Press, 1999). Often the linkage between camp and queer culture is attributed to Christopher Isherwood's *World in the Evening* (1954).

5 Booth, *Camp*, 17, 30; Greg Taylor, *Artists in the Audience: Cults, Camp, and American Film Criticism* (Princeton, NJ: Princeton University Press, 1999), 52. Note also Philip Core, *Camp: The Lie that Tells the Truth* (London: Plexus, 1984); Andrew Ross, "Uses of Camp," in Cleto, ed., *Camp*, 317.

6 Booth, *Camp*, 22–6, 77–8.

7 Booth, *Camp*, 87, 116, 132, 150, 152, 181–3, 179. Another less judgmental take on camp is in Andrew Ross, *No Respect: Intellectuals and Popular Culture* (New York: Routledge, 1989), 136–53.

8 Eco, *On Ugliness*, 408.

9 Rachel Adams, *Sideshow U.S.A.: Freaks and the American Cultural Imagination* (Chicago: University of Chicago Press, 2001), 13.

10 Sontag," Notes on Camp," 11, 4–17; Michael Dango, "Camp's Distribution: 'Our Aesthetic Category,'" *Social Text*, 35, 2 (June 2017): 39–67.

11 Quotations from Gene Thornton, "Diane Arbus: The Subject was Freaks," *New York Times*, August 22, 1971, D12 and Hilton Kramer, "From Fashion to Freak," *New York Times*, November 15, 1971, SM 38. Note also Jack Hunter, *Freak Babylon: An Illustrated History of Teratology and Freakshows* (New York: Creation, 2014), 106–9; Michael Hardin, "Fundamentally Freaky: Collapsing the Freak/Norm Binary in Geek Love," *Critique*, 45, 2 (Summer 2004): 337–46; Katherine Dunn, *Geek Love* (New York: Knopf, 1989); Rachel Adams, "An American Tail: Freaks, Gender, and the Incorporation of History in Katherine Dunn's Geek Love," in *Freakery: Cultural Spectacles of the Extraordinary Body*, Rosemarie Garland Thomson, ed. (New York: New York University Press, 1996), 277–90.

12 Daniel Foss, *Freak Culture* (New York: Dutton, 1972), 132, 145–80. Less positive views are found in Leslie Fiedler, *Freaks: Myths and Images of the Secret Self* (New York: Simon and Schuster, 1976), 306.

13 Fiedler, *Freaks*, 13–14; Robert Bogdan, *Freak Show: Presenting Human Oddities for Amusement and Profit* (Chicago: University of Chicago Press, 1988), 2.

14 Michael Chemers, *Staging Stigma: A Critical Examination of the American Freak Show* (London: Palgrave, 2008), Chapter 1; Zappa quotation in Foss, *Freak Culture*, 135 (also in http://aln2.albumlinernotes.com/Freak_Out_.html).

15 Gary Groth, *Complete Crumb Comics, Vol. 4, The Sixties* (Seattle: Fantagraphics Books, 2009), preface; Jean Pierre Mercier, *Who's Afraid of R Crumb: R Crumb Conversations* (Jackson: University Press of Mississippi, 2004), 191–223; Gary Griffith, "Truckin' Along with R. Crumb or Something," in *R. Crumb: Conversations*, D. K. Holm, ed. (Jackson: University Press of Mississippi, 2004), 6; Edward Shannon, "Shameful, Impure Art: Robert Crumb's Autobiographical Comics and the Confessional Poets," *Biography*, 35, 4 (Fall 2012): 627–49.

16 Tom Wolfe, *The Kandy-Kolored Tangerine-Flake Streamline Baby* (New York: Noonday, 1963), 87–98.

17 Obituaries for Ed Roth: *Baltimore City Paper*, December 12, 2001, 4; *Los Angeles Times*, April 6, 2001, B6; *The Washington Post*, April 7, 2001, B7; *New York Times*, April 7, 2001, B6.

18 Foss, *Freak Culture*, 199–202.

19 Fiedler, *Freaks*, 18–19; Vincent Canby, "Why *Freaks* is Still a Great Horror Film," *New York Times*, November 11, 1970, 103; Hunter, *Freak Babylon*,

150–1, 106; J. Hoberman and Jonathan Rosenbaum, *Midnight Movies* (New York: Harper and Row, 1983), 95, 99; James Monaco, *American Film* (New York: New American Library, 1979), 66.

20 Hoberman and Rosenbaum, *Midnight Movies*, 30; David Gomery, *Shared Pleasures: The History of Movie Exhibition in the United States* (Madison: University of Wisconsin Press, 1992), 194.

21 Harry Benshoff, "1966: Movies and Camp," in *American Cinema in the 1960s*, Benny Grant, ed. (New Brunswick, NJ: Rutgers University Press, 2008), 150; Lawrence Cohen, "Ten Years of Off-Beat Midnight Movies," *Variety*, November 11, 1980, 36.

22 Eco, *On Ugliness*, 423; Michael Wolff, "So What Do You Do at Midnight: You See a Trashy Movie," *New York Times*, September 7, 1975, 121.

23 Benshoff, "1966: Movies and Camp," 150; Jim Anderson, "Grossing Out Replaces Making Out at the Movies," *Chicago Tribune*, August 17, 1978, S2, 7.

24 Eric Schaefer, *"Bold! Daring! Shocking! True!" A History of Exploitation Films, 1919–1959* (Durham, NC: Duke University Press, 1999), 103.

25 Schaefer, *"Bold! Daring! Shocking! True!,"* Chapter 1, 103, 106–13, 129, Chapter 9; Glenn Ward, "Grinding Out the Grind House: Exploitation, Myth, and Memory," in *Grindhouse: Cultural Exchange on 42nd Street, and Beyond,* Austin Fish and Johnny Walker, eds. (New York: Bloomsbury, 2016), 13–30.

26 David Church, "Freakery, Cult Films, and the Problem of Ambivalence," *Journal of Film and Video*, 63, 1 (Spring 2011): 3–17; Martin Norden, *The Cinema of Isolation: A History of Physical Disability in the Movies* (New Brunswick, NJ: Rutgers University Press, 1994), 68, 71.

27 David F. Friedman, *A Youth in Babylon: Confessions of a Trash-Film King* (Buffalo, NY: Prometheus, 1990), 172; Church, "Freakery, Cult Films," 3–17; Schaefer, *"Bold! Daring! Shocking! True!,"* 7.

28 Fred Nadis, *Wonder Shows: Performing Science, Magic, and Religion in America* (New Brunswick, NJ: Rutgers University Press, 2005), Chapter 2; LeRoy Ashby, *With Amusement for All: A History of American Popular Culture since 1830* (Lexington: University Press of Kentucky, 2006), 206; Beth A. Kattelman, "Magic, Monsters, and Movies: America's Midnight Ghost Shows," *Theatre Journal*, 62, 1 (2010): 23–39.

29 Sexploitation may have begun with Rus Meyer's *The Immoral Mr. Teas* (1959) that made no moral pretense and instead "played for ironic laughs" as Mr. Teas stumbles through sexually charged but still non-explicit situations. Schaefer, *"Bold! Daring! Shocking! True!,"* 337–8.

30 Schaefer, *"Bold! Daring! Shocking! True!,"* 39, 340; Hoberman, *Midnight Movies*, 39–76; Robert Weiner, "The Prince of Exploitation: Dwain Esper," in *From the Arthouse to the Grindhouse,* John Cline and Robert Weiner, eds. (Lanham, MD: Scarecrow Press, 2010), 41–56.

31 Benshoff, "1966: Movies and Camp," 165; Arhoff cited in Hoberman and Rosenbaum, *Midnight Movies,* 116.

32 Mark Jancovich, "Cult Fictions: Cult Movies, Subcultural Capital, and the Production of Cultural Distinctions," *Cultural Studies*, 16, 2 (2002): 306–22;

Church, "Freakery, Cult Films," 3–17; Barry K. Grant, "Second Thoughts on Double Features: Revisiting the Cult Film," in *Unruly Pleasures: The Cult Film and Its Critics*, Xavier Mendik and Graeme Harper, eds. (Guildford: FAB Press, 2000), 122–37; Jacinda Read, "The Cult of Masculinity: From Fan Boys to Academic Bad-Boys," in *Defining Cult Movies: The Cultural Politics of Oppositional Taste*, Mark Jancovich et al., eds. (Manchester: Manchester University Press, 2003), 54–70.

33 Hoberman and Rosenbaum, *Midnight Movies*, 116; Benshoff, "1966: Movies and Camp," 156.

34 John Waters, *Shock Value* (New York: Dell, 1981); Maralyn Polak, "Interview: John Waters," *Philadelphia Inquirer*, May 23, 1976, 8; "Pink Flamingos," *Gay News,* December 15, 1977, 31; "Divine," *Gay News*, June 30, 1977, 24.

35 Hoberman and Rosenbaum, *Midnight Movies*, 5–6, 14.

36 Liz Locke, "Don't Dream It, Be It: *The Rocky Horror Picture Show* as Cultural Performance," *New Directions in Folklore*, 3 (May–June 1999): 1–21, quotations on 6, https://scholarworks.iu.edu/journals/index.php/ndif/article/view/19866/25961.

37 Bruce Austin, "Portrait of a Cult Film: *Rocky Horror Picture Show*," *Journal of Communication,* 31, 2 (June 1981): 43–54; Patrick Kinkade, "Toward a Sociology of Cult Films," *Sociological Quarterly*, 33, 2 (Summer 1992): 191–209; Locke, "Don't Dream It," 2; Sal Piro, *Creatures of the Night: The Rocky Horror Picture Show Experience* (Redford, MI: Stabur Press, 1990). Fan site: http://www.rockyhorror.com).

38 Molly McCourt, "Strange Journey: Finding Carnival in the *Rocky Horror Picture Show*," 49–57; Sarah Cleary, "Don't Dream it, Be It," 109–17, quotation on 113 both in *Fan Phenomena: The Rocky Horror Picture Show,* Marisa Hayes, ed. (Chicago: University of Chicago Press, 2015).

39 David Church, "Freakery, Cult Films," 3–4; Jeffrey Sconce, "'Trashing' the Academy: Taste, Excess, and an Emerging Politics of Cinematic Style," *Screen*, 36, 4 (1995): 371–93.

40 Wendy Munson, *All Talk: The Talk Show in Media Culture* (Philadelphia, PA: Temple University Press, 1993), Chapter 1; Julie Manga, *Talking Trash: Cult Politics of Daytime TV Talk Shows* (New York: New York University Press, 2003), 24–5; Phil Donahue, *My Own Story* (New York: Simon and Schuster, 1974); Howard Kurtz, *Hot Air: All Talk All the Time* (New York: Basic Books, 1996), 49–52, 59, 65; Jane Shattuc, *Talking Cure: Talk Shows and Women* (New York: Routledge, 1997), 1; Monica Collins, "Real Sick Freak Shows," *Boston Herald*, February 16, 1995, 59; Kathleen Lowney, *Baring our Souls: TV Talk Shows and the Religion of Recovery* (New York: Aldine De Gruyter, 1999). 55.

41 Jerry Springer, *Ringmaster* (New York: St. Martin's, 1998), 16, 45, 71–92, 101, 107.

42 William Bennett, "In Civil Society, Shame has its Place," *Los Angeles Times*, January 26, 1996, B9; Jonathan Alter, "Talk Shows," *Newsweek,* November 6, 1995, 46; Vicki Abt and Leonard Mustazza, *Coming after Oprah: Cultural Fallout in the Age of the TV Talk Show* (New York: Popular Press, 1997)

4, 26, 88; Manga, *Talking Trash*, 42–5; Kevin Glynn, *Tabloid Culture: Trash Taste, Popular Power, and the Transformation of American Television* (Durham, NC: Duke University Press, 2000), 184; Shattuc, *Talking Cure*, 171; Bernard Timberg, *Television Talk: A History of the TV Talk Show* (Austin: University of Texas Press, 2002), 176–7.

43 Paolo Carpignano, "Chatter in the Age of Electronic Reproduction," *Social Text*, 25, 6 (1990): 33–55; Gini Scott, *Can We Talk?: The Power and Influence of Talk Shows* (New York: Insight Books, 1996), 295–6; Andrew Tolson, "Introduction," in *Television Talk Shows*, Andrew Tolson, ed. (London: Erlbaum, 2001), 9–16.

44 "Notes from the Back," 11, *Freaks*, November 1997, 37 (Ringling Art Library, Sarasota, FL); Andrea Dennett, *Weird and Wonderful: The Dime Museum in America* (New York: New York University Press, 1997), 323; Laura Grindstaff, *The Money Shot: Trash, Class and the Making of TV Talk Shows* (Chicago: University of Chicago Press, 2002), 22.

45 Dennett, *Weird and Wonderful*, 142, 320; Joshua Gamson, *Freaks Talk Back: Tabloid Talk Shows and Sexual Nonconformity* (Chicago: University of Chicago Press, 1998), 165–7.

46 Glynn, *Tabloid Culture*, 4–7, 22–44, 143–4.

47 Dennett, *Weird and Wonderful*, 321; Gamson, *Freaks Talk Back*, 36–40, quotation on 166; Springer, *Ringmaster*, 151, 171–2, quotation on 238.

48 Springer, *Ringmaster*, 133, 160–1; Glynn, *Tabloid Culture*, 146–7; Manga, *Talking Trash*, 187–9.

49 Neal Gabler, "Talk Show Freak Shows," *Pittsburgh Post-Gazette*, March 26, 1995, F1; Louis Gates, "13 Ways of Looking at a Black Man," *New Yorker*, October 23, 1995, 60 cited in Shattuc, *Talking Cure*, 165–7.

50 Charles Oliver, "Television Freak Shows," *Daily News of Los Angeles*, April 2, 1995, V5; Manga, *Talking Trash*, Chapter 3; 113–4, 178–9, 195.

51 J. Dee Hill, *Freaks and Fire: The Underground Reinvention of the Circus* (New York: Soft Skull Press, 2004), 16, 18.

52 Chris Fellner, *Freaks*, 1, May 1995, Ringling Museum Art Library. The fanzine ended in November 1998; Chemers, *Staging Stigma*, 31–9.

53 Quoted (without citation) in Jay Ricky, *Jay Ricky's Journal of Anomalies* (New York: Quantuck Lane Press, 2003), 1–2; Jay Ricky, *Learned Pigs and Fireproof Women* (New York: Warner Books, 1986).

54 Hill, *Freaks and Fire*, 141; Jim Rose, *Freaks Like Me* (New York: Dell, 1995), 34, 103, 161; A. W. Stencell, *Circus and Carnival Ballyhoo: Sideshow Freaks, Jabbers and Blade Box Queens* (Toronto: ECW Press, 2010), 352; "The Jim Rose Circus Sideshow - 1993-Full Video. Beauuutiful," https://www.youtube.com/watch?v=DiclO5DQMcw.

55 Rose, *Freaks Like Me*, 34, 96–100, 103; Hill, *Freaks and Fire*, 55–6, 62–3, 68.

56 Rose, *Freaks Like Me*, 103–4, 108, 117–19, 125, 153; Kit Boss, "Freak Love," *Seattle Times*, July 17, 1992, 12.

57 Bindlestiff Family Cirkus website, http://www.bindlestiff.org/about/; Jay Blotcher, "Chaos with Purpose: The Redeeming Social Value of Bindlestiff

Family Cirkus," *Roll Magazine*, March 2011, http://www.rollmagazine.com/ar chive/mar11/articles/theatre.php.

58 "Bindlestiff Family Cirkus," *Wisconsin State Journal*, August 3, 2000, 22; Chauncey Hollingsworth, "The Oddest Show on Earth," *Chicago Tribune*, October 16, 1997, 1, 5; "The Magic Hat Bindlestiff Family Cirkus Summer Variety Show Tour!," *Business Wire,* June 1, 2006, 1; "Circus in Review," *Bandwagon,* March 4, 2006, 20; Hill, *Freaks and Fire*, 127, 131.

59 Hellzapoppin Circus Sideshow website: https://www.hellzapoppin.com/; George Archibald, "Bryce 'The Govna' Graves of Hellzapoppin Circus Sideshow," February 12, 2018, https://killthemusic.net/blog/interview-bryce -the-govna-graves-of-hellzapoppin-circus-sideshow; Hill, *Freaks and Fire*, 13–14, 59–70.

60 Elizabeth Stephens, "Cultural Fixions of the Freak Body: Coney Island and the Postmodern Sideshow," *Continuum: Journal of Media & Cultural Studies*, 20, 4 (December 2006): 485–98; 2019; "Coney Island Sideshow" website: https:// www.coneyisland.com/programs/coney-island-circus-sideshow.

61 Lenny Stoute, "Sideshow Gets Set to Freakout," *Toronto Star,* April 9, 1992, H3; Rose, *Freaks Like Me,* Dunn, "Introduction," 10, 119, 147.

62 Hill, *Freaks and Fire,* xi–xii.

63 Interview with Jim Rose, *St Paul Pioneer Press*, August 23, 1992, 113; Rose, *Freaks Like Me,* back cover; Hill, *Freaks and Fire,* 136.

6

The Creepy

Freaks as Flesh-Eating Zombies

The surge of shock in 1960s movies is still another manifestation of the irresistible freak. This intensification has its roots in the Gothic horror film tradition of the 1930s and 1940s of which *Freaks* was a part and extended into the sci-fi monster movies and horror classics of the Hammer Film Productions of Britain of the 1950s and 1960s. However, these films were constrained by the Production Code Administration, to which major studios subscribed, and more broadly by the same taste standards that made freak shows taboo. From the end of the 1960s, however, with the loosening of censorship and the rise of a countercultural audience, the old horror was often viewed by young audiences as camp while a new brand of horror eliminated many of the old boundaries, meeting the desire of new audiences to be grossed or creeped out. Again, irrepressible freaks.

A huge literature analyzes this transition that culminated in the 1970s. I will not try to best, much less systematically challenge, these writings (though I will draw on many for my own interpretation). Students of horror usually zero in on the horror narrative, the psychosocial meanings of encounters between the monster and the victim in the light of the literary history of the genre. Instead, I will focus on a sometimes neglected, but still complex, trend: the increasing intensity and pace of the cinematic evocation of fear, shock, disgust, the uncanny, and other emotions as audiences encounter the monster. These efforts at evoking the creepy shared with, but ultimately far outdistanced, the emotions aroused in *Freaks* and freak shows.

My starting point is simple: Horror met two irrepressible psychological needs. The first, inherited from our distant ancestors, was to encounter and prevail over the outside threat, the predator. The second was to confront the abject figure or situation that challenges our understanding of normality. The first commonly evokes fear and the second, disgust. Pleasure comes in surviving these experiences when they are simulations. In effect, the genteel attempt to ban this longing to be scared by the creepy and to show that one can "take it" ran against powerful impulses, rooted in evolution or in centuries of culture. What shocked and disgusted sensibilities in the freak show could not be suppressed. It had to be confronted and enjoyed.

But why did the liberation of fear and disgust come about so forcefully and vividly at the end of the 1960s as it obviously did with films like *Night of the Living Dead*? A simple claim of evolutionary anthropology doesn't fully explain this. Why is the attraction to the scary not constant over history? Marxian/Freudian theories of super-repression (as promoted by film historian Robin Wood) claim that cultural and political controls that had long dampened down these impulses (often identified with sexuality) were released.

But why did this release of the creepy occur when it did and why hasn't there been a return to cultural repression since then? Historians generally agree that the lifting of censorship from above in the late 1960s (along with economic pressure on the studios) reduced the power of the genteel admonition against horror. At the same time came countercultural pressure from below: Children of the middle class rejected their elders' abhorrence of the freak, expressing a willingness, even desire, to encounter the fearful and repulsive, made possible by the realistic illusions created by motion pictures.

But this surge of shock didn't disappear, as one might have expected, when it no longer was a novelty or when the boomer generation of thrill seekers grew up and retreated to the suburbs and television. Despite the nostalgic call for a return to the "50s" in the 1970s and the retrogressive appeals of the Reagan 80s, there was no restitution of the old "repression." Instead, the mechanisms for evoking shock, fear, and disgust escalated in the decades following the 1960s, not despite, but because, the shock culture had become jaded. While the old freak show flourished in a world where encounters with the exotic were rare and seasonal, the "new" display of cinematic monsters became an everyday occurrence, inevitably leading to consumer satiation. With this came the need to invent new, still more intense, forms of excitation in slasher films and digitized gore.

Ultimately, I argue, that this seeking of the gross out was more than a countercultural rejection of middle-class taboos or even an expression of the self-interest of moviemakers. It was a product of a long trend in consumer culture that escalated in the era of the counterculture and loosened controls. With Robert Proctor, I find that consumer culture was rooted in the packaging of sensations in new consumer goods that began around 1900. This coincided with the emergence of the first movies that featured visual effects, stimulating a sensual and emotional response, especially in the form of horror. And this potential was finally realized by the 1970s, when visual action in films came to prevail over dialog in many movies and, with it, the rush to intensification. All this made the traditional freak show tame and even boring.[1]

Across the last century, horror movies (and before that commercialized freak shows) were really a part of a broader trend toward the packaging of sensual intensity. A veritable assembly line of horror fully emerged by the late 1960s that offered a nearly predictable parade of "hits" of shock, disgust, and fright. In many ways, these consumptive pleasure points were more important that the oft-analyzed narratives of horror spectacles—at least to audiences. This drive toward the outer edge of the creepy was part of the logic of fast capitalism and was linked to a wide range of commercialized experience—from the surge of tubular roller coasters and the increasing kills of action-adventure films to the high of recreational drugs and even the accelerated pace of TV sitcoms and advertising. The return of the freak in post-1968 creepy horror was part of a broader intensification and acceleration of fast capitalism. The new monsters took the old freak show to new levels of fear and disgust that made it hardly recognizable.

There were, however, limits, both emotionally and aesthetically, to this drift to the edge, even for seasoned and jaded audiences. The creepy in the late twentieth century was modulated with the camp and other genres that mollified the dreariness of horror and its unrelieved intensity. In a focused analysis, intended for the general reader, I will explore the contours of this third element in the irrepressible appeal of the freak—the creepy.

Why Horror and Why Pleasurable

For me, horror, like the freak show, is best understood as an audience response. As James Twitchell notes, the Latin origin of the word *horrere* means to bristle, as in hair standing on end in the shivering of excitement when encountering the terrifying. The constricting of skin creates a "ripple sensation," the creeping flesh (the creeps or creepy). This is a biological response of self-defense automatically produced when encountering a life-threatening event, especially a predator, the most obvious object of horror. Biologically, the creeps is part of the process of the body producing the chemicals needed to respond with "fight or flight" when facing danger.[2] Horror as art or entertainment then is ultimately about arousing in audiences the sensation of facing and fearing death. Evoking fear, of course, is a complex business: This encounter can be attractive as well as repulsive, even when it makes us feel powerless.[3]

The object of fear takes many forms, only one of which is the classical freak (and then often mixed with other responses). But the most basic instigator of fear is the predator. The evolutionary approach of Mathias Clasen elucidates the centrality of predation in horror. In contrast to most horror scholars, Clasen emphasizes how horror fiction targets biologically rooted defense mechanisms by "activating supersensitive danger-detection circuits" in the brain. These originated in "vertebrate evolution" that helped our hominid ancestors survive when they were prey, before they evolved into predators. While the object of fright has changed over time, it isn't arbitrary or simply "socially constructed." Even modern humans remain fearful of snakes and reptiles in dark bodies of water just as did our ancestors who spent 2.5 million years close to these dangers; and we respond forcefully to the cinematic settings of jungles or forests where we identify with human prey (featured in *Cabin in the Woods, Lake Placid*, etc.). We fear what our forest-dwelling ancestors feared much more than what today are real threats—speeding automobiles or even guns. We have inherited immediate, prerational responses to the unexpected—sudden noises, looming objects. Like our ancestors, we are "trip wired for agency detection"—we expect nature to be intentional (even out to get us), making us proto-animistic, with a proclivity to believe in ghosts, demons, or other supernatural forces intent on harming (though more rarely helping) us. And we have evolved, Clasen notes, to be repulsed by that which can cause us disease and death: feces, vomit, and decomposing flesh.[4] Not only has biology given us a physiological proclivity to reacting to predation (in both fear and exhilaration) but so has history as in the initiation rites of many premodern cultures, blood sports (e.g., cock fighting), gladiator games, and, of course, horror films.[5]

Clasen, like others that stress the evolutionary roots of horror, is critical of psychological (especially Freudian) explanations, purely historical understandings (claiming that horror was a literary reaction to the Enlightenment), and claims that the monster is always dependent upon the cultural context.[6] He notes that these interpretations don't explain the mechanisms of fright; instead, their arguments often reveal more about the intellectual politics of horror scholars than the biologically rooted experience of horror viewers.

I agree with this perspective, but I think that it best explains the horrific fear of the predator. However, the psychological argument (though overdrawn often) is needed to understand fully a second object of the horror—the repulsive or disgusting. Revulsion at decaying flesh, as Clasen notes, may be an evolved response rooted in the biological reaction to the threat of exposure to disease. But there is more to the response of the disgusting. We are often repulsed by viewing that which challenges or threatens the secure sense of the self: corporal integrity (like a missing head or limbs), expected human behavior and appearance, and other deviations from the norms of life, even when there is no threat to survival (as with a predator). Of course, this feeling of disgust is at the heart of the anxiety experienced at the sight of conjoined twins, three-legged men, or even tattooed ladies (at least historically). Horror stories and movie productions toy with this response far more vividly than do freak shows. This is partially because they can do what freak shows cannot—subject audiences to the illusion of decaying human bodies, exposed internal organs, and artificially and grotesquely constructed bodies, as when movies show humans giving birth to monsters and beasts extruding from human bodies.

All these are examples of what Julia Kristeva famously calls the "abject"—that which undermines our insecure egos. The ultimate form of the abject is death (and this helps explain fear and fascination with the "interstitial," the ghost, zombie, and vampire that present the upsetting ambiguity between life and death). But the abject can be whatever "disturbs identity, system, order," notes Kristeva[7]—the killer, for example, in the form of an "innocent" child or "jolly" clown. Such characters are more than predators, they are abject. All this inevitably recalls Freud's oft-cited essay on the uncanny, the experience of what at first seems familiar, but in reality is disturbing.[8] The monster that is often the most frightening is the beast that first appears to be ordinary or even attractive, but turns out to be threatening or even just a challenge to the accustomed order of things.[9]

I share with critics of Freudians a skepticism toward arguments that link the monstrous with the release of repressed Oedipal longings, for example; but it is hard to ignore the irrational character of much horror, and its commonality with nightmares. Especially noteworthy is the attraction as well as repulsion experienced in encounters with the monstrous or, as Stephen Asma notes, "the instinctual awe of the unknown," especially in supernatural horror.[10]

So then why is horror so pleasurable, winning billions in ticket sales and online purchases? This question has inspired much debate. The "narrative" is crucial in the enjoyment of horror, Noël Carroll argues. The story produces anticipation, curiosity about who will be the victim, and even who is the monster; and this makes horror more than a terrifying event (like the attack on the Twin Towers).[11] Yet others, like Elizabeth Covie, argue, that the pleasure in horror comes not from the story but from the "cessation of unpleasure"; and still others, say the enjoyment is mostly in knowing that monsters and their predation are pure fiction.[12]

The attraction of horror may come from encountering and overcoming fear, a sequence of scenes in which, as Dennis Giles observes, "fear will be aroused, then controlled" or, as Clasen notes, the evocation of "strong and rich emotions in a safe context occurs." Other factors may explain the persistent appeal of horror: the "need" for the "supernatural" to replace the mysteries of a traditional religious culture, now in rapid retreat. Finally, horror can be a way of venting evolved or culturally acquired anger and aggression (as, for example, the appeal of men to slasher films in the feminist era when the victims are women).[13] Horror evokes multiple pleasures.

As the young Stephen King (1981) notes in *Danse Macabre*, in horror we can even identify with the predator as well as those who destroy it, as long as it's fantasy: "The horror film is an invitation to indulge in deviant, antisocial behavior by proxy—to commit gratuitous acts of violence, indulge our puerile dreams of power, to give in to our most craven fears . . . [T]he horror story . . . says it's okay to join the mob, to become the total tribal being, to destroy the outsider."[14] The key to this pleasure was its unreality. Interestingly this may explain why *Freaks* was so disturbing in 1932. King understands that circus freaks are monsters, often classic examples of the abject. Yet King admits that he never had the courage to see the freak show as a child, though he has been writing horror since he was eight. The problem for King was that freaks were real as were the cast from Brownings *Freaks*. "We may only feel really comfortable with horror as long as we can see the zipper running up monster's back, when we understand that we are not playing for keepsies." Ultimately, King argues, the "main purpose" of horror "is to reaffirm the virtues of the norm by showing us what awful things happen to people who venture into taboo lands" for "the evildoers will almost certainly be punished . . . Steady state has been restored. We have watched for the mutant and repulsed it. Equilibrium never felt so good."[15]

Very interesting. But all this doesn't go very far in explaining the *change* in horror or why it in fact has become more "real," closer to the real freak of the sideshow, why equilibrium in fact sometimes is not restored, and why that freak is irrepressible.[16] Let's briefly consider some common thinking about the historical context of modern horror, especially in regard to my focus on the 1960s transition.

Robin Wood's Freudian analysis of late 1960s and 1970s horror offers us one answer. He argues that the wave of new horror films is largely a response to the prevailing "surplus repression" of Western culture that has stifled individuality in service to capitalist possessiveness and patriarchal dominance. As part of a general revolt against the repressiveness of bourgeois culture in the 1960s and early 1970s, horror challenged this denial of human need. Monsters, according to this view, intruded on "normality" and were often met by audiences with ambiguity. Some movie monsters challenged this surplus repression (in Wood's characterization of progressive horror); other predators were agents of punishment against those who broke from surplus repression, especially the young or female (reactionary horror that was more common in conservative 1980s and 1990s). For Wood, the observation that a goodly share of modern horror films had a family theme (site of repression and its consequences) helps make his case.[17] Wood's analysis conforms to the common view that the late 1960s and 1970s challenged the repressive culture and society of the 1950s.

James Twitchell takes all this a step further by his observation that horror was primarily directed toward youth in this period; and, following a common Freudian path, Twitchell finds much horror to be a response to the traumas of youth, especially the emergence of adult sexuality. Werewolves and vampires are projected wishes of the young.[18] Mikita Brottman sees horror as a fairy tale for teens; and like the traditional fairy tale for children, slasher films teach teens a lesson, in this case, of the dangers of sex and other adult behavior.[19]

Unsurprisingly, evolutionary/biological theorists reject these Freudian interpretations as contrived and unscientific. Others dispute these psychological arguments for ignoring the historical and social context of changes in horror.[20] Paul Wells finds modern horror to be a reflection of the "collapse of spiritual and religious values in the face of seemingly indifferent progress of modernity." Todd Platts notes the linkage between the breakdown of the optimism of the youth movement of the 1960s and pessimistic tone of *Night of the Living Dead*. Others relate the new horror to the rising tide of nihilism from the seeming collapse of the family and other institutions in the 1970s (as in *Texas Chainsaw* Massacre and *The Hills Have Eyes*). Kendall Phillips sees American horror movies as projections of a succession of collective cultural anxieties across time.[21]

While these linkages of horror and history should not be entirely discounted, they are too specific to be persuasive. As a historian with a long point of view and who wants to put the "new horror" into the context of the irrepressible freak, I think that we need a longer perspective to explain the changing place of the creepy from the late 1960s.

Monsters of the Mind: Modern Origins of Fear and Disgust as Entertainment

As Stephen Asma notes, we all are equipped with "furnished minds," full of biologically and culturally inherited "furniture" in the form of our ancestors' fears and repulsive imaginings. "African adaptations" to our biological evolution direct us to react to and anticipate predators like snakes or tigers. But most monsters come from culture: for example, stories of alien races such as the Gogs and Magogs that generations believed lurked in the Caucasus Mountains to threaten ancient Greek cities. These predators return to excite modern peoples in films about creatures from black lagoons or monsters from outer space. And, as noted earlier, modern anxiety in encountering the abject has deep roots in ancient stories of liminal creatures—hermaphrodites, gorgons, griffins, zombies, and, of course, freaks—beings that are non-categorizable. Moreover, the modern horror theme of the monster within the normal person (as in *The Exorcist*) is deeply rooted in ancient and medieval folklore as well as religious texts that perpetuate fears of demons, witches, and other monstrous creatures.[22] There has always been a close link between the relentless predator and the disgusting freak.

And such superstitious stories long survived the Enlightenment and the abandonment of the medieval worldview. As W. Scott Poole notes, Americans of the eighteenth and nineteenth centuries may have abandoned witch crazes but transferred ancient and medieval fear of the alien monster to the native American "savages" and Africans. Shelly's Frankenstein monster was not only a classic form of the alien predator and liminality but represented the very opposite of Enlightenment optimism about human potential to shape and control nature.[23]

But, more important here, the English gothic novels of Ann Radcliff, Horace Walpole, and William Beckford of the late eighteenth century and the later writings of American authors like Edgar Allan Poe revived folkloric traditions of irrational fear and disgust. They also *intensified* them, doing far more than perpetuating ancient fears and disrupting Enlightenment optimism. Gothic horror novels created, Twitchell notes, "jolting expectations" and "fright fragments" that powerfully "re-create [audience] fears in pictures." Gothic novels featured the "furnishings" of modern horror—"blue smoke, mazes, mirrors and trapdoors," all engineered to excite a thrill. These works created the "aesthetics of fright" that set the stage for the late nineteenth-century flowering of horror with *Dracula, Dr. Jekyll and Mr. Hyde,* and *Island of Dr. Moreau* as well as the dramatization of Shelly's earlier *Frankenstein*. And, of course, the attraction of horror fiction paralleled the nineteenth-century rise of the freak show.[24]

Horror was an integral part of an early phase of filmmaking, often dedicated to exciting emotions, including fear and disgust through visual effects. Horror was part of the early twentieth-century "cinema of attractions" that dominated early films before the rise of narrative. Horror in concentrated visual pulsations began with Georges Méliès two-minute short *The Devil's Castle* (1896) featuring a vampire. Thomas Edison's first film version of *Frankenstein* (1910) was only the culmination of his early fascination with the monstrous and graphic death on film (*The Execution of Mary, Queen of Scots,* 1895 and *Electrocuting an Elephant,* 1903). In a sense, contemporary horror is a perpetuation (or revival) of this early appeal of the cinematic creepy by its emphasis on special effects rather than on the story and dialog.[25]

Still, even after the era of the cinema of attractions, the movie camera had a particular power to intensify visual (and later audio) sensation—liberating the eye and ear from natural constraints of live theater (or freak show). The camera could go where the eye couldn't normally go—up close as no one could comfortably experience in real life, top-down views as if the audience was a bird in flight, and into a fantasy world (making it visually real). Still, the most striking feature of the filmed visual was that it could be packed— compressing time and thus intensifying the visual effect. Eight years after the introduction of sound in 1927, Walter Benjamin wrote that movies could have a "percussive effect on the spectator," extending the ocular sensation into the haptic as in the creeps.[26]

This blending of audio and visual effect dramatically ramped up the sensuality of the audience's encounter with the monster. Virtually all of the major Hollywood studios produced horror in the early 1930s, although Universal is often credited with leading the way (with *Dracula* and *Frankenstein* in 1931, *The Mummy* in 1932, and *The Invisible Man* in 1933, followed by sequels and monster combinations like *Bride of Frankenstein* in 1935 and *Frankenstein Meets the Wolf Man* in 1943).

However, several trends stand out that muted the sensual/emotional impact of horror in the 1930s and 1940s: Many of the leading actors (e.g., Bela Lugosi and Boris Karloff) and directors (James Wale and Karl

Freund) were European, speaking with foreign accents and drawing on German expressionist techniques (foggy or misty settings, shadows, and extreme camera angles). And most of the settings were European (or in the case of *White Zombies*, Caribbean and *The Mummy*, Egyptian). All this, especially for American audiences, made horror movies distant from their lives and easy to romanticize and stereotype with their "traditional grotesquerie of graveyards, gloomy castles, mad scientists' labs, counts in capes, hunchbacks, and crazed villagers with pitch forks." The monster plays the expected nightmare theme of the predator, but the impact is lessened by the weight of a story and stock of conventional and predictable characters (deformed servants, scoffing authority figures, and often beautiful screaming females). And the story usually ends with the restoration of order as the monsters get their just deserts.[27] All this suggests the considerable constraints placed on cinematic evocation of fear and revulsion.

As with the attack on the freak show at the same time, genteel censorship further restricted the intensity and frequency of fright/disgust moments. The Production Code Administration (or Hays Office, named after Will Hays, president of the consortium of major motion picture companies who voluntarily adhered to its censorship) was instituted in 1930, though Code standards were enforced only in 1934. A team of mostly pious Catholic men in charge sought to prevent a presumably vulnerable audience from imitating acts of sex, blasphemy, and violence. The Code did not refer specifically to horror (only prohibiting "brutality and possible gruesomeness"). Still members of Hays Office expressed concern about the rise of horror films in 1931 and 1932; and several states censored early monster movies. When *Freaks* appeared in 1932, *The Motion Picture Herald* called on Hollywood to "stem this rising tide of goose-flesh melodrama." Records of the Code

FIGURE 6.1 *A promotional poster for Universal's 1935 remake of the famous* Frankenstein. *The garish color image has little to do with the black-and-white critically acclaimed story. Wikimedia Commons.*

Administration's treatment of *Bride of Frankenstein* suggests that Code officials agreed. Joseph Breen, leading figure in the Catholic Legion of Decency and Administration official, was concerned about isolated scenes of horror (frames showing a human heart taken from a jar and an idiot nephew strangling his uncle). Interestingly, censorship boards in Asia and Europe were even more diligent, especially in Britain in banning much horror until regulations were relaxed in the late 1950s.[28]

Pressure from the Code Administration seems to have constrained Hollywood, for as the 1930s progressed, the trend was not to ramp up horror (as was the case from the 1960s), but to reduce its production and to offer predictable sequels. The studios mixed increasingly familiar horror themes and characters with comedy, designed to appeal to children (as in Son of Frankenstein in 1939 and especially Abbott and Costello Meet Frankenstein in 1948). Despite relatively sophisticated treatments from RKO (starting in 1942 with *Cat People*), the horror genre stayed within the boundaries of genteel decency into the 1950s.[29]

By mid-century, horror had become repetitive: "same props, stars, camera tracks, and sets," notes Twitchell. As late as 1960, horror movie themes were often drawn from 1930s features that themselves were adaptations of 1890s novels with ultimate roots in "Elizabethan blood and thunder tragedies." Veteran monsters played by Bela Lugosi and Boris Karloff had been long reduced to caricature and horror freaks like the mummy and the werewolf were mere variations on old themes. To be sure, there were new themes, addressing 1950s fears of extraterrestrial aliens as space travel became more plausible. Anxiety over threats from the Cold War and nuclear radiation to the blissful security of suburban America was expressed in tales of body-invading pods from outer space (*Invasion of the Body Snatchers* of 1956) or stories of mutant insects caused by atomic radiation as in *Them!* of 1954. Even ancient anxieties about monsters from the deep (*Creature from the Black Lagoon*, 1954) were roused. These films, at least, brought horror into the contemporary world and familiar places. But the "classical" characters came back too, much as the conventional freak types remained at carnival sideshows. Even new monsters were placed in "very traditional iconography"—mad (and sometimes heroic) scientists, for example, with a return to normalcy at the movie's end.[30]

Moreover, among the most successful of these 1950s and early 1960s horror films were revivals of old themes such as Hammer Films' *Curse of Frankenstein* of 1957, followed by many redoes of *Dracula* and *The Mummy*, often with the same two lead characters—Peter Cushing and Christopher Lee. To be sure, Hammer introduced color and a bit more gore, but the pace and intensity remained conventionally slow and low, and the story lines and characters were familiar. Roger Corman's collection of Poe-derived movies (*Pit and the Pendulum* and the *House of Usher*) in the early 1960s were hardly spine-tingling, despite garish advertising posters.[31]

The New Creepy: Makers, Audiences, and Critics

While enhanced technology (such as the special effects in Hitchcock's *Birds* of 1963) upped the ante of horror, more substantial change came with the transformation of the movie business and the rise of a new generation eager for more edgy encounters with monsters. And these changes culminated in the 1960s, though it had roots in the late 1940s. The 1948 "Paramount Decision," where the courts broke up the vertical integration of the movie industry, cut many theaters from studio control. This led to the reduction of the output of major studios and diminished access of local cinemas to films to exhibit. This, along with the withdrawal of adults from theaters for the comfort of home TV, forced the major studios into producing fewer, but more expensive, blockbuster films that still could draw a multigenerational and cross-class audience. In the long run, this was a losing strategy. By 1970, the traditional downtown theater could no longer draw that family audience, even to a movie in CinemaScope. This situation created space for independents like American International Pictures and Allied Artists to move cheap carnivalesque films into local theaters (and drive-ins), eager for features to show. Along with this change on the supply side was a transformation of demand—the growth of a youth audience for whom family TV was a bore and who were open to sexploitation comedy and more graphic horror.[32]

This appeal to youth in these movies was more than a manipulation of youth identity (e.g, teenage werewolves) or the supposed age-old attraction of youth to outrage and shock as a rite of passage of rite out of childhood. These new movies were, as Mark Jancovich and Barbara Ehrenreich note, part of a broader generational shift of youth that was unique to the mid-twentieth century—an expansive critique of middle-class values and especially taste. These young people, as Jancovich notes, did not become "hip intellectuals," who prided themselves on their ignorance of popular culture. Instead, a portion of this generation of youth adopted a strategy of the "lower class hipster," being well versed in that culture, especially of horror: "They knew the forms of horror so well that they could recognize their artificiality and preposterousness, and this allowed them to celebrate these texts without being cultural dupes." Here the creepy met camp, but the genre was also accompanied by a ramping up of horrific sensation.[33]

Impresarios of the campy-creepy included William Castle, a producer of cheap studio mysteries and crime movies from the late 1940s. He is best known for a series of gimmicky horror films in the late 1950s: *House on Haunted Hill* featured a plastic skeleton that was supposed to fly over the theater audience at a dramatic part of the film. In *The Tingler*, some seats in the movie auditorium were wired to give viewers a minor shock. Castle himself appears on film at the beginning of the movie, like a sideshow talker, warning the audience that some will receive "some of the sensations . . . which the actors on the screen feel," advising them that if they did not scream, it may be fatal. Another contributor was AIP, famous for their ultra-cheap drive-in double features (like *A Bucket of Blood* and *Attack of the Giant Leaches* of 1959). These movies featured publicity posters with garish "carney come-ons," similar to the exaggerated images on the bannerline of sideshows. This drift to the grotesque also paralleled trends in the carnival freak show. This genre, notes Jancovich, ignored "standards of maturity" as it was directed toward teens. These movies moved to the "very boundary between horror and parody," observes Martin Barker, and in so doing intensified the creepy.[34]

After 1960, even the mainstream studios began to adapt this new aggressive approach (as in Hitchcock's *Psycho* of 1960 that introduced the sexual psychopath). The inability of the major movie makers to draw a mature audience led them to join the exploitation movie makers. Warner even offered *Two on a Guillotine* in 1965 with garish publicity though little horror. This trend culminated in the Paramount's big-budget success, *Rosemary's Baby*, in 1968. Produced by William Castle, *Rosemary's Baby* elevated a master of the exploitation "B" movie into the "A" category.[35] All this signals the abandonment of the old family/middle-class/adult audience, which had once been willing to buy reserve seats for biblical epics or romantic comedies, and the beginning of the mainstreaming of the carnival.

An essential part of the desertion of the old Hollywood model was the collapse of the Production Code that had protected the moralistic branding of the American cinema. As often noted, the old rules of 1934 regarding "direct" displays of violence were being eroded from the early 1960s (beginning with *Psycho* but continuing with *Fistful of Dollars, Bonnie and Clyde*, and *The Wild Bunch*). The nearly quarter-century dominance of the Code Administration by Joseph Breen ended in 1954 with his retirement. Economic pressure from television for audiences and competition from independent filmmakers, eager to accommodate a less genteel audience, inevitably led to Jack Valente's ascendance to head the Motion Picture Association of America in 1966. Seeing the writing on the wall, Valente supported Code approval of *Rosemary's Baby* in 1968, thus legitimizing more edgy, but still mainstream, horror. This paved the way for the legitimization of *The Exorcist, The Omen*, and *Poltergeist*. Most important, Valente replaced the Code with a rating system (still run by the studios) that attempted to separate "mature" from family audiences (with ratings of "R" that allowed gore, violence, and nudity, if not pornography, distinct from "PG" and "G"). It isn't surprising that the new rating system came into effect in 1968 about the time of the release of *Night of the Living Dead*.[36]

This loosening of constraint certainly opened the floodgates of horror, but the key was the attraction of youth (and minority) audiences to the new horror. AIP had already succeeded with a string of teenage horror features (*I Was a Teenage Werewolf* of 1957 being only the best known). As Thomas Doherty and Peter Stanfield note, teens flocked to drive-ins to see these and other thrillers, in part in defiance of adult notions of taste and propriety. And these movies frequently addressed teen feelings of alienation from family and peers. They appealed also to teen humor by being clearly self-parodic, especially in their deliberate silliness and cheap special effects (such as with Roger Corman's *Attack of the Crab Monsters* and *The Man with the X-Ray Eyes*). And late 1960s horror played especially well in "kiddie matinees" in Philadelphia, sometimes followed in the evening by hard core pornography. These cinemas especially attracted African American audiences (who, though only about 10 percent of the population, were estimated to be 30 percent of movie patrons at the end of the 1960s).[37]

But the new crowds for horror went beyond thrill-seeking minorities and the lower classes. That appeal extended into the broader group of youth in the 1960s who had grown up with old horror films, some dating from as far back as *King Kong* and *Dracula*. In 1957, the TV program distributor Screen Gems obtained from Universal International 550 pre-1948 films (52 of which were "shock" films) for syndication on local TV for the late show. Often horror films were featured on weekend "shock theater" programs with campy introductions and skits during commercial breaks by local celebrities dressed as Dracula and other familiar characters from horror classics. For the younger set, monster toys and monster fan magazines like *Famous Monsters of Filmland* had made Dracula "cool" to preteen kids of the middle as well as working classes. And, in the early 1960s, "horror" even invaded the world of the TV sitcom with *The Munsters* and *The Addams Family*. Kids who felt like outsiders in the conformist late 1950s and early 1960s identified with the monsters. A wave of horror comics (produced by William Gaines and others) thrilled kids in the early 1950s while "freaking out" adults (leading to a restrictive "Comics Code"). Despite this, these comics were still around in 1960. I read them in a magazine section of a grocery store that year for the price of a fifteen-cent soft ice-cream cone.[38]

As we have seen, youth affinity for horror took the form of camp and rebellion, but here I would like to stress another element—the "gross out" that William Paul argues is the central element in the new horror of the late 1960s. Paul focuses on the centrality of the emotional release of the horror-induced "scream," especially as it was collectively experienced in theaters. Scream movies, he argues, were closely associated with outrageous comedy movies of the era and the uproarious laughter that they induced. Horror as gross out reverses conventional values, making the gross good and the disgusting pleasurable. The gross out allows audiences to scream (and laugh) in a return to the "tradition of the vulgar arts" of the carnival and its freaks. This inversion, however, was and is not necessarily subversive (just as camp was not). The gross out "does not seek purgation so much as indulgence." It's simply fun.[39]

While the gross out was deliberately taboo-breaking, the viewer remained safely within the dominate culture. As Barry Grant notes, horror is a kind of "transgressive tourism," a brief vacation from rationality, allowing viewers to "vicariously delve into forbidden and dangerous territory only to return

FIGURE 6.2 *Poster for* I Was a Teenage Werewolf *(1957). A successful feature for Samuel Arkoff's American International Pictures for the young crowd out for a lark. Reynold Brown, Wikimedia Commons.*

to a world of reason." Part of the audience's boundary-breaking is its noisy and boisterous behavior at viewings of cult horror.[40] Brottman goes further, arguing that horror can take the form of *Cinéma vomitif*, resulting in "the arousal of strong sensations in the lower body—nausea, revulsion, weakness, faintness and a loosening of bowls or bladder control." Indeed, the trend in horror has been to focus graphically on the body: "the opened body, the body in panic, the body in threat, the body in death."[41]

For critics, as opposed to "in the know" viewers, this understanding of horror is often objectionable because, as Paul notes, critics insist on "making art serious . . . by downplaying play, by making art something other than fun." Of course, well-known horror scholars like Carol Clover have recognized that audiences are seeking an "affective response," but they still insist that the story and the familiarity of the audience with horror's codes and tropes that are expressed through the narrative are essential to evoke this "affective response."[42]

Still, whatever the story, that response is largely visceral and psychological. Clover admits that horror characters all "do more or less the same job, narratively speaking" be they gorillas, blobs, sharks, or motel attendants. Clover recognizes that slasher movie crowds are watching "heads squashed and eyes popped out, faces flayed, limbs dismembered, eyes penetrated by needles in close-up." Todd Platts recognizes that what drove crowds to horror movies was the gratuitous gore and "diarrheic spectacle."[43]

These movies evoke fear and disgust. In effect, the narrative and the characters carry the audience to the payoff moments of shock. In an informal survey of horror audiences around 2000, Wells found that viewers between the ages of sixteen and twenty-five focused on the spectacle of horror rather than the story, finding pleasure in the "excess more than the narrative," even taking special pleasure in the humor mixed in "scare effects." These young viewers appreciated the "grotesque body," while older audiences did not. And yet Wells, like others including Paul, focuses primarily on the narrative in delineating horror. Wood breaks down horror by featured monsters ("the human psychotic," "revenge of nature," "Satanism, diabolic possession," "the terrible child," and "cannibalism"). Yet, beneath these variations is the same "gross out."[44] To many scholars, horror must be understood as an artistic genre to be analyzed like any other. But what the modern horror crowd wants is the gross out (by whatever narrative vehicle)—essentially an updated encounter with the sideshow freak—just more terrifying, more disgusting, than the freak of old because the audience has seen all that and wants more.[45]

Escalating/Intensifying Creepiness in the 1960s

The modern gross out is more than a return to the traditional carnival or even update of the "cinema of attractions." It is part of the logic of sensual intensification to which youth was especially attuned in this age of fast consumer capitalism. That logic plays out especially in profit-seeking entertainment industries that engineered sensuality through video. This acceleration of sensuality has developed over the course of a century but took off in the 1960s. The disappearance of the carnival sideshow was very much a part of this process. Popular culture gradually ceased being experienced locally and intermittently. The centralized and continuously flowing world of modern media replaced that localized festival culture, of which the freak show was a part. By 1900, the movies introduced a new world of universality/uniformity and incessancy. But middle-class tastemakers and consumers in the early twentieth century feared that the movies would take a carnivalesque form of sensuality in sexuality and violence. Just as these people upheld propriety and "family values" by marginalizing the freak show, they averted the carnival in the movies with the help of nongovernmental censorship in the Production Code. The 1960s brought the collapse of these controls and the release of the full logic of fast consumer capitalism—even a return to the carnival in the form of youth rebellion. Along with this came unbound horror, "packed" with gross out sensation.

Let me illustrate with a few familiar horror movies and explain how they laid the groundwork for the modern culture of intensification. Herschell Gordon Lewis certainly understood this appeal when he produced *Blood Feast* (1963) and *Two Thousand Maniacs* (1964). An outsider in the movie business with a background as a literature professor and advertising promoter, Lewis was even less bound to the dictates of Hollywood taste than was Corman. He used animal intestines to make his gore seem realistic (and half-naked women to offer an added sex attraction). A coherent plot would have gotten in the way. What people remember about Lewis's movies is the ritual dismemberment of a women and a man pushed down a hill in a barrel lined with spikes that turned him into a bloody mess. Advances in makeup and special effects, especially in latex and mechanical illusions, made the gore of Lewis's early 1960s movies far more realistic and intense than what preceded. Lewis succeeded especially in drive-ins that catered to youth. Such films paved the way for franchise movies, "in which only violence matters," notes horror scholar Wheeler Dixon. "These became increasingly mechanical as audiences became progressively inured to watching pain and suffering on the screen as a means of escape from their own lives—an escape through indifference to the suffering of others."[46]

Night of the Living Dead (1968), however, had a far wider impact than did *Blood Feast*. As Clasen notes, the film is not about "the defeat of the counterculture" (as often claimed) but about the unrelenting fear that the movie evokes in an entirely realistic setting without the comfort of a happy ending.[47] It's about zombies, radical extensions of the traditional freak. Its maker, George Romero, was a Hollywood outsider, but his background was in sync with a rising generation of horror hounds. Born in 1940, he began making amateur horror at fourteen and shared with his generation an admiration not only for Elvis and Brando but also for the Crime Suspense comic book maker, William Gaines (whose early 1950s stories sometimes featured family murder and cannibalism); and he enjoyed AIP double features. Schooled in Pittsburgh, Romero followed college with making industrial films and shooting TV advertising. Drawing on local talent, he produced *Living Dead* with a budget of roughly $125,000 dollars. As was true of many independent filmmakers, Romero had difficulties finding a distributor, made much harder by the movie's outrageous content. Columbia refused it as did even AIP (who wanted a positive ending). Romero settled on distribution by a small theater chain out of New York. *Living Dead* received negative reviews when it first was released in December 1968 (displaying "unrelieved sadism" according to *Variety*). By the summer of 1969, however, Romero's film was on its way to becoming a cult classic, a top money maker in Europe as well as in urban theaters in the United States. It even played at the Museum of Modern Art in New York and received a second, now positive review from *Variety*. Admired for its gritty realism, *Living Dead* appealed both to the art crowd and to the kids, just as did the revival of *Freaks*.[48] In fact, *Living Dead* appeared in early 1971 in midnight movie theaters like the Waverly in New York's Greenwich Village, just after a successful run of *Freaks*. *Living Dead* ran continuously in midnight movie theaters until July 1973. Thereafter, it was a regular feature of college film societies.[49]

While appealing to the camp crowd, the *Living Dead* experience was far from camp. It systematically broke the old boundaries of horror. First, its setting was contemporary, not some foreign place and time. This is made clearer when the zombies in Romero's movie are compared to earlier uses of this theme. The classic *White Zombie* of 1932 is set in Haiti where the zombies were kept in thrall by a voodoo priest (a variation on the mad scientist). Romero's zombies may remind viewers of a dark take on the Christian "resurrection of the dead." The film certainly evokes apocalyptical hopelessness where all the old rules are gone, and the world has come to an end. But the very lack of a controlling agent and clear backstory of the origins of the zombies makes the emotional intensity of the zombie onslaught all the more powerful. The graphic violence is obviously excessive, serving no narrative purpose, as zombies eat the intestines of a young couple and a deranged daughter repeatedly stabs her mother with a garden trawl. Such gory punctuations in horror films soon became common and more frequent. The old indirection is gone: No more are the killings shown in a shadow; instead, blood and guts are disgustingly and graphically revealed. Gone too are fantastic monsters or animals; instead, the predators look and dress like the audience. The horror is unmitigated and unrelenting. There is no buildup to the horrific climax, as in so many earlier horror movies. Within several minutes of the opening, Barbara's brother is killed at the cemetery they are visiting and she is pursued by a zombie as she seeks cover in a dreary white clapboard farmhouse. As R. H. W. Dillard notes, "the film is primary one of ceaseless and unremitting struggle"—in an intense form of our biologically rooted anxiety over the pursuing predator. This is compounded by the total inability of the inhabitants of the farmhouse to come to any common plan for survival. This stands in contrast to the "traditional" smart team that rescues the prey from the predator through wit and luck. Even the classic love interest has a gory conclusion: A young couple who try to escape end up burnt to death in their truck and eaten by zombies. The dead brother of Barbara returns as a zombie to attack his sister. Most astonishing of all, the black hero, Ben, who alone survives the night, is killed by a team of "red neck" volunteers who arrive to destroy the zombies, mistaking him for a zombie and casually burning his body with the slain zombies. Not only is there no "comic relief," nothing relieves the tension.

Some critics see an implicit social message in the racism of the white vigilantes and police, but this may not have been intentional.[50] It isn't surprising that commentaries see this movie as a product of a growing cynicism emerging out of the failure of liberal and radical movements for racial and social change at the end of the 1960s.[51] But the audience reaction of terror (but also sometimes laughter) suggests a simpler explanation: The guardrails that had traditionally softened the "gross out" of horror had been removed. Nothing held back its acceleration. The creepiness of the freak show and the horror of the movie *Freaks* shifted to high gear.

Living Dead was only the beginning and just one example of this trend. As we have seen, major studios joined Romero with *Rosemary's Baby* (also in 1968), an atmospheric story of devil possession, set not in the past or Transylvania, but in an upscale Manhattan apartment building. Five years later, with *The Exorcist*, Warner Brothers offered a story (based on a best-selling novel) of an innocent preteen possessed by the devil and the efforts of a priest to "exorcise" the demon. Unwilling to completely abandon the traditional guardrails of a familiar backstory, *The Exorcist* was couched in a heavy overlay of Catholic themes concerning the struggle of the sacred versus the demonic, familiar movie star leads, and muted ads that further legitimized the movie. Still, the producers were seeking the patronage not only of middle-class adults but also of teens and even minority youth. *The Exorcist*'s success was ultimately linked to its disgusting special effects— the girl vomiting on the priest, masturbating on a cross, and urinating on the floor at a posh party (earning a ban in Britain until 1999). She was even more disgusting than the mouse-devouring geek. William Paul suggests that the religious dialog and story were really devices disguising what audiences really came to see, the gross out of green vomit and spinning heads.[52]

An equally important landmark was Tobe Hooper's *Texas Chainsaw Massacre* (1974). It shares much with *Night of the Living Dead*: a no-name cast, a documentary look, and ultimately a similar nihilism. Nothing to distance viewers from their own real worlds. It's a story of a group of hippie-like youth who, while traveling through rural Texas, come upon a family of unemployed slaughterhouse workers, who slaughter them with a chainsaw. Only one, a young woman, survives. Hooper makes little effort to explain the murdering family's behavior.

Critics pounced. Wood sees in *Texas Chainsaw Massacre* little more than the "sheer undifferentiated lust for destruction that seems to lie not far below the surface of modern collective consciousness." And Chris Sharret finds in it a "cynical nihilism with criticism of the order of things." But again, this negativity (and even the lack of much memorable dialog) reinforces a raw sensuality. Wood even notes how the occasional "grotesque comedy" (such as in the repeated inability of the aged and encumbered grandpa to kill the

FIGURE 6.3 *Zombies on the march in* Night of the Living Dead, *1968. Film Still, Wikimedia Commons.*

surviving young woman with a hammer) in "no way diminishes, rather it intensifies [the scene's] nightmare horrors."[53]

Texas Chainsaw Massacre, like *Living Dead*, is horrifying because, like sideshow freaks, the monsters are not supernatural or extraterrestrial beings, or even hungry animals. They are like us, and, at the same time, utterly deprived of the humanity that we consider is at our core. Moreover, both movies (and even *The Exorcist*) are "body horror films." There is little spiritual pretense, not even a suggestion that the monster is a victim of moral degradation or external corruption. Like the modern freak show, any hint of a humanizing backstory is eliminated, reducing the stare at the freak or the viewing of the screen monster to the most basic biological/emotional encounter with fear, disgust, and the attending pleasures of the corporal spectacle. Wood finds "relentless and unremitting intensity" in *Chainsaw Massacre*—even though significantly today viewers might not even have found it shocking given the paucity of actual graphic violence. However, for audiences in 1974, the utter excess in the pursuit and tormenting of Sally (the final survivor) marks the movie's "total negativity."[54]

Accelerating Horror in the 1970s

The implications of the gross out and its intensification are played out in the late 1970s. The best example of "body horror" perhaps is *The Alien* of

FIGURE 6.4 *Cast of* Texas Chainsaw Massacre *posing in costume (1974), Silver Screen Collection/Getty Images.*

1979 with its grim sci-fi setting in a spaceship where a reptilian monster kills the crew (in one terrifying scene tearing itself out of the body of a member). Of course, there is no character development. Again, the emotional hook is making audiences face an attack on their "sense of bodily integrity" and a grotesque mockery of childbirth. This grim story generated three direct sequels. *Shivers* (1975) revives the animal horror of the 1950s (*Them!*, *The Fly*, and *The Giant Claw*, for example) but with far more graphic displays of predation as parasites invade human bodies. Other examples of the new horror feature human bodies being violently transformed into monsters as in *The Howling* (1981), *The Beast Within* (1982), and *The Thing* (1982).[55]

Perhaps more influential was the revenge horror of Wes Craven's *Last House on the Left* (1972), and the slasher films of John Carpenter (*Halloween* of 1978) and Sean Cunningham (*Friday the 13th* of 1980). Craven's *Last House* begins the cycle, with teen girls on their way to a party being raped and murdered by a gang of "hippies," after which the middle-class parents of one girl take justice in their own hands. They lure the murderers into their houses for deliciously ghastly revenge. The father kills one with a chainsaw and the mother, after luring the other into a sexual encounter, castrates him with her teeth and kills him. "Everything is shown in vicious, unsparing detail; there is not a drop of sympathy, humanity, or compassion in the film's world of unrelenting cruelty," notes Dixon. Revenge horror found a long-lasting audience with a series beginning with *I Spit on Your Grave* (1978), where a rape victim takes retribution on her attackers in drawn-out scenes of torture and death.[56]

But likely the most influential were the "slasher" pioneers: *Halloween*, *Friday the 13th*, and another Craven hit, *Nightmare on Elm Street* of 1984. They were so popular that they led numerous sequels—ten for *Halloween*, eleven for *Friday* (including *Freddy vs. Jason* of 2003 where the monsters in *Friday* and *Nightmare* duel it out in killing sprees), and eight sequels for *Nightmare*). These remakes incredulously kept bringing back the monsters (Mike Meyers, Jason Voorhees, and Freddy Krueger), who became as familiar to horror fans as sitcom characters to TV fans. A new set of horrific conventions were firmly established in these slasher movies. An inexplicably evil young male unrelentingly pursues victims to murder (mostly women) in grossly graphic ways (usually with sharp objects—sometimes seen as "phallic" by commentators). The terror of predation was central, often intensified by surprise attacks in closed spaces. Almost invariably, as a climax, the human monster chases down his final victim (often called "the last girl") in drawn-out scenes with repeated violent encounters, evoking fear for the victim and fear of the monster. Despite seemingly being defeated, the predator rises again and again in vicious pursuit. The monster is unpredictable; and even his destruction is no guarantee of restored peace and order (setting up the audience for still another sequel).[57]

Commentators often conclude that these films reflect the late 1970s and 1980s—times presumably when the social and political upheavals of the 1960s were over and thus the bogeyman had become apolitical, representing pure evil instead. Perhaps reflecting a less socially engaged time, horror was often set in a family context—such as the oft-repeated theme of the "innocent" child who turned out to be the monster as in *The Omen*, *It's Alive*, and *Children of the Corn*. A variation was the demonic doll as in the multi-sequeled success of Chucky, a doll possessed by the soul of a dead murderer in *Child's Play* of 1988.[58] In some cases, slasher horror manifested a not-too-subtle condemnation of the sexual promiscuity of the monster's victims (especially if female)—as in the first *Halloween*—reflecting a more conservative time, perhaps even a negative reaction to the feminism of the early 1970s. And, of course, discussion of this genre heavily focuses on questions like which of them were "reactionary" and "progressive." Was the repeated appearance of the "last girl" pursued by the killer a manifestation of misogyny; or did male consumers identify with the ultimately victorious female; or even, despite appearance, did young women embrace the slasher?[59]

Let's leave these debates aside (which, in my view became somewhat arcane). What isn't disputable is that these films represent an intensification of horror—and this was part of a broader and longer trend in the history of fast capitalism that accelerated from the late 1960s. Of course, not all of these movie monsters fit easily into the category of "updated freaks" (though some certainly did). But the change in horror films (like the increasingly grotesque carnival freak show) is really part of a broader trend toward the packaging of sensual intensity, part of the defeat of a middle-class culture that attempted to crush the carnival culture of the freak show. And this defeat was essentially linked to the triumph not merely of the bad taste of the masses or immaturity of the young or even the greed of the "horrorspoitation" moviemaker. It was built into the logic of fast consumer capitalism in which youth from the 1960s were fully engaged.

A veritable assembly line of horror emerged by the 1980s that offered a nearly predictable parade of concussions or "hits" of shock, fright, and disgust that were carried by equally predictable characters and stories. In many ways, these pleasure points that ran throughout horror films from the 1960s were more important than the oft-analyzed narratives of horror spectacles—at least to audiences, if not scholars. All this was part and parcel to a dynamic of a consumer culture driven by the packing and packaging of sensation, the long, if distant, culmination of the freak show.

Modern horror was only part of a wide range of commercialized sensuality in the era of modern fast capitalism. The 1970s also witnessed a new generation of roller coasters that abandoned the old wooden frames and elaborate scaffolding for tubular steel suspended on giant steel poles. Featured in new amusement park construction, these "iron rides" no longer had story themes (as did Disney and later Universal Studios). Instead they simply offered speed, height, and twists, creating new thrills like the feeling of weightlessness as the coaster catapulted riders high in the air.[60] Similarly, the pace and intensity of action-adventure movies like *Dirty Harry* (1971) and its sequels dramatically increased while stories and character diminished. By the mid-1970s the action-filled heroisms of Sylvester Stallone and Arnold Schwarzenegger won audiences with aestheticized violence.[61] Even on TV, the pace of ads increased while their length shortened, intensifying their impact. The same pattern of briefer, more intense, scenes is obvious in the contrast between sitcoms of the 1950s and those after 1970. With the coming of the TV remote, it became all-too-easy for viewers to channel surf, a habit advertisers and programmers wanted to discourage by eliminating "slow" and "boring" action. But viewers found longer shots and scenes "slow" because they had grown to expect them to be "fast."[62] The thrill of the kill in horror was an extreme form of all this.

This process was obviously generated by consumer satiation. From the 1960s, audiences had become jaded with the old horror, obliging moviemakers to invent new forms of excitation as in slasher films and digitized gore. But, in the process, the power of shock had been reduced. Satiation here as elsewhere in consumer capitalism had set in and novelty was required of horror makers.[63] In an age of packaged pleasures, that meant more and more intense "hits" of fright and disgust. And, despite the drift toward the grotesque, the freak show, with its limited repertory of characters, its dependence on real people, and its traditionalism, could not provide this. But the escalation of horror in cinematic form was both doable and almost inevitable.

Horror scholars note the rise in the "body count" of slasher victims, increasing from a mere five in *Chainsaw Massacre* to the 14 in the first *Friday the 13th* six years later. *The Omen* of 1976 might be the first horror film made by a major studio with no elaborate plot, just a satanic child committing murder in the most graphic of ways every ten minutes of running time. While it took thirty-five minutes in *Chainsaw Massacre* (that clocked in at 123 minutes in toto) to build up to the first killing, latter slasher films get to it within the opening minutes. Twenty years after *Chainsaw Massacre*, Craven's *Scream*, featuring the usual masked killer (in the classic look of Edvard Munch's painting by that name), opens with the murder of the star Drew Barrymore and her boyfriend in a harrowing first ten minutes. As Dixon notes, "This is *Psycho* in fast forward." No longer is anticipation as important as is the moment of shock. And the traditional calming tone of the endings of traditional horror is often replaced by a final burst of shock (as in the final scene of *Carrie* in 1976).[64] Some might call this "apocalyptic." A simpler name for it is the endless pursuit of shock. And even this trick soon evokes laughter rather than screams. A sign of this process is the fact that *The Exorcist*, banned in 1974 in Britain, was greeted with laughter after censorship was lifted in 1999. The trend was clear. Body horror, body counts, and the realism of the gore became more intense with subsequent remakes.[65]

Modulated Horror

But inevitably there were limits to intensification: Unrelenting shock in horror is emotionally unsustainable just as vertigo is in roller coasters. A measure of that limit is the decline of slasher movies in the 1980s. Even in modern times, there are psychological constraints on emotional onslaught. Still necessary were the traditional dramatic device of "comic relief," narrative episodes and even love interest, however brief and contrived, to give the audience respite from the emotional and visceral impact of the action. Horror, as any form of sensual intensity, had to be modulated and it was increasingly in the 1980s.[66]

An essential form of that mollification was built into an extraordinary, and for some, a surprising feature of modern entertainment—the balancing of novelty with repetition. Reprise was inevitable in the economy of film making (both to tap into the proven success of the original and to eliminate some of the costs of innovation). More interesting here, however, is that repetition was accepted—even embraced—by audiences. There is much evidence that besides the shock of the monster encounter, audiences were draw to the basic predictability of horror. Horror director John Carpenter recognized that young crowds were content to see basically the same movie over again (as in the frequent sequels to *Halloween*). In fact, they actually wanted to return to the same scenes and characters much as their elders had long embraced the predictable sitcoms and police procedurals on radio and television. Wes Craven admitted that his franchise slasher Freddy Krueger in the sequels "wouldn't disturb you but . . . would make you jump and make your date hold you a little closer. It was like making cheeseburgers. You get a formula for something that satisfies the appetite and then you make it over and over again and make a business out of it."[67]

But modulation went further, when horror makers sought the laughter of knowing audiences. As Paul argues, both the scream and the laugh were closely related as responses to the horrifying and vulgar, and both produced a release of tension. But laughing at horror went further: It is and was closely connected to the camp response; and, as we have seen from the days of the 1960s AIP movies, horror makers learned to embrace the camp response of viewers by offering intentional camp. In 1959, audiences responded in mock terror at Castle's "Emergo Skeleton" coming out of the screen in *House on Haunted Hill*. They knew it was a joke. Corman understood that by the 1970s there was a thin line between camp and horror and that this paralleled an equally narrow line between "B" and "A" movies. In 1990, Corman cites famed movie critic Vincent Canby: "What is *Jaws* but a big-budget Roger Corman movie?" Corman rather modestly admits, "The whole idea was to tell an interesting, visually entertaining story that would draw young people to the drive-ins and hardtop cinemas, and not take yourself too seriously along the way."[68]

Corman's successors introduced camp humor with more technology and bigger budgets—and more knowing (or jaded) audiences. Accompanying escalating gore came comedy as in George Romero's 1979 *Dawn of the Dead*. It is a zombie film, but, unlike *Night of the Living Dead* of a decade earlier, takes place in daylight in a shopping mall with much hilarity. Though disgusting, *Basket Case* of 1982 by Frank Henenlotter (featuring a deformed Siamese twin who had been separated from his brother and kept in a wicker basket) is still another example of comedic (camp) horror. Especially notable in this combination are Peter Jackson films *Bad Taste* (1988), *Meet the Feebles* (1989), and *Braindead* (1992) that Jackson calls "splat-stick," (a blend of gory splatter and slapstick comedy a la "The Three Stooges"). Unlike the seriousness of slasher films, these movies make light of the transformation of "the body into flesh." Jackson uses what he called "absurdism" in gore films like *Bad Taste*, for example, where aliens invade earth in pursuit of a new "fast food craze: human meat." The gags come fast and furious, detaching viewers from the "normal" horrified response of fear and even disgust. The technique continues to be sprinkled into even the mainstream

FIGURE 6.5 *Robert Englund portrayed as Freddy Krueger in* A Nightmare on Elm Street, *c. 1989. Hulton Archive Staff/Getty Images.*

of cartoon sitcoms like the Halloween episodes of *The Simpsons*. The creepy is met with humor and disengagement.[69]

The creepy is also mollified by camp in appealing to the "knowing crowd" as when postmodern slasher films make reference to their predecessors. In *Fade to Black* (1980), a crazed movie fan reenacts famous monster murder scenes, and in his *New Nightmare* (1994), Wes Craven and his stars from earlier *Nightmare* movies play themselves as they are stalked by the "real" Freddy Krueger. Knowing audiences are in on the joke. Perhaps most iconic of the postmodern slasher movies that heavily relies on past horror themes and scenes (nostalgia really) is Craven's *Scream* (1996), which opens with a killer on the phone demanding a teen answer questions about slasher films to stop the murder of her boyfriend.[70]

As Peter Hutchings notes, camp audiences scream or "faint to order" when the scene requires it, without necessarily any real emotional engagement. By the 1990s, postmodern slasher movies helped audiences distance themselves from fear and disgust. Following active crowds at showings of The *Rock*

Horror Picture Show in the 1970s, new horror audiences sometimes even asserted themselves in mock battles with the mock predator on the screen. Ultimately all this was part of horror's modulation.[71]

Behind the self-asserting (or self-protecting) laughter of the audience of horror was an accumulation of viewer knowledge of horror—the characteristic scenes, the setups for monster encounters, and the "bad decisions" of ultimate victims. This knowledge and the campish response marked the maturation of young horror fans as they transitioned from their early initiation into the "naughty world" of horror. This "knowing" both empowered the horror audience and perpetuated a market for a seemingly endless flow of modulated, if still intense, horror. The seasoned fan both demanded more gore and had the armor to take it, making horror essentially a ritual experience.[72]

Interestingly, well-healed horror commenters, including Twitchell in 1987, believed that horror cinema was running out of new "fright tropes." Similarly, Wells in 2000 claimed that horror had little more to say, and Paul in 2004 anticipated that gross out would "burn itself out by its very excesses."[73] They all assumed that horror genre had exhausted its potential for innovation to reach an increasingly jaded audience.

However, that certainly hasn't happened. Instead, the camp horror of the 1990s gave way to a period of relatively humorless and extremely violent horror in the first decade of the 2000s. Movies like *The Hills Have Eyes* (2006), a redo of Craven's hit of 1977, dish up unprecedented gore and disgust, including graphic episodes of rape and murder (as in the scene of a mutant lizard sucking milk from the breast of a woman before shooting her in the head). As Angela Ndalianis notes, the appeal of body horror has hardly declined: "The bite that ravages fragile skin, the hands that tear open an abdomen to reveal slippery internal organs, the same hands that rip limbs from pulsating bodies" continue to attract audiences.[74]

Why is the horror genre as unrelenting as are the monsters? Partially, it is because new generations of youth emerge, perhaps not to work through the psychological traumas of transitioning to adulthood as Twitchell suggests, but rather to test their metal in interacting with shock (just as youth climb aboard ever more thrilling and daring roller coasters or play ever more immersive and intense video games). But the modulation of horror is also part of that continued appeal. The creepy blends with the camp (and even the cute), as well as other aesthetic appeals (romance, mystery, nostalgia, etc.). As suggested in the prologue, the freak show, broadly understood, survives in all this variety because modern culture has so successfully blended these appeals. Let's return to that subject briefly for my final thoughts on the irrepressible freak.

Notes

1   Walter Benjamin, *The Work of Art in the Age of Its Technological Reproducibility, and Other Writings on Media*, Michael Jennings, Brigit

Doherty, and Thomas Leven, eds. (Cambridge, MA: Harvard University Press, 2008), 39–41; Robert Jütte, *A History of the Senses: From Antiquity to Cyberspace* (Cambridge: Polity, 2005), 300–1.

2   James Twitchell, *Dreadful Pleasures: An Anatomy of Modern Horror* (New York: Oxford University Press, 1985), 10; Barbara Ehrenreich, *Blood Rites: Origins and History of the Passions of War* (New York: Metropolitan, 1997), 80.

3   Some sources are W. Scott Poole, *Monsters in America* (Waco, TX: Baylor University Press, 2014), 14; Paul Wells, *The Horror Genre* (London: Wallflower Press, 2004), 8, 15; Noël Carroll, *Philosophy of Horror* (New York: Routledge, 1990), 192, 200; Rich Worland, *Horror Film* (London: Blackwell, 2007), 11.

4   Mathias Clasen, *Why Horror Seduces* (New York: Oxford University Press, 2017), 3–5, 24–7, 29–30, 35, 97, 126; Denis Dutton, *The Art Instinct: Beauty, Pleasure and Human Evolution* (London: Bloomsbury, 2009), 96, 204; David Buss, *The Murderer Next Door: Why the Mind is Designed to Kill* (New York: Penguin, 2005), 929. A very interesting survey of this theme is in Stephen Asma, "Monsters on the Brain: An Evolutionary Epistemology of Horror," *Social Research*, 81, 4 (Winter 2014): 941–67.

5   And the thrill comes not only from surviving predation but in the collective destruction of the predator. As Barbara Ehrenreich argues, "Give us an 'enemy' and a team or tribe with which to face that enemy down, and all anxiety dissolves, temporarily in a surge of collective aggression against the threat." Ehrenreich, *Blood Rites*, 91–4.

6   Jeffrey Jerome Cohen makes the case that the monster is always "pure culture," an embodiment of desires, fantasies, and fears emanating from a specific culture. J. J. Cohen, ed., "Monster Culture (Seven Theses)," in *Monster Theory: Reading Culture* (Minneapolis: University of Minnesota Press, 1996), 4.

7   Julia Kristeva, *Powers of Horror: An Essay on Abjection* (New York: Columbia University Press, 1982), 4.

8   Sigmund Freud, "The 'Uncanny,'" in *The Standard Edition of the Complete Psychological Works of Sigmund Freud, Volume XVII (1917-1919): An Infantile Neurosis and Other Works*, J. Strachey, ed. (London: Hogarth Press, 1955), 217–56.

9   Wells, *Horror Genre*, 16; Poole, *Monsters in America*, 14; Peter Hutchings, *The Horror Film* (Harlow: Pearson), 35, 69; Carroll, *Philosophy of Horror*, 187, 190, 209.

10   Stephen Asma, *On Monsters: An Unnatural History of Our Worst Fears* (New York: Oxford University Press, 2009), 187; Charles Derry, "More Dark Dreams: Some Notes on Recent Horror Films," in *American Horror*, Gregory A. Waller, ed. (Urbana: University of Illinois Press, 1987), 162–74; Margrit Shildrick, *Embodying the Monster: Encounters with the Vulnerable Self* (London: Sage, 2002), 3.

11   Noël Carroll, "General Theory of Horrific Appeal," 1–9 and Robert Solomon, "Real Horror," 232 both in *Dark Thoughts: Philosophical Reflections on*

Cinematic Horror, Steven Schneider and Daniel Shaw, eds. (Lanham, MD: Scarecrow Press, 2003). Dennis Giles, "Conditions of Pleasure in Horror Cinema," in *Planks of Reason: Essays in the Horror Film*, Barry Grant and Christopher Sharret, eds. (Lanham, MD: Scarecrow Press, 2004), 38–40. Note also Carroll, *Philosophy of Horror*.

12 Elizabeth Cowie, "The Lived Nightmare," 25–43 and Daniel Shaw, "Reply to 'Real Horror,'" 260–2 both in *Dark Thoughts*; Julian Hanich, *Cinematic Emotion in Horror Films and Thrillers* (New York: Routledge, 2011).

13 Giles, "Conditions of Pleasure in Horror," 46; Clasen, *Why Horror Seduces*, 54. Similar views are in Dutton, *Art Instinct*, 135; Twitchell, *Dreadful Pleasures*, 65–6; Waller, "Introduction," in *American Horror*, 11.

14 Stephen King, *Danse Macabre* (New York: Everest House, 1981), 43.

15 King, *Danse Macabre*, 44–5, 268–9.

16 Stephen King makes the conventional point: periods of increased popularity in horror "seem to coincide with periods of fairly serious economic and /or political strain" as these movies and novels "seem to reflect those free-floating anxieties." Still horror during the strain of the Second World War did less well and was in fact banned in Britain. King, *Danse Macabre*, 40.

17 Of course, this psychoanalytic interpretation was hardly confined to the new horror from the late 1960s. Classical monsters, from Dr. Frankenstein's creature to Dracula and King Kong, have been understood by historians like Reynolds Humphries as embodiments of repressed libido. Robin Wood, "Introduction to The American Horror Film," in *Planks of Reason*, 107–52, especially 111–15, 120; Robin Wood, *Hollywood: From Vietnam to Reagan . . . and Beyond* (New York: Columbia University Press, 2003), Chapter 5; Asma, *On Monsters*, 191, 197–8; Reynold Humphries, *American Horror Film* (Edinburgh: Edinburgh University Press, 2002), Chapter 1.

18 Twitchell admits that horror is about more than sexual repression; it is also an expression of a youthful quest for visceral excitement. But he still insists that horror films have something to do with the encounter with the "incest taboo." Twitchell, *Dreadful Pleasures*, 10, 69, 74–84, 77–8, 86–9, 93.

19 Mikita Brottman, *Offensive Films: Toward an Anthropology of Cinéma Vomitif* (Westport, CT: Greenwood, 1997), 8, 108.

20 Arthur Tudor, *Monsters and Mad Men* (London: Blackwell, 1989), 3; Solomon, "Real Horror," 18.

21 Wells, *Horror Genre*, 5; Wheeler Dixon, *A History of Horror* (New Brunswick, NJ: Rutgers University Press, 2010), 142–3; Todd Platts, "New Horror Movies," in *Baby Boomers and Popular Culture*, Thom Gencarelli, ed. (Santa Barbara, CA: Praeger, 2014), 5, 8–9; Waller, "Introduction," in *American Horror*, 1–4; Kendall Phillips, *Projected Fears: Horror Film and American Culture* (Westport, CT: Praeger, 2005).

22 Asma, *On Monsters*, 3–4, 24, 30, 87, chapter 8; Poole, *Monsters in America*, 5–6; Ehrenreich, *Blood Rites*, Chapters 3, 5.

23 Poole, *Monsters in America*, Chapter 1.

24 Worland, *Horror Film*, 27–35; Twitchell, *Dreadful Pleasures*, 26, 41–5, 49, quotation on 7; Asma, *On Monsters,* 153.

25 Tom Gunning, "The Cinema of Attractions (s): Early Film, Its Spectator and the Avant-Garde," in *Early Cinema: Space Frame Narrative*, Thomas Elsaesser, ed. (London: British Film Institute, 1990), 56–62; Tom Gunning, "Rethinking Early Cinema: Cinema of Attraction and Narrativity," in *Cinema of Attractions Reloaded*, Wanda Strauven, ed. (Amsterdam: Amsterdam University Press, 2006), 389–416; Gunning, "An Aesthetic of Astonishment: Early Film and the (In)Credulous Spectator," *Art & Text* 34 (Spring 1989): 31–45.

26 Benjamin, *Work of Art*, 29, 35, 37. On the tactile quality of film visuals, note Angela Ndalianis, *The Horror Sensorium: Media and the Senses* (Jefferson, NC: McFarland, 2012), 2–3.

27 Kevin Heffernan, *Ghouls, Gimmicks and Gold: Horror Films and the American Movie Business* (Durham, NC: Duke University Press, 2004), 5–6; Worland, *Horror Films*, 55–69; Hutchings, *Horror Film*, 14–15, 23; S. M. Conger, "The *Comic* and Grotesque in James Wale's Frankenstein Films," in *Planks of Reason*, 24; Kim Newman, *Nightmare Movies: A Critique of the Horror Film* (London: Bloomsbury, 1988), 2.

28 "Production Code of 1930" published in Jon Lewis, *Hollywood v. Hard Core: How the Struggle over Censorships Saved the Modern Film Industry* (New York: New York University Press, 2000), 302–7; *Motion Picture Herald*, January 23, 1932 cited in David Skal, *Monster Show* (London: Faber and Faber, 1993), 155 (note also 162, 171, 182); PCA quotation cited in Worland, *Horror Film*, 66; Gerald Gardner, *Censorship Papers: Movie Censorship Letters from the Hays Office, 1934-68* (New York: Dodd, Mead, 1987), xvi–xxi, 67–72; Jennifer Fronc, *Monitoring the Movies: The Fight over Film Censorship in Early Twentieth-Century Urban America* (Austin: University of Texas Press, 2017), 3, 7; Sheri Biesen, *Film Censorship Regulating America's Screen* (London: Wallflower, 2018), 17–23.

29 Worland, *Horror Film,* 68–70.

30 Twitchell, *Dreadful Pleasures*, 5, 57; Mark Jancovich, *Rational Fears: American Horror in the 1950s* (Manchester: Manchester University Press, 1996) challenges the conclusion that "invasion" horror encouraged a 1950s conformity, 11, 15, 18, 26, 29, as argued in Peter Biskind, *Seeing Is Believing: How Hollywood Taught Us to Stop Worrying and Love the Fifties* (London: Pluto, 1983), Chapter 3; Andrew Tudor, *Monsters and Mad Scientists* (Oxford: Blackwell, 1987); Dixon, *History of Horror*, Chapter 3; Hutchings, *Horror Film*, 27–8.

31 Roger Corman, *How I Made a Hundred Movies in Hollywood and Never Lost a Dime* (New York; Random House, 1990), Chapter 7; Jancovich, *Rational Fears*, 268–83; Mikita Brottman, "AIP's *Pit and Pendulum*: Poe as Drive-in Gothic," in *Planks of Reason*, 283–99; Heffernan, *Ghouls*, 44.

32 Heffernan, *Ghouls*, 7, 64–7; Waller, "Introduction," in *American Horror*, 5; William Paul, *Laughing, Screaming: Modern Hollywood Horror and Comedy* (New York: Columbia University Press, 1994), 15; Axel Madsen, *The New Hollywood* (New York: Crowell, 1975), 22–3.

33 Jancovich, *Rational Fears*, 85–7; Barbara Ehrenreich, *The Hearts of Men: American Dreams and the Flight from Commitment* (London: Pluto, 1983), 17; Andrew Ross, *No Respect: Intellectuals and Popular Culture* (London: Routledge, 1989), 83.

34 Murray Leeder, "Collective Screams: William Castle and the Gimmick Film," in *ReFocus: The Films of William Castle*, Murray Leeder, ed. (Edinburgh: Edinburgh University Press, 2018), 76–98, Castle's quotation cited on 76; Jancovich, *Rational Fears*, 88–9, 199–200.

35 Heffernan, *Ghouls*, 67, 185; Worland, *Horror Film*, 75–92, 116; Paul, *Laughing, Screaming*, 30-33.

36 Lewis, *Hollywood v. Hard Core*, Chapter 4; Platts, "New Horror Movies," 5; Paul, *Laughing, Screaming*, 28, 30–2; Skal, *Monster Show*, 328.

37 Heffernan, *Ghouls*, 203, 207, 212; Jancovich, *Rational Fears*, 199–218; Thomas Doherty, *Teenagers and Teenpics* (Boston: Unwin, 1988), 146–61; Peter Stanfield, *The Cool and the Crazy: Pop Fifties Cinema* (New Brunswick, NJ: Rutgers University Press, 2015).

38 Poole, *Monsters in America*, 151, 197–9; Skal, *Monster Show*, 272–3; Heffernan, *Ghouls*, 156, 181, 185, 221, 224, 228.

39 Leeder, "Castle and the Gimmick Film," 93; Paul, *Screaming, Laughing*, 13, 21, 34, 47, 419. Gunning, "Cinema of Attractions," 61 notes that spectacle films of the 1980s (including horror) had "roots in stimulus and carnival rides."

40 J. P. Telotte, "Beyond all Reason: The Nature of the Cult," 5–27 and Barry Grant, "Science-Fiction Double Feature: Ideology in the Cult Film," 122–30 both in *The Cult Film Experience*, J. P. Telotte, ed. (Austin: University of Texas Press, 1991); Jamie Sexton, *Cult Cinema* (New York: Wiley-Blackwell, 2011), 102–4. On the link between "freakery" and cult/horror, note David Church, "Freakery, Cult Films and the Problems of Ambivalence," *Journal of Film and Video*, 63, 1 (2011): 3–17.

41 Brottman, *Offensive Films*, 11–12.

42 Paul, *Screaming, Laughing*, 422. Carol Clover, *Men, Women, and Chain Saws* (Princeton, NJ: Princeton University Press, 1992), 41.

43 Clover, *Chain Saws*, 49, Platts, "New Horror Movies," 7–8.

44 Heffernan, *Ghouls*, 11–13; Hutchings, *Horror Film*, 88; Clover, *Chain Saws*, 12–13, 41; Wells, *Horror Genre*, 27; Wood, *Hollywood*, 75.

45 Hutchings, *Horror Film*, 82; Paul, *Screaming, Laughing*, 13.

46 William Kerwin, *The Herschell Gordon Lewis Feast*, blu-ray collection of films (Arrow Video, 2020); Dixon, *History of Horror*, 124–5.

47 Clasen, *Why Horror Seduces*, 95. Among the many interpretations are R. H. W. Dillard, "Night of the Living Dead: It's Not Just like a Wind Passing Through," in *American Horrors: Essays on the Modern American Horror Film*, Gregory Waller, ed. (Urbana: University of Illinois Press, 1988), 14–29; Phillips, *Projected Fears*, 82 especially.

48 J. Hoberman and Jonathan Rosenbaum, *Midnight Movies* (New York: De Capo, 1983), 110–11, 113–15, 120–1, 126; Worland, *Horror Film*, 36–8; Dillard, "Night of the Living Dead," 14–15.

49 Kristopher Woofter, ed. "'The Death of Death': A Memorial Retrospective on George A. Romero (1940-2017)," *MONSTRUM* 1, 1 (April 2018), https://www.academia.edu/37197922/_The_Death_of_Death_A_Memorial_Retrospective_on_George_A._Romero; Hoberman and Rosenbaum, *Midnight Movies*, 125–6.

50 Dillard, "Night of the Living Dead," 28; Poole, *Monsters in America*, 252; Hoberman and Rosenbaum, *Midnight Movies*, Chapter 5; Clasen, *Why Horror Seduces*, 95-99.

51 The famed Humberto Eco, *On Ugliness* (New York: Rizzoli, 2011), 422 reads Romero's film as a take on the failure of revolution in 1968 and the pessimistic view of the prevailing "presence of evil" in the world.

52 Wells, *Horror Genre*, 84; Paul, *Screaming, Laughing*, 288–9, 293–4, 312.

53 Wood, "Introduction," in *Plank of Reason*, 132–3 for quotations, also 134–8; Chris Sharret, "The Idea of Apocalypse in *The Texas Chainsaw Massacre*," in *Planks of Reason*, 301–219; Brottman, *Offensive Films*, 107–26.

54 Wood, "Introduction," in *Planks of Reason*, 130.

55 Paul, *Laughing, Screaming*, 390.

56 Dixon, *History of Horror*, 117; Katarina Gregersdotter, "A History of Animal Horror Cinema," in *Animal Horror Cinema*, Katarina Gregersdotter, Johan Höglund, and Nicklas Hållén, eds. (London Palgrave, 2015), 19–36.

57 Among the many commentaries on slasher films are Ian Conrich, "Seducing the Subject: Freddy Krueger, Popular Culture and the *Nightmare on Elm Street* Films," in *Trash Aesthetics: Popular Culture and Its Audience*, Deborah Cartmell et al., eds. (London: Pluto, 1997), 118–31; Phillips, *Projected Fears*, Chapter 6; Clover, *Chain Saws*, 33; Humphries, *American Horror*, Chapter 7.

58 Dixon, *History of Horror*, 168-69; especially focused on child killer films is Paul, *Laughing, Screaming*, Chapters 15, 16.

59 Wood in *Hollywood*, chapter 8, advances the distinction between reactionary horror (especially in the slasher genre) where religious themes and a monster who punishes promiscuity and independent females are common vs. "progressive horror," where the monster represents repressed desire and the story seems to critique cultural and social norms and conformity. He condemns later slasher films like *Creep Show* for "its empty anecdotes in which nasty people do nasty things to other nasty people," 173. Carol Clover famously argues that male viewers identify with the "last girl," not with the male predator (as claim others) in *Chain Saws*, 17–33. Richard Nowell, *Blood Money: A History of the First Teen Slasher Film Cycle* (New York: Continuum, 2011), argues that slasher film makers actually shaped their product to appeal to teen females. Even more distinctions are made by Judith Halberstam, *Skin Shows: Gothic Horror and the Technic of Monsters* (Durham, NC: Duke University Press, 1995).

60 Todd Trogmorton, *Roller Coasters* (Jefferson, NC: McFarland, 1993), 8–11, 32–3, 35; Robert Cartmell, *Incredible Scream Machine* (Bowling Green: Bowling Green State University Popular Press, 1987),182; Gary Cross, *Men to Boys: The Making of Modern Immaturity* (New York: Columbia University Press, 2008), Chapter 6.

61 Eric Lichtenfeld, *Action Speaks Louder: Violence, Spectacle, and the American Action Movie* (Westport, CT: Praeger, 2004), 22–5, 186–7; John Taylor, "Dirty Harry," in *Movies of the Seventies*, Ann Lloyd, ed. (London: Orbis, 1984), 172–3.

62 J. MacLachlan and M. Logan, "Camera Shot Length in TV Commercials and their Memorability and Persuasiveness," *Journal of Advertising Research*, 33, 2 (1993): 57–63; Simon Gottschalk, "Speed Culture: Fast Strategies in Televised Commercial Ads," *Qualitative Sociology*, 22, 4 (1999): 312.

63 As Colin Campbell notes, in a consumer age spending is driven not only by anticipating the satisfaction of desire but by disappointment when the desirable object is consumed, creating the incentive to find still another item of consumer fulfillment. Colin Campbell, *The Romantic Ethic and the Spirit of Modern Consumerism* (New York: Palgrave, 2018, originally published in 1987).

64 An early example is the final scene of *Carrie* (1976), the story of a nerdy and humiliated high school girl who destroys everyone at the prom with her telekinetic powers. The movie concludes with the beautiful and dreamy goodie-goodie Sue Snell knelling at Carrie's grave only to be grabbed by a bloody arm as she lays flowers down. A similar shock scene ends *Friday the 13th* as a rotted corpse rises from a lake to grab the final female victim.

65 Paul, *Laughing, Screaming,* 420; Dixon, *History of Horror,* 12, 17, 152.

66 Clasen, *Why Horror Seduces,* 71.

67 Craven cited in Wells, *Horror Genre*, 93; Hutchings, *Horror Film*, 212; Andrew Britton, "Blissing Out: The Politics of Reaganite Entertainment," *Movie*, I31, 32 (1986): 1–7.

68 Corman, *How I Made a Hundred Movies*, ix, 33–4, 61–3.

69 Donato Totaro, "Your Mother Ate My Dog! Peter Jackson and Gore-Comedy," *Offscreen*, 5, 4 (September 2001): 1–24, https://offscreen.com/view/peterjackson.

70 Wes Craven and Kevin Williamson, *Scream,* DVD (Dimension Films, 1996); Jane Maslin, *Tricks of the Gory Trade, New York Times*, December 20, 1996, https://www.nytimes.com/1996/12/20/movies/tricks-of-the-gory-trade.html; Worland, *Horror Film*, 109.

71 Dixon, *History of Horror*, 136. Judith Mayne, *Cinema and Spectatorship* (London: Routledge, 1993); Valerie Wee, "The Scream Trilogy: Hyperpostmodernism and the Late Nineties: Teen Slasher Films," *Journal of Film and Video*, 57, 3 (2005): 44–61; I. C. Pinedo, *Recreational Terror: Women and the Pleasure of Horror Film Viewing* (Albany, NY: SUNY Press, 1997), 9–50.

72 Wells, *Horror Genre*, 23, 32–3.

73 Twitchell, *Dreadful Pleasures*, 63; Wells, *Horror Genre*, 35, 108; Paul, *Laughing, Screaming,* 430.

74 Ndalianis, *Horror Sensorium*, 16, 26–8.

7

Taking the Sideshow to the Big Top

Freak Culture in the Mainstream

The twentieth century did not bring the triumph of the high modernist culture of natural history museums or even of the middlebrow culture of family sitcoms over the freak at the carnival. Instead, a new freak show emerged, drawing upon the old, but shaped by and patronized by elements of the very middle class that earlier in the century had shunned it. That new freak show—sometimes with characters and themes that were very different from the original—became an important element in a highly contested modern popular culture. That culture largely emanated from a broad middle-class, which was divided against itself by generation and values. The sideshow show had moved to the "Big Top."

The middle class that had embraced the "philistine" or family middlebrow (as opposed to highbrow modernist elite) rejected the disgusting freak, but, at the same time, accepted oddity in the delight of the cute. This had its roots in the late nineteenth century and ran parallel to the elite condemnation of the traditional freak show. While the family-centered middle class abhorred the geek and pinhead, in the 1930s it embraced the cute in the childlike innocent (if sometimes impish) image of Disney's freakish characters and even the gleeful troupes of singing midgets. Later in the 1960s in rebellion from middle-class convention, literary elites like Susan Sontag and Diane Arbus re-embraced a wider range of the freak-show bannerline and were joined by some of the rebellious children of that middle class. Again, this was not a full restoration of the traditional sideshow; instead, it was a substitution of the marvel-seeking gawking of plebes for the campish irony of counterculturists in defiance of their middle-class origins. Put another way, youth rejected the cute for the cool freak. And finally, in a second form of middle-class rebellion, youth abandoned the emotional and somatic restraint of genteel tastemakers (and conventional kitschists) for unleashed sensation. One form of this was to turn the creepy encounter with the traditional freak into the embrace of unrestrained horror.

The cute, camp, and creepy rehabilitated traditional carnival culture, but did so only within the broad framework of an emerging consumer culture. Commercial enterprise marketed the cute and camp in extremely varied venues ranging from Disney's Worlds to midnight movie theaters. The intensification of the creepy in the new horror synced with another dynamic of consumer culture—the acceleration and compression of sensation in experiential goods. The freak show of 1910 was almost unrecognizable in its modern commercial forms as cartoon characters, cross-dressing performers, and zombies. Yet the rejected freak returned, transformed in the fragmented and divided culture of the middle class.

The result was striking: The early twentieth-century bourgeois values that had marginalized the freak show were themselves marginalized in the cute, camp, and creepy of contemporary popular culture. For even the middle-class consumer, the somber and cultivated culture of high modernism was sometimes passed over for the more playful, even mildly impish, culture of the cute. Thus, the irrepressible popularity of Disney and its many successors. Similarly, the middle-class counterculture from the 1960s rejected genteel cultural hierarchy and emotional restraint in a "return" to the long-marginalized sideshow (albeit in new forms) in camp and the creepy. The outcome is a popular culture that encompasses a full aesthetic range: from the sentimental, reassuring, and nostalgic to the endlessly novel, irreverent, and sensuously uncorked.

Traditional and Contemporary Freakishness

Clearly, the modern middle-class transformation of the freak show has changed what it means to be or to encounter a freak. Today's freak has become less abnormal (or creepy) and this has undercut the line that separated the conventional from the taboo. For example, the recent popularization of piercing, tattooing, purple hair, and so on (as modeled in celebrities like Dennis Rodman) has eroded the "shock" of the stigmatized other. What once was scandalous often has become camp. In time, the freak photos of Diane Arbus have ceased to disturb the public, obliging freak performers to extremes that the tradition-bound sideshow never engaged in. On the screen, the new freak (as zombie or cartoon monster) has become even more abject. The simultaneous reduction and increase of freakishness defines our age—and doubtless contributes to the anxiety of those of us raised on restraint and customary identity.

Obviously, the modern freak has broken from the constraints of tradition, even of the freak show from the past. Though drawing on tradition (as did Jim Rose's cavalcade of blockheads and pincushions), the new freak show in all its variety is fundamentally innovative as the traditional show was not. The new version is, like much modern consumer culture, based on novelty, rapidity of change, and intensification in response to satiation. This is part of the modern speed up of the entertainment and consumption cycle (as novelty begets more novelty). Other related factors also come into play, including the new plasticity in image-making in the digital age that introduces new forms of freakishness that far outpace the bizarre products of irregular birth in the traditional sideshow. Digitized special effects make gore more horrifying and cartoon characters more bizarre. But the key point remains: With increased exposure, the creepy has become less frightening and disgusting, encouraging, in turn, more direct, frequent, and extreme productions of creepiness.

The traditional sideshow had its roots in the country fair and festival, and, like other festival attractions, it drew audiences expecting an annual return of the unchanging bannerline. The modern freak show, be it produced by Disney, Jim Hensen or other fabricators of the freakishly cute, staged by camp-impresarios Jerry Springer and John Waters, or commercialized by creep-makers Wes Craven and George Romero, has a much more tenuous tie to the past and to the memory of its crowd. And, as rising generations were exposed to this accelerating turnover of freaks, identification with and memory of traditional stories and characters declined or were reduced to camp. When the young lost ties to freak traditions, freakishness often went to extremes.

Of course, the new freak show is not just about novelty. Modern horror often references the past, at least, to knowing crowds recollecting iconic scenes from the repertory of horror movies. Yet this leads not to a traditional form of nostalgia (as in the repeated and accustomed visit to the sideshow of old), but to a new way of engaging the past—a nostalgia triggered by re-encounters with media moments from childhood or youth (such as from viewing a succession of versions of *Friday the 13th*). Instead of a return to a site of wonder (perhaps shared with a novice viewer) at the circus or carnival, the modern form of nostalgia is usually camp, often a resistance to wonder.

In the final analysis, the difference between the old and new freak show is found in the change of audiences and how the new crowd encountered the Other. Gone is the country rube or immigrant. Instead, in the new freak show the audience has largely been comprised of a jaded middle-class youth (but also minority and working-class whites), gleefully mocking convention while searching endlessly for new thrills. The gawking at the oddity was central to the traditional sideshow. That encounter produced wonder but it was also driven by the viewer's search for assurances of personal normality and even superiority. This ritual has been partially replaced by a more tolerant and open gaze, including the embrace of the stigmatized in somewhat bowdlerized form (the cute), the suspension of convention and a playful joining in the freak community (the camp), and the attraction to a bracing emotional intensity (the creepy). Yet, as the new freak show has become more "freaky," it has also become more mainstream, less sideshow, and more, big top.

Televised Freaks: Ghosts of Barnum Today

Of course, the traditional freak show has not lost all its appeal. As noted in Chapter 3, it is featured repeatedly in documentaries and even in the nostalgic reality TV series *Freakshow*. The classical freak was the theme of thirteen episodes of the anthology cable series (FX) *American Horror Show* in 2014, loosely imitating Browning's idea in *Freaks* of conflict between normal people and human oddities.[1]

However, most contemporary manifestations of the freak show are part of tabloid cable TV. Still, they reveal striking parallels with the traditional show, even that of Barnum. For example, *My 600-Lb Life* that began in 2012 on TLC, formerly known as The Learning Channel, combines the voyeuristic appeal of viewing the showering and dressing of real 600-pound women (mostly) along with sympathetic images of their struggle with weight-loss programs, with which many viewers certainly identify. The featured reality stars try to become "normal" through will power, gradual self-understanding, medical intervention (especially in graphic scenes of surgery), and inevitable setbacks. It is a type of reality and documentary TV that updates the Barnumesque freak show by attempting to humanize the disturbing oddity, who, beneath the mounds of flesh and awkward movements, is still just a regular person with recognizable longings for love, achievement, and integrity. Unlike the "jolly" or "baby" fat ladies of the traditional sideshow, these women were not supposed to be "happy" in their weight or mocked when posed as chubby babies as in the old freak show. This change is perhaps a measure of more positive attitudes about difference. But, in part, because of the modern valorization of thinness for medical as well as aesthetic reasons, 600 pounders were "normal" only in their striving to be like "everyone else" in weight. With less heft, they return to the fold of independent self-determining selfhood. The audience is to cheer them on, even as they look on, like the freak show crowd of old, aghast at their bodies.[2]

Other programs offer similar blends of voyeurism and pseudo-medical documentary. For example, *Supersize vs Superskinny* on the UK's Channel 4 (2008–2014) pairs off participants with contrasting body sizes who swap their usual meals for a week to see if they reassess their attitudes toward food. The purported purpose is to explore the responses of people with extreme relationships with food. But the freakish appeal of the anomalous body remains. These are the fat lady and skeleton person of Barnum's freak show in modern guise.[3]

These takes on body weight correspond with a modern moral judgment: the presumed responsibility of the individual to maintain an ideal body size.

Fat is no longer a mark of success or affluence as it sometimes was in the past when it distinguished the rich from the poor who could not afford food. Rather, obesity has become a mark of lack of self-control. It certainly isn't something to laugh at or to assume that the overweight person is a contented self-indulgent (like Santa Claus). The stare has changed since Barnum's day. It has been reconfigured in the terms of modern concerns—especially an all-too-common temptation to binge in a world of easy access to temptation. Many viewers can both judge and identify with these overweight women. But it is a stare just the same.[4]

The treatment of midgets in TLC and other channels is quite different: Their body anomalies are treated as natural (as they are); and in their reality shows, small people are portrayed as normal. Following the tenets of the disability-rights movement, these small people are presented positively and, despite their difficulties in dealing with the full-sized community, they are shown in well-adjusted and conventional lives (even if that normality in itself may appear "freakish," as seen when a small person has a regular-sized offspring). All this is played out in the portrayals of the economic and personal successes of the Roloff family in *Little People, Big World*.[5]

There are, however, limits to even positive presentations of the anomalous body in these TV freak shows. In this light, Krystal Cleary considers *Abby and Brittany*, a TLC reality presentation (2012) of the American conjoined twins Abby and Brittany Hensel, who have been media curiosities since their birth in 1990. Cleary notes how the twins (sharing a lower body) are presented as "just like us" and challenge "oppressive depictions of people with non-normative bodies." But the "us" that the Hensel twins resemble is characterized by "whiteness, upward class mobility, and fulfillment of conventional gender and sexual norms." The twins aspire to marry, go to college, travel, and live normal lives. Their disability is a matter of how they cope individually, rather than politically, and is limited only by "antagonistic haters," rather than by wider social biases. I would add that covering these physical anomalies with conventional middle-class values harks back to the Victorian portrayal of human oddities, in effect "normalizing" them and reducing the anxiety of the gaze.[6]

If the recent televised freak, in effect, modernizes the Barnum formula, the TLC also appeals in some measure to the campy version of the stare that was featured in the tabloid TV of Jerry Springer. Campish takes on the freak are central to the recent transformation of narrowcast and cable TV. Like others, The Learning Channel began with an educational mission in 1972 with ties to the federal government to promote science, nature, and medical programming to a general TV audience. Though privatized in 1980, the format began to change only when it was purchased by the Discovery Channel in 1991. Slowly the general educational format was replaced by reality TV programming. In addition to televising classical freaks like the Hensel Twins, TLC featured the antics of outrageous family groups like *Jon & Kate Plus 8* (from 2007) and *17 Kids and Counting* (which became *18 Kids and Counting* and then *19 Kids and Counting,* running from 2008 to 2017). These reality programs combine the self-display of the type of psychological freak that appeared on 1990s tabloid TV with soap opera as fans identify with and mock these personalities and their dilemmas.[7]

Classic perhaps is *My Husband's Not Gay,* a TLC special that aired in 2015. This show features four Mormon men from Utah (three married) who admit to being attracted to the same sex but deny their homosexuality. To create a tabloid interest, the show focuses on how their Mormon wives, families, and neighbors cope with this obvious anomaly in conservative Mormon society.[8] Arguably, TLC has become progressively more bizarre and campish after 2010. *Meet the Putmans* features three generations and twenty-six people living in chaos in the same house. The more recent Netflix hit (2020) *Tiger King* follows the same path with warring promotors of wild animal shelters (as Carole Baskin of Big Cat Rescue accuses Joe Exotic of abusing wild animals). The series offers bemused viewers (34.5 million according to a Nielson survey) contrasting "philosophies" and personal styles that are equally extreme.[9]

Most of these cable shows either modified the Barnumesque formula to fit contemporary expectations of the "normal" or featured psychological freaks in a reality TV format that revived the tabloid TV of Jerry Springer and company. The TLC and other freak programming may make Ward Hall's point that there remains a market today for the sideshow. A century of genteel condemnation of the freak show and ever more extreme spectacles have not made the midget's daily life or the travails of the 600-pound woman boring or distasteful to a jaded modern audience. The continued success of these programs reveals once again the persistence of the carnivalesque, sometimes as a thumb in the eye of genteel culture (or the PC) and sometimes as an impulse that simply has survived cultural "progress" and decades of "fast" entertainment.

Yet surely a greater takeaway from our exploration of the "irrepressible freak" has been how the old sideshow has been transformed by the bourgeois turn to the cute and the countercultural adoption of camp and the creepy. Moreover, these aesthetics have been combined in contemporary popular culture. These amalgams (intertextual collages if you will) should not be surprising in a postmodern age. The decontextualization of old appeals and their recombination into new and shifting presentations is a hallmark of our times. It's worth a few moments in the closing of this book to look a little closer at how and why this pastiche of the cute, camp, and creepy works.

The Cute Morphs into the Creepy

As we have seen, the cute in the midget was among the last of the live (and born) freaks that kept the loyalty of a broad middle-class audience. And the aesthetic of cuteness spread far beyond the sideshow. From the 1930s, the cuteified freak took the form of a wide range of media characters and stories that toyed with and challenged expectations about body size and behavior. And these especially appealed to children. Examples are animal cartoon characters, Louis Marx toys, Disney's Lands, and recently preschool cable cartoon networks, and children's Pixar movies.

However, the cute has not remained unchanged. While the Disney formula survived and even flourished into the twenty-first century, the cute has taken new forms less amenable to traditional middle-class sensibilities, blending with the cool (often adult- and boundary-defying images and attitudes as seen in long-running cartoon sitcoms like *The Simpsons* and *Family Guy*), and this melding has extended even into the realm of horror.

Let's consider briefly the example of the Jim Henson's monster menagerie, the Muppets,. a soft blending of the cute and the creepy. Henson's creations often went through a process of cuteification. Consider Big Bird, whose first appearance on Sesame Street was frightening to children. Like Mickey Mouse in the 1930s, Big Bird was modified to make his/her size seem gentle and childlike with the introduction of a shorter beak and wider eyes in 1970. Count von Count was modeled after Bela Lugosi's Dracula with an eastern European voice and dress in 1972, but gradually the Count became more benign, a childlike caricature of the horror film star. And while the Cookie Monster was obsessed with cookies, he never knocked down anyone to devour their sweets. Children saw themselves in the Cookie Monster, but they knew also that they had greater self-control than he did (just as was the case with Donald Duck for an earlier generation).[10]

Historian Chandra Mukerji's brief foray into the cultural sociology of the Muppets as children's monsters makes a critical point: Modern adults see young children as "cuddly little creatures containing the marks of an untamed beast." Children see themselves similarly and recognize themselves in the Muppet "monster." The cute in monster form is a contradictory mix of natural goodness and impulsiveness. This is reflected in the child who adults view as innocent but who has yet to learn self-control and to positively express emotions and desires (a view that long has shaped the meaning of the cute). Thus, Oscar the Grouch who is slovenly, uncooperative, quick to anger, and lives in a garbage can is the embodiment of impulsiveness. Yet, he is innocently contained and unthreatening. Children can identify with him and accept their "bad" side as part of growing up in a permissive American childhood. Miss Piggy represents the nonconformist child who is both the girly girl and the wild masculine force, a classic monster ("made up of different elements from nature that do not belong together"). Yet again, she is loveble, in part, because of her affection for the everyman hero, Kermit the Frog. For Mukerji, the Muppets characters help children to learn to navigate through childhood. In their cuteified form, the Muppets also make this process unthreatening to adults who insist on the "innocence" of children. Yet the Muppets remain monsters.[11]

Horror historians have often noted the attraction of children to monsters and the creepy. Since *Dracula* and *Frankenstein* in the early 1930s, young people have filled the theaters showing horror. But that childish fascination has been adapted and dampened by the cute, reducing fear and disgust in encountering the monster. The cuteification of horror also gives parents' permission to allow their kids to watch creepy movies. From the late 1930s and 1940s, horror was adapted to humor in classics like *Abbott and Costello Meet Frankenstein* (where the young audience delights in the "scaredy-cat" behavior of the child-man Lou Costello). The "new horror" in 1968 and the rating system, which excluded children from "R" movies like *Night of the Living Dead*, opened space for a more "child friendly" form of horror that was rated PG (*Ghostbusters* and *Gremlins* of 1984, for example). Even more, the introduction of the PG-13 rating in 1984, designed for the older child, encouraged horror productions that avoided sex and graphic gore, but offered fright and the disgusting.[12]

Because kids' horror has to be both scary and suitable for the innocent child, it must be domesticated or tamed. The easiest way of doing this is to make the monsters humorous and unrealistic, and so earn the PG rating.[13] Such movies frequently reach kids "by placing children at the centers of the narratives as independent, resourceful, and identifiable characters who do not need the help of adults." This rehabilitation of horror, notes Susanne Ylönen, steels children against their fears of the unknown, but does so because the monster has been cuteified, made sympathetic, even endearing. However, by cuteifying the monster, film makers not only housebreak the fearful and disgusting, they make horror transgressive. As Catherine Lester notes (following Carroll and other horror scholars), "horror monsters are disgusting because they are impure": They are often amalgamations of opposites like the living and dead (vampires, zombies) or human and unhuman like werewolves, but also combinations of the fearful and cheerful. This allows children especially to "balance 'negative' feelings of fear and disgust with 'positive' ones of amusement and relief."[14]

But the cute entry into the world of horror goes beyond finding a marketing sweet spot for PG horror. As Maja Brzozowska-Brywczyńska observes, the cute and the creepy can be understood through one another. The aesthetics of cuteness has curious linkages with "deformity and dejection," classic expressions of the creepy. Think only of Hello Kitty, on the face of it a "loveable white kitten," but freakishly deformed and creepy without a mouth or hands. This combination works to define many contemporary freaks.[15]

The tense linkage between the cute and the creepy becomes even clearer when we return to the concept of the "uncanny," an unnerving creepy feeling that occurs when what appears familiar turns out to be strange. Robots and talking dolls have made people feel the uncanny because they challenge our accustomed divisions between the inanimate and alive. The same response occurs at viewing Arbus's photographs of a smiling child with a toy hand grenade. Both disturb our expectations. This disruption happens frequently in modern media and consumer culture. Scott Eberle observes, "The uncanny works best when the dissonance is sharpest: the innocent turned monstrous as in a doll." Here, once again, the cute meets the creepy. Film has long played with this such as in *Bad Seed*, where the seemingly adorable child turns out to be murderer.[16]

Given this, it shouldn't be surprising that "dark toys" have increasingly appeared in children's playrooms. As Katriina Heljakka remarks (2017), "The toys of today have come to communicate attitude, spunk and subcultural styles of a darker, morbid nature. As horror is becoming increasingly toyified, it is simultaneously cuteified as well." These toys "soften the dark and monstrous elements of the characters by . . . adding plumpness and more vulnerable expressions to their facial features." This can be found in toy figures of vampires, werewolves, and Voodoo dolls that "blur the boundaries" between the "sick" and the "cute." These evil effigies give agency to kids by serving as "vehicles that mirror projections of [children's] dark side." Still for children horrifying dolls must not slip into the unplayably terrifying. Moreover, the line between the cuteified monster and the terrifying monster shifts as youth become jaded.[17]

The cute can slide in an instant from the innocent and even pitiful to the impish and "naughty," from the passive and yielding to the demanding and willful. The cute is ambiguous (suggesting the passive, but again with origins in the word "acute" meaning sharp or edgy), and thus, it can shift into the monstrous. Moreover, the anti-cute is not simply the opposite of cute, but, as Maja Brzozowska-Brywczyńska observes, "the empowered cute." Such was the function of the Chuckie series as the adorable doll turns into a monster.[18]

Finally, the cute character can be a prompt for a monstrous assault on the cute. The notorious example is *Happy Tree Friends*, an "adult cartoon" series involving cute and cuddly animal characters who, while playing, shopping, and engaging in other everyday safe activities, find their "Disneyesque" lives ended (temporarily and in cartoonish ways)—with decapitations, hangings, and so on. Presumably, viewers take delight in the upending of these syrupy characters and situations, an update of Ed Roth's whimsical mockery of Mickey Mouse with his Rat Fink images from the 1970s. *Happy Tree Friends* also points to another side of the cute—its curious tendency to evoke a monstrous response. As culture critic Daniel Harris notes, "Adorable things are often most adorable in the middle of a pratfall or a blunder: Winnie the Pooh with his snout stuck in the hive." Curiously, the cute is most cute when it is hurt; even more, many of us in play (hopefully not reality) enjoy imposing that hurt on the cute. It is a particularly nasty expression of aggression toward the freak.[19]

Genteel society of the past found ways of ignoring and suppressing the monster apart from but also within us. But modern commerce finds ways of letting this demon out of the bag. Yet, with the cute, it does so in ways that are not too disturbing or threatening. The uncanny was present in the old freak show, with the "cute" and babylike midget who turned out to smoke cigars and display lecherousness. But with the shift to the hypercute as in new animation, and the shift from the intermittent and rare carnival experience to hours of daily screen entertainment, the old uncanny becomes familiar and thus no longer uncanny. As a result, the new freak show, like that of *Happy Tree Friends*, has to become ever edgier as it reduces the distinction between the cute and the creepy.

All-Pervasive Camp

Just as the cute and creepy have melded in the contemporary freak, camp has become nearly omnipresent. Since the 1990s, but building on trends from the 1960s, camp has moved to greater extremes in everything from "ironic" and self-deprecating advertising to genre-mocking sitcoms (like *Family Guy*), transforming the countercultural into the mainstream. As we have seen in Chapter 6, camp has worked like the cute to facilitate the creepy (especially in its intensification) as camp horror has transformed the emotionally charged experience of the disgusting and fearful into a joke. Camp has also empowered self-proclaimed freaks on the stage and screen but also in the audience. The latter trend is most obvious in campy "cosplay" (costumed participation) at showings of the Rocky Horror Picture Show and elsewhere.

The campish performances of self-declared freaks who haunted theaters for weekend showings of *The Rocky Horror Picture Show* survived the decline of the counterculture. *Rocky* reappeared for decades after its 1975 premiere in screen revivals but also as cosplay spectacle. These viewings became a cult, attracting the generation who went to rock clubs to see Jim Rose's new age freak show in the 1990s. In subsequent years up to the present, the *Rocky* "experience" has become sort of a nostalgic event as children (maybe even grandchildren) of the 1960s and 1970s "freaks" tried to get some of the fun back. It has reached even into Halloween performances in small-town colleges like Morehead State in Kentucky in 2011 (as reported by a young librarian I met at the Ringling Art Library). In 1991, sixteen years after its first exhibition, *Rocky* still attracted a cult of about 30,000 people with enthusiasts claiming to have seen the film a thousand times. In 2016, a TV film, *The Rocky Horror Picture Show: Let's Do the Time Warp Again* offered still another way of reembracing the old cult of *Rocky*.[20]

Of course, there were other signs of the survival of the campish freak culture of the 1960s and 1970s. One is "Geek Culture" that closely aligns with the creepy theme. An example is Qui Nguyen's *She Kills Monsters* (2013), at the "off-off Broadway" site of Steppenwolf Garage Theater in Chicago. In this and his many other productions, Nguyen attempts to bring gamers, cosplayers, and science fiction/fantasy/noir fans to the theater. Of special interest, of course, are horror characters. Nguyen is coproducer of the New York theater group Vampire Cowboys, founded in 2000 and located in New York since 2002. His plays draw on comic books and role-playing video games, appealing to self-described "geeks." Vampire Cowboys has attracted the comic book fan crowd with workshops and presentations at comic book conventions.[21]

These conventions date back to the late 1930s as gatherings of science-fiction enthusiasts. The most famous is the Comic-Con International that dates from 1970 in San Diego. Over time, it and its many imitators have offered panel presentations and commercial displays, but more recently also cosplay with fans dressing up as zombies and other monsters (as well as superheroes and other comic book characters). In September 2011, Stan Lee, famed Marvel comics creator, produced the Comikaze Zombie Apocalypse at the Los Angeles Convention Center, attracting thousands, many in costume. Celebrity guests included for nostalgia the aged Adam West from the 1960s TV version of *Batman* but also Norman Reedus, current star of *Walking Dead* on AMC. Featured was an obstacle "survival course infested with zombies" who chased participants, obliging them to "crawl, climb, and slide to safety."[22] Horror has become play, and with this a means of putting on the freak (at least for a long weekend).

Irrepressible Freaks and Contemporary Popular Culture

The revived freak show in all its forms is certainly disappointing from the standpoint of natural history museum curators, advocates of high modern art, and proponents of the dignity of the different. And I share many of these concerns. Yet this trend is hardly all negative. The gawking at the oddity was central to the traditional sideshow and, with it, the viewers' longing to feel superior and even to humiliate the different. This has been partially replaced by a more tolerant gaze, even if the predominate form of this embrace of the different is in a distorted, bowdlerized form (the cute). We still like our freaks to be small people or the cheerfully odd. Also, we can suspend convention and playfully join the freak community in the campish crowd, even though, as with the college students who attended Jerry Springer spectacles, we often do so from an emotional distance. The cosplay of youth "performing" zombie stories may be harmless, but when do we get serious? We can abandon the repressive squeamishness of the past and embrace an emotional intensity (the creepy), even if we sometimes sacrifice narrative and experience sensual overload to no moral end.

These trends run through much of contemporary popular culture, sometimes producing entertainment that is unconventional and often titillating, if not often uplifting or wondrous. Yet this infusion of the latter-day freakery provides contemporary culture with a dynamic and creativity that neither genteel nor traditional carnival culture could ever offer. Our encounter with the irrepressible freak can be playful, eye-opening, and just plain fun, liberating us from the often elitist restraints of the respectable (be it in modern art museums or sentimental country music concerts). The modern oddity can free us from the tired fare of the circus, whose delights are lost to modern audiences. The irrepressible freak recovers for us the vitality of the historic carnival but in ways befitting our modern attraction to endless novelty. The decline of a cultural hierarchy that once put the sideshow at the periphery has made the rebellious descendances of earlier middle-class tastemakers today more tolerant and playful. The sideshow is no longer sidelined, and its pleasures have enlivened popular culture—even if at a price.

Notes

1 The "Freak Show season" of *American Horror Show* was set in 1952 in Jupiter Florida, revolving around the story of one of the last freak shows struggling to survive and coping with the fears and hostility of locals toward these "monsters." Borrowing from Browning's *Freaks,* featured characters include conjoined female twins, a bearded lady, a "lobster boy," and other classic freaks, along with a self-centered and volatile "owner" Elsa Mars. Though much of the violence and convoluted plot development centers around others (including a mysterious "killer clown"), Browning's identification of the freak show with horror remains. *American Horror Show: Freak Show*, October 8, 2014–January 21, 2015, FX network, created by Ryan Murphy and Brad Falchuk (available on Prime Video, 2020).

2 A variation is *My Big Fat Fabulous Life,* featuring a somewhat more upbeat personality Whitney Way Thore, who at 380 pounds (perhaps caused by Polycystic ovary syndrome) challenges body shaming and longs to return to her love of dance and relationships. She "is no longer letting her fear of people's judgment dictate the way she lives her life." https://www.tlc.com/tv-sh ows/my-big-fat-fabulous-life/about. See also https://www.tlc.com/tv-shows/my -600-lb-life/.

3 Allison Leadley, "Supersize vs. Superskinny: (Re)framing the Freak Show in Contemporary Popular Culture (2008–2014)," *Journal of Popular Television*, 3, 2 (October 2015): 213–28; R. Sandell, "In the Shadow of the Freakshow: The Impact of Freakshow Tradition on the Display and Understanding of Disability History in Museums," *Disability Studies Quarterly*, 25, 4 (2005), http://dsq-sds.org/ article/view/614/791.

4 Peter Stearns, *Fat History: Bodies and Beauty in the Modern West* (New York: New York University Press, 2002).

5 Laura Backstrom, "From the Freak Show to the Living Room: Cultural Representations of Dwarfism and Obesity," *Sociological Forum*, 27, 3 (September 2012): 682–707.

6 Krystal Cleary, "Misfitting and Hater Blocking: A Feminist Disability Analysis of the Extraordinary Body on Reality Television," *Disability Studies Quarterly*, 36, 4 (2016), https://dsq-sds.org/article/view/5442/4471; Krystal Cleary, "One

of Us?: Disability Drag and the Gaga Enfreakment of Fandom," in *Disability Media Studies: Media, Popular Culture, and the Meanings of Disability*, Elizabeth Ellcessor and Bill Kirkpatrick, eds. (New York: New York University Press, 2017), 177–96.

7   Emma Teitel, "What Exactly Are We Learning from The Learning Channel?" *McCleans,* February 14, 2015, https://www.macleans.ca/culture/television/wh at-exactly-are-we-learning-from-tlc/.

8   Joanne Ostrow, "Latest TLC Freak Show: 'My Husband's Not Gay,'" *Denver Post,* January 7, 2015.

9   Ian Fortey, "5 Signs TLC Shows Have Gone From Stupid To Evil," *Cracked*, September 16, 2018, https://www.cracked.com/blog/5-signs-tlc-shows-hav e-gone-from-stupid-to-evil/; Todd Spangler, "'Tiger King' Nabbed Over 34 Million U.S. Viewers in First 10 Days, Nielsen Says (EXCLUSIVE)," *Variety*, April 8, 2020, https://variety.com/2020/digital/news/tiger-king-nielsen -viewership-data-stranger-things-1234573602/.

10   Michael Davis, *Street Gang: The Complete History of Sesame Street* (New York: Viking, 2008), 193, 197, 240, 247.

11   Chandra Mukerji, "Monsters and Muppets: The History of Childhood and Techniques of Cultural Analysis," in *From Sociology to Cultural Studies*, Elizabeth Long, ed. (New York: Blackwell, 1997), 158, 160.

12   Catherine Lester, "The Children's Horror Film: Characterizing an 'Impossible,'" *The Velvet Light Trap,* 78 (Fall 2016): 22–4; Filipa Antunes, "Children and Horror after PG-13: The Case of The Gate," *Networking Knowledge,* 6, 4 (2014): 18–28.

13   Harvey Roy Greenberg, "Heimlich Maneuvers: On a Certain Tendency of Horror and Spectacular Cinema," in *Horror Film and Psychoanalysis: Freud's Worst Nightmare*, Stephen Schneider, ed. (Cambridge: Cambridge University Press, 2004), 123.

14   David Buckingham, *Moving Images: Understanding Children's Emotional Responses to Television* (Manchester: Manchester University Press, 1996), 111–12; Susanne Ylönen, "Lower than Low? Domesticating the Aesthetics of Horror in Childish Remakes," in *Aesthetics of Popular Culture*, M. Ryynänen and J. Kovalcik, eds. (Bratislava: Academy of Fine Arts and Design; SlovArt Publishing, 2014), 124–49; Lester, "Children's Horror," 25–8, 34; Noël Carroll, *The Philosophy of Horror, or Paradoxes of the Heart* (New York: Routledge, 1990), 15, 35.

15   Maja Brzozowska-Brywczyńska, "'Monstrous/Cute:' Notes on the Ambivalent Nature of Cuteness," in *Monsters and the Monstrous: Myths and Metaphors of Enduring Evil*, Niall Scott, ed. (Amsterdam: Rodopi 2007), 4–5.

16   Scott Eberle, "Exploring the Uncanny Valley to Find the Edge of Play," *American Journal of Play*, 2, 2 (2009): 167–94, quotation on 174–6. For a sophisticated treatment of the boundary between the cute and the sublime see Elizabeth Legge, "When Awe Turns to Awww . . . Jeff Koons's Balloon Dog and the Cute Sublime," in *The Aesthetics and Affects of Cuteness*, Joshua Paul Dale et al., eds. (New York: Routledge, 2016), 130–50. For another example of how the uncanny cute can unnerve rather than attract, note how the characters in

a Pokémon movie were "too realistic" for the expectations of consumers who grew up with the cartoon: Bill Bradley, "Here's Why Realistic Pokémon From 'Detective Pikachu' Are Creeping People Out," *Huffington Post*, November 11, 2018, https://www.huffingtonpost.com/entry/realistic-pokemon-from-detec tive-pikachu-are-creeping-people-out_us_5beb41e1e4b0caeec2bef1ff.

17 Katriina Heljakka, "Disliked and Demonized Dollies: Pedophobia and Popular Toys of the Present," *WiderScreen*, March 2017, http://widerscreen.fi/numerot/ 2018-3/disliked-and-demonized-dollies-pediophobia-and-popular-toys-of-the-p resent/.

18 Brzozowska-Brywczyńska, "Monstrous/Cute," 4–5.

19 Brzozowska-Brywczyńska, "Monstrous/Cute," 8–9; Daniel Harris, *Cute, Quaint, Hungry and Romantic: The Aesthetics of Consumerism* (New York: Da Capo, 2001), 1–21, citation, 6.

20 Liz Locke, "Don't Dream It, Be It: RHPS as Cultural Performance," *New Directions in Folklore*, 3 (May–July 1999): 1–21, https://scholarworks.iu.edu/ journals/index.php/ndif/article/view/19866/25961. See also Sal Piro, *Creatures of the Night: The Rocky Horror Picture Show Experience* (Redford: Stabur Press, 1990). Fan site: http://www.rockyhorror.com.

21 John P. Bray, "'There's Too Many of Them!' Off-Off Broadway's Subversive Performance of Geek Culture," *Theatre Symposium*, April 2013, 120–33, https://muse.jhu.edu/article/556623; Vampire Cowboys website: https://www .vampirecowboys.com/about.htm.

22 Lori Weisberg, "Comic-Con Registration Crashes for Second Time," *San Diego Union-Tribune*, November 22, 2010, 24; Mark Hughes, "Stan Lee's LA Comic Con Brings Huge Costumed Crowd To Downtown," *Forbes*, October 31, 2016, https://www.forbes.com/sites/markhughes/2016/10/31/stan-lees-la-c omic-con-brings-huge-costumed-crowd-to-downtown/#2780e3f037f3/.

BIBLIOGRAPHY

Adams, Rachel, *Sideshow U.S.: Freaks and the American Cultural Imagination* (Chicago: University of Chicago Press, 2001).

Asma, Stephen, *On Monsters: An Unnatural History of Our Worst Fears* (New York: Oxford University Press, 2009).

Bogdan, Robert, *Freak Show: Presenting Human Oddities for Amusement and Profit* (Chicago: University of Chicago Press, 1988).

Booth, Mark, *Camp* (London: Quartet Books, 1983).

Brzozowska-Brywczyńska, Maja, "'Monstrous/Cute:' Notes on the Ambivalent Nature of Cuteness," in *Monsters and the Monstrous: Myths and Metaphors of Enduring Evil*, edited by Niall Scott, 213–28 (Amsterdam: Rodopi, 2007).

Carroll, Noël, *Philosophy of Horror* (New York: Routledge, 1990).

Chemers, Michael, *Staging Stigma: A Critical Examination of the American Freak Show* (London: Palgrave, 2008).

Church, David, "Freakery, Cult Films, and the Problem of Ambivalence," *Journal of Film and Video*, 63, no. 1 (Spring 2011): 3–17.

Clasen, Mathias, *Why Horror Seduces* (New York: Oxford University Press, 2017).

Cleary, Krystal, "Misfitting and Hater Blocking: A Feminist Disability Analysis of the Extraordinary Body on Reality Television," *Disability Studies Quarterly*, 36, no. 4 (2016), http://dsq-sds.org/article/view/5442/4471.

Cline, John and Robert Weiner, eds., *From the Arthouse to the Grindhouse* (Lanham, MD: Scarecrow Press, 2010).

Clover, Carol, *Men, Women, and Chain Saws* (Princeton, NJ: Princeton University Press, 1992).

Conn, Steven, *Museums and American Intellectual Life, 1876–1926* (Chicago: University of Chicago Press, 1998).

Cook, James, *The Arts of Deception: Playing with Fraud in the Age of Barnum* (Cambridge, MA: Harvard University Press, 2001).

Cook, James, ed., *The Colossal P.T. Barnum Reader* (Urbana: University of Illinois Press, 2005).

Corman, Roger, *How I Made a Hundred Movies in Hollywood and Never Lost a Dime* (New York: Random House, 1990).

Cross, Gary, *The Cute and the Cool: Wondrous Innocence and American Children's Culture* (New York: Oxford University Press, 2004).

Cross, Gary, *Kids' Stuff: Toys and the Changing World of American Childhood* (Cambridge, MA: Harvard University Press, 1997).

Dale, Joshua, Joyce Goggin, Julia Leyda, Anthony P. McIntyre and Diane Negra, eds., *The Aesthetics and Affects of Cuteness* (New York: Routledge, 2017).

Daston, Lorraine and Katherine Park, *Wonders and Orders of Nature, 1150–1750* (New York: Zone Books, 1998).

Davis, Janet, *The Circus Age: Culture and Society Under the American Big Top* (Chapel Hill: University of North Carolina Press, 2002).

Dennett, Andrea, "The Dime Museum Freak Show Reconfigured at the Talk Show," in *Freakery: Cultural Spectacles of the Extraordinary Body*, edited by Rosemarie Garland Thomson, 315–26 (New York: New York University Press, 1996).

Dennett, Andrea, *Weird and Wonderful: The Dime Museum in America* (New York: New York University Press, 1997).

Drimmer, Frederick, *Very Special People* (New York: Bell Publishing, 1985).

Eco, Humberto, *On Ugliness* (London: Rizzoli, 2011).

Erenberg, Lewis, *Steppin' Out: New York Night Life and the Transformation of American Culture* (Chicago: University of Chicago Press, 1981).

Fiedler, Leslie, *Freaks: Myths and Images of the Secret Self* (New York: Simon and Schuster, 1978).

Foss, Daniel, *Freak Culture* (New York: Dutton, 1972).

Freud, Sigmund, "The 'Uncanny,'" in *The Standard Edition of the Complete Psychological Works of Sigmund Freud, Volume XVII (1917-1919): An Infantile Neurosis and Other Works*, edited by J. Strachey, 217–56 (London: Hogarth Press, 1955).

Gabler, Neal, *Walt Disney: The Triumph of the American Imagination* (New York: Vintage, 2006).

Garland-Thomson, Rosemarie, *Staring: How We Look* (New York: Oxford University Press, 2009).

Glynn, Kevin, *Tabloid Culture: Trash Taste, Popular Power, and the Transformation of American Television* (Durham, NC: Duke University Press, 2000).

Grant, Barry and Christopher Sharret, eds., *Planks of Reason: Essays in the Horror Film* (Lanham: Scarecrow Press, 2004).

Grier, Katherine, *Pets in America: A History* (Chapel Hill: University of North Carolina Press, 2006).

Hall, Ward, *My Very Unusual Friends* (Sarasota: Self-published, 1991).

Harris, Daniel, *Cute, Quaint, Hungry and Romantic* (New York: Basic, 2000).

Hatch, Kristen, *Shirley Temple: The Performance of Girlhood* (New Brunswick: Rutgers University Press, 2015).

Heffernan, Kevin, *Ghouls, Gimmicks and Gold: Horror Films and the American Movie Business* (Durham, NC: Duke University Press, 2004).

Hill, J. Dee, *Freaks and Fire: The Underground Reinvention of the Circus* (New York: Soft Skull Press, 2004).

Hoberman, James and Jonathan Rosenbaum, *Midnight Movies* (New York: Da Capo, 1991).

Holtman, Jerry, *Freak Show Man: The Autobiography of Harry Lewiston* (Los Angeles: Holloway House, 1968).

Humphries, Reynold, *American Horror Film* (Edinburgh: Edinburgh University Press, 2002).

Hunter, Jack, *Freak Babylon: An Illustrated History of Teratology and Freakshows* (New York: Creation, 2014).

Kasson, John, *Houdini, Tarzan, and the Perfect Man* (New York: Hill and Wang, 2001).

Kasson, John, *The Little Girl Who Fought the Great Depression: Shirley Temple and the 1930s* (New York: Norton, 2014).

Kasson, John, *Rudeness and Civility: Manners in Nineteen Century Urban America* (New York: Harper Collins, 1990).

King, Stephen, *Danse Macabre* (New York: Everest House, 1981).

Kristeva, Julia, *Powers of Horror: An Essay on Abjection* (New York: Columbia University Press, 1982).

Levine, Lawrence, *High Brow/Low Brow: The Emergence of a Cultural Hierarchy in America* (Cambridge, MA: Harvard University Press, 1988).

Liz Locke, Liz, "Don't Dream it: Be it: *The Rocky Horror Picture Show* as Cultural Performance," *New Directions in Folklore*, 3 (May–June 1999): 1–21.

Manga, Julie, *Talking Trash: Cult Politics of Daytime TV Talk Shows* (New York: New York University Press, 2003).

May, Simon, *The Power of Cute* (Princeton, NJ: Princeton University Press, 2019).

Monod, David, *The Soul of Pleasure: Sentiment and Sensation in Nineteenth-Century American Mass Entertainment* (Ithaca, NY: Cornell University Press, 2016).

Munson, Wendy, *All Talk: The Talk Show in Media Culture* (Philadelphia, PA: Temple University Press, 1993).

Ngai, Sianne, *Our Aesthetic Categories: Zany, Cute, Interesting* (Cambridge, MA: Harvard University Press, 2012).

Nickell, Joe, *Secrets of the Sideshows* (Lexington: University of Kentucky Press, 2008).

O'Brien, Tim, *Ward Hall: King of the Side Show* (Nashville: Casa Flamingo Literary Arts, 2014).

Paul, William, *Laughing Screaming: Modern Hollywood Horror and Comedy* (New York: Columbia University Press, 1994).

Platts, Todd, "New Horror Movies," in *Baby Boomers and Popular Culture*, edited by Brian Cogan and Thom Gencarelli, 147–64 (Santa Barbara: Praeger, 2014).

Poole, W. Scott, *Monsters in America* (Waco: Baylor University Press, 2014).

Rader, Karen and Victoria Cain, *Life on Display: Revolutionizing U.S. Museums of Science in the Twentieth Century* (Chicago: University of Chicago Press, 2014).

Raffel, Dawn, *The Strange Case of Dr. Couney* (New York: Blue Rider Press, 2018).

Reiss, Benjamin, *The Showman and the Slave: Race, Death, and Memory in Barnum's America* (Cambridge, MA: Harvard University Press, 2001).

Rose, Jim, *Freaks like Me* (New York: Dell, 1995).

Roth, Hy and Robert Cromie, *Little People* (New York: Everest House, 1980).

Rydell, Robert, *All the World's a Fair: Visions of Empire at American International Expositions, 1876–1916* (Chicago: University of Chicago Press, 1987).

Schaefer, Eric, *"Bold! Daring! Shocking! True!" A History of Exploitation Films, 1919–1959* (Durham, NC: Duke University Press, 1999).

Skal, David, *The Monster Show: A Cultural History of Horror* (New York: Norton, 1995).

Skal, David and Elias Savada, *Dark Carnival: The Secret World of Tod Browning* (New York: Anchor, 1995).

Sontag, Susan, "Notes on Camp," in *Susan Sontag Reader*, edited by Susan Sontag, 105–20 (New York: Vintage, 1983).

Stencell, A. W., *Circus and Carnival Ballyhoo: Sideshow Freaks, Jabbers and Blade Box Queens* (Toronto: ECW Press, 2010).

Stewart, Susan, *On Longing: Narratives of the Miniature, the Gigantic, the Souvenir, the Collection* (Durham, NC: Duke University Press, 1993).

Thompson, Neal, *A Curious Man: The Strange and Brilliant Life of Robert "Believe it or Not!" Ripley* (New York: Three Rivers Press, 2013).

Twitchell, James, *Dreadful Pleasures: The Anatomy of Modern Horror* (New York: Oxford University Press, 1985).

Wells, Paul, *The Horror Genre* (London: Wallflower Press, 2004).

Wood, Robin, *Hollywood: From Vietnam to Reagan . . . and Beyond* (New York: Columbia University Press, 2003).

Worland, Rich, *Horror Film* (London: Blackwell, 2007).

Ylönen, Susanne, "Lower than Low? Domesticating the Aesthetics of Horror in Childish Remakes," in *Aesthetics of Popular Culture*, edited by M. Ryynänen, and J. Kovalcik, 124–49 (Bratislava: Academy of Fine Arts and Design; SlovArt Publishing, 2014).

INDEX

Abbott and Costello Meet Frankenstein 184, 213
Abt, Vicky 159–60
action-adventure movies 177
Adams, Rachel 23, 57, 144
Addams Family 187
Admiral Dot (Leopold Kahn) 107
Alien 194
Allied Artists 185
American Horror Show 210
American International Pictures (AIP) 153–5, 185–6
American Museum 5, 28
animal freaks 77, 83–4, 88
Arbus, Diane 9, 79, 145–7, 207
Arhoff, Samuel 153
Asma, Stephen 179, 181
Astley, Philip 32

Baby Burlesks 129
baby incubators 127–8
Baby Irene 44
Bad Seed 215
Bad Taste 198
Bakhtin, M. M. 12
Barnum, P. T
  circus 32
  cross-class appeal 34–5, 50, 103
  dime museum 28–9
  and freaks 28–30, 34, 211
  and new freak show 167
  and Tom Thumb 30–1
Barnum and Bailey circus 37, 48, 49, 58
Barty, Billy 118, 126
Basket Case 198
Batman (TV show) 154, 217
Baudelaire, Charles 143

Beckford, William 181
Bell, Daniel 15, 16, 143
Benjamin, Walter 182
Benshoff, Harry 149
Bergman, Ingmar 150
Bindlestiff Family Cirkus 165–6
Birds (Alfred Hitchcock) 185
blockheads 48
Blood Feast 190
Bone, Howard 82
Booth, Mark 143, 147
Bowen, Eli 40
Bowery 30
Breen, Joseph 184, 186
Breen, Tom 93, 96
Bride of Frankenstein 182–3
Briggs, Ellen, The German Dwarf 112
Brottman, Mikita 180, 188
Brownies 24
Browning, Tod 1, 5, 6, 149
Brunel, Luis 149
Brzozowska-Brywczyńska, Maja 214–15
Bucket of Blood 186
Bunker, Chang and Eng 41–2
Bunnell, George 30
Burmese women, giraffe-necked 72–3

camp
  and the avant garde 143–6
  compared to the cute 141, 168–9
  in cosplay 156, 216–17
  in the counterculture 15, 133, 144–8
  critiques of 141, 143–4, 157
  definition and origins 9, 14, 141–2
  in grindhouse films 151, 153
  intentional *vs.* naïve 144, 153

"knowing" crowd as   143–5, 150,
        153, 156, 199–200
    in the movies   149–51, 153–7,
        216–17
    in New Age freak shows   163–7
    and punk music   148
    theory   142–5
    in trash talk TV   161–2
Canby, Vincent   149, 198
carnival (festival)   12
carnival (traveling), *see also* circus; sex
        shows
    freak shows   80–1, 83
    origins   33
Carpenter, John   194
Carrie   196
Carrington, Hereward   54
Carroll, Noël   179, 214
Castle, William   185–6, 198
Cat People   184
Chained for Life   152
Chaplin, Charles   117
Chemers, Michael   146
Chicago World's Fair   76–7, 120
children
    advertising to   127
    associations with twentieth century
        midgets   17, 121–2
    association with Victorian
        midgets   103–6, 110–11, 113
    cuteification   17, 104, 126–30, 132
    and Disney cartoons   130–2
    sacralization of   126
    and *Snow White and the Seven
        Dwarfs*   6–8
Children of the Corn   195
Child's Play   195
Christ, Chris   88–90, 93
Church, David   151, 157
cinema of attractions   182, 189
Circassians   37
circus, *see also* Barnum and Bailey;
        Ringling Brothers Barnum and
        Bailey
    decline   70–1, 73
    origins   32
    sideshows   32–3, 49, 72–3
Cirque du Soleil   71
Clasen, Mathias   177–9, 190

Cleary, Krystal   211
Cleary, Sarah   156
Clicko, the Bushman   72, 87
Clofullia, Madame   39
Clover, Carol   189
college film societies   149
Columbia Exhibition of 1893   32
Comic-Con International   217
Comikaze Zombie Apocalypse   217
Coney Island   33, 52, 54, 114, 128
Coney Island Sideshow   166
conjoined (Siamese) twins   41–2,
        211, *see also* Bunker, Chang and
        Eng; Hensel, Abby and Brittany;
        Hilton, Daisy and Violet;
        McKoy, Millie and Christina
Conn, Steven   56
Coogan, Jackie   117
Cook, James   28–9
Coolah, Lala   39
Corman, Roger   153, 156, 184, 187,
        190, 198
cosplay (costumed performance)   156,
        216–17
Costentenus, George   47
Couney, Martin   52, 127–8
counterculture, *see also* Crumb,
        Robert; midnight movies
    and camp   144–50
    definition and origins   9, 146
    and horror   15, 187
    as middle-class youth
        rebellion   146
    and midnight movies   149
    and self-declared "freaks"   146–8
Covie, Elizabeth   179
Craven, Wes   194–6, 198–9, 208
Creature from the Black Lagoon   184
creepy, *see* horror
Crumb, Robert (R)   141, 147, 163
*Cultural Contradictions of
        Capitalism*   15
Cunningham, Sean   194
Cushing, Peter   184
cute, *see also* children; Couney, Martin;
        Mickey Mouse; midgets; Temple,
        Shirley
    as "acute"   126
    in art   125

in biological evolution   124–6
in cartoons   130–2
controversies   124–6
and the cool   133
definitions   104–5, 115
edginess of the   115, 118, 126,
    130, 133
as a historical construct   105,
    125–7
in horror   213–16
in legitimizing the freak   14, 133,
    207
and the middle-class   14–15, 113,
    132–3, 207
and modern childrearing   7, 17,
    123, 126–7, 132–3
in modern pets   104, 128–9
and playthings   117, 123, 130
in *Snow White and the Seven
    Dwarfs*   6–8
uncanny forms of   126
and women   104–5
Cute and the Cool   125

Dale, Joshua Paul   105, 125–6
Daston, Lorraine   25, 51
Davis, Lennard   48
Dawn of the Dead   198
Decker, Charles   108–9
Dennett, Andrea   91
Diane D'Elgar (George Searles)   81,
    88
Dickens, Charles   27
Dillard, R. H. W.   191
dime museums   28, 30–1
Disney, Walt   6–8, 130, 207
Disneyland   133
Disney World   133, 208, 213
Dixon, Wheeler   190
Doll, Harry (Harry Earles,
    Harry Schneider)   3, 115–16,
    123
Doll family   3, 115–17
Dollie Dutton (Alice Marie)   113
dolls   113, 130
Donahue, Phil   158–9, 161
Donald Duck   131–2, 213
Dracula   2, 150, 182, 213
Dreamland amusement park   33, 120

Dr. Jekyll and Mr. Hyde   182
Dr. Strangelove   146
Dufour, Lou   77, 79, 82,
    87, 91
Dunn, Katherine   146, 166

Eberle, Scott   214
Eck, Johnny   4
Eco, Humberto   144, 150
Edison, Thomas   182
Ehrenreich, Barbara   185
El Topo   150
Enigma (Paul Lawrence)   163–5
Esper, Dwain   8
Ethnological Congress of Savage
    Peoples   37
eugenics   53
evolutionary theory   36–7
Exorcist   192, 196

Family Guy   9, 213, 216
Famous Monsters of Filmland   150,
    187
Feil, Ken   143
Fellner, Chris   163
Fiedler, Leslie   16, 33, 77, 143
flea circus   83
Foss, Daniel   146
Frankenstein   2, 4, 182, 213
freaks, *see also* carnival (traveling);
    circus; conjoined twins;
    dime museums; freak show;
    giants; midgets; missing link;
    psychological freaks; staring;
    tattooed; teratology; trash
    talk TV
ancient origins   23–7
body-invasive   46–9
born   5, 38–46
definition   1
exotic   34–7, 39
gaffe   5, 39–40
as pets   25
as prodigies   58
on reality TV   160, 210–12
and science   23, 51–3, 55–7
self-made   5, 46
traditional and modern
    contrasted   17, 208–10

Freaks (film), *see also* freaks; freak
    show
  cast   3, 4
  on the grindhouse circuit   8, 151
  origins   1, 2
  plot   2–3
  reception in 1932   1–4
  revival   9–10, 141, 149
Freakshow (reality TV series)   210
freak shows, *see also* animal freak;
    Gumpertz, Sam; Hall, Ward;
    Lewiston, Harry; New Age
    freak shows; pickled punk;
    psychological freaks; sex shows,
    torture shows
  audience in the nineteenth
    century   34, 36, 39, 42, 44
  audience in the twentieth
    century   18, 79–80, 83–5,
    87, 91
  changes in Victorian era   49, 55
  continuing appeal after
    1930   90–3
  decline 1930–70   69, 71–3, 80
  eclipse after 1970   93–6
  nostalgia for   93–4, 163
  operators and barkers   85–90
  performances   32–3, 49, 80,
    88–90
  shift to the grotesque   69, 78,
    80–5, 87, 91
Freudian theory   127, 176, 179–80
Friday the 13th   194–5, 208

Gabler, Neal   6, 161
Gaines, William   187, 190
Gainsborough, Thomas   125
Gamson, Joshua   160
Garland, Judy   123
Garland-Thomson, Rosemary   42,
    52, 58
Gates, Louis   161
geek culture   216
geeks   48, 79, 84, 91–2
General Mite (Francis Flynn)   111
genteel values, *see also* middlebrow;
    natural history museum; staring
  adaptations to freaks   34–6, 39,
    42, 44, 48, 50

challenges to   56–7, 133, 207–8
definition and origins   5, 12
rejection of freaks   4, 5, 12–14, 51,
    53–4, 208
Gest, Morris   121
Ghostbusters   214
Ghost in the Invisible Bikini   150
giants   46, 59–60
Glynn, Kevin   160
Goffman, Erving   58
Gold Diggers of 1933   118, 126
Gorham, Maurice   91–2
gothic novels   181–2
Gould, Jay   131
Graham, Stanley   120
Greeley, Horace   51
Gremlins   213
grindhouse (theaters)   149, 151–3
Gumpertz, Sam   85, 120

Haeckel, Ernest   36
Hall, G. Stanley   36
Hall, Ward, *see also* Christ, Chris;
    freak shows
  and the decline of the freak
    show   90
  as empresario   69, 81–3, 88–90, 94
  on the freak show   80, 90–1, 95–6
  as performer   88
Halloween   194–5
Hammer Film Productions   175, 184
Happy Tree Friends   215–16
Harris, Daniel   104, 215
Hatch, Kristen   129
Hawthorne, Nathaniel   27
Heljakka, Katriina   215
Hennen, Peter   82
Hensel, Abby and Brittany   211
Henson, Jim   15, 208, 213
hermaphrodites   4, 39–40, 73, 79, 81
Hermines, Bob   122
Herodotus   24
Heth, Joice   28
highbrow, *see* genteel values
Higonnet, Anne   125
Hildebrandt, Nora   47
Hill, J. Dee   162–3
Hilton, Daisy and Violet   3, 78–9,
    151–2

horror, *see also* camp; *Night of the Living Dead*; slasher films
  as the abject   175, 179
  ancient origins of   181
  audience   180, 187, 213–14
  body   193, 198, 200
  as camp   187, 199
  for children   213–16
  as cinéma vomitif   188
  comics   150, 187
  countercultural impact on   15, 187
  early film   182–3
  evolutionary origins   16, 177–8, 179–81
  and fast capitalism   176, 197
  and freakery   179, 193
  Freudian interpretations of   176, 178–80
  and gothic novels   181–2
  as "gross out"   187–9
  humor   192, 198–200
  intensification of, after 1970   193–7
  intensification of, in the 1960s   185–9
  mollifying tendencies after 1980   197–200
  mollifying tendencies before the 1960s   183–5
  persistence of   200
  pleasures of   179–80
  predator   176, 178
House on Haunted Hill   185
Howard, Joseph   107
Huber, George   30
Hubert's Museum   3, 79, 145
human ostriches   48
Hunter, John   52
Huntler, Joseph   111
Hutchings, Peter   199
hypercapitalism   16
hypertrichosis   38

Ingrassia, Paul   91
Invasion of the Body Snatchers   184
Invisible Man   150
I Was a Teenage Werewolf   186, 188

Jackson, Peter   198
Jameson, Frederic   143

Jancovich, Mark   185–6
Jay, Ricky   163
Jim Rose's Circus Sideshow   163–7, 216
Jodorovsky, Alejandro   150
Johnny Jones Exposition   83
Jo-Jo the Dog-Faced Boy   39
Jon & Kate Plus 8   211

Karloff, Boris   182
Kasson, John   57, 59
Katzenjammer Kids   126
Kelson, Keith   165
Kid, The   117
Kimbal, Moses   28
King, Don   167
King, Stephen   179–80
King Kong   2
Knievel, Evel   167
Kristeva, Julia   179
Krueger, Freddy   195, 199

Lake, Ricki   158, 160–1
Lambert, Daniel   45
LaRue, Lash   71, 84
Last House on the Left   194
Leak, Ann   40
Learning Channel, The (TLC)   210–12
Lee, Christopher   184
Lee, Stan   217
Lentini, Francesco   41, 43
Lester, Catherine   214
Levine, Lawrence   13
Lewis, Herschell Gordon   190
Lewiston, Harry   80–1, 84–5, 87
Liberace   143
Lilliputia   85, 120
Little Lord Fauntleroy   124, 130
Little People, Big World   211
Locke, Liz   156
Lorenz, Konrad   125, 131
Lucasie, Rudolph   35
Lugosi, Bela   182

McCourt, Molly   156
McCullers, Carson   146
McDaniels, Grace, The Mule-Faced Woman   79, 85–7

McKoy, Millie and Christina 41
Marxist theory 143, 176
May, Simon 105, 126
Meet the Putmans 212
Méliès, Georges 182
Merrick, Joseph 24
Meyer, Louis B. 2
Meyers, Russ 153–4
MGM 1, 2, 4
Mickey Mouse 130–1, 215
middlebrow 133, 207
midgets
    on advertising 115, 124
    cuteification 115–18, 122
    vs. dwarfs 106
    as "innocent children" 111–13
    as miniatures 108
    in movies 123–24
    vs. other freaks 109
    in premodern times 26–7
    and religion 108, 113
    as uncanny 106
    in vaudeville 114
    as Victorian bourgeois 106–8, 112
    and Victorian children 110–12
    in Victorian genteel culture 103,
        106–9
    villages 118–22
midnight movies, *see also* grindhouse
        (theaters)
    and camp 149–51
    and counterculture 149, 153–4
    featured films 150
    and *Freaks* revival 149–50
missing link 36–8
Monseu, Stephanie 165
Moses, Robert 54, 78, 79
Motion Picture Production Code 2,
        3, 175, 183–4, 186, 190
Movie ratings 186, 214
Mukerji, Chandra 213
Mummy, The 182
Munsters 187
Muppets 132, 213
Museum of Anatomy 31
Museum of Modern Art 15
Mustazza, Leonard 159–60
My 600-lb Life 210
My Husband's Not Gay 212

National Association of Women 2, 4
Natural history museums 55–7
Ndalianis, Angela 200
Nestel, Charles 106, 108
New Age freak shows
    as camp 166–7
    compared to traditional freak
        shows 162–3, 167
    origins 162–5
    performers 163–6
New York World's Fair of 1939–40
        79, 120–1
New York World's Fair of 1964 78
Ngai, Sianne 16, 104
Nguyen, Qui 216
Nicol, Philippe 114
Nightmare on Elm Street 195
Night of the Living Dead
    audience 11
    compared with earlier horror 11,
        190–3
    as midnight movie 149
    origins 10
No Not Nanette 142
Nutt, George 30
Nutt, George (General) 108–9

obesity 44–5, 210–11
oddities, *see* freaks
Odditorium (Robert Ripley) 76–7
Oliver, Charles 162
Omen, The 195
ossified men 43–4

Paramount Decision 185
Paré, Ambroise 24
Park, Katherine 25, 51
Paul, William 187, 189, 192, 197–8
Peale, Charles Willson 27–8, 55
Pearlroth, Norbert 76
People for the Ethical Treatment of
        Animals 71
Pfening, Fred III 71
Philadelphia Centennial Exhibition of
        1876 32
Phillips, Kendal 181
pickled punks (freakish human
        embryos) 77, 82–3, 89–90
pinheads (microcephalics) 34–6

Pink Flamingos   150, 154
Planet Nine from Outer Space   150
Platts, Todd   181
Poe, Edgar Allan   182
Polyester   154
Poole, W. Scott   181
popeyes (performer)   72, 88
Prince Randian   3, 80
Proctor, Robert   176
Psycho (Alfred Hitchcock)   186
psychological freak shows   159–61, 211–12
punk rock   148, 162
Pushnik, Frieda   73
Pyle, C. C.   74, 76

Quetelet, Adolphe   48

Radcliff, Ann   181
Rader, Karen   56
Raphael, Sally Jessy   158, 165
Rat Fink   147–9, 215
Ray, Todd   94
reality TV   210–12
Reefer Madness   8, 151
Reiss, Benjamin   28
Renton, Al   84
Reynolds, Joshua   125
Ricketts, John   32
Ringling Brothers Barnum and Bailey circus   59, 70–2, 85, 89, 94
Ripley, Robert   24, 69, 74–7
Rivera, Geraldo   158, 161
rock clubs   164, 167
Rocky Horror Picture Show   149, 151, 155–8, 216–17
Rodman, Dennis   208
Romero, George   10, 190–1, 198, 208
Roper, Fred   121–2
Rosemary's *Baby*   186
Ross, Andrew   143
Rossitto, Angelo   123
Roth, Ed (Big Daddy)   147–8, 215
Roventini, Johnny   124
Royal American Shows   93
Ruschenberger, William   55

St. Bartholonew's Fair   27
Saint-Hilaire, Geoffroy   52

Sandow, Edward   59
Saturnalia   12
Schaeffer's Fairy Tale Town   11
Schlitzie   3
Sconce, Jeffrey   157
Scream   196, 199
Screen Gems   187
sexploitation movies   153, 185
sex shows   80–1
Shelly, Mary   181–2
Shivers   194
sideshows, *see* freak shows
Simpsons   165, 199, 213
Singer, Leo   120–1, 123
sitcoms   177, 187
slasher films   194–6
Smithsonian Institution   55
Snow White and the Seven Dwarfs   6, 7
Sontag, Susan   9, 142–5, 148, 150, 207
spookers   153
Sprague, Isaac   43–5
Springer, Jerry   158–60, 208, 211–12
staring
    at freaks   29, 48–9, 57–60
    and genteel civility   57–8
Stern, Howard   167
Stratton, Charles   30–1, 109–11
strong people   48, 59
Supersize vs. Superskinny   210
sword-swallowers   47

tableau   109
tattooed   46–7
Taylor, James   163
Teddy Bears   130
Temple, Shirley   129–30
teratology   52
Terhune, Pete   89, 93–5
Terror of Tiny Town   123
Texas Chainsaw Massacre   150, 192–4
Thalberg, Irving   1
Thompson, Neal   76–7
Tiger King   212
Tingler   185
Tomaini, Al and Jeanie   72
Tom Thumb, *see* Stratton, Charles
torture shows   83
trash talk TV   157–62, 212

Twitchell, James   177, 180, 182, 200

Ubangis, saucer-lipped   73
Unholy Three   1
U.S. Farm Security Administration   90

Valente, Jack   186
Vampire Cowboys   216–17
vaudeville   3, 13, 79, 114
Velázquez, Diego   25
Venice Beach   165
Venice Film Festival   149
Victoria (Queen)   30

Wadlow, Robert   59–60
Waino and Plutano, The Wild Men of
       Borneo   36, 46
Wale, James   182
Walking Dead   11, 217
Walpole, Horace   181
Warhol, Andy   142
Warren, Lavinia   30, 112
Waters, John   150, 154, 208
Waverly Theater (Greenwich
       Village)   155

Weber, Max   12
Wells, Paul   180, 189
West, Rick   83
White Zombies   183, 191
Wiktin, Joel-Peter   146
Wild Children of Australia   33
Wilde, Oscar   143
Winfrey, Oprah   158, 161
Wizard of Oz   120
Wolfe, Tom   147
Wood, Robin   176, 179, 189
world's fairs   32, 76–8, 120–1

Zappa, Frank   146–7, 162
Zarate, Lucia   113
Zelizer, Viviana   126
Zigun, Dick   166
Zip, What Is It?   37, 85
zombie
    as the abject   178, 180
    and camp   217
    as freaks   9, 174, 190,
       208, 214
    in George Romero's films   10–11,
       191–2, 198

CPSIA information can be obtained
at www.ICGtesting.com
Printed in the USA
LVHW080445140621
690154LV00006B/309

9 781350 145122